D1478355

# The Evolution of Pragmatism in India

954.
0350
9
STR

Stroud, Scott R.

The evolution of
pragmatism in
India.

Guelph Public Library

$29.00

33281930115248

| DATE | | | |
|---|---|---|---|
| | | | |
| | | | |
| | | | |
| | | | |
| | | | |
| | | | |
| | | | |
| | | | |
| | | | |
| | | | |
| | | | |

MAY - - 2023

# The Evolution of Pragmatism in India

## Ambedkar, Dewey, and the Rhetoric of Reconstruction

SCOTT R. STROUD

The University of Chicago Press
Chicago and London

The University of Chicago Press, Chicago 60637
The University of Chicago Press, Ltd., London
© 2023 by The University of Chicago
All rights reserved. No part of this book may be used or reproduced in any
manner whatsoever without written permission, except in the case of brief
quotations in critical articles and reviews. For more information, contact the
University of Chicago Press, 1427 E. 60th St., Chicago, IL 60637.
Published 2023
Printed in the United States of America

32  31  30  29  28  27  26  25  24  23      1  2  3  4  5

ISBN-13: 978-0-226-82388-1 (cloth)
ISBN-13: 978-0-226-82432-1 (paper)
ISBN-13: 978-0-226-82389-8 (e-book)
DOI: https://doi.org/10.7208/chicago/9780226823898.001.0001

Library of Congress Cataloging-in-Publication Data

Names: Stroud, Scott R., author.
Title: The evolution of pragmatism in India : Ambedkar, Dewey, and the
    rhetoric of reconstruction / Scott R. Stroud.
Other titles: Ambedkar, Dewey, and the rhetoric of reconstruction
Description: Chicago : The University of Chicago Press, [2023] | Includes
    bibliographical references and index.
Identifiers: LCCN 2022022557 | ISBN 9780226823881 (cloth) |
    ISBN 9780226824321 (paperback) | ISBN 9780226823898 (e-book)
Subjects: LCSH: Ambedkar, B. R. (Bhimrao Ramji), 1891–1956—Philosophy. |
    Ambedkar, B. R. (Bhimrao Ramji), 1891–1956—Political and social views. |
    Dewey, John, 1859–1952—Influence. | Pragmatism. | BISAC: LANGUAGE
    ARTS & DISCIPLINES / Rhetoric | PHILOSOPHY / Movements /
    Pragmatism
Classification: LCC DS481.A6 S77 2023 | DDC 954.03/5092—dc23/
    eng/20220616
LC record available at https://lccn.loc.gov/2022022557

♾ This paper meets the requirements of ANSI/NISO Z39.48-1992
(Permanence of Paper)

*For Clara Stroud*
*Reconstruct your world, leaving room for friend and foe*

CONTENTS

# Exploring the Evolution of Pragmatism in India

By all accounts, Bhimrao Ambedkar (1891–1956) is one of the towering figures of modern India. Born an "untouchable" in India's complex and hierarchical caste system, he was subject to intense and pervasive discrimination that was underwritten by a common interpretation of a religious tradition that has roots stretching back for thousands of years. By the 1950s, the twilight of his all-too-short life, he had experienced many victories and many defeats. The victories were grand, however, and largely orbited around pushing Indian politics toward protecting the interests of his fellow Dalits (Marathi for "crushed," a modern, self-chosen term replacing the pejorative label "untouchable"). He had a vigorous career as a lawyer arguing for the rights of Dalits and was a sometime teacher, an organization builder, and an able statesman whose crowning achievement, perhaps, was orchestrating the form and substance of much of the Indian constitution. Ambedkar was the central figure in the push against caste oppression in India in the twentieth century, and he was one of the most influential figures in the formation of India as the largest democracy that the world has ever seen. Beyond his anticaste activism and his role as the architect of the Indian constitution in the 1940s, he spoke and wrote on behalf of Buddhism in the 1950s—a campaign for mass conversion as a way out of caste oppression that was concretized in his "Buddhist Bible," *The Buddha and His Dhamma*, published in 1957. It is because of these influential roles of activist, liberator, religious figure, and lawgiver that he was voted the "Greatest Indian" in postindependence India in a 2012 poll in which more than twenty million votes were cast.[1]

Underwriting these accomplishments was an expansive education. Ambedkar was one of the most educated Indians of his day, earning multiple advanced degrees from institutions such as Columbia University, the

London School of Economics, and Gray's Inn. By 1952, Ambedkar was called back to what could arguably be called his educational home, the one that first introduced him to the power of progressive thought and the role of intellectual rebels in transforming society: Columbia University. For his contributions to the drafting of India's constitution, he was set to receive an honorary degree from his alma mater. His flight back to New York in June 1952 was far from smooth. Intense sandstorms delayed his arrival at the intermediary stop of Basra, causing his plane to circle the airport for two hours before returning to its previous departure point, most likely Bahrain. What did Ambedkar think of during these flights? What did he expect from New York and Columbia University, ground that he had not trod since the early 1930s? Perhaps he hoped all of his teachers and friends from his time at Columbia (1913–1916) would be waiting for him at the glorious ceremony that would partially recognize the statesman and thinker he had become. After all, he had tipped his hand about his feelings toward his Columbia family in 1930, fondly writing in the alumni newspaper that "the best friends I have had in my life were some of my classmates at Columbia and my great professors, John Dewey, James Shotwell, Edwin Seligman and James Harvey Robinson."[2]

Although we can't know what he was thinking as he bounced around in his airplane, we do know that Ambedkar was supposed to arrive in New York in the dark of night on June 2, 1952, but the sandstorm and his tortuous flight path deposited him in America on June 3 at 8:00 in the morning. Either way, the die was already cast. John Dewey, Ambedkar's teacher from his Columbia days, had died of pneumonia in New York on June 1, 1952. Ambedkar would never see the sage of Morningside Heights in person again. From his correspondence penned during this 1952 trip, we can see how much Dewey's death stung the mature Ambedkar. Ambedkar wrote his wife, Savita, from New York on June 4, sitting in the King's Crown Hotel across from Columbia University's campus, lamenting the lacunae that news of Dewey's passing presaged. "There are many old friends who have gathered around me and [who are] helping me in all sorts of ways," Ambedkar reported, but then his correspondence took a morose turn: "I was looking forward to meet[ing] Prof. Dewey. But he died on the 2nd when our plane was in Rome." Ambedkar had many teachers in New York, but as his next words revealed, none compared to Dewey: "I am so sorry. I owe all my intellectual life to him. He was a wonderful man."[3] At this stage in his accomplished life, Ambedkar had little reason to exaggerate what Dewey, a teacher he had not been in the same room with since June 1916, meant to him and his intellectual development.

I am not the first to notice these powerful lines about his teacher, the most effusive praise that I can identify from Ambedkar about any of his intellectual guiding lights from the West. Eleanor Zelliot notes Ambedkar's relationship to his academic mentors and similarly concludes that "John Dewey seems to have had the greatest influence on Ambedkar."[4] Other studies have mentioned the relationship between Dewey and Ambedkar; Anand Teltumbde, in the course of his research interrogating the logics of caste in modern India, recognizes that "under the influence of John Dewey, his professor at Columbia University, he remained a pragmatist in dealing with history. If one examines his methodology, one cannot miss this philosophical strand. What is called Ambedkarism actually boils down to pragmatism, a way of practically resolving particular issues with available resources, rather than relying on grand narratives and a politics of overhaul."[5] Teltumbde's project carries him in other directions than the analysis of this claim, but he brings to our attention the "recurring motif in Ambedkar's public life" that "was the deep impact of his professor, John Dewey while he was a student at Columbia University."[6] How this impact or influence unfolded, however, is not explained in these studies. Some have devoted attention to the philosophical overlaps between Dewey and Ambedkar, such as Meera Nanda's focus on Ambedkar's attempt to "'hybridize' John Dewey's conception of scientific temper with the teachings of the Buddha" and his use of "the reinterpreted Buddhist tradition to challenge Hindu metaphysics and the ethics of natural inequality it sanctions."[7] Beyond the identification of Deweyan themes in Ambedkar's vision of Buddhism, Nanda's account is useful because it highlights the paucity of details scholars provide about Dewey's connection to critique in modern India: "While Dewey's influence on the Chinese Enlightenment, the May 4th Movement, is very well documented," Nanda argues, "his indirect connection with the aborted *Indian* Enlightenment is hardly known outside the small circle of scholars. Unfortunately, even these scholars tend to treat Ambedkar's American experience and his great regard for Dewey as just one more biographical detail."[8] An in-depth engagement with Dewey *as Ambedkar knew him* is integral to understanding what is so original in this Indian thinker, as K. N. Kadam argues in one of the first explorations of this topic: "Unless we understand something of John Dewey, one of Dr. Ambedkar's teachers at the Columbia University, it would be impossible to understand Dr. Ambedkar."[9] Arun Mukherjee likewise cautions scholars against engaging Ambedkar and his thought "in isolation, without paying attention to his dialogue with Dewey."[10]

The importance of Dewey to Ambedkar's thought has frequently been mentioned, but it has not been deeply mined beyond the confines of a few isolated chapters or disconnected articles. While useful, this work represents only a start to plumbing the depths of Ambedkar's reception of American pragmatism. Put bluntly, we have no sustained or in-depth accounting of Ambedkar's engagement with Dewey's pragmatism, including what he appropriated, rejected, or altered. We also have no evidence-based accounting of *what* in Dewey's classes, or all the works that Dewey published over his lifetime, actually reached Ambedkar and affected his writing, speaking, and activism. Ambedkar was a prolific, complex, and highly educated figure, so we need a similarly detailed and evidenced accounting of how he encountered and even resisted parts of Dewey's work at Columbia and beyond. We do not even know the lay of the land here; thus, we must set aside worries that promise more premature closure than enlightenment. Let us thoroughly answer the questions: What did Ambedkar hear and read from Dewey? How is this reflected, changed, or resisted across his body of work? How did it influence his methods of argument, and how might it have informed his novel idea of social democracy and the sort of oppression that India—and other democracies—ought to resist?

Given Ambedkar's formative role in Indian thought and politics in the twentieth century, exploring these questions with an honest look at the available evidence that we can identify will also fill in crucial details about the pluralistic tradition of pragmatism that has emerged across the globe. Ambedkar's story is told from many angles, with different emphases placed on various themes and aspects of his life and work. For instance, Dhananjay Keer and Narendra Jadhav admirably describe the various movements of Ambedkar's life and thought in their magisterial biographies.[11] Christophe Jaffrelot, Gail Omvedt, and Eleanor Zelliot have written extensively about Ambedkar's activism and political thought and its impact on the Dalit movement.[12] Others, such as Anupama Rao, have written on the question of caste and democracy in India in its more general scope, including Ambedkar as a central figure and agitator for caste rights.[13] All of these are well-argued contributions to what we know about the importance of Ambedkar to the issues of oppression and emancipation in the Indian setting. But there is a side to Ambedkar that has yet to be unearthed, one that starts with his early educational impressions abroad in the 1910s and has a significant impact that stretches throughout his entire life and body of work, political and scholarly. The story that is yet to be told is a grand tale, one that begins to tell us about the development of Indian pragmatism through Ambedkar in the twentieth century. Ambedkar was many things, so it is natural that there are many ways to tell his story. The range of retellings, however, does not yet include the tale of Ambedkar as a pragmatist. His story, in a deep sense, is the tale of pragmatism's entrance into Indian intellectual and political circles. Gesturing at a story's existence, however, is not the same as telling it. This book is the first sustained and in-depth study of the historical relationship of Dewey's pragmatism to the creative thought of the great Indian statesman, Ambedkar. It is also the first book to explore the historical evolution of pragmatism in India through the creation of Ambedkar's new form of pragmatism.

## "A New Turn to His Life": New Clues to Ambedkar's Pragmatist Quest

This book explores the evolution of pragmatist thought in India in the life, works, and thought of Bhimrao Ambedkar. Why do I think that such a story is waiting to be told? More than enough clues rest in plain view, if we are but open to exploring the questions they elicit. The letter to Savita in 1952 is one such clue that begs for more exploration of what Dewey and his thought mean for such an accomplished thinker. We also have material traces that Ambedkar was fascinated with Dewey's thought. He was an avid reader of Dewey and pragmatism long after he left the pragmatist's classes in Morningside Heights. In various archives around India, one can still find dusty copies of Ambedkar's various editions of Dewey's books, including *Ethics* (1908, two copies), *The Influence of Darwin on Philosophy* (1910), *German Philosophy and Politics* (1915), *Democracy and Education* (1916, 1925; four copies in total), *Essays in Experimental Logic* (1916, 1953), *Experience and Nature* (1929), *The Quest for Certainty* (1930), *Freedom and Culture* (1939), *Education Today* (1940), *Problems of Men* (1946), *Human Nature and Conduct* (1948), and Joseph Ratner's edited collection *Intelligence in the Modern World: John Dewey's Philosophy* (1939). Books about Dewey's pragmatism were also cherished by Ambedkar, including Sidney Hook's *John Dewey: Philosopher of Science and Freedom* (1950), Jerome Nathanson's *John Dewey: The Reconstruction of the Democratic Life* (1951), Paul Arthur Schilp's *The Philosophy of John Dewey* (1951), and A. H. Johnson's *The Wit and Wisdom of John Dewey* (1949). Ambedkar's copy of Dewey's 1939 address, "Creative Democracy—The Task Before Us," typed by the dedicated student V. B. Kadam, is jammed in an iron trunk in archives in Maharashtra.[14] Multiple books by William James and George Santayana round out Ambedkar's collection of American thought. Sizing up the stack of works by or about Dewey, one is hard pressed to find another modern author as well represented in any of the archives or private collections that preserve Ambedkar's precious library.[15]

Another clue—more revealing of young Ambedkar's personality, perhaps—resides on a scrap of paper I found lodged inside one of these books. Inside Ambedkar's decaying copy of Dewey's 1910 book *The Influence of Darwin on Philosophy*, now preserved at Siddharth College, are Ambedkar's own annotations and his indication of when he acquired this book: "Columbia/New York/12th October 1914." This book was acquired at the beginning of Ambedkar's first seminar with the American pragmatist, a course on psychological ethics held in the fall of 1914. Of more interest to me, however, was what I saw upon unfolding the century-old piece of paper wedged into the back page folds of Dewey's book. The scrap of paper contains an ink blot, indicating the provisional nature of what it was used for, and it also holds Ambedkar's own signature penned out partially or completely in the same ink at least four times with one of his beloved fountain pens. I realized that I was witnessing, through this quotidian artifact, Ambedkar practicing his signature, his mark, and refining his style, a living metaphor for what was going on in his education and his first years back in India afterward. But next to these signature attempts was something more intriguing: "John" written out in cursive multiple times by Ambedkar using the same pen and ink. The young Indian student worked hard, but he also dreamed, he also played with language and honed his own artistic script. He did this by refining his now-famous signature, an early, less artful version of the one that adorns the signature page of the Indian constitution in the 1940s, but he also did this by doodling *John* Dewey's name in a book acquired while he was taking the pragmatist's course. Dewey and pragmatism, it seemed, were making their own mark on Ambedkar as early as 1914.

What other clues, should we have the imagination to hear them out, tell us about the interactions between Ambedkar's thought and the diverse tradition of American pragmatism? In the course of my digging about Ambedkar's experience at Columbia in archives related to Dewey's history, I have come across a tantalizing new clue that convinces me that there is much more to be said on Ambedkar's relationship to Dewey than what has appeared in the handful of studies so far; it also shocked me as to the possible reading we can give to the *pragmatist* nature of Ambedkar's lifelong project of emancipation. Everyone agrees, it seems, that Dewey had *some* influence on Ambedkar, that Dewey's idea of democracy made *some* impact on Ambedkar, and that Ambedkar later promulgated his own revision of Buddhism to his followers in the 1950s. But what if all of these points and projects, disparate in time as they were, were somehow related, but not reducible, to Ambedkar's exposure to and reception of Dewey? Even the merest possibility of such a connection could be epochal, shaking common narratives of Dewey as being only one of many (equal) influences on the Indian reformer or of Ambedkar deciding on Buddhism as his favored religion for conversion in the late 1940s and as only tangentially affected by Dewey.

It is just this possibility that jumped out at me when I heard an audio recollection by Nima Adlerblum (1881–1974) held by the Center for Dewey Studies at Southern Illinois University, Carbondale. Adlerblum was a philosopher and activist who wrote on Jewish philosophy, but her importance for this project on Ambedkar lies in the fact that she was a devoted student of John Dewey's during his years at Columbia University. Much later in her life, on May 6, 1966, Adlerblum recorded her memories of studying with Dewey. This recording was apparently made at the request of Dewey's second wife, Roberta, and Columbia University, for a proposed Dewey museum that never materialized.[16] The simple but detailed recording is valuable because it recounts Adlerblum's wide range of experiences in Dewey's classes and at Columbia, which started with her enrollment in 1905 and continued past her time as a student at Columbia later in Dewey's life, when he was married to Roberta. Adlerblum had much experience with Dewey, taking and auditing his classes year in and year out; dropping in on dinners at the home of Dewey and his first wife, Alice; and writing a dissertation on the fourteenth-century Jewish philosopher Gersonides with Dewey's interest and guidance, a work that was finalized and published in 1926.[17] Adlerblum even served as the chair of the international committee formed in 1948 that was tasked with planning Dewey's ninetieth birthday celebration, an event attended by the first prime minister of India, Jawaharlal Nehru. As she puts it in her 1966 recollection concerning Dewey, "My memories therefore cover more than a half a century."[18]

What caught my attention in her recollections was not the stories about Dewey, but rather the memories of international students at Columbia University during her many years as a student there (1905–1926). At one point she begins to talk of the many Japanese and Chinese students that Dewey attracted to his courses, and she recalls that she "used to meet those students frequently in the Library Seminar Room, on the campus, [and in] the cafeteria." Alongside the recollections of this group of East Asian students, Adlerblum speaks of one solitary and motivated—but unnamed—student from *India*. My heart raced—could this be *Ambedkar*? Her memories of this individual are worth recounting whole:

> There was also a student from India whom I saw daily, as I happened to sit at the same table with him at the Seminar Library. Always with pen and paper he was reading Dewey's articles, which so swiftly followed one another. He would sometimes ask me for some explanations, and we would ponder together the many ideas. He recopied the class notes after each lecture. Whenever he read some to me, it felt as if I heard Dewey himself talking—not a single word omitted. He also showed me his attached comments, searching for a bridge between Dewey and Buddhism. Both, he said, aim at the highest morality. But Dewey's drive for a good society might be more conducive to happiness than nirvana. Providence, he felt led him to the United States. His father wanted him to study in England, but he was biased against the British Government for keeping the Indian people backward. In the United States he met Dewey who gave a new turn to his life. He was promised a post at the University of Delhi. He planned to give courses on every phase of his philosophy. In infusing Dewey's concept of an idealistic democracy, he may be of some help in easing the ugly, ingrained tradition of the Untouchables,—probably not too soon. He himself belonged to the upper class.[19]

If this recollection—recorded some fifty years after his stay at Columbia University—was referring to Ambedkar, it could change many things we know about him and the ways we tell his story. Do the dates line up? We know Adlerblum took and audited classes with Dewey for many years, and that she often frequented the Columbia University campus. In her recollection, Adlerblum reveals that "since then [after entering Columbia in 1905] I took all his courses year in and year out, even after I got my degree, was married and a mother."[20] Nima was married to Israel Adlerblum, an insurance consultant in New York who was a student of Edwin Robert Anderson Seligman (also Ambedkar's adviser), on May 14, 1914.[21] From the return address indicated on a May 19, 1915, letter Israel wrote to Seligman, we know that Nima Adlerblum resided at 370 West 116th Street in New York City, less than one mile from Columbia's campus and library.[22] According to a January 28, 1915, letter to staff at Columbia's Department of Economics written by Israel, the couple moved into this nearby residence in the fall of 1914.[23] Thus, it is likely that Nima Adlerblum was around the campus, as she claimed in her 1966 recollection, before and after her 1914 marriage; this, of course, is the exact period when Ambedkar was exposed to Dewey's courses at Columbia (1914–1916). She even recalls elsewhere in her recollections taking courses such as Dewey's Psychological Ethics, which we know he was teaching while Ambedkar studied at Columbia.

Many details in the passage—and facts that we know about Dewey and Ambedkar—line up with the hypothesis that Adlerblum was referring to Ambedkar as the Indian student. First, Dewey had no other Indian students in the 1910s, or even the 1920s, that I can identify beyond Ambedkar.[24] One of the leading Ambedkar scholars, Eleanor Zelliot, has written that she can recall two other preindependence Indians who had a taste of American education comparable to Ambedkar's, but neither attended Columbia University, choosing midwestern and western universities instead.[25] From his biographers, we know that Ambedkar frequently occupied the library, even to the point of forcing the librarian to evict him at closing time. We also know that Ambedkar's father and grandfather benefited greatly from British sources—indeed, it was the military that gave them and him his English education—so it seems reasonable that his father would have "wanted him to study in England." In general, it was much more common to study there than in America because, as Brant Moscovitch puts it, "most families encouraged their children to study in Britain in the hope of advancing their career prospects and possibly enabling them to eventually join the Indian Civil Service."[26] Beyond these facts, some parts of this description concerning the "Indian student's" performance and personality struck me as denoting Ambedkar. Adlerblum's recollection that "whenever he read some [of Dewey's lectures] to me, it felt as if I heard Dewey himself talking" echoes Zelliot's report of "Savita Ambedkar's [Ambedkar's second wife] . . . touching story of Ambedkar's happily imitating John Dewey's distinctive classroom mannerisms—thirty years after Ambedkar sat in Dewey's classes."[27] The descriptions of his studious reading, annotating, and mannerisms also cohere with K. N. Kadam's curious claim that "Dr. Ambedkar took down every word uttered by his great teacher [Dewey] in the course of his lectures; and it seems that Ambedkar used to tell his friends that, if unfortunately Dewey died all of a sudden, 'I could reproduce every lecture verbatim.'"[28] In sum, what little we know about the general intellectual impact Dewey's words and personage had on Ambedkar aligns perfectly with Adlerblum's description. Also like Ambedkar, with his unique focus on ending caste—instead of the more common fixation on Indian independence—Adlerblum recounts that the "Indian student" was dedicated to "easing the ugly, ingrained tradition of the Untouchables."

The letter is startling precisely because of the many details that line up so well with Ambedkar's story: a unique figure among Indian students in the 1910s in both his focus on caste oppression and his experience with Dewey. I cannot think of any other Indian student who would check so many of these boxes. The few specifics that do not line up with what we know of Ambedkar's life—the mention of the student being from the upper castes and his having a promised position at the "University of Delhi"— could be artifacts of Adlerblum's struggling to remember details large and small from over fifty years in her past. There is evidence that Ambedkar wanted to be a professor from early on, however.[29] Or the mismatching details could be an indication that Ambedkar took liberties with his caste description and the possibilities that awaited him back in India once in America, where there was still little accurate information about India and its traditions. It would have been humiliating—not to mention unneces- sary—to foreground his status as an "untouchable" and as a victim of caste oppression to an American student like Adlerblum, sharing his reading ta- ble and his admiration for Professor Dewey. In various ways, Ambedkar felt a new type of freedom in Morningside Heights, and it is certainly possible that he extended this appreciation of his new agency to creative redescrip- tions of who he was and his aspirations when speaking to his new Ameri- can colleagues at Columbia.[30]

The most significant details of this letter line up with what we know about Ambedkar and Dewey and reveal new ways of understanding the importance of Dewey and American pragmatism to young Ambedkar. The probabilities here are intriguing. We imagine a young Ambedkar fascinated with Dewey, spending long hours in the library "reading Dewey's articles," recopying "the class notes after each lecture," and querying nearby students like Adlerblum to "ponder together the many ideas" in Dewey's classes and writings. As I saw on that scrap of paper still held at Siddharth College, Ambedkar was doodling Dewey's name next to his own, most likely during his first semester with the pragmatist in fall 1914. The Adlerblum recollec- tion lines up too well with too many other hints of Dewey's importance to Ambedkar to ignore. We have no comparable primary sources—scrap pa- pers, letters talking of his intellectual debt, or the recollections from class- mates like Adlerblum—that attest to this level of intense engagement with any of his other teachers. We must take Dewey seriously in our accounts of Ambedkar, and such seriousness entails detailed and sustained attention.

Adlerblum's recollection is epochal because of what it can add to the narratives of Ambedkar's life we can imagine and tell. It reveals a vision of a young Ambedkar animated by a quest to find "a bridge between Dewey and Buddhism" during his time with Dewey in 1914–1916. Every bio- graphical account notes that K. A. Keluskar—a reformer, schoolteacher, and mentor to Ambedkar—gave the Marathi book he authored on the life of the Buddha to young Ambedkar in 1907, but there is not much indication that Ambedkar was invested in recovering and promulgating Buddhism in the 1910s or 1920s. There is the tantalizing hint provided by the Buddhist monk, Walpole Rahula, that Ambedkar was reported to have said that he "became a Buddhist when I was a boy of sixteen," at the time that he received Keluskar's book.[31] The bulk of narratives on Ambedkar's intellectual development, however, place his decision to commit to Buddhism in the late 1940s. The Adlerblum letter opens up the possibility that not only was Ambedkar familiar with Buddhism early in his life, but he was actively seeking to reconstruct it even then.

Adlerblum's recollection opens up the very likely possibility that Ambedkar evinced a passion about Buddhism *and* pragmatism as early as his time at Columbia. This jars against our received inferences about Ambedkar and Buddhism, but it does cohere with a few stray, and easily overlooked, comments that Ambedkar made during speeches in the 1950s. At a Diamond Jubilee celebration held in honor of Ambedkar in Bombay on October 28, 1954, Ambedkar addressed the crowd of around three hundred individuals and, according to a report on the festivities, revealed "that he had gone through religious books like *Mahabharat*, *Bhagwat Gita* in his young days but when he came across the book about *Gautam Buddha*, it had [made a] great impression on him and since that time he had been the follower of *Buddha*."[32] The book he referenced is most likely the one given to him by Keluskar in 1907, when he was sixteen years old. In a January 14, 1955, Marathi speech at a rally in Bombay organized by the Advisory Committee on Buddhism, Ambedkar admitted a long-standing passion for Buddhism, even before his days at Columbia: "I had gone to America for my higher education. There I read a lot about Buddhism to satisfy my curiosity created by my initial reading of Buddhist biography, and also to further understand Buddhism." If this late utterance is taken to be accurate, what he said next confirms what Adlerblum observed and remembered decades later: "My passion for Buddhism is therefore quite old."[33]

What the Adlerblum recollection adds to these statements made by Ambedkar in the last years of his life, a period that focused on his promotion of Buddhism above all else, is the importance of pragmatism to this project. As we shall see in later chapters, Buddhism, as Ambedkar retasks and reconstructs it, is thoroughly intertwined with pragmatist ideas, methods, and themes. Young Ambedkar at Columbia was at the very beginning of this journey of creative appropriation, one that saw the potential in Dewey for the recovery and adaptation of Buddhism; as Adlerblum reports the young student saying, "Dewey's drive for a good society might be more conducive to happiness than nirvana." This was a not a *replacing* of Buddhism with Deweyan pragmatism, however, but a *merging* or *synthesis*. The student in Adlerblum's description saw Dewey's thought as a reservoir of creative resources, one that could be evangelized back in India, as the student's reported plan "to give courses on every phase of his [Dewey's] philosophy."[34] As we shall see, Ambedkar—in all likelihood the student being described—demonstrably appropriated and resisted parts of Dewey's thought once he was back in India battling against caste injustice. As Adlerblum reports five decades later about this student who struck her as so memorable, "In infusing Dewey's concept of an idealistic democracy, he [the Indian student] may be of some help in easing the ugly, ingrained tradition of the Untouchables,—probably not too soon."[35]

Such provocative primary sources as Adlerblum only add to the textual and archival case that I build throughout this book: Dewey should not be dismissively judged as simply one of many influences, he is the *best documented influence* on Ambedkar's development at Columbia, the *most evident source of inspiration and material* for important parts of vital writings and speeches by Ambedkar, and *a vivid inspiration* to Ambedkar's revisioning of Indian traditions such as Buddhism. To fully understand Ambedkar as an anticaste activist and theorist, and to see what informed his passion and creativity in regard to Buddhism, one must come to terms with Dewey and his form of pragmatism as Ambedkar saw, heard, and read it early in his educational development. Pragmatism therefore represents a thread that runs through many of Ambedkar's projects, activities, and works. Ambedkar, from his earliest days to his final years, can be understood under many labels: *activist, politician, anticaste intellectual*, and *Buddhist*. But as Adlerblum opens up for us, among those descriptions and hopes must be represented an embodied quest to bridge the worlds of Dewey's pragmatism and Indian Buddhism. Ambedkar, in short, was also a *pragmatist*.

## The Intersection of Ambedkar, Pragmatism, and Rhetoric

To tell the story of Ambedkar as a pragmatist—or Ambedkar as closely in conversation with Dewey's philosophy—we must avoid paths that lead to nowhere or strategies that shut down our imaginative grasp of the possibilities of Ambedkar's thought and history. First, we must not think that talking of Dewey as an influence on Ambedkar precludes recognizing the influence of other figures—Vladimir Simkhovitch, say, or Gabriel Tarde. Influence, and the depth of meaning behind someone as well-read as

Ambedkar, will not be a zero-sum game. That being said, when one aims to do justice to a thinker who has written and said as much as Ambedkar has, and who has evolved as much as Ambedkar has, one must make choices: if we bring in all the authors that he has read, or all of the teachers that he has studied with, then we will have much less room to delve into each of these authors, with their myriad texts and their own historical courses of evolution. Broadness in the stories of Ambedkar's influences and the trajectories of his work inevitably sacrifices some possible senses of meaningful depth. While both sorts of approaches to Ambedkar are valuable, this study focuses mostly on the Dewey-Ambedkar relationship to provide a new meaning and narrative arc to the general claims about Ambedkar's deep relationship with Dewey and his thought. Let no reader, however, think that this is the *only* account that can be given about Ambedkar. I look forward to other scholars finding comparable archival resources to those which I employ in this study, and book-length inquiries on the influence of Edwin Seligman on Ambedkar, or Henri Bergson, are sure to be useful projects to pursue. This book tries to present the most thorough, evidence-based reading of Ambedkar's reception of—and in some cases resistance to—Dewey's pragmatism *as it was encountered at different points by Ambedkar.* The last qualification is vital, since it is all too easy to simply hold up part of Dewey's corpus that seems similar to something in Ambedkar's body of work. This might be provocative and conceptually useful, but it is not the project on which I am embarking. Ambedkar did not know of, hear, or read all of Dewey's works—said to be over eight million words contained in the thirty-eight volumes of his collected works. I am particularly attentive to what evidence we have concerning what Ambedkar actually read of Dewey's vast corpus and what evidence we have that parts of those books or lectures actually mattered for parts of Ambedkar's complex body of work. Ambedkar did not read everything Dewey wrote or spoke, nor did he read all parts of the books he owned, let alone find all those parts useful in his own battle against caste oppression in India. We must maintain a focus on the question: What specific evidence undergirds our attempts to deepen the story of Ambedkar and Dewey?

This book attempts to answer these questions of reception, influence, resistance, and reconstruction with as much archival and textual evidence as possible. This project fits into two general lines of scholarly approach, each with its prevailing habits, advantages, and limitations. The method of argument accordingly synthesizes both of these approaches. First, this book constitutes a *philosophical* examination of Ambedkar's work, one with a particular reference to those parts and themes that have a meaningful relationship to parts of Dewey's philosophy. This approach focuses on arguments and positions, especially as they are ensconced in specific *texts*. One can talk in general about Ambedkar's arguments against the caste system, but he presents these in specific ways in different books or speeches; accordingly, I try to explicate the content, commitment, and evolution of Ambedkar's philosophy as it is discussed, argued, and asserted in the details of specific works. There will always be books, speeches, and passages left out of this approach, but what it loses in generalities it gains in a specific sensitivity to texts that contain arguments that can be placed as unique positions within a thinker's developing body of philosophical argument. By the end of this book, I hope to have provided a historically informed account of what Ambedkar's philosophy looks like if we are sensitive to its extensions, adaptations, and resistances to themes in Dewey's complex thought. In this way, this book hopes to serve as an addition to the literature in the history of philosophy, especially that part concerned with the interactions between American and Indian philosophies in and around the twentieth century.

Another important characteristic that distinguishes this book and its argument is its *rhetorical* focus. Rhetoric, or the art of persuasion and meaning-making through language use in community settings, has a long and distinguished history in the West, as well as in India. Hindu, Jaina, and Buddhist philosophers have long argued about the nature of rationality, argument, and debate; some of the greatest thinkers in the Indian tradition were also powerful speakers or teachers. Ambedkar, I argue, is part of this tradition of thinkers who were also great public communicators. Beyond his fiery orations, the concept of rhetoric focuses us on something that often goes overlooked: Ambedkar's love of words, and what they can do if they are used in the right way to address the right people. Eschewing pejorative notions of "rhetoric" as simplistic manipulation, instead taking it as pointing toward certain *ways* or *styles* of argument or persuasion, allows us to see Ambedkar as a rhetor adapting his books and speeches to various audiences and situational needs. A useful, albeit ultimately simplistic, notion of rhetoric to start with is Aristotle's idea of "the faculty of observing, in any given case, the available means of persuasion," or Donald C. Bryant's conception of rhetoric and persuasion as "the function of adjusting *ideas to people* and *people to ideas*."[36] More recent views of rhetoric see persuasion as practices of meaning-making and the performance of individual and systemic power. Both of these conceptions of rhetoric are used here as guides in seeing how Ambedkar makes specific arguments in certain ways, as well as how he reshapes terms and traditions to recapture self-respect for himself and his Dalit audiences. The rhetorical approach taken by this book dovetails with the philosophical approach in that both call for a sensitivity to texts: sites of rich linguistic choices, arguments, and presentation of words that convey powerful values and emotions and that present positions and philosophies through concrete, and contingent, arrangements.

A focus on rhetoric adds the idea of *persuasion* to this situation, focusing on analyzing Ambedkar's *texts*, with all the moves and arguments contained therein, in a specific *context*. Most evidently, the context of specific texts involved certain intended or assumed audiences. It is this feature, combined with Ambedkar's stunning number of public speeches, that also makes this study a valuable addition to the study of public address in India. Ambedkar's books, as well as his many speeches, were typically calculated and intentionally designed to speak to certain kinds of audiences with specific interests and needs. The approach taken in this inquiry explores Ambedkar's philosophical pragmatism in conjunction with its *rhetorical* commitments to a certain style of arguing to various audiences and in regard to various situations he encountered throughout his life. Whereas approaching Ambedkar as a philosopher tends to concretize his many arguments and texts into one "philosophy" or position, taking him as a rhetorical figure allows us to see the tensions within and among his various messages as being related to his changing and evolving goals and interests, as well as the varying interests of those he aimed to reach with his messages.

What will emerge from this study of Ambedkar's education, the books he read and those he wrote, and the many speeches he gave is a powerful image of his reception of pragmatism in his Indian context. Pragmatism, specifically the version ensconced in the Deweyan texts to which he was privy, is shown to affect Ambedkar's arguments and style of argument in determinate ways. It affects important parts of what he says in many texts and how he makes his points across these texts. Telling the story of Ambedkar and his relationship with Dewey—as well as the story of pragmatism's evolution in India—is a complex undertaking. It will surely take more than this book to do it justice. But it must start with Ambedkar's first contact with John Dewey at Columbia University. We must not let our current state of knowledge about Ambedkar dictate what we could know. For instance, Ambedkar's time at Columbia and his engagement there with Dewey seems lost to time, so much so that Ananya Vajpeyi proclaims, "Details of their initial encounter are not known and cannot be reconstructed."[37]

While Vajpeyi is right that we presently lack details on what Ambedkar said to Dewey in their first conversation, surely we can ascertain more information on Ambedkar's experience in Dewey's courses at Columbia, and from that basis, examine its echoes and impacts on Ambedkar's later work. In chapter 1 I begin this difficult process. I set the scene of what courses Ambedkar took with Dewey and what the Columbia philosophical faculty was like at the time. More importantly, however, is the detailed examination of the content of the three courses that Ambedkar took from Dewey. Using a variety of lecture notes scrawled and typed by Dewey, as well as pre-prepared handouts he produced and notes taken by Ambedkar and his fellow students, I chronicle for the first time the precise content of what Ambedkar heard in Dewey's courses. Such a level of detail on Ambedkar's educational experience is, to my knowledge, absolutely unique. This exhaustive look into Ambedkar's time with Dewey is also valuable in that it grounds and adds meaning to Ambedkar's activities and rhetoric once he was back in India, as he began engaging the psychology and customs of the caste system. As we shall see, Dewey's discussion of the interrelation of the individual and community, force and effective freedom, and individualism and collectivism would inform many of Ambedkar's innovative notions of democracy and social justice. We shall also canvass what Ambedkar heard about Dewey's psychology of the individual and of group custom, topics that would be enhanced, expanded, and employed in Ambedkar's later critiques of the caste system. In these early courses, Ambedkar began to see the integrative and reconstructive impulses of the pragmatist tradition as spelled out in figures such as Dewey, a synthesizing orientation that gave additional meaning and direction to so many of the other courses he took from the progressive intellectuals at Columbia University.

In chapter 2 I examine one of Ambedkar's first publications, a review of a book by Bertrand Russell. While most accounts of Ambedkar's life pass over this minor publication, we must reevaluate it as it represents an important start to Ambedkar's lifelong interest in public acts of melioration and reconstruction aimed at Indian society. Here, he advises his readers on what is of value in Russell's book, a work that is inherently concerned with oppression and cycles of oppression that could accompany reform efforts. Ambedkar draws on Dewey's ideas of force that he heard from the American professor in his 1916 course and begins to synthesize ideas of constructive or intelligent force with the emphasis on individual reformers as educative that he sees in Russell's book. For Ambedkar after his time at Columbia, reform becomes a form of education outside of formal institutions, and reformers must be concerned with the sort of force or means that they employ in striving for ends as crucial as equality and social justice. It is here that we can see that *persuasive force* is a valuable, but unstable, path around end-destroying fanatical violence or coercive shame.

Ambedkar's meliorism holds a special place for persuasion as one of the best means for social change. Dewey's pragmatism partially inspired this commitment, along with the engagement with thinkers such as Russell. It began to affect Ambedkar's *method* or *way* of arguing—his rhetorical style—as early as 1919. Chapter 3 explores Ambedkar's first public appearance of note in India, his testimony to the Southborough Commission in 1919 concerning voting reforms for India's various constituencies. It is in this public testimony that we first see Ambedkar echoing Dewey's ideas and texts at vital points to enunciate his novel notion of social democracy and his own critique of caste oppression. I chart these echoes in parts of his testimony and explore the rhetorical functioning that quotation—and echoing—plays in constituting the soft force of persuasion. This contributes to what I call Ambedkar's *reconstructive rhetoric*, a technique that channels the meliorative themes of pragmatism through creative uses of text, authors, and past traditions. Reconstruction for Ambedkar the Indian pragmatist engaged both certain *ideals* to which democracy should aspire and a certain *method* of advocating and creating these conditions.

Ambedkar's version of pragmatism, along with his full use of reconstructive rhetoric, matured in the 1930s when he turned to a full-throated critique of caste and the Hindu tradition that he believed authorized it. The 1930s also encompassed some of his most powerful oratory criticizing caste oppression. Chapter 4 explores Ambedkar's unique version of pragmatism as it emerges in texts such as his famous undelivered address, *Annihilation of Caste*. Dewey's pragmatism was not the only influence or tradition inspiring Ambedkar, of course, but it was a significant one. To make this case for its importance to Ambedkar, I provide a detailed and thorough accounting of Ambedkar as a *reader* of pragmatist texts—including Dewey's 1908 *Ethics* and *Democracy and Education*—with a concern for what constellations of themes and ideas he found valuable in his former teacher's work. These ideas are not only marked by Ambedkar as a reader; they also impact him as an orator or rhetor. Accordingly, I provide the most exhaustive analysis to date of passages from pragmatist works that intersect with and are echoed in Ambedkar's *Annihilation of Caste* text, illustrating two vital points: first, that Ambedkar's critique of caste and approach to democracy synthetically extend some ideas in Dewey's work while simultaneously going beyond the American's philosophy, and second, that pragmatism's method of reconstruction also encompasses the ways that Ambedkar argued and used sources such as Dewey's books. Considering his *Annihilation of Caste* text as a rhetorical artifact intended for a specific audience, we can begin to discern Ambedkar's concern with the habits of individual reflective morality and how these relate to making dominant group customs more reflective and progressive. From a rhetorical perspective, this well-known text thereby reveals a model of conversion that reflects Ambedkar's concerns with inquiry, rational thought, and the role of reflective criticism in examining Hinduism and the caste system. His rhetoric became one of reconstructive meliorism as it sought to promote *reflection* on problematic situations, *renunciation* of problematic religious attitudes, and, eventually, *conversion* to more useful religious orientations.

Seeing Ambedkar as a rhetorical figure also attunes us to the differences in the enunciation of his views and philosophy in various time periods and to varying audiences. Chapter 5 examines Ambedkar's speeches and writings targeting his Dalit followers, including powerful addresses in the 1930s arguing for Dalit conversion from Hinduism and various speeches in the 1940s and 1950s that argued for conversion to Buddhism. What we shall see in analyzing the arguments and appeals contained in these rhetorical artifacts adds further support to the idea that Dewey mattered for the direction and content of Ambedkar's philosophy of emancipation. Resisting simplistic readings and objections that paint influence as a matter of imitating or copying wholesale, this chapter begins by charting out the influence of Dewey's early—and neo-Hegelian—idea of "personality" on Ambedkar in the 1930s. Using textual and archival evidence, I show that Ambedkar used some aspects of Dewey's concept of personality from his early writings in the 1880s but also resisted or refused other parts of the American's early pragmatism. As demonstrated in previous chapters, Ambedkar's reconstructive method picks and chooses ideas, ideals, and texts from Dewey and strategically reworks them into various parts of his arguments concerning democracy, caste, and social justice. The idealist philosophy that Dewey largely discarded before he stood in front of Ambedkar and his classmates thereby assumes a new importance in charting Ambedkar's intellectual engagement with Dewey. The quest of Ambedkar and his fellow Dalits to reclaim personality leads us to consider Ambedkar's epochal push for conversion to Buddhism in the 1950s. We will see how, culminating with his conversion at Nagpur on October 14, 1956, Ambedkar's rhetoric, his performance of conversion, and his philosophy all intersected in a liberatory practice of reconstructing the self.

While his advocacy for conversion makes important use of various early and later parts of Dewey's pragmatism, it offers us a vision of a lived pragmatism that is distinctly Ambedkar's and is unique to the Indian context. Ambedkar appropriated parts of Dewey's early and later psychology, combined them with his own interests in willfulness and effort, and produced a pragmatic version of Buddhism that offers a path toward reclaiming Dalit respect and self-respect. In the conclusion to this comprehensive, but ultimately incomplete, study of Ambedkar and Dewey, I draw out the general contours of Ambedkar's form of pragmatism—what I label his *Navayana Pragmatism*, echoing the labeling of his Buddhism as *Navayana* or "new vehicle" Buddhism. The commitments of Ambedkar's Navayana Pragmatism are explored, showing that Ambedkar is an anticaste thinker who also holds a general philosophy of democracy and emancipation. Ambedkar's Navayana Pragmatism is part of the global evolution of pragmatist thought, and it emerges in its distinctness within the turbulence of twentieth-century India, but its implications and applications for reconstruction and democratic meliorism are by no means limited to only those contexts and topics. Such a general accounting of Ambedkar as a Navayana pragmatist does not exclude all the other ways to categorize and explore his thought, but it does give us additional traction in placing Ambedkar as a global philosopher.

## Ambedkar as a Pragmatist: An Opening, Not a Conclusion

Of course, Dewey and his pragmatism are not present in every part of Ambedkar's corpus, and objections to any inquiry into his relationship with Dewey that assume such a demand do not engage the case I lay out in this book. Also without basis are the demurs to projects that link Dewey and Ambedkar that assert Dewey was simply one among many, or that, as Aishwary Kumar claims, "Focusing solely on Dewey's influence, however, obscures many untraced supplements of Ambedkar's thought, for there were figures from different, often irreconcilable, traditions that he was engaged with during the interwar years, and with whom his relationships were far from settled. Often he would refuse to choose one thinker over the other."[38] This is a perplexing position. Must every book account comprehensively for *every* influence on Ambedkar? Must influence be reduced to a state of identity, with the standard being that thinkers like Ambedkar engaged with only one thinker and always sided with that figure? These are ultimately nonuseful stances to take in fleshing out the specific and actual relationship between Dewey and Ambedkar. There is also no reason to think that spending time on detailing and connecting all the archival and textual evidence linking Ambedkar and Dewey precludes acknowledging the existence of other influences, just as Kumar's insightful book limits its focus to Ambedkar and Mohandas Gandhi without precluding other scholars (like me) fully exploring other influences.

I believe what lies below such complaints is the idea that claiming that Ambedkar is a pragmatist or that he was influenced by Dewey really means that Ambedkar is *only* a pragmatist, or that Ambedkar's philosophy is *the same as* Dewey's pragmatism. Anyone who reads the chapters that follow will realize I am not interested in such simplistic and useless reductions. The pragmatist tradition is pluralistic and diverse, and being part of this tradition of thought and intellectual history neither implies nor demands a uniformity in thought. Both Dewey and Charles S. Peirce were pragmatists, and the latter influenced the former as his teacher, but their thought is radically different. Dewey's Chinese student Hu Shih—who shared Dewey's class with Ambedkar in 1915–16—has been placed as part of the pragmatist tradition without asserting the impossible claim that his form of Chinese pragmatism was simply Dewey's thought repackaged. Pragmatism is creative and synthetic, and as it spread through global contacts its hybridity became even more intriguing, innovative, and pronounced. When I explore Ambedkar's pragmatism, I am really exploring his thought as *historically* related to Dewey's thought (as his teacher, as the author of books that mattered to Ambedkar), as *conceptually* related (as using some common ideas and ideals such as social democracy), and as *methodologically* related (as sharing a process of reconstructive meliorism). This multifaceted approach displays how Ambedkar adapted, reconceptualized, and reimagined what a pragmatist philosophy could mean for social democracy and the fight against oppression. Just as calling Ambedkar a "Buddhist" does not preclude exploring him as an "activist" or "lawyer," discussing him as a "pragmatist" does not close off other ways of telling his story. Indeed, readers will see new vistas opened up in the course of this book concerning the interrelations possible and actual between Dewey's and Ambedkar's complex philosophies. Let us proceed to suspend what conclusions we think we know about Ambedkar and Dewey and give the lifelong intellectual relationship between Dewey and Ambedkar the attention and care it so rightly deserves. Ambedkar never had the time to tell the intellectual history of his relationship with Dewey and his thought. This book represents an attempt, albeit imperfect, to imagine one way that such a tale could be told.

# ONE

# Ambedkar and Dewey
# at Columbia University

"We became fearful of the loneliness which surrounded us." This was how Ambedkar recounted—most likely in the 1930s—one of his earliest childhood experiences of what it meant to live, travel, and be "untouchable" in India during his childhood.[1] It is not too much to say that one cannot understand Ambedkar's life or writings, or untouchability in general, if one does not understand the deep existential loneliness he felt throughout his life. He had his community of untouchables, but each person felt alone and devalued by a system that assigned them worth, occupations, and prohibitions based on their birth family. Fear and loneliness surrounded Ambedkar even when he was among his most intimate acquaintances: his family. Later in life, Ambedkar would see philosophical tools such as John Dewey's notion of democratic community as an ideal or hope that loneliness could be erased and bridges with dignity be built between agreeing and disagreeing community members. But the diametric opposite of communication's focus—lacking a community of action and meaning *with others*—constantly haunted Ambedkar.

The roots of Ambedkar's search for dignity and community, and an escape from loneliness, started early in his life. Others have explored the details and particulars of Ambedkar's life story and his lived experiences of caste injustice more thoroughly than I am able to in this book focusing on his relationship to American pragmatism.[2] New York itself surely affected the young Indian; as Christopher Queen puts it, "Ambedkar cannot have missed the progressivist and modernist *zeitgeist* that permeated Morningside Heights."[3] Ambedkar's time at Columbia University would shake his prison of loneliness and isolation in ways that his experiences as a child in India could not. During Ambedkar's time in Morningside Heights (1913–16) he met a curious cast of progressive-minded figures.[4] He was one of the few Indians living in colonial India to seek an education in America, as opposed to solely a European education, and he was in all likelihood the first Dalit intellectual to receive advanced degrees from an American university. The intellectuals he encountered in New York included his adviser, Edwin Seligman, an expert on finance and the history of economic thought; the ornery anti-Marxist socialist and part-time gardener Vladimir Simkhovitch; perhaps Vladimir's wife, Mary Kingsbury Simkhovitch, who ran a settlement house and was a friend of Dewey's; and a range of other leading lights in economics, sociology, and beyond. Books could be written on each of these figures and what each meant to Ambedkar's later writings and pursuits.

If the recollections aired in the introduction are accurate, one of the more important figures in this intellectual community-making exercise that was Ambedkar's education in the West was John Dewey (1859–1952), "Ambedkar's most influential professor at Columbia University."[5] Dewey—perhaps the foremost thinker in American philosophical circles of his time—impressed Ambedkar. About this, most biographers and scholars of Ambedkar agree; the few details we know of this relationship, however, leave inquisitive minds hungry for more. As we shall see in this book, the young Indian student would see in Dewey and in his ideas and method a vision of deep community and real democracy, an antithesis to collections of individuals that would still leave some feeling lonely, abused, and disempowered. Ambedkar surely felt out of place in some ways while in New York, but in other ways the space was cleared for ideas and philosophies to collide with the views bequeathed to him by Hindu tradition.

Young Ambedkar was steeped in a progressive environment during his time at Columbia and in New York City. But what of his specific experiences with his beloved teacher, John Dewey? What was Dewey like in the classes that Ambedkar took in 1914 and 1915–16, and what did the young student from India learn from this prominent philosopher? While we don't have accounts of their classroom interactions from Ambedkar, we do have accounts from other students of Dewey that help us flesh out what Ambedkar must have experienced in these classes. To put it politely, it must have been the message and philosophy that so grabbed Ambedkar when he was in Dewey's presence, because by all accounts Dewey was no dynamic orator.[6] As we shall see throughout this book, Ambedkar did become a captivating speaker and orator, able to command audiences of many thousands of rapt listeners. In class, however, Ambedkar was confronted with a speaker whom Sidney Hook remembers as largely boring:

He [Dewey] made no attempt to motivate or arouse the interest of his auditors, to relate problems to their own experiences, to use graphic, concrete
illustrations in order to give point to abstract and abstruse positions. He
rarely provoked a lively participation and response from students, in the absence of which it is difficult to determine whether genuine learning or even
comprehension has taken place. Dewey presupposed that he was talking to
colleagues and paid his students the supreme intellectual compliment of
treating them as his professional equals. . . . Dewey spoke in a husky mono-
tone. . . . There were pauses and sometimes long lapses as he gazed out of the
window or above the heads of his audience.[7]

Other students recall similar experiences with Dewey. Horace Kallen noted
that there "was a kind of withdrawn quality in all his communication,"
both inside and outside the classroom, and that it seemed as if Dewey
"was much more at ease in communication with his typewriter than he
was face to face, person to person."[8] The lack of dynamism in Dewey's style
and the halting cadence of his lectures was perceived by some, however,
as integrally connected to Dewey's image as a profound thinker. As James
Gutmann recalls, "I think there was no other teacher I ever had who gave
such a sense that for fifty minutes you were watching a man think."[9] This
impression was not unique to Gutmann; Sidney Hook refers to and agrees
with Ernest Nagel's description of "Dewey in the classroom" as "the ideal
type of man thinking."[10]

Dewey's image as a thinker—based as it was on many texts and ideas
that were profound—seemed to outweigh or countervail any lack of oratorical skill he might suffer from during his teaching or speaking. Ambedkar
was selective, at least when it came to his philosophers at Columbia; his
transcript indicates that he dropped the two-course sequence in 1915–16,
Philosophy 179–180, Present Day Philosophy and the Problem of Evolution, taught by William Pepperell Montague, a colleague and philosophical
opponent of John Dewey.[11] When it came to his philosophical preferences,
Ambedkar voted with his feet.

It is no wonder that the serious and studious young Ambedkar fell
into what was to be a lifelong intellectual relationship with the *thought* of
Dewey; Dewey's classroom was not meant to grab and convert the philosophically uninterested, but it could function as an experience of sustained
thinking about pressing problems. And as was the nature of Dewey's pragmatism in these courses, philosophy always arced toward the practical,
a feature that also surely attracted Ambedkar toward its ideas and ideals.

Ambedkar would never forget these points, as evidenced by a handwritten notecard labeled "John Dewey Philosophy" hailing from his final years. On this notecard—one of his various ways of notetaking—he handwrote two passages and a list of two books. One sentence can be identified as a quotation from Dewey's *The Influence of Darwin on Philosophy* (1910), a book Ambedkar owned and had marked as purchased in New York on October 12, 1914: "As the philosopher has received his problem from the world of action, so he must return his account there for auditing and liquidation."[12] The other sentence Ambedkar penned seems to be his summary of Dewey's philosophy, simply noting, "The consequences, he felt, were the final test of all the thinking and experience [is] the ultimate authority." The notecard ends with two references to two books by or about Dewey published in 1949.[13]

Dewey's lack of facility in communicating might have had a beneficial side. It seemed to sort out those committed to pragmatism in his courses from those not willing to put in the effort to think along with him. As Herbert Schneider notes, Dewey's classes "were well attended but the lectures weren't well listened to, so that he was popular in one sense, but not as a lecturer. But the notes! If we stayed awake enough to take notes, the notes that we got were wonderful to read."[14] Dewey's slow-paced and tortuous style made note taking challenging but necessary; his approach revealed all of his moves and commitments, a fact that Milton Halsey Thomas remembers as confusing but valuable in spurring the students who connected with him to greater intellectual heights: "He was so honest, he had to define everything, he had to think around it, and when he had finished his excursion, he would resume the main thread of his remarks in the next sentence without warning. It was not only confusing, but [it] placed a heavy strain on orderly note-taking."[15] Notes from these classes became the cherished trophies of his dedicated students, and it is from some of these notes that we can divine what young Ambedkar heard while he sat enraptured by Dewey's ineloquent, but thoroughly pragmatist, philosophical musings. Ambedkar did not draw on every thinker or teacher as much as he would in the case of Dewey, and this says something: Ambedkar recognized something useful in Dewey's classes, and later in his books, that could serve his own purposes in the fight against caste injustice back in India.

The courses that Ambedkar took with Dewey represented the pragmatist's standard offerings at Columbia for the 1910s and surrounding years. Philosophy 231—most often referred to as Psychological Ethics—and Philosophy 131–132 (Moral and Political Philosophy) formed a comprehensive two-year sequence that interrogated practical philosophy from the standpoints of the *psychological* and the *social*.[16] Herbert Schneider notes that Dewey was particularly excited about these courses and took great care in preparing an outline of the semester for students (which he often did not follow that closely in particular class sessions) and in sketching out the bare bones of individual lectures that would often feature his own extemporaneous thinking aloud as their content.[17] Nima Adlerblum also confirms this unique method of preparation and delivery, noting that "he did not improvise his lectures. They were thoroughly prepared with painstaking care. He was really not lecturing in the conventional way, but weaving out his prepared thoughts aloud."[18] Hu Shih, a classmate of Ambedkar's in Philosophy 131–132 in 1915–16, also observed the lack of dynamism in Dewey's oratory. He later recalled the generative power of Dewey's lectures: "John Dewey, with his slow way of lecturing and conversation, was always throwing out right and left these 'seed ideas'—ideas which may fall on fertile soil in the mind of some of his students and grow into intellectual structures probably beyond the dream of the originator."[19]

What "seed ideas" in Dewey's philosophy might have struck Ambedkar as valuable in his own anticaste pursuits? How did Dewey's teaching matter for Ambedkar's development? In the course of all previous work on Ambedkar's education, these questions were answered by turning to *Dewey's* published works, if they were asked at all. Answers were buttressed by the assumption that what Dewey was writing about (especially around this period of Ambedkar's development) was what he was teaching in his classes and that these would be the details from the course remembered by Ambedkar. These assumptions are questionable. Can we answer this riddle of the Dewey and Ambedkar relationship in a more thorough fashion? Using Ambedkar's transcripts and the Columbia University bulletins to ascertain which Dewey courses he enrolled in, I was able to identify the best materials we have about what Ambedkar heard or discussed in these specific classes. Exploring archives at the Center for John Dewey Studies and Columbia University, I was able to locate notes written and typed by Dewey in preparation for his lectures and those recorded by students in these specific terms. Some of these notes are incomplete, and some must be dated by inference. But some contain the exact dates of Ambedkar's specific semesters with Dewey; a few even include notes recorded by Ambedkar himself, whose name is indicated as the substitute note taker.

The value of these resources cannot be overestimated; to my knowledge, *they represent the only detailed record of what Ambedkar heard in any of his courses during his education in the West*. Perhaps additional notes and documents will be identified concerning the content of his other classes in

New York and London, but these Dewey-related materials give us incredibly unique access to the content of his education, and they will surely allow us to ground and pursue an analysis of his relationship to Dewey's pragmatism in an entirely new way. Let us examine what we can to understand the scope and content of these three courses with Dewey as a way to ground the further chapters that show the influence of, and sometimes resistance to, parts of Dewey's vast corpus. We must never forget, of course, that Dewey's collected works span more than thirty-eight volumes and contain over eight million words; not all of these ideas, arguments, and views existed at the time that Ambedkar sat in his philosophy class, nor could Dewey have incorporated all of them had he wanted to in those periodic hours of instruction.

## Philosophy 231: Dewey on Psychology, Society, and the Individual

Even though he only attended the first semester of Dewey's Psychological Ethics series (Philosophy 231), Ambedkar heard enough to see the contours of Dewey's later, and more naturalistic, psychology. We shall explore in future chapters how Dewey's earlier, and more Hegelian, psychology still exerted force on Ambedkar's arguments and positions, but here I provide the contours of what Ambedkar heard about psychology at Columbia in the classroom. How can we reconstruct or access what was possibly uttered in that classroom over a century ago? For Philosophy 231, the fall or winter semester of Dewey's Psychological Ethics course, I have identified a range of archival documents that give us a better idea of what Ambedkar heard from Dewey. Some of these documents come from years adjacent to the period when Ambedkar was enrolled in Philosophy 231; for instance, an incomplete typed page from 1912 (*References*) seems to list the readings that Dewey assigned to his students in the Psychological Ethics course (then listed under the course numbers 121–122).[20] One sees Dewey assigning works by William James on psychology, George Elliot Howard on social psychology, and Gabriel Tarde on imitation; Dewey's own students from his Michigan days are also present, with books from Charles Horton Cooley and Charles A. Ellwood showcasing the range of possible Hegelian rereadings of sociology. Dewey even recommends his own work with James H. Tufts, the 1908 *Ethics*, which we shall see Ambedkar leaning heavily on in future chapters. It is safe to infer that many, if not all, of these same books were recommended to Ambedkar's class with Dewey in 1914. As is obvious from his respect for work from directly before and after the turn of the century evident in his later syllabi, Dewey did not abandon older works that he saw as possessing reconstructive value.

Beyond the 1912 *References* document, other archival resources became apparent as ways to get more insight into Ambedkar's semester with Dewey. Some give us a likely idea of what Ambedkar was taught by Dewey. For instance, a forty-three-page syllabus bearing the titles "Columbia University" and "Psychological Ethics" appears to be the sort of précis of a course that Dewey was said to distribute to his students in advance of the semester's specific sessions as early as his teaching days in Michigan.[21] It does not list a date, but it has typed references to Dewey's 1916 book, *Democracy and Education*, and a handwritten note about Bertrand Russell's January 1917 book, *Why Men Fight*, the American edition of Russell's 1916 book (discussed in the next chapter), the focus of one of Ambedkar's early experiments in publication. Using the Columbia course bulletins and what we know of Dewey's travels, we can infer that this amended document, perhaps best called the *1917 Syllabus*, was most likely from the 1917–18 iteration of Philosophy 231–232.[22] Aligned with this useful document is an undated, but likely constantly reused, document that Dewey handed out to his students, titled "Notes on Psychological Ethics: Historical."[23] This seventeen-page *Background Handout* provides the context for Dewey's exploration of psychology and ethics in his course, surveying a range of important philosophical figures from the ancient world that lay behind Dewey's modern problematics: Plato, Aristotle, the Stoics Epictetus and Marcus Aurelius, the Epicureans, and the Skeptics. Such a condensed and generic background handout was surely used in multiple versions of Philosophy 231–232, and it would have been particularly valuable to a young Ambedkar wanting and needing to know more about the tradition of philosophy in the West.

More direct access to Ambedkar's specific semester can be gained from lecture notes from Dewey and his students that I have located. Dewey's own lecture notes, prepared in advance of his classroom ruminations, clearly hail from Ambedkar's course. They are labeled, both in his own handwriting and then later with his typewriter, as "Fall 1914" and "1914–1915 Psy of Ethics (231–232)."[24] Individual lectures bear the dates on which Dewey gave them, allowing us to determine which fell after Ambedkar's 231 fall session concluded and what lectures (and topics) he missed when he replaced Dewey's Philosophy 232 course in the spring with Vladimir Simkhovitch's Economics 242 course on radicalism and social reform.[25] Complementing the instructor's notes (what we can label *Lecture Notes*) are notes taken by students or stenographers during the 1914–15 academic year. Titled "Notes on Psychological Ethics—John Dewey," these were most likely taken or used by students in Ambedkar's class in the fall of 1914; they contain multiple references to Dewey in the third person and bear references dated as late as January 1914.[26] Taken together with the generic supplemental handouts and documents from adjacent years that have been identified (*References, Background Handout,* and *1917 Syllabus*), these *Student Notes* and Dewey's own *Lecture Notes* provide a very detailed and reliable guide to what young Ambedkar heard in his first course with the sage of American philosophy, John Dewey.

What did Ambedkar hear in, and what might he have learned from, this course? As we shall see throughout this book, Dewey's psychology—and its relation to ethics—served as an important touchstone for Ambedkar's quest for social justice within caste-structured Hindu society. By the time he was teaching at Columbia, Dewey's psychological thought had traveled through idealist circuits in Michigan, evolving from its more Hegelian form in his 1887 *Psychology,* and discharged into a fuller, but still evolving, naturalistic instrumentalism that took seriously Darwin and humans as natural organisms. It had surfaced, in a slightly earlier form, in the immensely popular *Ethics* that Dewey authored with his Chicago colleague James H. Tufts in 1908, a book that was reprinted twenty-five times before a significantly revised version was issued in 1932. We shall encounter this 1908 text again when we examine Ambedkar's rhetoric and activism in the 1930s. But in the fall of 1914, Ambedkar and his fellow students were led, most likely for the first time, through the basics of Dewey's approach to ethics informed by psychological science.

Dewey's early approach to psychology—in the 1880s and early 1890s—emphasized what he called the "psychological standpoint." This was the perspective that started where both the British empiricists *and* the new wave of Hegelians began: with consciousness and its contents. According to this stance, we are only to consider our knowledge of external things as integrally related to an individual's consciousness. "The relation of subject and object," Dewey states in an essay on the psychological standpoint from 1886, "is one which exists within consciousness. And its nature or meaning must be determined by an examination of consciousness itself."[27] After his move to Columbia, Dewey began to take empirical science—including the specific areas of evolution and sociology—much more seriously, and he incorporated these approaches into his reading of ethics. The psychological standpoint did not disappear by the time Ambedkar took Dewey's class in 1914; it was further enmeshed or entangled in the social standpoint. The emphasis on consciousness, a vital term for Hegelian approaches that fetishize the Absolute, was significantly reduced for a more socialized account of the individual self or agent. The self as individual was there, but for the Dewey of the 1910s and beyond, the opposition between the individual and the group was a nonstarter. The individual was and is always constituted by group membership. The individual is also a separate creature or living organism, though, so Dewey's account of ethics in Philosophy 231–232 will still account for the group-influenced *psychology* of the individual acting and reacting agent. Science and ideals combine in this approach to ethics, as is evidenced by Dewey's framing of his approach to his students in his *Lecture Notes*: the course was to cover "what is and what ought to be—science and philos [philosophy] as normative."[28] Sciences, like psychology and social psychology, described how things operate and what mechanisms drive our actions. But Dewey, like Ambedkar, was interested in the *normative* aspects of life as well: What is wrong with experience, how can we determine this, and how can we make it better? What is distinctive about Dewey's pragmatism, especially in this course on psychological ethics, is the combination of descriptive and normative endeavors. Dewey consistently resisted a strong "is-ought" distinction, maintaining that science has something to tell us about how humans act, which leads to scientifically informed philosophical accounts of how they ought to act. This is why he immediately follows this statement of the course problematic by recommending the scientific work of Hugo Muensterberg (*Psychology and Life*) alongside Plato's ancient dialogue, *Meno*.[29]

The "self" still matters in this naturalistic approach, but it is nuanced in two dimensions. First, the self that Ambedkar heard about in Philosophy 231 is the self of impulses, instincts that become increasingly habitualized in social settings. It is an inherently *social* or *socialized* self. As Dewey puts it in the *Student Notes*, psychology "is an account of animal nature as modified by operating under social environments."[30] Second, the process of habituation is temporal and contingent on its specific details. In a real sense, ethics from a psychological standpoint in the 1910s for Dewey emphasized the kind of *self* we make through our own actions and through the influence of our society. What is this model of the social self that Dewey laid out for his students? It starts with the basic biological accounting of the individual as creature. As Dewey puts it in his *Lecture Notes*, activity is integrally connected to the biological and involves "stimulus and response—adaptation, adjustment."[31] Of course Dewey was no crass behaviorist, sucking agency and intelligence out of human action. As he put it as early as his important 1896 article "The Reflex Arc Concept in Psychology," the human is an active part of the environment, seeking and searching out stimuli to react to; his *Lecture Notes* show him recommending this work to Ambedkar and his peers as early as September 18, 1914.[32] Beyond mere reactivity on the part of organism, our past experiences and future hopes and expectations condition and define what is a stimulus among the many details available in a surrounding environment.[33] This emphasis on the active organism continues in Dewey's lectures in 1914, where he indicates that reactions to stimuli alter already existing courses of activity—they are, more accurately, a "redirection of action" and "readjusting" of an organism's existing path of action in an environment.

Dewey's psychology, like the political thought that Ambedkar would hear from him, orbits closely around the idea of force. The individual becomes a channel for forces at work in the organism's push for survival, since it must do something rather than nothing in the face of an environment that quickly alternates from boring to deadly in its meaning for a creature. As the *Student Notes* record, "the primary function of life is action and repression [of the urges to act] is painful."[34] What animates the organism—in this case, the human self or agent? The outgoing force grounding human action is what Dewey calls "impulse," a term connected to the limited range of human "instincts" and our wide range of "emotions."[35] Dewey is always concerned, as a pragmatist should be, with his acts of theorizing closing off the richness of present and possible experience, so we must be careful in describing the notion of "instinct" or "impulse" at play. Some of the most fundamental impulses are those related to "food and sex," although Dewey quickly tells his students that these can be "diverted and supplemented by other secondary impulses."[36] Dewey does not reduce life, for instance, to a push for mere survival and procreation. This position would surely have pleased Ambedkar, given his treatment of reductionist accounts of impulses as causes, which we shall encounter in our future explorations of his texts concerning Bertrand Russell and Ambedkar's own *Annihilation of Caste* text. Impulses, as "general springs to action" as Dewey puts it, can be usefully characterized among three other general dimensions. Most impulses possess a mix of the following "emotional tones": "they are displayed 1. in acts of aggression or defense; 2. Are attractive or repulsive; 3. Have the quality of elation or depression."[37] Later in the semester, according to the *Student Notes*, Dewey analyzed impulse into a related, but slightly different, trichotomy: "seeking-shunning, restlessness-quiescence, attraction-repulsion."[38] All of these involve pleasure or pain, and all serve as a useful way to discuss in a scientific way the blind impulses driving preanalyzed human action. What we can take from this is an incipient, but naturalistically grounded, pluralism in accounting for human behavior. We are moved to action as creatures, but we must always be wary of accounts that reduce our urges to *one* impulse or drive such as "acquisitiveness" (as we shall see Bertrand Russell does in a work that caught Ambedkar's attention around 1917–18).

Ambedkar perceived in 1914 that Dewey was no biological reductionist who cared very little for culture or social organization. "These biological traits of impulses and emotions," Dewey is recorded as stating on the first page of *Student Notes*, "are not suppressed in a vacuum, but have relations to social environment which at once qualifies and colors them and gives them meaning."[39] Impulses provide the starting force for action, but they are conditioned and created by our natural *and* social environments, which include everything from the chilling frost of the mountain air to the lurid details of gossip in newspapers. He tells his students bluntly that "we must study how the social environment acts generally and specially."[40] How the environment, with the cooperation of an active and anticipatory organism, operates is through the fixing of stimuli. In general, a "stimulus excites *change*," but its specific meaning—and the specific direction of change or activity—differs radically based on the environment and the meaning it possesses and gains through the formation of "habits."[41] According to Dewey's own *Lecture Notes*, a habit involves "modification of structure" inherent in the plastic organism; it is a change that is based on experience and endures to condition future stimuli and experience.[42] This is the psychological version of what he would later state in his 1916 *Democracy and Education:* that all experience is educative. Stimuli, conditioned by our habits, "cause dis-equilibrium or tension," which our habits guide us in reacting to and hopefully in restoring a state of satisfactory equilibrium.

Where Dewey's psychology meets the normative expectation of ethics comes in his notions of *reflection*. Habits are contingent; experience does not need to be formed in the same ways, yet it is formed in some specific fashion. Individual and group action plays an integral role in shaping habits in certain ways. It is through our conscious analysis of causes and effects, past experiences and their propensities for future action and effect, that the process of inquiry or reflection works. Ambedkar would hear a vital theme of the value of reflection in Dewey, one that was there in a more idealist sense in the 1880s and that remained with Ambedkar through his last decade: *reflection* and *inquiry* involve a conscious removal from the work of habitualized action and reaction in order to render our habits more *intelligent* in future experiences. *Intelligence* is another word Dewey used for the human capacity to abstract oneself from a present situation to reformulate habits and meanings; human impulses drive us, but "they represent often disorganized modes of activity."[43] "Intelligence," according to

Dewey in 1914, is an adaptive response driven by the search for bettering experience and results "from failure of instincts to function adequately."[44] As the *Student Notes* record his thought, Dewey was committed to the idea that "intellect is not highly organized instinct, but the solution which has been found to the difficulties caused by the failures of instincts. Intellect comes with the multiplication of instincts, it is true, but the more instincts we have the more are the conflicts and wars between them, and hence the need of intellect[ual] control."[45]

*Intelligence* or *reflection*, or *inquiry* as Dewey would increasingly put it after Ambedkar's time with him, was the way to instantiate this intellectual control over our habituated ways of dealing with our outgoing impulses or springs to action. The *1917 Syllabus* shows how Dewey talked about matters of inquiry in line with this notion of reflection: "The act of inquiry," Dewey explains to his next batch of psychological ethics students immediately after Ambedkar departed for London,

> proceeds by finding, hitting upon certain factors, particular and general, which are not disintegrated or analyzed. They serve as limits of the reflective process. Reflection is tentative, hypothetical; these are final, categorical, assured, unquestioned, taken for granted. To *know*, as distinguished from to think (doubt and inquire) refers to the things which limit inquiry, and which are certain-ascertained. Knowledge in this sense is intuitive, and reflective inquiry starts from and ends in these assured objects, at every stage of inquiry things being taken for granted both implicit and explicit. They are acknowledged, observed, conformed to in what is done. Analysis makes some of them explicit, and reflection terminates in finding a stimulus which releases a direct response.[46]

This clear statement of reflection as inquiry coheres with what we see in the confirmed notes from Ambedkar's semester with Dewey in 1914 and shows the difference between knowing and reflecting. The former exudes certainty and focuses on one channeled path of reaction to a stimulus, whereas the latter is characterized by openness and the search for new meanings, connections, and possible reactions.

Ethics in this account of the psychology of human action becomes a multitiered affair, one that prizes (for Dewey, and eventually for Ambedkar) the stages that feature a central role for reflection as channeling and refining the impulsive forces immediately marshaled by established habits. As Dewey's students record him, the battles of ethics become battles of education: "Morality is [a] product of educational modification in a social organization."[47] The best, or most intelligent, education involves reflective processes that "mark" the plurality of experience in terms of "anticipated consequences, certain meanings" that are then used to generalize "the significance of the situation." In the course of the reflective process, "this empirical situation is rationally or conceptually controlled," and ideally, "the course of events is favorably influenced."[48] Reflection is integrally related to conscious judgment, of both descriptive matters of the world (as might be the paradigm case in scientific inquiry) and practical matters (as would be needed in ethics and axiological decisions).

Reflection, according to Dewey, is a psychological process that differs from the immediacy of everyday experience because it purposefully inquires into the habits and concepts that guide immediate experience. As he put it in the passage from the *1917 Syllabus*, knowing means immediately acting and reacting; reflection involves what Charles S. Peirce called the "irritation of doubt."[49] It signals a stoppage, or more aptly, the necessitated reaction on the part of an organism to deal with the meanings and potentialities involved in situations that confound habituated expectations. When it comes to moral or ethical experience, "situations of doubt, uncertainty, indeterminateness" as Dewey describes them in his *Lecture Notes* from December 15, 1914, evoke cognitive or reflective effort.[50] What undergirds the notion of reflection as Ambedkar heard it in 1914 is a deeply Deweyan theme: that of moral situations inherently involving deep conflict among elements. This conflict is "deep" precisely because simple solutions cannot solve or dissolve the tensions in the situation confronting the organism; reflection evaluates (or "valuates" as Dewey calls it in his 1914 notes) various aspects or objects previously valued in a hierarchical fashion, allowing for more intelligent trade-offs to be reached. Reflection also ascertains the marks that indicate causal propensities, allowing the human agent to better determine a way through the conflicting instincts, values, and parts to the situation while being *effective*—in achieving results they really desired and that others around them can live with in future experience. For Dewey, as Ambedkar heard him, reflection involves the navigation of tensions that arise from our biological impulses in a social setting; as Dewey wrote in his *Lecture Notes* from October 7, 1914, it "is the peculiar modification of biological responses which come thru their being encased in a social medium and becoming factors in conjoint activities that gives them the mental or psychological quality." This is what Dewey refers to as "meaning," which "implies a shared activity, an activity in which each participant refers his own response to that of another and that of another to his own. Both from the common situation."[51] These meanings, given the interactions among a range of agents with different impulses, habits, and purposes, inevitably are not completely shared by all involved; they also come into conflict in social experience. Thus, moral judgment is needed to settle *problematic situations* (the term that Ambedkar would later read in his copy of Dewey's 1925 *Experience and Nature*) that involve the conflict among values, desires, and purposes in social environments. Dewey would eventually divide up the moral situation into the "independent factors" of the "good," the "right," and the "virtuous" in a 1930 address and in the revised 1932 *Ethics* with Tufts.[52] But around Ambedkar's time with Dewey, this trifold manner of reading moral complexity was not explicitly asserted in the pragmatist's expositions. The reading of the moral situation that Ambedkar heard was one of conflict among the *good* and the *virtuous*—respectively, those things that an agent accepts or values in action, and what others think of that agent's action or valuing.[53] By paying attention to the exact part of Dewey's evolving pragmatism Ambedkar actually attended to, we can stay clear of mistaken attributions of part of Dewey's later thought to the aspects of pragmatism that struck young Ambedkar.

Out of these reflective situations in social settings of conflict among self and others emerges the product of reflective activity, what Dewey calls "habits" and "concepts" at various points in his 1914 course. Reflection settles things in a previously unsettled situation; this settling either creates habits or reconstructs past habits. Thus, the meaning and expectancies in habits strike a level of generality that must transcend one concrete situation of conflict if they are to be useful in another particular situation, whether it is problematic or not. As Ambedkar heard Dewey put it, "The effect of habit is to generalize the case—[the] object is recognized or identified[.] It is of the kind of sort that we respond to in a certain way. A dog, a Boston bull, my Boston bull. May mean simply calling more and more specific habits of reaction into play as the stimulus becomes more differentiated and a more complex set of habit called into play."[54] Thus, habits become meaningful and useful in a range of experiences by being tethered to abstract objects—*concepts*—that can then be used to explain and control other situations of a similar nature. These concepts can be very truncated (like the notion of Dewey's specific dog), or they can be more general and more widely applicable in experience (like the notion of "dog" in general). All involve expectancies of what the object will mean to us and how we are to react to it. As Dewey sketched out in his own notes for the class returning from its Christmas break to finish up the final weeks of its fall semester (which continued into early February 1915), a "concept [is] a rule for observation and experiment; what to look for—what is significant the key traits—marks.

But also of what may be expected, inferred, predicted—classification on the basis of the observed traits."[55] Earlier, on December 15, 1914, he had bluntly told his class, "Conclusion[:] a concept is a rule for the determination of particular cases."[56]

Our concepts, with their meanings of future expectations of how the object will behave in experience and how an agent ought to react to it, are *immediate* once habitualized. They become a *mediated* immediacy in human experience; they are natural, but socialized and constructed through the operation of past experience and, sometimes, past reflection. They are part of the "knowing" that Dewey talked about in the *1917 Syllabus* passage presented, and they are immediately acted on or assumed by an agent without reflective questioning or investigation. These also implicate *value:* these objects strike us *as* good, *as* useful, or *as* repulsive. Good is immediate, but Dewey warned Ambedkar's class in January 1915 that just "because goods are intrinsic, it does not follow that they cannot be criticized, compared, or even rejected; even intrinsic goods may be reorganized or transformed, and judgment, valuation, may be the chief factor in such development."[57] Our present habits, concepts, and values take place in present settings, but certain situations become problematic for the present *or* the future and demand reconstruction: "While the immediate must always be the standard of reference, it may be the future immediate instead of the now present immediate."[58] The goal of reevaluating our concepts and the value stances they imply toward objects and states of affairs is simple and presents what can be called Dewey's idea of reconstructive meliorism to young Ambedkar: the process of reflective valuation aims at "the reorganization of present goods in the light of future consequences."[59]

Habits and specific concepts, as a young Ambedkar heard in Philosophy 231, are useful beyond *psychology;* they implicate the self as social, as a product of interaction and associated life. These themes would be explored by Dewey in *Democracy and Education* and, to a lesser extent, the 1908 edition of *Ethics;* both of these works, as we shall learn, were prized and used by Ambedkar once back in India. But in the fall semester of 1914, Ambedkar witnessed Dewey making the jump from individual psychology to social matters, all the while not dissolving the concreteness of human lived experience (and *suffering,* a young "untouchable" Ambedkar might have added) in vague and general abstractions of classes and types. Individuals are social, and society is comprised of individuals who feel, aspire, react, and reflect. In the January 1915 weeks that concluded the fall 1914 session, Ambedkar saw Dewey link reflection and immediate meaning to past instances of culture. Dewey noted in preparation for his lecture that "in so far as the habits have been formed under influence of reflection–social custom and tradition as itself affected by prior inquiry," certain "objective stimuli" in situations and their associated individual "habits" can be "affected" by "education" of the course of formal or informal experience.[60] This *education*, however, of experience and collective experience (via culture and associated living) holds differing grades of *intelligent* adaptation to situations, present or possible. As Dewey puts the matter, one can distinguish among "brute habits—unenlightened, uncriticized" patterns of acting and value, "intellectualized habits" that are the product of past mediated thought by some members of the community, and "critical inquiry—deliberation guided by principles."[61] We shall see the idea of *principle* arise later in Ambedkar's work, primarily in the 1930s when he draws upon the 1908 *Ethics* discussion of *principles* as useful intellectual *methods* of reflectively engaging problematic present situations. Here, however, in his time with Dewey at Columbia University, we see that he is introduced to both the ideas of reflective thought *and* the notion of principle, but they were not as explicitly connected as they would be in the passages about them that he would annotate in his well-used copies of the 1908 *Ethics*.

Ambedkar also saw the idea of *custom* being used by Dewey as a natural outgrowth of the psychological phenomenon of habit. We must never forget that habit resides at the level of the biological organism, including those beings enmeshed in associated life like humans. Ambedkar surely was impressed by Dewey's way of accounting for individual habits *and* larger cultural patterns captured in the notion of "custom" or "tradition." As we shall see in later chapters, Ambedkar became particularly interested in getting specific individuals (such as high-caste Hindu reformers) to *reflect* on their problematic *habits* in order to reconstruct society and received customs. In texts such as his 1936 *Annihilation of Caste*, he refers to caste as a state of mind or as a notion. This has roots in Dewey's discussion of habit as concept and as instantiating certain *attitudes* in the individuals who comprise associations and groups. For Dewey in Philosophy 231, "attitude" represented "a readiness or tendency to act," and "emotion is [the] accompaniment of organic attitude."[62] Attitudes are habits, and involve concepts, but are marked by Dewey as a crucial part of psychological ethics since they are particularly important to our reactions and immediate evaluations:

> Conscious life is essentially an attendant upon our play of attitudes. An Attitude is always one, *towards, at, away* from, an object. The proposition is emphatic. Generically the emotion is as a whole an attitude-toward-an-object.

An attitude is not to be defined without consideration for the object. The concrete situation is attitude-object. One can't simply have an attitude—it must be an attitude toward or from etc. something.[63]

Unlike the more direct notion of "dog," what Dewey is getting at with attitudes is something more expansive, and perhaps more meaningful, for our experience in social settings. This sort of focus on attitude will have its echoes in Ambedkar's critique of caste, because in it lies an explanation of why groups of individual organisms (humans) could maintain similar, but not identical, patterns of negatively reacting to other human individuals as "untouchable" or impure. Caste is a state of mind because it implicates an *attitude* toward certain objects, in this case those labeled *as* "untouchables." Ambedkar was surely impressed by Dewey's respect for the openness of experience, even when habits and collective customs threatened to reduce it to one meaning, one emotional valence, or one way of valuing its objects and individuals. Indeed, Dewey's students heard not only his reading of the inherent complexity of moral situations but also his warnings about the "fallacy of assuming that when we have a single unified word that there is a corresponding unified fact. Words necessarily abstract."[64] Such abstraction involved in concepts and labels is often useful, but it can be limited if we take the abstractions as exhausting what reality and its objects are. Later in the Philosophy 231 course he would call this "the philosopher's fallacy," which involves "denying the context and taking that which is intellectually differentiated intellectually as the thing."[65]

As we shall explore, one can come across this point in Ambedkar's attacks on caste in the 1930s, where the *names* of the various castes will be taken as exhausting *the* meaning and value of those concrete human individuals bearing them. Dewey's point also extends to our ideals and ends, a point that comes across in the *1917 Syllabus* and that was probably broached in Ambedkar's semester: there, he warns that "any conceptual end or good is only a tool of analysis for the use in particular cases" and that such "ends-in-view" always run the risk of going from useful abstraction to being regarded "as ultimate ends instead of as instrumental to a reflective analysis. . . . They are so fundamentally important as methods that this pragmatic importance leads to their being elevated into a distinct kind of superior existence."[66] Dewey's target was the Platonic way of hashing out values and ends, but it could easily be applied to Ambedkar's critique of the ends and values implicit in the Hindu caste structure.

Indeed, in Ambedkar's seminar paper for his teacher Alexander Goldenweiser, read on May 9, 1916—a paper that lacks many of the critical emphases of Dewey's 1908 *Ethics* and Ambedkar's later works—we see echoes of this reading of ends and harmfully concretized ends and value terms. In that paper giving an explanation of the "mechanism, genesis and development" of caste in India, Ambedkar connects the Deweyan concepts of custom as collected habits of action to the discourse of ends and means: "These customs are essentially of the nature of means, though they are represented as ideals. But this should not blind us from understanding the *results* that flow from them. One might safely say that idealization of means is necessary and in this particular case was perhaps motivated to endow them with greater efficacy. Calling a means an end does no harm, except that it disguises its real character; but it does not deprive it of its real nature, that of a means."[67] While he does not use the term "ends-in-view," Ambedkar is making a point similar to Dewey's: taking ends as more than as a temporary means or guide to action falsely makes a contingent attitude or habit into some concrete and eternal existent. In the case of caste practices, it is more than a false concretization of an abstract concept; it is the existential justification of a habitual attitude that does great harm to the lived experiences of those who are trapped under its labels. As Dewey puts it in the course Ambedkar enrolled in, "All implements of civilization exist because past actions of [a] race have constituted certain effective stimulus out of complicated and wasteful stimuli," but the choice of how seriously and inflexibly to take these habits of reacting to stimuli is one of collective and individual importance.[68]

What we see emerging from the unique insight provided by the constellation of these archival sources documenting Dewey's Philosophy 231 course in 1914 is important. We now know that Ambedkar was exposed early in his Western education to Dewey's psychology of habit and attitude, and that this reading of ethics can be psychologically sophisticated and move beyond mere platitudes or the continuation of cultural values and ends that have gained a deceptive certainty over the years. In other words, Ambedkar saw Dewey's complex meliorism, a reconstructive program that embraced the social construction of the individual and aimed at the improvement of communities and aggregates, *without denigrating, devaluing, or deemphasizing the import of individual organisms and their specific courses of experience*. Life was an affair experienced by specific individuals, a point that Ambedkar, the lonely Dalit adrift for a short period in the free and chaotic American experiment, surely appreciated. One way of reading his future activities was as a struggle to get out of the tyranny of the customs and labels of caste attitudes, which destroyed the quality of so much of his experience. His life—as well as the lives of those like him—could be im-

proved, if these habits of individuals and collective customs of Hindu society could somehow be changed; as Dewey emphasized, it was natural for
creatures to take habits, but it was not set as a natural or eternal truth that
they should take *one* specific set of habits. Intelligence, or reflection, was
a tool in reshaping our habits, and if used widely and broadly enough, it
might hold out the hope of reconstructing the collection of habits labeled
as a society's "customs" or "traditions." Thus, Dewey's psychology began
to glimmer with the prospects of being potentially useful in a battle that
the American professor never anticipated—that of the struggle against the
millennia-old caste system in India.

## Philosophy 131–132: Dewey on Individuals, Force, and the State

In the fall of 1915, Ambedkar enrolled in the yearlong series of two courses
that Dewey offered under the heading Philosophy 131–132, Moral and Political Philosophy. Although he had not taken Philosophy 232, the course
that followed Dewey's Philosophy 231, Ambedkar stayed the entire year
in this course series on Dewey's social thought, soaking in one of Dewey's
most intense syntheses of psychology, social ethics, and economics, with
a rare jaunt (for Dewey) into the philosophy of law. This was a fortuitous
course sequence for Ambedkar's final year in New York, as it completed
the account of psychology and the socialized individual he had heard
in the previous fall with an account of political action and its paradoxes
that would help him define and push the limits of his advocacy for caste
justice later in his life. Philosophy 131–132 was an important course for
Dewey, who had offered it year in and year out since he started teaching
at the University of Chicago in the 1890s. Judging from surviving lecture
notes from 1895–1896, 1898, and 1900–1901, the early versions of the
course included three topics: the logic of ethics, the psychology of ethics,
and social or political ethics.[69] At Chicago, it was embedded in the quarter
system, and the coverage of each topic was compressed into this trifold
division. By the time Dewey moved to Columbia, this course had evolved
into a two-year sequence that focused primarily on the psychological and
social aspects of morality, and he had moved much of the analysis of moral
evaluation and judgment that was implicated by the "logic" of ethics into
the psychology course. As is evidenced by the three fairly complete—and
earlier—manuscripts of Dewey's notes in the psychological/social ethics sequence at Chicago, he was not afraid to change topics and explanations; this should serve as a vivid reminder to be wary of commentators
who concretize Dewey's "pragmatism" into one specified doctrine or set

of arguments. Topics such as force appeared in the 1896 and 1898 lectures on political matters but disappeared in the section on political ethics in the 1901 lectures; instead, a new section on art was added, which in turn would disappear by the time Ambedkar enrolled in the Columbia version of this course. All of this shows the importance of attending to which specific version of pragmatism Ambedkar absorbed in what concrete context; Dewey, like any complex thinker, was constantly evolving and changing his thoughts and arguments.

By the time Ambedkar sat down in the philosophy seminar room, Dewey had adapted this course in very specific ways to the time preceding American entry into the First World War. We know this because we have an excellent grasp on the content that was presented in the exact course Ambedkar sat in during 1915–16. Extensive notes survive from two fellow students, Robert Lee Hale (1884–1969) and Homer Hasenpflug Dubs (1892–1969).[70] Hale was studying economics at Columbia during Ambedkar's time there, and he would receive his doctorate in 1918. He would teach in Columbia's law and economics programs afterward. Dubs was less inclined toward the study of economics, instead earning his MA in philosophy from Columbia in 1916. Spending his childhood in China with his parents—both missionaries—inclined Dubs toward studying China both in the United States at the University of Chicago and as a missionary himself in China around and after the First World War.[71] Incidentally, he would see his professor, Dewey, once again, when the American pragmatist was lecturing in China around 1920. Dubs would return from China to teach at a variety of American universities, eventually ending up in the orbit of Columbia once again toward the end of his life. Despite their own status as underexplored thinkers, both Hale and Dubs assume a vital role as chroniclers of Dewey's Philosophy 131–132 course in 1915–16. Hale's notes cover only the first half of the course, whereas Dubs's more extensive notes allow us to see Dewey's teaching across the entire series of two courses. Both give us invaluable access to something we lack: what Ambedkar actually heard in his incredibly formative education on a class session by class session basis. Any doubt that their notes reflect what Ambedkar heard in the presence of Dewey is dispelled with certainty when one reaches Hale's notes for the class sessions on November 9, 24, and 30, 1915: Ambedkar is listed as the substitute note taker for those class periods.

Unlike for Philosophy 231, the precursor to the 131–132 series, we lack any lecture notes or outlines written by Dewey for the seminar in moral and political philosophy. We do have session-by-session student lecture notes that give us an incredibly detailed idea of what Dewey said to Ambedkar and his classmates. The notes span hundreds of pages, and much can come from mining them for the sort of pragmatism that Ambedkar was exposed to at Columbia. Some useful themes emerge for the analysis of Ambedkar as an Indian pragmatist that is to follow. Whereas the 231 course examined the individual as a *socialized* individual bearing habits and integrating with its surrounding environment, social and natural, the 131–132 course series starts from a different perspective, that of the group or social community surrounding, and comprised of, individuals. As he puts it in the first class session on October 4, the course would focus on "the *interaction* on, mutual action and reaction of all kinds of social arrangements, organisms and institutions, and man's moral ideas and judgment."[72] As Dewey puts the importance of the individual *in* group life, "Social ethics deals of course with the individual, but only with those traits of the individual which develop because of his association with others."[73] Thus, this lecture series serves as a thorough examination of the evolution of the individual in Western political thought and as an account of Dewey's naturalistic take on associated life and its relation to morality. This theme will play out, as he indicates on the first day of the course, in the form of "the state and the individual" and also in the interplay between "nationalism and internationalism."[74] The spring course would shift the focus to the philosophy of law and economics, even though Dewey would lag behind in finishing the fall's interrogation of individualism a significant way into the spring semester. The fall course, from its very beginning, highlights a crucial point for the Deweyan pragmatism that would inspire Ambedkar going forward: its unique reconciliation of the individual and the community. As we shall see, this reading emphasizes the melioristic, and moral, aspects of philosophy and practical action.

For Dewey's pragmatism, moral ideals and standards did not transcend historically situated contexts and practices; morality was a feature of groups. Dewey begins these lectures in 1915 by noting the sort of tension between morality and associated life (e.g., existing groups and communities). He notes that some approaches wish to "apply moral principles to evaluation of institutions. Seems [to] imply we have certain principles relatively fixed, [with] social arrangements variable," whereas others want to "consider effect of relatively fixed social arrangements on our moral ideas."[75] Must one choose between these exclusive paths? As his note takers record, "Dewey would prefer (if he had to conceive these views as antithetical) the second. But they are not antithetical, for the moral ideals produced by a given social state react on that state."[76] Dewey, ever the naturalist, wants to conceptualize moral norms as emerging from historical societies *and* to provide a basis for the immanent critique of such societies. As we shall see, this surely caused tension in Ambedkar, given that he hailed from a culture whose religious tradition (including its caste structuring) infused it with a potentially nonprogressive character that was all too often immune to reform efforts. Yet Dewey held out hope that no society was totally resistant to progress and reconstruction: "While it would take a perfect society to afford material for a perfect moral theory; yet a progressive society may afford an improving moral theory."[77] Moral theory came from the matter of historically conditioned societies comprised of aspiring and suffering and striving individuals; it conditioned their individuality, but it did not exhaust it. Reconstruction and improvement through moral inquiry was always a possibility, or at least this was the faith of Dewey's pragmatism as imbibed by Ambedkar in Morningside Heights.

Another organizing theme of Philosophy 131–132 that was unique to the iteration that Ambedkar heard in 1915–16 was the context of the world war. America had yet to enter the largest conflagration the world had ever seen, but war talk was already infiltrating popular and scholarly discourses in America. While some in the West and Midwest were sympathetic with the Germans, many more of those in the East saw the struggle against the Germans as a struggle for democratic society. Dewey, around 1915, was one of these enthusiastic proponents of entry into the war. The war was deadlocked in trench warfare, and the Lusitania had been sunk in May 1915. American losses on that vessel, as well as others attributable to German submarine warfare, all combined to push many to support American use of force in support of its western European allies.[78] These lectures, unlike previous surviving versions from 1898 and 1900, show an increasing interest in the interplay of societies and the forces that keep them together, or that cause them to struggle against each other. As we shall see in this chapter and future chapters, this necessity for force in accomplishing moral reform was an important theoretical touchstone for Dewey, and it continued to operate explicitly or implicitly in Ambedkar's diverse writings and activities. On what grounds do we deduce and apply moral standards: from the heavens, from a tradition that rings of eternal certainty, or from imperfect but evolving historical communities? These issues of social ethics are combined with means and ends implicated by the question of force: How does one reform society, and what limits should one be subjected to in these efforts to reconstruct communities?

One of the themes that guides the course—especially in the fall semester—is the supposed opposition between individualism and collectivism. As we shall see in a future chapter, Dewey had long been intrigued by the socially inflected nature of the individual, even in his early neo-Hegelian days at Michigan. At Columbia, Dewey continued his interrogation of what it means to be an individual, albeit less structured by Hegel's idealistic framework and more engaged with the developing sciences of psychology, social psychology, and anthropology. The crucial question for Dewey is not the opposition between the individual and their society; instead, it is what kind of socialized individual associated life creates. As he puts it in October, "Associated life brings about certain modifications in those who take part in the association and that they vary with the kind of associations. Instead of discussing in terms of antithesis between individual and social we would get more enlightenment if we substituted the distinction between the original native qualities and the acquired or learned qualities."[79] What sort of individual does a particular historicized form of group or associated life create or enable? The individual is already a social being, since it is "just as true to say we are born social and acquire individuality as to say [the] reverse."[80] Individualism, in the most useful sense, becomes a concept that shows certain paths forward in terms of contingent policies. As Dewey puts it, "The question of individual versus social is as irrelevant to moral questions as it is to discussion of physiology, where one wants to know the specific structures involved and [their] interactions. To say digestion was an individual phenomenon means nothing whatever. Only as a question of the relative merits of policies to be pursued is there any sense in distinguishing individual from social."[81] The problem becomes one of taking "individualism" as denoting "fixed metaphysical or psychological principles" that supposedly give us a grasp on some certain and unchanging "reality" beneath human culture, community, and experience. The individual is habituated in their psychological characteristics by and through a group, an associated form of life that stretches back beyond that individual into some shared history and projects future courses of group behavior, action, and reaction.

The hypostatizing of individualism into a metaphysical entity is what worried Dewey, given the conflicts his pragmatism was embroiled in with the Western philosophical tradition. While not all of these battles are ones that Ambedkar wished to or needed to fight, he surely saw the implication and flexibility of Dewey's approach to individualism and group experience. For Dewey in 1915, individualism and collectivism denoted two ways— not mutually exclusive—of taking the phenomena of human experience: "The terms individual and social go together—they are both adjectives; the individual and society are both nouns created out of adjectives and are abstract. If they are really adjectives—express qualities or attributes of some noun[—]the question of their relationship to each other is the relationship of two qualities of the same thing to each other."[82] Experience taken in its *individualized* sense places more stress on peculiarities of the individual organism: habits, upbringing, ends-in-view, and motives. Experience taken in its *social aspects* emphasizes collective patterns of action (customs and traditions), histories of groups, and general patterns of reaction among many (but not all) individuals making up certain groups. "Theoretical individualism" becomes problematic when it takes metaphysical account of the *individual* as central; this sort of error is replicated, according to Dewey in these lectures, when one focuses on *groups* or *classes* as the foundational and central category of analysis or existence. Instead, analyses of the psychology of the human, such as that dissected in Philosophy 231, are just as relevant and useful as the interrogation of laws and customs that Dewey would undergo in Philosophy 131–132. Neither excludes the other, and neither makes some claim to independence or primacy over the other. The individual is thoroughly social, but one can still examine the ways that socialized individuals differ from other individuals across a group, or even across historical contexts.

It is this latter commitment to historicism that pushes Dewey to spend much of the fall—and its concluding weeks in January 1916—on the historical development of themes of individualism and the state in the West. It is here that we have precise evidence of young Ambedkar's exposure to the leading figures of the Western political and philosophical tradition in his education, including John Locke, Thomas Hobbes, Jean-Jacques Rousseau, Immanuel Kant, Johann Gottlieb Fichte, G. W. F. Hegel, Karl Marx, Jeremy Bentham, Auguste Comte, John Stuart Mill, and Herbert Spencer, among many others. While Dewey's analysis is too detailed to recreate in this chapter, it is useful to note that he posits individualism as a historical phenomenon that relates to how much freedom, initiative, and agency individuals have in social settings. Individual powers and rights became protected by the state, Dewey argues, insofar as these capacities became valued and enshrined in doctrines that focused more on the individual than on the collective. Like many movements, this focus on individualism led to error in some cases (namely, the idea of theoretical individualism), but Dewey stresses its historical evolution in a nonjudgmental fashion. Along the way, Dewey broaches some other topics that will become important in understanding Ambedkar's pragmatism as it develops later in India.

For Dewey, the concept of the state gradually emerges in Western political thought as separate from the individual, and even as a way to promote or enable individual development itself. Figures like Locke and Hobbes began the story by tailoring the state to protect property and individual happiness. Sovereignty came in as something subservient to, but eventually beyond, incipient notions of individualism in the social contract tradition. On the continent, figures like Rousseau are important insofar as they began to psychologize this story—and the state. According to Dewey, Rousseau connected political *force* used to create and sustain certain forms of community or association with the psychological capacity of *will*, albeit in a general form. He also was the first to note that education can shape the will of all through its effects on the individual's constitution. It was Kant, a long-standing opponent of Dewey's philosophical inclinations whom he nonetheless highly respected, who combined the individual will with force in moral matters; Kant turned the question of rightful political force in a moral direction, limiting its application and hopes with the capacities of spontaneous human freedom and willful agency. As Dewey puts it, Kant's "Formula of Humanity as an end in itself" portrayed the state or community as one of a kingdom of *personalities*, each uniquely represented by the character and capacities of that historical agent.[83] Morality was general and universal for Kant, but it applied to imperfect and varying human beings. Johann Gottfried Herder, an important student and eventually an opponent of Kant, garnered a few days' worth of lectures, as he represented the increasing historical focus of German philosophy for Dewey. Human community was evolving through history, and the struggles that Kant placed at the heart of morality were also part of this ever-changing middle ground between abstract moral matters and the messiness of individual life. Individualism, morality, and group experience were all matters that these different thinkers explicated, each with their own values.

When Dewey reaches Fichte, a philosopher following in Kant's wake, we begin to see the pieces come together with this historical story of individualism and the promised analysis of the nation-state. Fichte, as Dewey portrays him over the course of five class sessions, sees the philosophy of history as the development of the nation-state. Extending Kant's tenuous connection of the individual moral will and the historical community of the state, Dewey sees Fichte as making the "state" into the "central factor in philosophy of history—central in execution of goal, not in being goal—goal = humanity. In truly religious and moral community, individuals would not need the external coercion of the State. State as 'artistic' institution—, i.e., an arrangement working by force, but having a distinct purpose, which is a humanity working out its ideas through choice (voluntary action). Certain things, however, [are] beyond the State's province— science, religion and virtue."[84] Whereas Kant's notion of "unsocial sociability" seems to posit the individual as opposed to society, Fichte makes the nation-state the primary way or means for the individual to realize their individuality and freedom.[85] Indeed, for Fichte, the nation-state allows for expression of more complete visions of individuality among the members that comprise its populace. Young Ambedkar hears Dewey's rendition of the historical evolution of individualism across varying cultures and philosophers—whereas the English and the French posited an opposition between freedom *and* state authority, the German thinkers such as Fichte and those who followed him tended to "assume that only where there are these universal regulations [of the authoritative state] can there be any freedom" among individuals.[86] Fichte, according to Dewey, seemed to be the first to connect the concept of *Kultur*, mediated by the nation state, to enabling the powers of the individual: "Culture is the realization of every capacity of every individual."[87]

Dewey spends a significant amount of time on Fichte, as he capped the development of Rousseau and Kant (in Dewey's mind) and set up the problematics for Hegel, Ferdinand Lassalle, and Marx.[88] For Fichte, the nation-state offers the realization of Kant's hope, namely that "in this life they may order all their relations with *freedom* according to *reason*."[89] Reason, for Fichte, is embodied in the external law of nation-states and eventually sparks a transformation in egoistic humans such that "*man does consciously from reason what he did in the first stage* [a state of nature]—reason becomes second nature."[90] In the German tradition, as represented by Fichte, "freedom is a state attained only through obedience to law—it is something universal, but all universality means law. It is only where there is an organized state with its universal laws that there can be any such thing as freedom; the state is the reconciliation of the seeming antithesis between individual freedom and authority."[91] The nation-state allows for the expression or realization of human personality: "The state is the means of realizing every capacity of the individual and that capacity when realized, which he calls culture, must inure to society and society is identified with the state; to raise themselves with freedom to this state is the vocation of mankind."[92] This notion of personality is traced by Dewey—through his reading of Fichte—back to the Christian ideal of "each person as personality" and as possessing the "rights to personality" and the development of their individual capacity as a free agent.[93]

Fichte, for Dewey's presentation in January 1916, becomes an important intermediary link between one powerful vision of historically constituted moral philosophy and the powerful tradition of socialism that would culminate in Dewey's and Ambedkar's time as Marxism and communism.

Fichte saw the state as having an integral role in controlling or directing significant aspects of "the *industrial and economic life*" as "a means to comfort[,] happiness, pleasure, increasing liberty of action."[94] The state, and its direction of economic matters, was integrally tied to the moralized end of the development of individual personality. These Fichtean views of socialism would eventually influence figures such as Lassalle—whom Dewey identifies as the figure who makes Fichte's socialism "explicit." It would ultimately reverberate with later reformist socialists who served as foils to important parts of Marx's doctrine, such as Eduard Bernstein, an influence on Ambedkar's teacher, Vladimir Simkhovitch. We shall see the effects of this heterodox line of thought on socialism when we turn to communism and Ambedkar's rhetorical activity in the 1950s. But the essential point that Dewey highlights as a major purpose for bringing Fichte into his genealogical account of morality, individualism, and collectivism stands out clearly: "It is the moral duty of every individual to fully develop all his powers and become a complete personality; but by nature each individual is limited. Only where association supplements him is he capable of becoming a complete [personality]."[95] Humans can only become complete—and completely free as individuals—when surrounded by the right sort of community or associated form of living.

This emphasis on the nation-state as sovereign *and* as the vehicle for the creation and expression of individuality segues into a discussion of collectivism under the guise of *socialism*. Dewey was long attracted to socialism, but like Ambedkar, he had a troubled relationship with socialistic emphases as filtered through Marxist revisions of Hegel. In these lectures, Ambedkar would hear Dewey identify one of the problematic points, starting as early as the transition from Fichte to Hegel: whereas Fichte conceived of the force of the national state as enabled by individual effort, Hegel had little room for what he surely saw as an appeal to Kantian notion of individual will. While Fichte "insists upon voluntary individual effort," Hegel's doctrine of reason is instantiated in the real, effectively paralyzing individual development and action: "If the idea already is you cannot exhort the individual to bring it into being, you can only tell him that if he does not absorb what is then he is so much to the bad. The appeal and the individual is only to utilize and assimilate the ideas already embodied in nature. His effort does not bring it into existence, he merely takes it in."[96] As we shall see when we turn to Ambedkar's later reception of Dewey's earlier, and more Hegelian, work on political ethics, this emphasis on the ideality of the real is a major stumbling block for ethical development; for Dewey in 1916, it represented a view of philosophy as reconciling morality to the institutions of the status quo in a way that disabled critique. Dewey wanted immanent ways of critiquing social arrangements that disabled individual development, but he did not seek to do this through transcendent moral laws or aspects of particular historical traditions concretized into universals. Nevertheless, young Ambedkar saw his teacher's dissatisfaction with Hegel's historicizing insofar as it disabled even useful aspects of individual and collective initiative to reconstruct social life. It ultimately led to a disabling of meliorative action, either through a perfunctory use of the individual's "will to assimilate in himself the ideal already in existence in nature, institutions, etc." or through simply waiting for history to unfold.[97] Dewey recounts this as the split between left and right Hegelians: "The right wing stuck to the static element—that philosophy can only find what is accomplished, try to justify the existing order. The left wing took the other end—reality is a process or movement; the fact that the existing order was stated was proof that it was done with and we were entering another stage. 'Whatever is, is going to be overturned,' this is the Russian Nihilist school which came from Hegel."[98] Part of this unsatisfying twist initiated with Hegel, according to Dewey's reading, was the eventual reduction of group life almost exclusively to abstract concepts such as *class;* unlike Fichte, this turn in German philosophy that would so resonate later with Marx's philosophy abandoned much of the ethics of personality and a rich reflection of the individual in the social. The point surely struck the young Ambedkar, who would return home to battle Hindu tradition *and* Marxism; as Dewey bluntly tells his class at the conclusion of his account of Hegel, "This all indicates how easily idealism may become identical with an extreme form of realism—philosophy becoming a systematic apologetics for the accomplished facts of history, whatever they may be."[99]

Dewey's reading of nationalism—as culminating in the Fichtean version—represented a standing challenge to internationalist visions of reason and moral community proffered by Hegel and extending to Marx's communism. Referring to Laski's reading of social pluralism (Laski would later serve as one of Ambedkar's teachers while he studied in London), Dewey puts the challenge as one of how to use this increasing range of groups beyond the nation-state to expand what is given about theories of sovereignty and the state in the present; reflecting his own pushes toward American intervention in the Great War, all of this attention to ways that states are or could be composed operates as part of a program of creating groups and individuals that interact in better ways.[100] Underlying this concern with theories and realities of communal living is the dialectic between two vital features for the Western political tradition surveyed by Dewey, as well as his own historically situated moral philosophy as spelled out in Philosophy 131–132: *cultural groups* and *political institutions*.[101] These aspects represent two sides to the same coin, that of the use of *force* in the social world, or the ability of either groups or individuals to effect change in specified directions in their shared course of experience. Nationalism represents a case in which institutions (such as governments and legal systems) are coordinated with an emergent and unified cultural tradition; it also showcases Dewey's point that human psychology is a reflection of social groups and can in some conditions reshape a group's overall characteristics. Groups exert force on specific individuals and their psychological development, for instance, insofar as they can cause individuals to "react towards groups as entities," as is the case in what Dewey calls "race prejudice—it means essentially that there is a certain attitude taken towards the race as an entity; even when it is not a *prejudice*, there is an assumption that the race has a collective personality, etc., which we transfer to the individual members."[102] Thus, an individual American can be shaped by their surrounding culture to hate Germans as a group in the same way they may have hated their specific German neighbor. This is an emotionally charged attitude that, like the concerns in Philosophy 231, affects individual judgments of concrete *and* abstract entities. These ways of thinking as a member of some national group are located in the individual, but they are connected to associated life: the "habits of the individual [are] practically derived for the most part from the customs of the group."[103] Societies implicate *customs* or traditional ways of behaving, judging, and reacting that thereby form and inform the habits of the individual; group customs have no reality, purchase, or force in social life without their instantiation in actual *habits* operative in specific living individuals. Dewey therefore continues the reading of habit and social life that Ambedkar heard in the fall of 1914, albeit with an extended social inflection. Reflection becomes central as a way to shape and reform the forces of institutions, groups, and custom, but it is not an easy battle. Speaking in one of the final sessions of the fall term (which concluded in early February 1916), Dewey charts a pragmatic way out of this impasse:

> People's modes of action and of thinking get so ingrained that he can't criticize them any more than criticize himself. He can criticize certain external aspects of [him]self; but can[']t dig up core of [him]self. So when one's mental structure is formed in infancy by the environment of a certain country, while under some conditions he can criticize that environment, under others it is impossible to do so. While one can cultivate an open mind to some extent,

yet the fundamental question is the thing to which these emotions become attached. Practical remedy for patriotism is the creation of new groups of less competitive nature to which it can attach itself; you can[']t eliminate the reactions themselves though you can rationalize them to a limited extent. The reactions are intrinsic, but the objects to which they are attached are accidental and can be changed.[104]

Young Ambedkar heard Dewey in this conclusion to the first half of the Moral and Political Philosophy course dissect something surely of interest to him: the challenges and promises of how to get individuals to reflect on, and perhaps reject, pernicious aspects of their received (and formative) culture. Dewey saw the solution to the problem of nationalism and patriotism in the formation of more and more cross-cutting, and less competitive, groups. New stimuli and interests would replace older, less useful foci and impulses. More of this analysis of culture, force, and how it might be changed served as a focus of the second half of the course that engaged young Ambedkar for his final year at Columbia.

Before the problematics of force and associated life are explored in the guise of law and state institutions, it is helpful to reflect upon the general approach that Dewey as teacher and philosopher was taking while leading Ambedkar and his classmates through these theories, concepts, and historical figures. At points, Dewey makes his approach, and his voice, very clear to his students. Dubs records Dewey as pausing from his discussion of socialism's engagement with nationalism—socialism, according to Dewey, was challenged by the evasion of class and economic interests held by the nationalist movements involved in the Great War—to indicate the larger philosophical approach at play. All philosophies, whether those that Dewey has been surveying or the socialism that he feels much attraction to,

have done harm in the universal and absolute guise in which they clothed themselves. Philosophies which were quite needed in their own time and place, which within certain limits were thoroughly justifiable and which rendered a positive service, have compromised their good influence and turned it more or less to an evil one by being put forth as a sort of eternal and absolute truth, like mathematics—true at all times and in all places; consequently they inevitably came into complete conflict with each other, so that it has not been open to man to select the elements of value, of significance which might be found scattered [throughout] these philosophies; it has been simply a choice between the philosophies.[105]

This tendency toward universal and unchanging truths about the moral or physical world was a constant target of Dewey's pragmatism, and it would become a feature of Ambedkar's evolving and flexible critique of the supposedly *sanatan* or eternal Hindu tradition that authorized caste oppression as the inherent result of natural worth and karmic positioning of individuals within South Asian communities. For Dewey, and eventually for Ambedkar, philosophies should be read as reactions to their historical context and judged for what provoked their enunciation and what use they had given those exigencies. "If philosophies had recognized their historical relativity," Dewey opines to his students, "and if they had been put forward in more modest and qualified terms, there would not have been the antithesis or the alternative of swallowing the one and rejecting the other."[106] This recognition of historical placement would create a sort of fallibilism among those philosophizing and would render the engagement with rival philosophical accounts something other than a zero-sum game of right views or wrong theories. The deification of Locke's theory, say, as *the* right account of individualism, is problematic because it refuses the obvious; time, and with it human psychology and culture, continues on and changes. It is less than useful to think that a specific past account exhausted what there was to say about some aspect of present experience, let alone of past experience, given how liable to bias and prejudice and even blindness each individual thinker may be.

Instead of seeing philosophy as issuing pronouncements in the form of "universal principles," young Ambedkar heard his teacher postulate the pragmatist alternative: "One could easily make as his most general principle this fact that any social philosophy is bound to be closely connected with the troubles, needs of the times and to be propounded and promoted as an ideal and method for remedying the more present and urgent defects of the present."[107] The functional meaning of this stance so dear to Dewey's own rhetorical practice through the fall semester of 1915 was soon made clear; this "itself is a general philosophical statement which does not lead to this conflict and holding over of philosophies from the period in which they were useful to the period in which they become harmful and detrimental."[108] In other words, we should value the past as reactions to those specific situations and cultural needs and value it in the present only insofar as it fits and is useful to our own context and pressing problems. "If that were recognized," Dewey opines, "the conclusion would not be skepticism, but to make an analysis of the situation and formulate the philosophy with reference to its needs, and recognize that that was what was being done and that it had to be tested by its applicability to the situation, not in abstract."[109]

Dewey's own strategy of teaching and speaking about these past philosophies and philosophers illustrated the rhetorical nature of the fallibilism he desired. How does one speak or write about and use the past? How does one orient oneself toward the arguments of others—as an entry among a conflicting set of utterances spanning a range of time, out of which only one can be true or right, as the participants maintain? In Philosophy 131–132, Ambedkar witnessed Dewey take Locke and Hegel, for instance, seriously; he did not feel the urge to pronounce one as right for all time—or even for his time. The important point was realizing their ties to a specific historical context, among a series of other conversations that evoked them and built upon them. It is when arguments are said to transcend their historical context that one is led to deny that they have specific contexts; in a move particularly relevant to Ambedkar, interested as he was in resisting the millennia-old tradition of texts and customs that underwrote caste hierarchy, Dewey also notes that "when one says that the past is more divine than the present, that the present cannot be understood at all except in the light of the past, the thing is universalized beyond all limits, and you get these antithetical philosophies."[110] Dewey takes Hegel's philosophy, and with it many of the subsequent socialist and communist approaches to come, to task for "over-universalizing" beyond a time that fit a disunited Germany.[111] Speaking in his own voice, and advancing his own arguments beyond his historical survey, Dewey advises his class about the pragmatist middle path: recognizing the historical limitations of any given specific philosophy is a valuable choice open to those coming to terms with philosophers and philosophical problems. The result of this would be the construction of a useful philosophy out of parts that might be located in other contexts, or across a wide range of philosophers such as the tradition that Dewey interrogates and bends to his interests in ascertaining the interaction among society and the individual. This creative and appropriative characteristic is a hallmark of what Dewey would call *reconstruction*, and it would ground a method of speaking, arguing, and thinking that inspired Ambedkar after his time in Dewey's classroom concluded.

While Dewey was embodying creativity and agency in engaging and using the philosophies of the past, he was also concerned with the overgeneralizing in these philosophies that hampered and hindered individual flourishing. Indeed, he ends his partially sympathetic exploration of socialism or collectivism in the first half of the course by summing up what had emerged from his survey of the emphases of eighteenth-century individualism and the nineteenth-century shift to collectivism. The practical idea that he finds as recoverable from this progression from individualism to collectivism relates to the individual as agent in a surrounding community; the key feature of this sort of individual socialized agent, according to Dewey's lectures, is what he calls "effective freedom." This is not the "hands-off" freedom of individualism as laissez-faire philosophy or the freedom of an individual to submit to the collective for the collective's benefit. Instead, Dewey captures the sense of positive freedom he seeks in the ideal sort of society as emerging from four characteristics. First, as shown in the historical development he has charted, the state is a necessary (but perhaps not sufficient) condition for individual freedom. Attention must be paid to political institutions, since "the highly organized state was a necessary means to individual freedom, instead of being antithetical to it."[112] Second, this recognition of the importance of the state or group to the life of the individual is a historical matter; we err if we take our concepts of socialized individuals as not "associated with a sense of historic continuity, and the accompanying conceptions of growth, development, evolution, as over against the notions of conscious calculated artifice and manufacture."[113] The fallibilism of Dewey's pragmatist approach means he can reconstruct or synthesize such traditions in his analysis, but he and his listeners must never forget the historical situatedness of the ideas and materials used in reconstruction. Third, the evolution toward collectivism emphasizes the vital idea for Dewey of *"organization,* which is almost everywhere connected with the sense of *efficiency* that comes with division of labor."[114] Dewey, along with Ambedkar, was continually occupied with the organization of groups and how this spilled over into their interactions with other groups, and with how they formed the individual members composing them. Democracy, as we shall see, was an attempt to achieve a sort of internal and external organization among groups that enhanced the lives of all individuals implicated. Yet one idea that Dewey vacillated on throughout his career appeared in his summary of freedom: the "metaphor of the social organization with the bodily organism."[115] Dewey was attracted to this way of relating the individual and the political community in his early idealist days, the period in which he produced such texts as the 1888 essay, "The Ethics of Democracy," a work we shall see appear in Ambedkar's later engagement with Dewey's pragmatism. Here, however, he appears skeptical of this metaphor taken too far; the organic aspects of German philosophy led, in his reading, to a nation-state that swallowed up flourishing individuality, and it was also correlated with Spencer's postulation of an active environment that operated at the expense of a putatively passive organism.

Dewey wanted strong individuals emerging from the right sort of social environments, and he always saw the organism as active and as capable of a functional independence if given the right habits. Nevertheless, the point that survives is that there is some basic *functional* integration of the individual agent and the surrounding group; the social always conditions the individual agent.

The fourth characteristic of effective freedom that young Ambedkar heard in March 1916 struck a chord in him that would resonate throughout his many later writings and speeches. Dewey capped off this list of characteristics with his evocation of the "conception of the *moral standard, aim,* as a *common good,* as the general welfare and the notion consequently of the *control of the individual in name of the common good.* Liberty, equality, fraternity, and [the] name fraternity means common good."[116] These three values, central to the French Revolution and the collectivist movements that Dewey had just finished surveying, make many reappearances across Ambedkar's later works. They become for him the central characteristics of the ideal society, appearing in many of the works we shall explore throughout this book and even in the preamble to the Indian constitution that Ambedkar would orchestrate in the 1940s.[117] Dewey does not make much of these three values across his writings, and they do not serve as a moral or political touchstone for the pragmatist, but here they present themselves as this sort of useful standard. This should stand as a caution to those who assume that Dewey's influence stems from Ambedkar mindlessly repeating the American's every commitment. Ambedkar heard Dewey use them to criticize the collectivism movements (including many historical forms of socialism): "the tendency of the philosophic movement," says Dewey about collectivism, "was to subordinate the first two to the third [fraternity], to the general will, the social organism, or the greatest good for the greatest number, which is a collectivistic feature."[118] Dewey stops abruptly here, since he is already a month behind schedule in shifting to the half of the course that was to focus on the philosophy of law. But the point has been made: freedom of socialized individuals that is *effective,* or that which we ought to aim for because it matters in practical experience, involves a harmonization among liberty, equality, and fraternity in habitualized agents and among agents in associated life. Freedom matters to individuals, and freedom can only be effective and meaningful if we pay attention to how groups are organized and how individuals can further reconstruct or meliorate these communities.

The idea of effective freedom that Ambedkar heard Dewey conclude Philosophy 131 with grew out of the ideas of historically situated individuals, as well as the earlier social psychology that had appeared in his Philosophy 231 course. The emergent point was simple but powerful: all individuals are social, but not all manners of socialization enable the full use of an individual's capacities and personality. And individuals and groups of individuals can alter how they are socialized in certain conditions and environments. In other words, Dewey was concerned with the forces that shaped individuals within groups and how those individuals— representing habitualized and channelized vectors of force themselves— could alter or reconstruct their social groups. This summed up to a practical question, one that continued to inspire Dewey to some extent but that captivated Ambedkar: When did the force of social or cultural institutions enable the force of the individual, and when did they truncate or constrain it? Of course, Dewey was a pluralist about the sort of force that was operating within and among societies and states. In these lectures, he rejects the economic interpretation of history proffered by dogmatic Marxists and points his students toward Harold Laski's 1916 article "Sovereignty of the State," which, as Dewey glosses it, "suggest[s] that upon the whole *there has prevailed a tendency* in the discussion of the state and in law to *oversimplify* the problem to looking for a *very few* definitely limited number of *forces and factors* which have to be taken account of in the theory of state and of law and if one looks at history of theory there have been *quarrels about which one of the forces* assigned of the two or three of them *have been the ones which explain* the matter and have an exclusive right to be considered."[119] Of course, Dewey would also reject such a reading of historical causation, because it would overlook its own status as a contingent, purpose-driven act of reflection on behalf of the inquiring historian or theorist, or even critic. Perhaps there is a purpose to reading historical evolution in light of one variable or force, but it involves an abstraction and generalization that could be harmful if it rises above the concrete situation of analysis and stays there floating above the specifics of lived experience. "One implication of what Laski calls a pluralistic theory," Dewey states while drawing the political scientist into his pragmatist fold, "is that the situation is not so simple as that—there are very great diversities, a variety of factors which one might add. That the particular one which is uppermost may well shift from time to time. Even though there are [sic] a diversity of factors, one may take the lead. So that the theory which would be less simple would be more empirical."[120] Any analysis of force in the individual agent and the group must recognize its contingency and be based on a qualified push to make *this* specific community better.

Dewey does think we can extract *useful*, even if not universally *true*, concepts and ideas from historical settings and figures to use for our own present battles and purposes. This is precisely what he was doing in leading Ambedkar and his fellow students through the Western encounters with individualism and the state, and this is ironically what Ambedkar would do with his appropriation of the lectures, texts, and theories of Dewey once he was involved in Indian politics. But here in the truncated second half of the course, Dewey returns to the idea of "human nature," or perhaps less misleadingly put, the fact of habit-bearing "human beings living in juxtaposition, thrown into very different modes of organization by various factors."[121] What he explicated in the idiom of "habit" in the Philosophy 231 course the previous year, here he couches in the larger-scale notions of custom and social tradition. Humans are liable to take a variety of habits that can be explained in a range of conflicting ways, but often certain patterns or constellations emerge among the members of a group. The general patterns or trends denoted by the concept of "custom" relate to the formation of individuals at the organic level: as he puts it in his Philosophy 131–132 course, "habits of the individual [are] practically derived for the most part from the customs of the group."[122] Experience resides at the individual level of the striving organism in the social environment, but that environment—including the grouping of individuals they interact with or associate with—affects the action paths the individual is likely to follow. The group also conditions the meanings that the individual imputes to groups or members of groups, a point that Dewey made concerning the psychology of labels in Philosophy 231 and one that we shall see emerge later in Ambedkar's critique of the caste system and its normative labels that cut to the supposed essence of each individual.

Individual habits and social customs go hand in hand in Dewey's exposition. Customs emerge from, and then reinforce, contingent individual habits. As Dewey told his class, "People, when they live together, develop certain coordinated schemes of behavior—there is a certain amount of order, harmony,—there are rules, it is just the fact of the system."[123] These rules or norms form morality for Dewey; morality does not lie outside of the realm of action and force, it *is* the complex world of action among those group members. "If *morals* is not anything as precepatory, hortatory," Dewey opines, it is because it *"consists of the actual forces which are operative in any community irrespective of legal decisions and penalties to make people act in certain ways."*[124] It is a "complex of forces" that operates through formal institutions, such as governments or courts of law, and through informal function in the form of public opinion and social approval and disapproval. Dewey spends many class sessions exploring the nature of law, but he constantly returns to his larger point that positive law merely codifies prevailing social mores; it also makes clear wide patterns of social disapproval of certain actions.

While law and governmental action is cast as a reflection of custom, custom itself does not need overt governmental action to operate. On Dewey's schema of social ethics in 1916, custom grounded governments and individual habits and could operate within and through a collective group of individuals without formal or coercive government action. This, for Dewey, was the fundamental mistake of Kant's political philosophy. It separated the "legal and political sphere" from the "moral sphere" and thus introduced a sharp division between matters of "force and moral considerations" such as "ends or purposes."[125] For Dewey, the forces of custom and the norms of ethics are integrally related: "The larger question is that of the relation between force and a moral or ethical factor."[126] In the next day's class session, Dewey translates this question into another, that of "the place *of force in the moral economy.*"[127]

To understand the challenge that force represented for Dewey, and for Ambedkar, we must understand how force operates. For Dewey during the 1915–16 semester, society was a matter of forces pushing and pulling among individuals and groups. Force was not a bad thing; indeed, Dewey would resist the accounts of nonresistance promoted by Leo Tolstoy and others on the grounds that they rested on a reduction of force to *one* thing, and specifically to one *bad* thing at that: *violence.* With his commitment to the world being complex, Dewey tentatively divides force into constructive and destructive varieties—force as energy and force as violence—and posits this distinction as a useful and realistic way to come to terms with the operation of means in individual and social experience.[128] I return to this distinction between types of force in the following chapters, along with his critique of philosophies of nonresistance, since these concepts are engaged by Ambedkar in his writings and speeches after he returns to India. Here it is important to see, however, that Dewey contextualizes his analysis of law and social ethics in the realm of force, or the means to create certain ends or results that were not previously present.

What sort of force does custom represent or channel? For Dewey, custom operates as a *moral* force as channelized or habitual individual reactions to certain actions or results. It tells any member of that group what is acceptable or what will be met with criticism, penalties, or harsh reactions. In the case of law, penalties and coercive measures are previewed as a conscious stimulus *against* acting in certain ways; laws, in this account, formalize and make explicit the commands of dominant customs within a group.

But laws aren't needed for such force toward certain preferred pathways of action. Custom is self-enforcing since, as Dewey remarks, we always find ourselves in our social environment surrounded by individuals whose reactions to our activities will be affected by their habitualization in the group. Custom involves these contingent but ingrained expectations, and there are almost always "sanctions and penalties attached" to their transgression.[129] The monitoring of these breaks with custom occurs through the presence and agency of "some body of persons interested in enforcing that usage."[130]

Our peers are always watching, and force can operate through the actions and reactions of these individuals. In some cases, violence might be elicited. As we shall see in the next chapter, Dewey and Ambedkar were both skeptical of violent means since they foreclose more ends than the end that they realize. They tend to destroy community with others more than create or reconstruct it in a morally ideal fashion. But Dewey was not above connecting *coercion* to force; force wielded by the group, or by individuals other than myself, will always subjectively feel foreign to an individual's own forces and purposes. Force that operates on some disjunction or tension or problematic situation will be experienced as coercive and external to some extent. Groups normally tend toward an internal, free, and harmonious flowing of forces since "wherever there is a *social group* there is a *certain organization*, certain *uniform ways of acting*, [an] established order of activities."[131] But force—or perhaps, more accurately, forces—come into the picture at a conscious level when there is conflict or divergence from the customs of the group. These forces call for individual action to coerce divergent agents back into line; they also set the groundwork for Dewey's theory of law as an explicit way to settle disputes and to alter customs to fit changing circumstances. Laws, in the explicit sense, are formulated by state actors "only when there was some disturbance or deviation from the custom."[132] Laws are needed only when the reality or possibility of divergence from accepted custom becomes conscious to a group. It is only then, as Dewey puts it to his class, that groups or states feel "*a conscious need of establishing a uniform order.*"[133]

In this course, Ambedkar heard Dewey ruminate on a challenge that the Indian student surely had, given his reservations about Indian social mores surrounding caste hierarchy; Dewey acknowledges that "we become conscious that there is a great deal in this body of de facto morality which does not measure up to the standards of the more enlightened portions of the community—we want a standard by which to criticize this de facto morality."[134] Yet Dewey the naturalist is reluctant to provide any criterion of moral normativity outside of or above the community and its ethical path-ways. This surely perturbed Ambedkar, who would later constantly seek ways and grounds with which to critically engage the dominant Hindu re-ligious tradition surrounding him and the millions of other Dalits across India. Ambedkar did latch onto the closest thing in Dewey's philosophy of flux, dragooning the values of equality, liberty, and fraternity to serve as a moral criterion that transcends specific historical circumstances, at least to some useful extent.

How do customs—either through the reaction of others in a group or through the operation of enacted laws—function and prove effective? Dewey praises force as a coordinating feature or as an ever-present means that is operating in and through individual members of a group to form and maintain that group. Society always implies *"some actual coordination of the energies* exercised, force put forth by various people."[135] The integra-tion, and severability at some level, of the individual and the social are unmistakable here: social organization is an "organization of force," which effectively means "persons with their capacities for action."[136] Individual acts occur within a social environment and cannot but be noticed by other individuals in that group or association. Their judgments of, and reactions to, the actions of others constitute one primary way that the force of cus-tom replicates and enforces its previous instantiations. If an agent "goes beyond certain limits in any one of the established forms of coordinated organized activity," Dewey tells his class, "the group as a whole comes back at him—it is almost a physical process, like stretching an elastic band."[137] This is what Dewey calls *"coercive force, which is the constituting force which is the organized force of the group displaying* itself against the deviating mem-ber."[138] This coercive force operates *"by means of stimuli* which call into play the individual's *intelligence."*[139] It isn't a mere physical redirection of the individual's body, Dewey explains, but a direct or indirect *"holding out* [of] *certain consequences to the individual and telling him what is going to happen*— these consequences are consequences only because the individual has in-telligence and emotions."[140]

We shall return to this notion of reflection in the following chapters, since the search for more *intelligent* ways of reform will be seen as a prob-lematic that Ambedkar appropriates from Dewey's rather one-dimensional discussion of coercive force. For Dewey in 1916, coercive force was rela-tively simple, and relatively constructive: it leveraged the individual's abil-ity to direct and redirect their own action given their powers of foresight and of adjusting means and activities to their purposes and ends. Laws for-malize disapproval by extracting money or freedom from, or by causing pain to, individuals who diverge from the strictures of custom, but public opinion emergent in the form of individualized reactions can also do the same through the pain of shame and social ridicule. Indeed, Dewey specifically points out the communicative phenomenon of ridicule as one way that drinking and dueling are proscribed.[141] At the larger level, however, social disapprobation (the genus of shame and ridicule) operates through fear. Like coercive laws, social disapproval and ridicule involves the "pain of disapprobation, of being unpopular, at bringing disfavor of some one who one respects or has affection for," or perhaps even the "fear of physical suffering."[142] This "menace of a social group" must be morally evaluated, Dewey notes, based on its consequences: Does it maintain a range of ends among the populace, or does it truncate purposes and individuals who ought to be valued? In Dewey's straightforward way of describing it, "it may be that it [a group's reaction to divergence] also secures a lot of results that are undesirable," at least as judged by other ends and values held by that group.[143] Thus, vigilante justice that employs lethal force is likely to fall, eventually, into error in identifying the guilty party or in meting out an appropriately measured punishment, thereby harming the ends of the individuals targeted and those not targeted who wish to be free of such persecution at some potential time in the future. In the most difficult cases of possible or actual divergence from custom's advocacy, Dewey places courts of law and judicial judgments as institutionalized means for settling disputes *without* destroying more valuable ends.

Dewey's Philosophy 131–132 course concluded soon after this discussion of law, custom, and force. Two questions likely occurred to young Ambedkar, however, related to how he would extend, modify, and reject parts of Dewey's philosophy over the next four decades of his fight for social justice back in India. First, Ambedkar surely worried about the conundrum brought on by Dewey's reading of morality *as* existent social organization. How can society safeguard or enable progressive tendencies if the content of morality is society's dominant customs? What if the dominant customs dominate valuable parts of society? Of course, Ambedkar found himself as precisely this sort of individual, labeled as not being worthy of touch or social contact through such verbalizations of certain Hindu caste customs as those in the *Laws of Manu*. How could he *morally* chastise this system *and* adhere to the position that morality and its standards emerged *from* such systems? This search for norms and grounds of emancipatory critique would animate Ambedkar's rhetoric across many books, speeches, and activities. He constantly sought a way to think, act, and exist that was grounded in some pertinent reality; if Adlerblum's recollections are to be

trusted, perhaps young Ambedkar saw Buddhism as that existing philosophical discourse out of which a critique could be enunciated against the
structures of caste. In any case, however, Dewey's engagement with force
and coercion gave young Ambedkar a problematic, if not a solution, to
work with in his own way.

Dewey appears to have sensed this problem, even if his resolution of
it is less than thorough or spelled out. After noting that custom regulates
social groups, he acknowledges that "under certain conditions, especially
conditions of deviation, disorder within this order, there is a conscious taking [of] thought and formulation and the laying down of conscious commands."[144] In some cases, however, this process of reflection at the group
level does not merely replicate the previous customs; it can reconstruct
these materials of the past tradition. This implicates what Dewey calls a
"progressive society," or at least the process of societies embracing complexity and diversity among their constituting individuals: "As societies
become more progressive, more easily altered, there is of necessity greater
prominence put upon individual variations from which the inventions,
etc., may proceed."[145] This *reflective* or *intelligent* process grows out of social
mores and customs but allows for some amount of change and alteration
among these received structures. It also highlights something that we shall
see mattered deeply to Ambedkar: the changes allowed build upon and enable *individuals*. While classes and groups are important, Dewey recognizes
the importance of the individual as bearer of habits and as habitualized
enforcer of group customs; the individual, in the right circumstances, can
also be the cause of social innovation or change.

Customs, like habits, are based on the past (or tradition, in the parlance
of social analysis) and possess a certain projective power. Thus, they are
inherently conservative matters, in Dewey's reading, at the individual and
social levels. This is not a bad thing, as societies cannot subsist in the midst
of constant revolution and upheaval. Dewey, and Ambedkar, wanted to
maintain room for difference, however, since divergent individuals could
merit the label of *criminal* in some cases or *innovator* in others. One cannot
know in advance that a certain act will *always* be worthy of being judged as
criminal, so flexibility must be maintained in applying laws and reforming them in the future should the right cause arise. Similarly, there is no *a
priori* or eternal standard that adjudicates divergent personalities and individuals as *always* worthy of coercive correction; in some cases, perhaps the
group ought to become more like those individuals, or at the least, leave
them alone.

This focus on the individual is recognized in the first half of the course when Dewey talks of *individualism* as a historical movement. Speaking in November 1915, Dewey connects individualism to progressive tendencies in society, noting that "historically, individualism has been a struggle for a form of society which provides for its own modification."[146] The philosophies of figures such as Mill that appear in the debates about the nature and limit of the state in the West show that individualism does have a use in emphasizing flexibility in customs and their productive extension into future experience. Dewey recognizes that there is sometimes little to differentiate innovators and heroes from criminals and hated individuals, given the dynamics of custom and group reaction to difference. Ambedkar surely recognized this point and its concerns: How does one identify useful or innovative divergence from long-cherished group norms, especially when so much of custom, like habit, operates at a level below the conscious consideration of remote future results? As we shall see, Ambedkar not only saw himself as one of these innovators reforming cultures and group life, but he also saw that it was essential to possess the right sort of method in speaking and persuading when one went about challenging custom, lest one's effectiveness be dashed upon the rocks of idiosyncrasy and group counterreaction.

The second worry that emerges from this discussion is the challenge of force's specifics. When is force too coercive? Dewey's division of force as energy and force as violence only sets the problematic, it does not resolve it. How can one distinguish between better or worse ways of constructing or reconstructing society through force? Such energetic uses of force are not always physical, as is operative in many state laws invoking punishment. Some applications appear to be primarily *communicative* or *persuasive* for Dewey, such as those evoking expressions that shame individuals within a group or that persuade others to also disapprove of an agent's actions. But Ambedkar surely noticed aspects of what can be called *rhetorical force*, in distinction from physical forces, that also truncated valued ends or caused pain to those who didn't deserve it. Ambedkar, as an "untouchable," was constantly worried in India about social taboos and sanctions such as social boycott, a matter of life or death to individuals like him who depended on the mercy—and cruel favors—of a village of touchables to have food and water.[147]

Another way to illustrate the problematic Ambedkar was left with from Dewey's lectures is by relating it to the challenges of freedom within Dewey's lectures. How can the state through its legal instantiations of custom, the group through its social methods of voicing custom, or the individual through the reformation of their habits achieve what Dewey called "effective freedom"? Dewey engaged this concept earlier in the fall, but he also chose to return to it at the end of his analysis of the state and law in May 1916. Dewey surveys two senses of freedom, one that focuses on *metaphysical freedom* that concerns "a kind of unrestrained infinite possibility of action" and another that represents "actual freedom [as] a matter of control of conditions."[148] The former was the freedom of those focused on free will, or those like Kant who sought a way to escape the forces of the natural world and the natural body. Dewey, of course, would have none of that path. The latter conception is what the pragmatist found useful, since it is "the only real freedom" that makes agency *effective*.[149] It involves groups or classes of individuals insofar as these social environments render "an individual [as] free when he can command sources to carry out his purposes."[150] This is the version of individualism that was acceptable to Dewey in 1916, and it held some level of attraction for Ambedkar, since it allowed the Indian reformer to see how social matters and individualized habits in others could constrain an individual like him by undercutting the means and capacities needed to make him effectively free. How can force affect a collection of individuals and preserve these capacities for action among *all* agents, all *individuals*? Must the freedom of others be rendered ineffective to make the agency of the oppressed effective?

One can see the foreshadowing of many of Ambedkar's later arguments and concerns in the enigmatic but aspirational note on which Dewey concludes his Philosophy 131–132 course. Lecturing on the final day, May 16, 1916, just weeks before Ambedkar would sail for London, Dewey puts the matter bluntly: the challenges of political philosophy come down to the struggle now between scientific approaches to society and dogmatic systems that offer certain, and often certainly outdated or inflexible, answers to social problems. Dewey boils it down to "the gist of the matter—the ethical crux of the present social and economic situation is the intellectual factor." What he means by this is less than clear, but it seems to have related to social groups, and the individuals that comprised them, gaining and cultivating habits of reflective thinking and openness to reconstructing culture; indeed, he explains that "it is at that point that the trained mind ought to find its way out of mere conservativism and mere radicalism, its ultimate aim being in the possibility of the self-conscious approach to the affair." Young Ambedkar heard Dewey, the pragmatist committed to democracy, praise socialism, albeit tentatively: "Socialism stands in a symbolic way for the possibility of a social self-direction. The hope for the future is in the recognition of society taking control of its own factors, to direct its course, its impact."[151] It is important to note, however, that the socialism that Dewey praised was really a construct that occupied the middle ground between a conservative reaction to any attempts at change or reform and the other extreme of "mere radicalism" that sought revolutions that would inevitably step on the toes of other group members one ought to be valuing. Thus, self-conscious methods of individuals and societies taking control of their fate and reforming in progressive ways became the primary concern. It was a fragile quest that relied on social forces and that tried to regulate these same forces; it could also go too far based on dogmatism, zeal, or the failure to recognize human intellectual frailty in light of an unpredictable and ever-changing world.

This raising to consciousness of the methods, goals, means, and moral limits of social reform and reconstruction became, for Dewey, another way of describing "a process of *transition* from a personal to a social morality."[152] Evoking Jane Addams and her book *Democracy and Social Ethics* (1902), Dewey explains that both senses of morality are social, but the difference or "conflict is between the *morality which was attached to a narrower and more immediate set of social relations and a wider and more indirect system of social relationships.*"[153] As we shall see, Ambedkar confronted a similar, albeit slightly different, equation of what moral progress was when he read and annotated Dewey and Tufts's 1908 book *Ethics*. But here in 1916, we see Ambedkar being introduced to the idea that moral progress was something of this world, this messy social environment, and that it demanded a judicious use of force to create the most associated form of life possible among a collection of disparate individuals: a democratic community. Democracy, for Dewey in Philosophy 131–132, "means in theory the possibility of any individual having a share in this general redirection of society—a vote is an evidence of the fact that the area of the individual's influence has immensely increased and the average man instead of being bounded by the parish so that he takes more part than before."[154] Ambedkar's acquisition and avid reading of Dewey's *Democracy and Education* in London in 1917 would expand this idea greatly and further inspire Ambedkar toward an appropriation of the pragmatist views of democracy as a habit of engaging society and other individuals. Here, in 1916, Dewey places the concerns over democracy and the forces that can achieve it as part of "the demand for more social morality—adapted to wider relationships. You could turn the thing around—e.g., change of idea of education from the development of certain social duties to the development of personality—aiwdeing [a widening]."[155] The idea of *personality* behind and in each individual will emerge later in this study, but here it's important to note that Dewey feels obliged to use this term so common in his early idealist writings to expound his anthropologically sophisticated reading of custom and progress. "To say that the end is the development of personality," Dewey continues, "is an abbreviated way of saying that you cannot any longer enumerate the various social relationships into which a person will enter. The difficulty is due not merely to the complexity of the relationships, but more to their indirect character."[156] Individuals in complex, large societies are further enmeshed in social relationships they often are not conscious of, or that they cannot fully control or appreciate. While there is no evidence that Ambedkar ever owned, read, or cited Dewey's 1927 book *The Public and Its Problems*, we see here in May 1916 that he heard similar worries about the size and complexity of modern societies hamstringing the efforts to use force and reform to create the deep sense of democratic community that Dewey's pragmatism sought. The fundamental question of what *kind* of force one can use in the quest for this social ideal, however, is left unanswered. The worries about the *limits* to force in speech or action are also sidestepped. What Dewey leaves Ambedkar and his classmates with in the final minutes of the tortuous journey through individualism, collectivism, the state, and law in Philosophy 131–132 strikes one as prophetic for Ambedkar's later activities as a speaker, an organizer, and an educator: for those seeking democracy in the hectic and interconnected modern world, "the remedy is a development of imagination through education and of an organization through publicity."[157]

## Force, Community, and Communication

Ambedkar left Dewey's seminars—and Columbia University—with an acute realization that force matters for society. Dewey made this much clear in the courses that Ambedkar sat in during 1914–16. As a concept coupled with the idea of custom, it explained in intellectual terms what had held Ambedkar down for his entire life in the form of caste prohibitions and oppression. Connected to the idea of habit, he surely began to see how he and his fellow "untouchables" played some unknowing role in continuing their undignified isolation by internalizing the attitudes constitutive of caste behavior. While other classes and teachers at Columbia surely contributed to what Ambedkar was to become once his program of activism and reform gained steam back in India, it is undeniable, based on the evidence we have, that Dewey's pragmatic reading of society and the individual, covering the ground from individual psychology to group customs, mattered deeply for Ambedkar's analysis of how societies change and grow sedimented with certain patterns of action and oppression. As we have seen in the course of this chapter, Dewey's classes represent the only instance we have of direct records of what Ambedkar heard during the course of his education. While his engagement with (and adaptation of) pragmatism would blossom in the following decades (largely through Dewey's books), we can see specific themes that were presented in these early classroom experiences. One of those themes was the vicissitudes of force in individual and group action.

Ambedkar also was exposed to Dewey's philosophical prizing of intelligence or reflective thought. Dewey was enough of a philosopher to value the activities of the mind, since reflection offered one of the only comforting paths to reforming any problematic state of affairs in a constantly changing world without many absolutes. This notion of reflection involved an individual's standing back from some immediate situation and figuring out what might or might not be worth changing, but it was not solely a lonely endeavor. Implicit in Dewey—barely below the surface, really—is the idea of *democratic inquiry*. Reflection was a group or communal phenomenon, or at least it could be if contexts and habits were correctly adjusted. As Ambedkar would read in Dewey's *Democracy and Education* once he purchased his copy in London in January 1917, education is group experience formed and informed by human intelligence; education welldone thereby affects our habits and helps to create the sort of groups and communities we wish for in a democracy. This communal, or *communicative*, dimension of reflection resonated in Ambedkar's later activism, as well as in his appropriation and adaptation of Dewey's thought later in his efforts to fight caste injustice in India. Rhetoric or persuasive speaking could be calibrated to become the sort of stimuli that could jar the oppressed and the oppressors out of their habits and customs; speaking well could matter for how the oppressed are treated and how much self-respect they give themselves as agents.

All of this will be seen to extend throughout vital parts of Ambedkar's writing and speaking during the next four decades. Of course, one can point to other thinkers that might also be part of this story, or to texts that do not immediately reveal an intellectual, textual, or historical relationship to what Ambedkar heard in these three courses by Dewey or in the pragmatist's many books that the Indian student was to own. Such reactions miss the point, however. Dewey's influence matters, even if its presence does not exclude influences of others on Ambedkar. And unlike for all of his other teachers, we have specific records (some taken by Ambedkar himself) about what he heard in Dewey's courses. Also unlike for many other scholars and authors he was personally exposed to, Ambedkar often (but not always) returned to touchstone texts or ideas in Dewey during the course of his own persuasive activity in preindependence and postindependence India. And beyond specific texts or ideas, we shall see that Ambedkar saw a certain sort of *rhetorical method* of talking, arguing, and dealing with the texts of his past in India and his recent experiences in New York (viz. Dewey's works) that was distinctly pragmatist in spirit and origin. The story of pragmatism in India starts in Dewey's courses in 1914–16, but it by no means concludes there. As we shall see in the next chapter, Ambedkar had many additions and changes of his own to make that would make this story of pragmatism in India distinct from anything Dewey—or other pragmatists across the globe—could imagine. Part of what makes this *Ambedkar's* pragmatism, however, is his engagement with topics, concepts, problems, and injustices distinctly prominent in the South Asian context.

TWO

# The Genesis of Ambedkar's
# Reconstructive Rhetoric

After his time at Columbia ran its course, Ambedkar traveled to London in May 1916 to begin what he thought would be another extended period of graduate work. After a year of intense work in a range of programs, Ambedkar's money and luck ran out, and the Gaikwad summoned him back to India to repay his debts through service to the state of Baroda. Leaving Europe in July 1917, Ambedkar arrived back in Bombay on August 21, 1917. It was on this trip that he was fortunately separated from most of his luggage; the steamer containing his possessions was torpedoed by a German U-boat and sunk. The Great War that Dewey and his professors had argued about had finally come home for Ambedkar. Trunks of his beloved books, and presumably class notes, from his New York and London experiences sank to the bottom of the Mediterranean, a loss that the ever-studious Ambedkar must have felt deeply. Yet he was surely enlivened by the chaotic but promising situation he returned to in India. The British were being beaten down by the increasing costs of the war, and even the secretary of state for India, Edwin Montagu, was broaching the idea in the House of Commons of gradual self-rule for India within the British Empire.[1] When Montagu visited India in 1917, he witnessed firsthand the increasing assertiveness of the Indian home rule movement, along with the germination of a handful of groups asserting concerns of India's Dalits and tribal groups. Gandhi had reentered the Indian scene, stepping ashore in Bombay in 1915 and bringing his developing method of *satyagraha* with him. He would employ this method of passive resistance (a term he used with some reluctance, since he was in the process of discarding it) with noted success in Champaran, Bihar, in April 1917 to assist indigo sharecroppers in their struggles with local planters. As Dennis Dalton notes, this campaign propelled Gandhi into "a position of national leadership."[2]

Ambedkar entered into this scene, as Keer puts it, a "mere nobody in Indian politics."[3] He had been well educated in the West but was virtually unknown in the circles of power in India. He gradually would rectify this public image over the course of the 1920s and 1930s, but his low profile (and power) around 1917–19 is surely one of the reasons he was in no position to invite, or host, an international visitor like Dewey. Even if he wanted to follow the course of Hu Shih and his colleagues, Ambedkar lacked the time, connections, and clout around the time of Dewey's travels to Asia to pull such a visit together for his former professor. As his biographers recount, Ambedkar was simply struggling to create a viable financial situation for himself and his family around his arrival back in India in 1917. This is the time period of Ambedkar's humiliating and scarring encounter with the clashing features of his education and his "untouchability": even though the state of Baroda had called him back to a high-ranking government position, Ambedkar had trouble interacting with his subordinates and even finding housing. After failing to acquire shelter—he lodged under a fake name at a Parsi boarding house for a while, but he was eventually chased out by armed men—he returned to Bombay and variously worked as an investment consultant and as a professor at Sydenham College.[4] All of these endeavors became unbearable once the reality of his caste status overwhelmed his intellectual qualifications. Caste always caught up with young Ambedkar in India.

Amid all of this struggle for gainful employment and his family's shear survival, the educated Ambedkar decided to publish a short work in the *Journal of the Indian Economic Society* in its very first volume in March 1918. This was not his first publication—that honor rested with his "Castes in India" seminar paper, prepared in 1916 and published in the *Indian Antiquary* in May 1917.[5] The work that Ambedkar published in 1918 was a review article—effectively a book review—titled "Mr. Russell and the Reconstruction of Society." It was an account of a recent book authored by Bertrand Russell, a leading British philosopher active in the anti-war movement. Most accounts of Ambedkar's thought skip over this work; biographical accounts, driven by urges for completeness, note and summarize it, then move on. These approaches leave something important out of our stories of Ambedkar, however, since it is in this first review that Ambedkar's program of *meliorism* starts to be developed and worked out. In his early economic essays and his sociological work, "Castes in India," we do not see the fully developed normative or critical edge of the fiery Ambedkar as revealed in his 1936 Annihilation of Caste text. In "Castes in India," we see him diagnosing problematic customs and social arrangements, but he holds back from addressing readers forcefully about what should be done and what they can or should do. In this short review of a book that has so little to do, ostensibly, with India and its quest for self-rule, we see Ambedkar wade into the waters of normative advocacy: what Indians attentive to his arguments *should do and think now.* As we shall see, his review of Russell's book offers suggestions for constructive reactions to choices involving force and, I suggest, showcases an ever-evolving pragmatism that grows from—and sometimes resists—elements of Dewey's thought that he had heard and read. In other words, this review article in 1918 marks the most evident start of Ambedkar's project of *reconstructive rhetoric,* or his attempt to fashion and refashion problematic habits, customs, and institutions in readers or publics through acts of persuasive speech and writing.

## Ambedkar, Economics Discourse, and Indian Self-Help

It is interesting to consider why Ambedkar published in *this* journal and not others in India. We have evidence that his adviser, Edwin Seligman, was in conversation with other economics journals in India. For instance, H. Stanley Jevons, son of the economics thinker William Stanley Jevons and editor of the *Indian Journal of Economics,* carried on a correspondence with Seligman.[6] In a letter dated September 9, 1917, Jevons continues the conversation on a range of topics and at one point responds to Seligman that he is "glad to hear that you have some good Indian students working for the Doctor's degree with you."[7] Perhaps Seligman had been bragging about Ambedkar in a previous letter to this India-based European economist who founded this journal in 1916, along with being the first head of the Department of Economics at the University of Allahabad. The contacts existed for an easy path into the pages of this journal. Why didn't Ambedkar follow this route? Perhaps it was a concern with regionalism, as this journal was based in the north and stated in its inaugural issue that it was partly meant to provide "a convenient and compact vehicle of publication for the original investigations made by the staff of the Economics Department of the Allahabad University," as well as for "the more important researches of students of the Seminar class in Economics."[8] It also may have struck young Ambedkar as not fitting his focus of involving Indians in the reform of Indian life; its pages featured many British authors (most at Indian institutions), and the journal's guiding editorial statement indicated its purpose as "the dissemination of information about the economic activities of other countries. National progress can be made swiftly and surely only by utilizing the experience of other nations."[9] It even subscribed to a method most foreign to the pluralistic and historical methods evinced by Ambedkar's teachers such as Seligman and Dewey in their respective works: Jevons's journal aimed to advance India "by deductive reasoning based upon the comparative method."[10]

Ambedkar ultimately chose to publish his review article in the *Journal of the Indian Economics Society* in its inaugural issue in March 1918.[11] Soon afterward, he published his article "Small Holdings in India and their Remedies" in the next issue of the journal (1, no. 2) in June 1918. This journal surely captivated young Ambedkar's attention because of its reach in Indian economics circles; it was based in Bombay, Ambedkar's adopted hometown and an up-and-coming financial powerhouse of colonial India, and its articles were mostly written by Indian authors writing about Indian economic issues. There was no pretense that Europe or a comparative method would be able to "deduce" the solutions for India's economic woes. Furthermore, the journal was headed by Indian editors—the managing editor was C. S. Deole, and its editorial board consisted of V. G. Kale, N. M. Muzumbdar, P. A. Wadia, and V. G. Dalvi. There is evidence to suggest that Ambedkar knew many of these individuals personally: in the preface to Ambedkar's 1923 book (and doctoral thesis in London), *The Problem of the Rupee*, he thanks a "Professor Wadia of Wilson College" for help in correcting proofs, and in the book based on his doctoral thesis from Columbia, *The Evolution of Provincial Finance in British India*, he notes that he was "obliged to my friend Mr. C. S. Deole for assistance afforded in the dreary task of reading the proofs."[12] In a footnote on the final page of *The Problem of the Rupee*, Ambedkar criticizes the arguments that V. G. Kale made in his 1919 book, *Currency Reform in India*.[13] Beyond these personal and intellectual connections, this journal also seems to have been more attuned to Ambedkar's meliorist sensibilities. In its inaugural editorial message about the purpose of the journal, the editors frame its focus around the "monster of war" that had blighted the world; Indian economic reform was contextualized within this larger context, as one nation among other equals, using concepts that are strikingly compatible with Dewey's pragmatist vocabulary: "What is most certain is that work of re-construction and readjustment that lies ahead, is going to be tremendously difficult and nations must prepare to face it."[14]

Curiously enough, the inaugural issue of this English-language journal recounted an anonymized story that *could* have been drawn from Ambedkar's own history in the West. After reaffirming the journal's resistance to a deductive comparative method—"the experiences of other countries can help them [Indians] only to a limited extent"—the anonymous editorial statement continues:

> When an Indian pupil of an English Professor of world-wide repute, on the eve of his return to this country, went to seek his Professor's advice regarding the problems and needs of India, he was told *"no, no, my friend, we have no time to think for you. You must think out your own problems. No country's problems were solved by any other."* It was in the spirit of this sound and honest advice that the Indian Economic Society was started, and it was again in the spirit of the same advice that the idea of starting a journal of the Society was first mooted by some of its members. Self-help is the basic principle of life. All progress depends upon it and comes from within.[15]

No hint is given of who this "Indian pupil" or the "English Professor" is, and the wording leaves open the possibility that the person in question was not connected with the founding of this specific society. Given Ambedkar's personal connections to Wadia and Deole, it is not unreasonable to believe that this anecdote referred to something Ambedkar had experienced and reported once back in Bombay. If so, the "English Professor" referred to could easily have been one of Ambedkar's famous faculty mentors—such as Herbert Foxwell or his supervisor, Edwin Cannan—whom he learned from while in London.[16] As his biographers recount, Ambedkar had a penchant for continually placing the challenges of India's economic problems in front of them.[17] We shall encounter similar themes of self-help, self-respect, and individual initiative in Ambedkar's own biography, his writings and speeches, and his evolving messages in the following decades. Specifically, we shall see this idea of self-help merge with his own use of education and knowledge; even though he valued authors, concepts, and traditions of thought in the West—including Dewey and Russell—it was *Ambedkar* himself who was to put together novel and synthetic solutions to India's problems.

## Russell, Reform, and the Paradox of Force

At first glance, Ambedkar's review of Bertrand Russell's *Principles of Social Reconstruction* (originally published in 1916; Ambedkar reviewed the 1917 reissue) seems like an odd work.[18] Russell's book had little to do with India or with economics. He was not among the modern or classical crop of economic theorists that Ambedkar had cut his teeth on back at Columbia or in London. Yet Russell was a force to be reckoned with in philosophy, having a public stature in British intellectual circles as Dewey did in America. Perhaps Ambedkar saw that one way to hone his message was to build on, and resist, the thoughts of those whom large publics saw as somehow insightful. The rhetorical form of a review essay—or book review, given its focus on a published work—seems to incline the author's message toward following the thoughts of the reviewed author. Originality is not much expected of such works, nor would it be easy to achieve given the immediate choices of presenting, praising, or resisting the original author's published thoughts. The fact remains, however, that Ambedkar read Russell's work and chose to write down his thoughts on it and publish them in a journal with a significant readership among Indian audiences interested in economic reform. Thus, we can see this review as perhaps Ambedkar's earliest attempt to influence courses of reform in India with his words, arguments, and ideas. This is evident from the title he places on the short review, "Mr. Russell and the Reconstruction of Society."[19] As the opening editorial of the *Journal of the Indian Economic Society* proclaimed, the important challenge in India was *reconstruction* of what existed into something more ideal. This review not only highlights what Ambedkar as a *reader* might have seen in Russell's book, it also showcases Ambedkar as a *writer* bent on this reconstruction through rhetorical means. He wanted to change his Indian readers, not simply explain a foreign book to them.[20]

The choice of Russell as the target of Ambedkar's only review article is important. In many ways the London-based philosopher represented an intriguing figure for the young Indian reformer so intent on eradicating caste oppression in India. At this time, Russell was one of the leading figures in Western philosophical circles and was extremely interested in moral and political issues wherein philosophy met the practical world of politics. He was an ardent opponent of Britain's involvement in the First World War and a lifelong advocate for pacifism and anti-militarism. His books often could not find a home among British presses because of their content, and he served jail time for his anti-war activism—a fact that Ambedkar foregrounds for his Indian readers in the review. In terms of Ambedkar's intellectual guiding lights, Russell is also an important figure because he represents a line of thinking that ran close to—but that often jarred with—Dewey's pragmatism. Like Dewey, Russell valued education as part of his philosophical system, especially insofar as it was rendered secular and scientific. But the British philosopher was a relentless critic of Dewey's pragmatic instrumentalism, which undergirded so much of the American's thought. Epistemology, not moral commitments, seemed to divide these towering figures in philosophy. Dewey's view throughout much of his career was that notions such as "truth" and pursuits such as epistemology cost us more than we gained, as they drew our focus to some alleged feature of the world that goes beyond our experiences and our purposive judgments of them.

As a thoroughgoing naturalist, Dewey was committed to the position that our experience just *was*, and that epistemological markers such as "truth" only had a meaningful role to play in talking about our *judgments* on or about these experiences. There was nothing beyond human intelligence and its processes that was true or real in some grandly edifying sense, nor was there any touchstone that warranted the certainty that talk about truth entailed. For Dewey, the world could be carved up by humans and cultures in many contingent ways.

As a proponent of a view of logic that emulated the certainty evident in mathematics, Russell seemed displeased by this extreme reduction of truth and pursued a harsh critique of Dewey's pragmatist epistemology that was animated by Russell's "watered-down" Platonism.[21] Russell also seemed displeased by Dewey's seeming prioritization of individual experience and habit in the stories philosophy tells of the world, noting in a 1909 article that "the pragmatist's world will seem narrow and petty, robbing life of all that gives it value, and making Man himself small by depriving the universe which he contemplates of all its splendour."[22] Pragmatism idolized the world of action and practice, according to Russell, and perverted the honors that epistemology and the pursuit of truth could bestow upon humans. For him, Dewey and his fellow pragmatists (such as F. C. S. Schiller and William James) reduced philosophical inquiry to crass material matters and those orientations that seek to make claims to truth stick through superior force and willpower; simply put, "pragmatism appeals to the temper of mind which finds on the surface of this planet the whole of its imaginative material; which feels confident of progress, and unaware of non-human limitations to human power."[23] It was in this article taking aim at James and Dewey that Russell presented his infamous characterization of pragmatist epistemology as a "worship of force" that entailed that "ironclads and Maxim guns must be the ultimate arbiters of metaphysical truth."[24] Dewey, of course, reacted strenuously to these critiques of his pragmatic instrumentalism and its ways of sorting out justified beliefs from unjustified claims.[25]

Despite all the differences between Russell and Dewey, the British philosopher had important overlaps in emphases with his American nemesis. Russell, like Dewey, used terms like "growth" and a focus on education to combine with a melioristic sensibility of reform to critique society in the book that Ambedkar was to review shortly after his time with the American pragmatist. In the published review, Ambedkar notes all of these features, and it is fascinating to watch how he reacts to Russell's program of reform. It is also useful to note that Dewey portrayed Russell's book in a favorable light in a lecture in China in 1920, where he told his audience that even though Russell's theoretical philosophy was fixated on abstract, mathematical concerns, his social philosophy did have much to offer those confronting pressing social and economic issues.[26] Dewey also thought highly enough of Russell's book to pencil in a reference to the 1917 American reissue of it (titled *Why Men Fight*) in his typed notes for his Psychological Ethics course in 1917.[27]

Given the history and heat between Russell and Dewey, the question remains: Why would Ambedkar engage this book in one of his first acts of public scholarship back in India? Why would he concern himself with a book arguing about the Great War and its causes, especially in the pages of an Indian *economics* journal, after arriving home in India from his extended sojourn in the West? Russell's book gave young Ambedkar a conceptual vocabulary and testing ground to develop the prototype of what would become his fully employed reconstructive rhetoric. Russell's thought was focused enough on what mattered to Ambedkar but resided far enough from the approach and topics that Ambedkar had grown close to given his early formation under the hands of American teachers such as Dewey. It was, in a way, a useful goad that moved him to start exploring themes that would be important in his later, forceful and focused, works attacking the Hindu system of caste. Russell's book, however, might strike a reader as an ineffective starting point for those seeking answers to problems in India. As Ambedkar noted in his review, it was "a war book" placed in the "preventive" subcategory of "Bellicose literature."[28] And like much European philosophy of its time, it seemed intently focused on the problems and problematics of European civilization. There was no mention in its pages of India or of the problems of caste. But in its concern with the social institutions that had led to the outbreak of unprecedented levels of violence in the Great War was embedded a more general account of conflict, psychology, and reform. As Dewey was to note in a 1920 lecture in China, Russell tied the problems of institutions and nations to the problems of human instinct. Our impulses and instinctive urges are unconscious for Russell, and when thought intelligently controls them, they can become useful and conscious features of thought and desire.[29] This is related to what Russell calls the "principle of growth," or the free flourishing of human life in its creative dimensions. Institutions such as our government and economic systems can conspire against real growth, but there is a melioriative possibility that remains: "In the modern world, the principle of growth in most men and women is hampered by institutions inherited from a simpler age. By the progress of thought and knowledge, and by the increase in command over the forces of the physical world, new possibilities of growth have come into existence, and have given rise to new claims which must be satisfied if those who make them are not to be thwarted."[30] Society and its institutions can be altered through what Russell labels "reconstruction." The problem for Russell is that our institutions are based on authority and force and are grounded on concerns of a past remote from our present situation. In order for our personal psychology to be reconstructed in a more just and felicitous fashion, we must reconstruct our institutions. This is why his book so naturally divides its expositions into chapters on the state, war, education, property, marriage, and religion. All of these concern systems larger than any one person's mental makeup, yet all of these affect and condition the experiences and happiness of each individual person. The locus of change is illusive, and Russell searches to find such a reconstructive point of Archimedean efficacy.

What seems to flummox Russell's search for an effective way for people to change institutions to enable personal growth is simple: these institutions are represented and backed by people, and the common currency between people seems to be *force*. From the first chapter on, Russell focuses on religion as the site of both the most oppressive and most liberatory movements in the battle for individual growth. The West's long and tumultuous history with religious oppression is no deterrent to his argument, since history shows an ascending path of freedom here. Noting the forces that began to grow in resistance to religious hegemony, Russell points to

> Luther's assertion of the right of private judgment and the fallibility of General Councils. Out of this assertion grew inevitably, with time, the belief that a man's religion could not be determined for him by authority, but must be left to the free choice of each individual. It was in matters of religion that the battle for liberty began, and it is in matters of religion that it has come nearest to a complete victory.[31]

Reading such lines surely must have dismayed young Ambedkar, since he personally knew that his lack of freedom as an "untouchable" was primarily attributable to *religious* reasons.[32]

Russell's account of religious development in the West was a fairly optimistic story, despite contemporary setbacks involving support among religious leaders in Britain for the Great War. Russell thought little of the value and usefulness of religious belief for the efforts of civilization and peace. He was content if it simply stayed out of the business of oppression and rule. Ambedkar, however, would come to emphasize the potentially empowering aspect of personal choice in religions in his evolving writings, a choice that could be intelligently guided by reflection on the consequences of religious affiliation for those under its spell. Perhaps Ambedkar was already pining for a pragmatic form of Buddhism when he penned this review, if the Adlerblum recollection presented at the start of this book is accurate. For Russell in his book, similar to Dewey in his Philosophy 131–132 course, what characterized all of the battles for reform and justice in Europe—successful or not—was the feature of forceful action and reaction among interacting individuals, not just the empowerment wrought by individual choice. Europe went from extreme communalism in religion and state control to a more chaotic individualism, which led Russell to wonder about the next development at the hands of these forces: "The development through extreme individualism to strife, and thence, one hopes, to a new reintegration, is to be seen in almost every department of life."[33]

What is important for our understanding of Ambedkar's reaction to all of this is what Russell does next with this reading of force. Force underlies all of these changes among and between people and institutions. Institutions are abstract, remote things in a certain sense; people in front of you are the more concrete face of social reality. It is such individuals who make claims for reconstruction; it is also such individuals who make claims against one's reconstructive efforts. Russell acknowledges the general *form* such struggles tend to take, especially in heated disputes evoking the notion of social justice:

> Claims are advanced in the name of justice, and resisted in the name of tradition and prescriptive right. Each side honestly believes that it deserves to triumph, because two theories of society exist side by side in our thought, and men choose, unconsciously, the theory which fits their case. Because the battle is long and arduous all general theory is gradually forgotten; in the end, nothing remains but self-assertion, and when the oppressed win freedom they are as oppressive as their former masters.[34]

In other essays penned during the war, Russell takes both the German and British sides to task for continuing a cycle of violence grounded on partial but emotive views that one's own side is right, and unique, in its pursuit

of just ends, and the other side is reprehensibly exemplary in its use of immoral means and methods.[35] Here, he expands the scope of this critique
into general philosophical terms that go beyond the specific conflicts of
the world war; his account of social reconstruction becomes enmeshed in
a general notion of conflict and what it does to those who are targeted
by advocates of change. This abstract account is bracing in its honesty, or
perhaps cynicism, about human nature. Humans will tend to always think
they are right and good, even when they are diametrically opposed to others who think they are right and good. Theories are noted and then subli-
mated, but the assertiveness of the self in combat with the other remains.
This applies to an individual struggling against another lone individual or
to a group of individuals (such as a "nationality") resisting other similar
groups. At the most basic level, the reformer wants to remake society into
a set of institutions that gives them the justice they have so far lacked; in
doing so, Russell emphasizes that they will often become insensitive to the
injustices they will create once in power. The oppressed so easily become
oppressors, because the nature of oppression only cares about an assertive
self coupled with power to enforce its (but not others') will.

Russell's book, so eagerly attended to by both Dewey and Ambedkar,
wrestles with the ends of reconstruction and the uncertain means of achieving it. If all pursuits of justice through social reconstruction are likely to
result in a new form of injustice, how are we to proceed? The assertion of
self is the root of this problem, but this assertion enigmatically represents
the *means* for any attempt to create these ends:

> The tug of war of mutual self-assertion can only result in justice through an
> accidental equality of force. It is no use to attempt any bolstering up of insti-
> tutions based on authority, since all such institutions involve injustice, and
> injustice once realized cannot be perpetuated without fundamental damage
> both to those who uphold it and to those who resist it. The damage consists
> in the hardening of the walls of the Ego, making them a prison instead of a
> window.[36]

If activism and reform efforts lead to such undesirable effects, are we then
consigned to not acting? Russell was a pacifist, but his reformist agitations
show he was no quietist. He did not give up on reform or reconstruction.
There must be a way out of this conundrum, yet the rest of Russell's book
does not definitively answer this problem postulated by the use of force to
reconstruct society. What was sought was growth—an evolutionary term

that assumed more and more prominence in Dewey's naturalism after the war—but "unimpeded growth in the individual depends upon many contacts with other people, which must be of the nature of free co-operation, not of enforced service."[37] The quest for this endpoint, merging individual flourishing with group organization, does place limitations on the means of its realization, according to Russell:

> While the belief in authority was alive, free co-operation was compatible with inequality and subjection, but now equality and mutual freedom are necessary. All institutions, if they are not to hamper individual growth, must be based as far as possible upon voluntary combination, rather than the force of the law or the traditional authority of the holders of power. None of our institutions can survive the application of this principle without great and fundamental changes; but these changes are imperatively necessary if the world is to be withheld from dissolving into hard separate units each at war with all the others.[38]

Russell can see the way forward, but the exact moves to make along this path are unclear. What is apparent, however, is that we must be absolutely cautious with our use of *force* to realize this end. This is the path of authority, whether it uses the force of law or armed power, and this intimates the cycle of forceful oppression that Russell worries about in attempts at social reconstruction.

We must reconstruct society in the face of opposing others but not become as bad and exclusive in our uses of force as we see the others being. Russell's book acknowledges the tempting promise of force to be used for *only* just ends and ultimately shies away from its siren call. As his other essays specifically on the war note, British and German thinkers never failed to find the motive and the means to see their side as just and their use of violent force as righteous. By the final chapter of this book, Russell begins to take back what he has advanced in terms of his critique of various institutions in society, pointing out the "despair" that grips many people given that "their power seems infinitesimal."[39] He deflates hopes of immediate, noticeable social melioration, at least in the context of war-torn Europe, despairing that

> so long as we think only of the immediate future, it seems that what we can do is not much. It is probably impossible for us to bring the war to an end. We cannot destroy the excessive power of the State or of private property. We

cannot, here and now, bring new life into education. In such matters, though we may see the evil, we cannot quickly cure it by any of the ordinary methods of politics.[40]

The path of reconstruction is long, in other words, and some institutions will simply be beyond any group's finite power to change them. Institutions have a material reality, but Russell begins to use the recalcitrance of this material reality to argue for another path. Russell's suggested means begin to take the form of a mental instantiation of reformed impulses and instincts as a way to slowly reform institutions. Education and rational persuasion are slow, but vital, means for reconstructing society.

This turn toward the individual person and their habits is vital and will become particularly noteworthy once we start engaging Ambedkar's rhetoric of conversion in the 1930s. This emphasis is also significant as it draws Russell closer to the Dewey Ambedkar saw and heard in his time at Columbia. As we explored in the previous chapter, Dewey was concerned with expounding a view of humans as organisms driven by impulse yet subject to habit and its reshaping of individual impetus. Impulse, for both philosophers, is what gives drive and force to individual agency, as well as the collective phenomenon of custom among a group of individuals. Institutions shape custom and often coalesce a group's customs into a stable and enforced form; these institutions and practices also shape the habits individuals have that add up the aggregate customs of the group. Russell in his book, however, extends the nature of impulse beyond custom and connects it to the concept of "spirit," arguing that the problem of war and violence is one of the "wrong spirit" animating our interactions with others. The solution, in part, will be the reformation of mental habits in the individual:

> We must recognize that the world is ruled in a wrong spirit, and that a change of spirit will not come from one day to the next. Our expectations must not be for tomorrow, but for the time when what is thought now by a few shall have become the common thought of many. If we have courage and patience, we can think the thoughts and feel the hopes by which, sooner or later, men will be inspired, and weariness and discouragement will be turned into energy and ardour. For this reason, the first thing we have to do is to be clear in our own minds as to the kind of life we think good and the kind of change that we desire in the world.[41]

We must begin to model or instantiate the sort of reform in thinking and in dealing with our impulses that we want to see encouraged by institutions after they are reformed. This will require some amount of inward "intellectual detachment," since it is our attachment to habitual ways of thinking and valuing that leads to our "comfortable acquiescence" with unjust institutions. Combining this with Russell's earlier reasoning on self-assertion, one can see that these habits of thinking that our native ways of thinking and valuing are right in a deep sense can easily *extend* or *create* forms of injustice when coupled with effective force and authority.

Russell ends his book by listing specific characteristics that fleshed out the life of growth, or the sort of individual and community endpoint that reconstruction sought. The life to be desired, according to Russell, was the "creative life" and not simply the "possessive life." The former marshaled an individual's creative and constructive impulses, whereas the latter built up an individual's impulses to possess and own. The latter, of course, was what led to conflict between people so often animated by the desire to have something as their exclusive source of happiness. Russell leaves us—and readers such as Ambedkar—with a tantalizingly simple framework of how we are to pursue growth through these creative means. In pursuing such a life, and in turn the institutions that encourage it, we must heed "two general principles which are always applicable." The first of these is the stricture that "the growth and vitality of individuals and communities is to be promoted as far as possible." This occurs through feeding one's own creative impulses and reforming institutions in line with this imperative when one can. But there are limiting factors on this pursuit, even when the force available to one's reconstructive projects seems efficacious: "The growth of one individual or one community is to be as little as possible at the expense of another."[42] Even if we can change the impulses of others through institutional change—Russell's ideal outcome—we must respect the cycle of force that undergirds reform efforts like a social bedrock. The oppressed can easily turn into oppressors through the self-assertion of the ego and its conception of a just society. This problematic of force and reform is what underlies Russell's commitment to pacifism and nonresistance as the best methods of social change. What stands as a wall against the cycle of force is the second principle of growth, which represents "reverence" for the life of others as equal to our own in Russell's account. This reverence can be cashed out in a negative fashion as "liberty," which "tells us not to interfere, but does not give any basis for construction. It shows that many political and social institutions are bad and ought to be swept away, but it does not show what ought to be put in their place."[43] Thus, Russell leaves his readers with a philosophical system that performs a delicate balancing act. It cares enough about the experience of each human life to desire a reform of each toward the best, but it realizes that the process of reform might be conceived of differently in a diverse community and might lead to overzealous uses of force in pursuit of one limited notion of flourishing.

## Ambedkar, Russell, and Reformers as Educators

Ambedkar surely noticed this tentative but important ending to Russell's account of what social reconstruction entails. His review of Russell's book is important because it contains his first overt use of the philosophy of Dewey; more important, however, than these citations is the fact that it is the first example we have of Ambedkar thinking as a *meliorist*, or a thinker dedicated to giving a theoretical account of some matter that strives to actually improve future experience. Meliorism is a complex topic, but it is an important theme in pragmatism. James and Dewey place it as a middle ground between optimistic or pessimistic views of the world.[44] Simplified, meliorism can be said to orbit around a few basic commitments. First, the meliorist is committed to the idea that the world is not wholly good or bad; the charge of meliorism is to reconstruct the harmful elements of individuals and societies so as to constantly improve or optimize lived experience. Second, the goal of melioristic work is not simply to describe or "capture" a phenomenon, even a harmful one; this would make it indistinguishable from dominant approaches across philosophy and social sciences of its time. Instead, meliorist work remains cognizant of its functioning as advocacy or as a means to help change the realities and imperfections of the world it engages. It doesn't so much *describe*, it *re-describes* to affect beneficial changes in specific ways through specific agents being addressed. Third, meliorism tends to draw its standards for progress or improvement from useful values already immanent within existing communities; it does not appeal to transcendent or divine standards from outside of instances of experience. Meliorism, in other words, is a form of reconstruction that also entails a certain rhetorical style of argument or address. It is not abstract theorizing without cognizance of who the message is directed at in the performance of arguing or theorizing.

This early review article is an essential start to my effort to extract Ambedkar's form of meliorism—what I describe as his reconstructive rhetoric throughout the course of this book. Like Dewey, Ambedkar immediately recognizes Russell's work as a "war book."[45] But unlike Dewey's rather descriptive 1920 gloss, Ambedkar mixes his praise of Russell's project with his own creative line of criticism that enunciates and performs his melioristic commitments. As we shall see, Ambedkar's critique centers on two main concerns: Russell insufficiently explained the challenges of "force" as a concept, especially in light of his Indian audiences, and Russell's analysis did not respect the inherent complexity in human psychology and the need for pluralistic explanations it entailed.

Before enunciating his thoughts on force, however, Ambedkar immediately picks up on, and praises, Russell's starting point in human psychology. He summarizes Russell's method as focusing on the "springs of action" within humans and highlights the hope that modifications or redirections of these tendencies allow. Like the psychology Ambedkar heard in Dewey's Philosophy 231 course and the psychology he would deploy in works such as his 1936 *Annihilation of Caste*, the springs to human action and their habitual modifications were a vital part of diagnosing social maladies, as well as ascertaining what might address them. These modifications of the impulses to human action, according to Ambedkar's review of Russell,

> constitute Education in the broadest sense of the word. All modifications, however, are not equally valuable and it is the business of the reformer to eliminate the circumstances and institutions that modify these tendencies for the socially worse and preserve and introduce those that will modify them for the socially better. Whatever that may be, it is of immense social value that these tendencies are capable of indefinite modifications.[46]

While Russell had a specific chapter in the work on education, he employed it as a topic and institution (viz. formal education). Ambedkar is extending the meaning of Russell's project of reform to be one of education from the start. If education also refers to the range of projects implicated by the concept of meliorism, Russell's work can be read as one that transforms reformers into educators, especially when these reformers are able to discriminate between better and worse states of social affairs. Such a position extracted by Ambedkar from Russell's book harmonizes with how Dewey puts matters in his *Democracy and Education* of 1916.[47] There, Dewey is clear that all education is indirect and occurs through the influence of an environment: the "Social environment forms the mental and emotional disposition of behavior in individuals by engaging them in activities that arouse and strengthen certain impulses, that have certain purposes and entail certain consequences."[48] Formal education—that of the school house—occurs through the efficacies provided by a purposive, deliberate alteration of the classroom environment, but it is indirect as well. Dewey describes the power of the teacher as control over an environment: "The educator's part in the enterprise of education is to furnish the environment which stimulates responses and directs the learner's course. In the last analysis, all that the educator can do is modify stimuli so that response will as surely as is possible result in the formation of desirable intellectual and emotional dispositions."[49] This is consonant with the psychology and reading of habit reformation we saw Dewey deliver to Ambedkar and his fellow students in the Philosophy 231 course in fall 1914.

In his 1918 review Ambedkar merged the Deweyan position—one also intertwined in the settlement activities of Jane Addams and Mary Kingsbury Simkhovitch—that education occurs through an environment that can be manipulated with Russell's position that the reformer is primarily concerned with altering the social environment represented by institutions. Like Dewey in the Philosophy 131–132 course of 1915–16, Russell insists that institutions shape our habits and dispositions; reformers can be said to attempt to change human nature and experience by changing these conditioning institutions. Dewey did not quite reach this point in his lectures on custom, although he did leave room for progress through social reform; he even toyed with the paradox that some moral heroes or reformers are first considered outlandish criminals by a custom-sedimented society.[50] Russell's reading of reform, combined with his view of the reformer as a persuasive gadfly, allowed Ambedkar to see a new way to extend Dewey's dialectics of individualism and community, habit and group custom. In his creative way, Ambedkar uses this minor review as a site to reconceptualize *reformers* not simply as political actors but as *educators*. This point will become increasingly magnified in the trajectory of Ambedkar's rhetorical activity explored throughout this book, but this synthesis in 1918 holds the key to seeing his later *oratorical* and *political* activism as educational in the Deweyan spirit. Why did he speak so often and so forcefully to so many types of audiences? Beyond the schools he built or his difficult time spent as a professor, Ambedkar saw himself as an educator whenever he affected the social environment through the political or rhetorical altering of its landscape. Speeches and persuasive writing were ways to achieve such changes in attentive audiences. He emphasized in his life and arguments something that many miss about the dialectic between the social and the individual: the social forms and educates the individual, and the individual can reform the social through his or her person and through altering institutions that comprise various parts of the state.

The development of Ambedkar's complex view of the Indian tradition and the way out of the injustice of the caste system would come later; his path of activism and advocacy wasn't evident in its full form in the young Ambedkar making comments and connections with the text of Russell's *Principles of Social Reconstruction*. But the review shows his concern with a central commitment: the question about *means* that matters so much when one is trying to achieve some ideal endpoint. Even though he would largely eschew overt engagement with Russell's writings in his later publications, he remained intrigued by the British philosopher's life and thought through his final years.[51] Like Dewey, he could not completely turn away from this adversary of pragmatism. Agonism can be productive, however. This early published negotiating of the challenges that Russell's work evokes signifies the acceleration of Ambedkar's development as a public intellectual and synthetic pragmatist figure.

Ambedkar segues in his review from his discussion of reform as education to Russell's infatuation with growth as the outcome of reform. Such a program is not passivity, Ambedkar alleges, as Russell wants activity that leads to growth. The principles of growth that Russell maintains, according to Ambedkar, are related to the economic and psychological impulses revealed in the nations so eager to go to war in Europe. While Ambedkar implores his readers in this "economics journal" to attend to the entirety of Russell's book, and even though he claims that "we need only attend to the analysis of the institution of Property and the modifications it is alleged by Mr. Russell to produce in human nature" for the purposes of his review, he immediately launches into a fascinating discussion of ends and means.[52] This tense relation of means and ends, force and violence, became an enduring feature of Ambedkar's thought over the coming decades.

Ambedkar seems concerned in this review to not only convey Russell's views on growth to his Indian readers but also clarify the relationship of growth and successful reform action with undesirable or counterproductive activity. Thus, he warns that though this is an "anti-war book," the Indian readers "who read in him [Russell] the philosophy of quietism will have read him all wrong."[53] Ambedkar emphasizes with seeming approval Russell's point that life without impulse is death, and that even nations and states need impulse as "the expression of life."[54] He summarizes Russell's point—*"activity is the condition of growth"*—demonstrating that the British philosopher is "against war but is not for quietism."[55] Quietism, according to Ambedkar, would lead only to death or, perhaps put more broadly, national and cultural stagnation.

## Dewey, Force, and the Prospects of Reform

So far, Ambedkar's Indian readers should see his clear agreement or sympathy with Russell's point about the necessity of careful reform activity.

But then Ambedkar makes an odd move, one that becomes understandable only when one sees the full scope of the submerged relationship he had with Dewey and pragmatism. Ambedkar insists on translating Russell's point into the philosophical parlance of Dewey. On first glance, this does not seem to get him much. The invoking of Dewey's name did not have much rhetorical value in Indian circles, but it does reveal the fact that *Ambedkar* reasons through such thinkers as Dewey and Russell, whom he sees as relevant to the Indian context. As we shall see in the next chapter, this selective echoing (implicitly or explicitly) of parts of Dewey's thought reveals Ambedkar as a synthetic and appropriative thinker willing to take what is useful from his tradition, or the traditions of others, and marshal it for his own melioristic purposes. The point he makes using Dewey's distinctions might have import for India by extending the reception of Ambedkar's message beyond anything resident in Russell's book on war, impulse, and reform. Ambedkar uses "the language of Professor Dewey" to explain that Russell is "only against 'force as violence' but is all for 'force as energy.'"[56] Ambedkar uses this explanatory framework largely to prevent his Indian readers from taking the wrong message (quietism) from Russell's book. First, he notes that force of some sort is necessary in projects of normative progress toward an ideal: "It must be remembered by those who are opposed to force that without the use of it all ideals will remain empty just as without some ideal or purpose (conscious or otherwise) all activity will be no more than mere fruitless fooling."[57] Second, he connects the discourse of force to a long-standing philosophical concern, namely the relation between ends and means. This is of importance for philosophers such as Dewey, as moral thought in its Kantian and utilitarian instantiations has always been concerned with the justificatory relationship between ends and means. Does the value of an end trump concerns about worrisome means that appear necessary to reach these ideals or goals? Ambedkar reveals his commitments when he writes in his review, "Ends and means (= force in operation) are therefore concomitants and the common adage that the end justifies the means contains a profound truth which is perverted simply because it is misunderstood. For if the end does not justify the means what else will? The difficulty is that we do not sufficiently control the operations of the means once employed for the achieving of some end."[58] Indian readers of this review article on economic matters witnessed Ambedkar making a move integral to the sort of pragmatism he would develop in the coming decades through his activism: ends and means are not binary or separate, but instead they are closely connected and fall into different shades of synthesis. They imbue each other with meaning, and their value is interlinked.

And, as Ambedkar notes in this early piece, ends and means are connected to the types of force we may employ in our reform efforts.

Force is a perplexing topic. It is frequently evoked in physics and implicates causal powers of inanimate objects; physics in turn borrowed this term from more human concerns such as willpower, muscular effort, and spiritual influence.[59] In the realm of moral and political matters, these qualities shade over into the concepts of agency and responsibility for effecting changes in the world. It is also a topic of importance in Indian traditions and among thinkers such as Mahatma Gandhi.[60] In this early review article, Ambedkar explicitly links force as a topic of importance to pragmatic effectiveness. Means are forceful, and ends are not wholly separate from the notion of means. The effective achievement of an end or goal through the application of force does not *end* activity; it simply sets up future courses of pursuit. In Dewey's later terminology, an end is really an end-in-view, which serves as a means to some other end-in-view in later or larger contexts. Ends should not be separated from means, nor should they be held apart from force. Later in the 1918 review, Ambedkar turns his readers to reflecting on their reactions to books such as Russell's; he criticizes those who use "the present European war" to "censure the philosophy of force" and to advocate a "gospel of quietism and the doctrine of non-resistance."[61]

What motivates Ambedkar with this unusual line of critique in his review of a European war book in the pages of an Indian economics journal? Partly, it must be motivated by Ambedkar's desire to think through debates in the West and to further develop his stance on the rising independence movement in India that would increasingly take its lead from doctrines of *karma* or nonviolence (*ahimsa*) that simultaneously seem to erode significant motivations for active force or even violence. He appears driven to "present Indian readers of Mr. Russell with a correct interpretation of his attitude. Their innate craving for a pacific life and their philosophic bias for the doctrine of non-resistance, I am afraid, might lead them to read in Mr. Russell a justification of their view of life."[62] One must infer what "view of life" he is imputing here, but perhaps it is a view that emphasizes birth as a measure of one's value in previous lives and of waiting for rebirth or even *moksha* as effective means of escaping one's current predicament. Instead of such commitments that seem to disable much of the social activity or progress of individuals *and* societies, Ambedkar reorients the hope for change and betterment to activities that can create change. At the basis of activity is force, and force must be reckoned with by all agents. The tensions that Russell identifies must not be read as decisive, Ambedkar implies. He senses the need to find a sort of force that empowers reform, but he requires one that does not undermine its own long-term goals.

This commitment to the conceptual interconnection of ends and means, along with the value of ends imbuing means with value (and vice versa), would remain with Ambedkar his entire life. As we shall see at the end of this book, this same distinction is used and attributed to "Professor Dewey" in Ambedkar's final years when he was engaging the philosophy of Marx from the perspective of his reconstructive reading of Buddhism. It is helpful to ask, however, what conversation the young Ambedkar was participating in when he evoked the language of his Columbia teacher to shed light on the useful and nonuseful ways of taking Russell's critique of society and reform. Knowing what we now know from the identification of materials from Ambedkar's courses with Dewey at Columbia, we are in a position to mark out the exact portion of his teacher's thought that he was referring to in this review article. In a lecture on April 19, 1916, that young Ambedkar heard at Columbia, we see Dewey make the exact distinction that Ambedkar refers to in his critique of Russell. Dewey is recorded as asking whether the state's violence begets more violence (a position attributed by Dewey to Tolstoy) and whether the "extreme non-resistance doctrine" is the best way to meliorate evil in communal settings. Dewey is recorded as replying to this in a straightforward manner: all of these approaches should highlight "the underlying *falsity of any theory which makes a separation between purpose and aim*, and force."[63] End-directed activity must involve force, even if it wants to be passive or nonviolent: "An *end which has no means of realization direct or indirect* is not an end at all."[64] Ideals or ends without effective means are "mere sentimentality." Dewey then makes the distinction that Ambedkar reiterates in addressing Russell: "In the case of force which is a means you do have words which make a distinction—energy and violence. Energy—ability to do work. Violence connotes destructive power or force."[65] Both of these indicate some relation of ends to means, but the former indicates a useful relationship, whereas the latter entails a wasteful, inefficient relationship. To assert that one's ends can be realized without force of any kind, according to Dewey, is "to hold up an ideal which by definition excludes means of its realization [and] is going beyond anything that is legitimately utopian—[it] adopt[s] the policy of passive inaction. That theory has been associated with the conception of the world as totally evil. Mere recourse to passive introspectionism, Nirvana."[66] While Dewey's analysis of the Buddhist concept of *nirvana* is surely not thorough, Ambedkar could not help seeing Indian thought as connected to this problematic of force Dewey enunciated: all programs of reform or change must use force.[67]

Ambedkar is continuing a conversation that Dewey started concerning nonresistance and *"the place of force in the moral economy of force"* in his 1916 lectures.[68] There, Dewey situated the issue of force in Kant's bifurcation between moral virtue (*Tugend*) and matters of physical coercion (*Recht*, in Kant's thought). Ambedkar heard Dewey opine that Kant erred by instituting a sharp dualism "between force and moral considerations, between force and ends or purposes as the carriers of the ethical element."[69] Dewey then continued on to one of his neo-Hegelian sparring partners, T. H. Green, and Green's explicit discussion of "will not force" in one of his articles. For Dewey, the dialogue on force implicated the limits and agencies of individual members of a tradition-bound group and thereby served as another instance of the historical development of the individualism-collectivism dialectic evidenced in modern philosophy. Dewey's main target, however, seemed to be the philosophy of nonresistance espoused by Tolstoy. In an extended discussion during his April 19, 1916, lecture, Dewey tells his students that Tolstoy conflated the violent force of a robber with the violent force of the state in punishing such thieves. For Dewey, Tolstoy's position was based on two objections to violence. One was a utilitarian concern: Tolstoy seemed to believe that "violence begets violence, the state educates criminality."[70] Dewey admits that "there is a certain amount of truth" in this concern.[71] The second objection is more deontological in its nature, pointing to an inherent wrongness in using force on individuals. As Dewey glosses Tolstoy's concern, the "bringing to bear of force upon individuals is essentially immoral; the essence of personality is will, freedom and the use of physical forces upon personality, upon will is so formal, as to be inherently and intrinsically evil and the deliberate recourse to the kingdom of darkness."[72] Dewey was no stranger to the value of "personality," as it was a staple of his earlier, more idealistic ethics. We shall see this term appear later in our exploration of Ambedkar's developing rhetoric of religious conversion in the 1930s. But in 1916, Dewey notes the uniqueness of Tolstoy's extreme views of the harms of force and attempts to cull the unreasonable points out of it while saving room for force and effectiveness in action. Tolstoy is like the anarchists, Dewey lectures, as both claim that the state's entanglement with force renders the state evil; its natural use of force and coercion on individuals "infringes this sacred liberty or personality."[73] Force and the state, according to this "extreme non-resistance doctrine," harms the very thing that should be emancipated and enabled: the individual personality.

Ambedkar's critique in this 1918 review continues this conversation. Even though he bends Dewey's critique—via Russell—back to the life-world of his readers in India, important parameters are set by a focus on Tolstoy (bequeathed to him by Dewey) and not primarily on Gandhi or *satyagraha*.[74] Indeed, the term Ambedkar uses in his review—"non-resistance"—is the term used by Dewey in his reading of Tolstoy, as well as by Russell in his various works on the moral problems of force, violence, and war.[75] Dewey would later focus on this term in a modified version distanced from debates about the state's powers, as he did in 1930 when discussing Jane Addams's influence on him: "One of the things that I have learned from her is the enormous value of *mental non-resistance*, of tearing away the armor-plate of prejudice, of convention, isolation that keeps one from sharing to the full in the larger and even the more unfamiliar and alien ranges of the possibilities of human life and experience."[76] In contexts relevant to India, Gandhi experimented with various terms to describe his method before Ambedkar's review was printed, but he almost exclusively used "passive resistance" even though he issued a public call for renaming his method of nonviolent resistance in 1907.[77] *Satyagraha* can be found as early as 1909 in Gandhi's own work, but it takes the place of "passive resistance" in Gandhi's advocacy around the time of Ambedkar's review of Russell's book. While Gandhi was greatly influenced by Tolstoy, he shied away from adopting the conceptual handle of "nonresistance" in his public utterances.[78] Revealing his focus on the juxtaposition of Russell and Dewey on force, Ambedkar does not use *satyagraha* or "passive resistance" in his review, even though he explicitly reveals that this discussion should speak to concerns of his Indian audience.

Ambedkar believes that translating the issues of force and violence from Russell into Dewey, and then back to concerns his Indian audience might have, can result in important realizations of the nuances of force and violence. The key for Ambedkar is the idea that means and ends are interconnected, a connection that he realizes is vulnerable to harmful misunderstandings. He makes a related point in describing the workings of the caste system in his paper "Castes in India," prepared for Alexander Goldenweiser's Columbia University seminar. In that work, he makes the pragmatist point that the pernicious customs of caste were

essentially of the nature of means, though they are represented as ideals. But this should not blind us from understanding the *results* that flow from them. One might safely say that idealization of means is necessary and in this par-

ticular case was perhaps motivated to endow them with greater efficacy. Calling a means an end does no harm, except that it disguises its real character;
but it does not deprive it of its real nature, that of a means.[79]

His point is related to what he uses Dewey to say in this review. Ends are
only a certain temporary stoppage of activity; they guide our activity, and
might even be labeled as ideals, but we should not fool ourselves that they
are divinely entailed or that action ends after they are achieved. They become means for the next endeavor, even when they function as ends-in-
view that direct activity of an individual or group toward preferred states of
affairs. Thinking customs like *sati* (widow burning) are divinely authorized
is pernicious for Ambedkar, as it hurts our ability to achieve a range of ends
and goals and to refine our values and action strategies. It makes holy and
unalterable something that may be pernicious and that ought to be reconstructed. In other words, concretizing a strong dualism between means and
ends makes it easy to confuse matters of force, leading to the paralyzing
nonactivity of the extreme doctrine of nonresistance of Tolstoy and a likely
misreading of Russell's thought.

Ambedkar, along with Dewey in 1916, is also concerned with another
result of this confusion of ends and means, the promotion of violent and
forceful means. The challenge lies in avoiding the violent use of force that
implicates a rush toward an end that undoes other desired results or ends.
In his lectures, Dewey is recorded as explicitly challenging the objection
to "the doctrine that the end justifies the mean[s]." As Ambedkar would
echo in his review, Dewey states in his lecture that "if one takes it literally,
of course the end justifies the means, if it did not, what would justify the
means?" What Dewey is concerned about is a fixation on one end: "Practically it has been used to justify the doctrine that if you have a good end
in view you are entitled to overlook all the bad results you get."[80] Actions
produce a range of results, Dewey claims, so to fixate on one and ignore
the other consequences implies an unintelligent truncation of activity. He
advises his class, including an attentive Ambedkar, that "the end justifies
the means in the sense that you cannot make any separation between ends
and means, as are the means, so the ends, as the ends, so the means. . . .
Hence always be on the lookout for all of the consequences of the means
which you employ, not attempting to justify our means by selecting certain
results."[81] Ambedkar clearly agrees with this point and casts it in terms of
"fanaticism" that focused too much on one end and sacrificed other valuable ends in the course of forceful activity. This concern will return when

we move on to Ambedkar's later works, which will often try to balance concerns of liberty, equality, *and* fraternity as values guiding action in a social democracy.

This fanaticism is a worry insofar as it represents a state of mind that would employ violence to achieve a truncated set of ends. In both Dewey's 1916 lectures and Ambedkar's 1918 review, moral action does not consist in getting away from all uses of force; it becomes the pragmatic search for an *intelligent* use of force as a replacement for destructive force. The division of force and ends evinced by the doctrine of nonresistance only encourages a "sharp division of the mind and body," says Dewey in the lecture on April 25, 1916; instead, he asserts, "What is mind but a purpose or aim, end in view as the object or will?"[82] Mind and body are linked, just as are means and ends, and actions and endpoints. Here we recognize the pragmatist roots of Ambedkar's later focus on the conceptual or mental implications of the externally structuring caste system. Group customs are internalized as habits and attitudes, and these consequentially affect our actions and judgments. They can even tone our perceptions and expectations of others we encounter in experience. In his review of Russell, Ambedkar turns these points toward the rhetorical situation he finds himself in once back in India and implores his Indian readers to ask whether their ends "could not be achieved otherwise than by violence"; they are also warned to avoid if possible "the sacrifice of other ends equally valuable for the stability of the world."[83] It is clear that Ambedkar is in conversation with his teacher Dewey's own position on nonresistance, one that was primarily sparring with Tolstoy's thought and its echoes around the deliberations of American entry into the Great War.[84] Of course, the India Ambedkar found himself in during the 1910s was no stranger to violence, both by the imperialistic British and those who took up violence to resist their rule.[85]

Ambedkar's conception of fanaticism as the use of force in the service of end-fixated attitudes toward the world intersects with Dewey's investigation of individualism and collectivism in his Philosophy 131–132 courses. There Dewey situated the individual as implicated by and created through a tradition-bound group. Custom and individual habit were mutually reinforcing. During his time in Dewey's course, Ambedkar heard Dewey follow the discussion of force as energy and force as violence by expounding the unstable middle ground of intelligent action. What "end" talk emphasizes for Dewey—and Ambedkar, I would add—is really a focus on the power of the human intelligence for organizing and engaging the world. The very notion of end or object, or even the notion of will, is what Dewey notes as "foresight of results."[86] This foresight or recognition of a complex situation or object includes consequences as well as conditions and effects of action and inaction. It also points to an awareness of the causes of action and inaction. This intelligence is the reflective connection of a present situation with the forces and factors in remote states of the past or the future; it adds greater meaning to what is engaged in the present and thereby enhances the chances for adaptation and growth in that situation. Such an intelligent use of the embodied mind in the encultured individual, according to Dewey in the 1916 lectures, depends on attention to the means of *stimuli* observed, "which call into play the individual's intelligence."[87] Dewey's reading of means and ends indicates that all effective approaches to activity would use force; the key to nonfanatical employments of force, according to Ambedkar's reconstruction of this theme, is attending to the full range of consequences of an action to ensure that waste is not occurring among other ends-in-view—held by self or others.

Dewey leaves open the possibility of the intelligent use of force. Indeed, in his lectures he enunciates the unstable middle path of "coercive force," a certain energy that we find emergent in organized groups. This sort of force, according to Dewey's account, involves the coordination of individual energies and forces that produce the organization evident as custom and culture within a group. This gives, according to Dewey's exposition, "a certain total collective force which is not coercive but simply identical with the fact of social organization."[88] Any individual transgressions involve "the group as a whole com[ing] back at him," a process that Dewey compares to the rebounding of a rubber band. Custom organizes individuals, and it coercively maintains that organization; indeed, Dewey equates it to "the constituting force which is the organized force of the group displaying itself against the deviating member."[89] The precise way that coercion operates is through the mental capacities of the individual agent: "Coercion is not simply taking hold of man's physical [self] and making him go through certain motions. It does not operate so directly, it operates by holding out certain consequences to the individual and telling him what is going to happen—these consequences are consequences only because the individual has intelligence and emotions."[90] This connection to the intelligence of an agent, and to a range of ends that may be effectively attended to through the intelligence and emotions of agents, is what moves coercive force away from physical power to achieve ends. It is also what differentiates it from violent force, the sort of force that ruins too many valued ends in a fixated quest for one outcome.

Dewey characterizes coercion as a middle path in his 1916 article, "Force and Coercion," a work that was recommended to Ambedkar and his fellow students in the lecture on April 19, 1916. In this exposition, Dewey continues to make a clear distinction between force as violence and force as "power or energy," a "neutral or eulogistic term." The latter term indicates the use of force as "effective means of operation."[91] What Dewey adds in this article is an emphasis on "coercive force [which] occupies, we may fairly say, a middle place between power as energy and power as violence."[92] As Dewey describes it, coercive force operates as an intelligent middle ground, a way of forcing and enabling rational thought and foresight on the part of some agent to become an effective cause or means toward an end. It is not the forceful truncation of the valued end of that agent's intelligence or freedom: "Coercion, in other words, is an incident of a situation under certain conditions—namely, where the means for the realization of an end are not naturally at hand, so that energy has to be spent in order to make some power into a means for the end at hand."

As a middle path, coercion is an appeal to the intelligence of the individual by forces originating at the group level. The stimuli that coercion operates on in this Deweyan exposition are intimately tied to emotions, values, and language as authorized by the group's prevailing customs. Dewey argues to his students in his 1916 lectures that "societies only resort to physical force in the last resort."[93] Instead, groups and organizations such as states primarily use hope and fear, which "presents stimuli which involve a mental response" that can be predicted in a fairly recognizable fashion.[94] Of course, appeals to hope and fear are most often ensconced in *language*, a fact made obvious by Dewey's elaboration on two main ways that coercion occurs, through ridicule and shame. Elsewhere in his lectures, Dewey discusses the cultural prohibitions (in his day) against dueling and drinking; these practices are more effectively discouraged by the reactions of others—through language and reaction—than through any legal countermeasures. As he closes the section on legal sanctions, immediately before starting the discussion of types of force that Ambedkar drew from in his 1918 review, "An individual who departs from a recognized custom" will soon "have it made uncomfortable for him" through the reaction of others in the group. "These forces," claims Dewey, "are more prevasing [pervasive] and more subtle in their action than the forces set in motion by the court . . . social disapprobation is able to be brought to bear upon actions which are more delicate, refined than those with which the courts may deal."[95] The reaction of others becomes a consequence to the behavior of an agent; this then comprises a form of coercive force pushing the agent back in line with custom.

The Deweyan position that Ambedkar was exposed to at Columbia suggests a *continuum of force*, with *power* as immediate energy occupying one extreme and a fixated, end-erasing *violence* at the other extreme. How do social reformers or progressives such as Russell, Dewey, or Ambedkar delineate the unstable middle path of *intelligent force*? Ambedkar agreed with much of this framework, criticizing nonresistance with a proclamation that "the responsibility for an intelligent control of force rests on us all. In short, the point is that to achieve anything we must use force: only we must use it constructively as energy and not destructively as violence."[96] Why did Ambedkar reconstitute Dewey's point as one angling away from violence *and* as one that does not emphasize *coercion*? This creative rereading is surely due to two issues that Ambedkar had with coercion as Dewey explicated it; these objections were enough to prevent him from importing Dewey's whole schema alongside the pragmatist reading of ends and means and of force as energy and as violence.[97]

First, Ambedkar undoubtedly looked for force in the form of individual action, but he surely had reservations about the coercive uses of language that Dewey pointed to as exemplifying the middle point between energy and violence. Ridicule, humiliation, and shame were central parts of the practice and enforcement of untouchability in Ambedkar's world.[98] Indeed, matters of the enforcement of group custom through such methods as social boycott meant more than a group constituting or reconstituting itself; for Dalits like Ambedkar, it meant a social exclusion that eliminated the means for bodily survival such as food and water.[99] Short of total exclusion from the means of survival, the shame doled out to Ambedkar (as recounted in his autobiographical writings) illustrates how he both would agree that these were forceful ways of a group policing deviators from its customs *and* insist that this activity must be reconstructed. For Ambedkar, there must be uses of language that were forceful and that did not simply reconstitute the group as it was.

Second, Ambedkar's appropriation of Dewey in this 1918 piece was tempered by his focus on individual worth and agency. These are characteristics that Russell's book allows him to foreground, with his talk of reformers as educators. Russell himself provided the model of an engaged thinker jostling his readers in the book that Ambedkar engaged with in the course of the review. In Russell's final chapter, the issue of how much individual thinkers can affect the world is directly addressed. Ambedkar surely felt the way about caste that Russell felt about his—or any lone individual's—ability to stop the senseless war raging across Europe and its domains. "So long as we think only of the immediate future," Russell opines, "it seems that what we can do is not much."[100] Yet Ambedkar sees Russell continue striving for social reconstruction, in this book and beyond its pages. Why? As Russell informs readers in his final chapter, "The power of thought, in the long run, is greater than any other human power. Those who have the ability to think, and the imagination to think in accordance with men's needs, are likely to achieve the good they aim at sooner or later, though probably not while they are still alive."[101]

This optimism of the long-term efficacy of personal activity—including one's written and spoken words—is different from the prose that Ambedkar absorbed in Dewey's courses. Dewey's thought left room for meliorism, but Russell gave Ambedkar a model of what meliorism combined with eloquent rhetorical activity could look like, and what it might hope for in the future. Ambedkar, ever the believer in his own willful efforts, would likely discount the traces of pessimism in Russell's stance: Why not achieve the changes in an unjust society through one's effort now? As a rhetor, Ambedkar saw the need to educate his Indian audience through texts such as this review, a method of action that was not totally at ease with Dewey's reading of the psychology and sociology of custom, habit, and force. Dewey's reading of custom that Ambedkar heard in 1915–16 explained how *societies* constitute their organization through subtle and overt forces; Ambedkar sensed through his own suffering under the yoke of caste oppression that room must be made for *individuals* to change or reconstruct such societies.

## Individuals, Society, and Reconstruction through Rhetoric

It is helpful to return to the general question: Why might Ambedkar have chosen to review Russell's book? The answer most likely would be that Russell's book presented a system that forced Ambedkar into synthetic thinking that complemented Dewey's wide-ranging psychology and account of how individuals and societies evolve. Russell's psychology was very close to Dewey's account, postulating that impulses and habits are vital parts of individual and collective experience. The main difference was twofold. Russell saw basic foundational blocks in his reading of the human organism, a clarity that Dewey would reject. Ambedkar pounces on this point when he turns to the ostensive purpose of his review, the economic matters of Russell's war book. Examining what he glosses as Russell's "analysis of the effects of property," Ambedkar launches into an interesting discourse on poverty, economic forces, and the intertwining of economic matters with human psychology.[102] What seems to concern Ambedkar the most, however, is that Russell reduces so much of the human mind to fit his critique of the "existing economic organizations of society" and "the ills they produce."[103] Ambedkar praises Russell's critique of "the social effects of the Economic Institutions" but laments, "I wish the same could be said of his analysis of the mental effects of property."[104]

Ambedkar is bothered by Russell's reduction of economic matters in a way that leaves out interests of systemically oppressed groups in cultures such as India's. For instance, Russell criticizes the "love of money," but Ambedkar rightly pushes back, pointing out that Russell does not include consideration of the *purpose* of financial instruments or wealth. Following a line not dissimilar to Dewey on the emotions, Ambedkar argues "that there is no such thing as a love of money in the abstract. Love of money is always *for something* and it is the purpose embodied in that 'for something' that will endow it with credit or cover it with shame."[105] Ambedkar is opposed to valorizing impoverished states because this would devalue the interests of his constantly impoverished class members; money and wealth are not inherently evil, and those who would say this probably have not experienced the grinding poverty and helpless dependence that scavenger life entails, for instance. In his review, Ambedkar gives a similar response to Russell's assertion that property causes violence; it encourages not only enjoyment but also care and protection—in some cases, it is the *lack* of property that spurs violence. Think what you will of his arguments, one sees the challenge Ambedkar is placing in front of his readers: Why essentialize the value of property and make simplistic claims about its connection to violence when so many of the oppressed in India have not possessed real property rights in millennia? While "property may be aggressive," Ambedkar concludes, "it is not without its compensating effects."[106] Ambedkar is elaborating a position of *value pluralism* in this article in opposition to Russell's explication of social ills. Values and meaning depend on purpose, and purpose is an utterly contingent and malleable feature of human life according to pragmatists such as Dewey, James, and Ambedkar.

While Dewey and Russell agree on the importance of impulse in human psychology—and in the operation of groups, communities, and nations— the difference lies in how delineated these aspects are. Russell boldly reduces all impulses into *creative* and *possessive* impulses. This is a vital point for his project of social reconstruction, and Ambedkar focuses on it at the conclusion of his review. While other reviewers of Russell at the time largely agreed with the supposed discovery of these basics undergirding the current social system, Ambedkar bluntly questions whether it is "possible so to divide the impulses," and whether there is even "such a thing as an impulse to appropriate" that's built into the acquisitive or possessive impulses.[107] Ambedkar flatly rejects this simple way of parsing human psychology. Like Dewey, he believes that "every impulse, if uninhibited, will lead to some creative act." "Whether the product will be appropriated or not," Ambedkar argues, "is a matter wholly different from any act of impulse or instinct," and it entirely depends on the "nature of its use."[108] He buttresses his argument with reference to the social settings of a communal hunt—a favorite analogy of Dewey in works such as his *Democracy and Education*—and the setting of a family household. In the latter case, Ambedkar explains, objects are not inherently determined in their meaning or status as possessed objects. It is *use*, not *impulse*, that sets these objects up as individually owned or "*of the house.*"[109] Purpose and use establish the parameters for appropriation or possession and are separate from issues of creative impulse. Ambedkar rejects the reduction of impulses to these two simple kinds, and he also denies that creation and appropriation are in tension with each other. Human psychology is complex, and our analyses of it should also flexibly mirror its complexity and diversity.

It is this malleability within human psychology that inspires the notion of reconstruction that both Dewey and Russell discuss in part and that so inspires Ambedkar in his own creative rethinking. Ambedkar's revision of the Russell-Dewey intersection in this review is straightforward and powerful: if human psychology is the basis of social life, and if social structures both build upon and help shape existing human habits and impulses, is there not a way that an individual can act to reshape the habits of self and others by reshaping institutions and customs? And might not institutional or systemic change be affected by leveraging its reliance on habits and impulses in existing individuals and groups? How people act is guided by the individual-collective dialectic that Dewey set up in his account of social psychology during 1915–16. This approach is mirrored to a lesser extent in Russell's book, a fact noted by Ambedkar at the end of his review when he praises Russell as deserving "full credit for having emphasized the psychic basis of social life."[110] Ambedkar would continually return to this theme throughout the following decades, criticizing the ways that Brahminism and Hinduism shape the habits and attitudes of their adherents. According to Ambedkar, Russell saw the basic point, one that was explicated in detail in Dewey's lectures as well: "Social reconstruction depends upon the right understanding of the relation of individual to society—a problem which has eluded the grasp of many sociologists."[111] Russell understood that the problem was one of noting the relation of "impulse to institution,"[112] a function that worked both ways: impulses form institutions and organized groups, and institutions and organized groups form or shape individual impulses.

What was missing from this equation was supplemented by Ambedkar's words, synthetic arguments, and performance in this review. Russell's own rhetorical activity, in the book and beyond, convinced Ambedkar that *reform* can be forcefully and effectively pursued by *individuals*. Furthermore, if education was the reshaping of social and natural environments such that desired changes in individuals and practices can be realized, and if a vital part of our social environment was the meaningful communicative stimuli experienced in interaction with other agents, *reform* pursued through *rhetorical action* could be seen as a form of *education*. Russell was vigorously speaking and writing to so many audiences affected by the Great War in an effort to change minds, habits, and institutions; his book was an effort at social reconstruction as much as it was an account of social reconstruction. This lesson was not lost on Ambedkar, as evidenced by the repeated appeals to his readers and what they should think about Russell's book and their approach to Indian problems. Ambedkar saw a path for an individual to be both an intellectual and activist at the same time and to use their words and ideas as weapons in fighting the battles of social reconstruction.

But taking part in such a struggle required force. This is why Dewey's distinction of force as energy and force as violence so struck young Ambedkar, and why it would stick with him until his final years. It gave him a way of conceptualizing his agency, as well as the way that social mores and customs could affect individuals like him in overt or covert fashions. Ambedkar as an "untouchable" individual was created by the customs flowing through himself and those around him, including his own family members in their actions and reactions to "upper caste" Hindus. Ambedkar sensed enough about the problematic nature of this situation to yearn to escape it; the dry theories of sociology, philosophy, and economics provided such a path once they became mated with a personal meliorism, a sense that his actions and words could matter in reshaping what needed to be reformed in himself and in others.

In other words, important moments such as his 1918 review reveal Ambedkar's realization that the reconstruction of society was something that must be pursued through individual effort; one cannot wait for it to happen or for some abstract concept such as a "class" to do something concrete. But what of the forces that an individual—or a group of individuals acting more or less in concert—might marshal? Ambedkar's penchant for pluralism, or a recognition of the complexity of human experience, surfaces again with his engagement with force. Like Dewey, he is unwilling to simplify—and then reject—the varieties of force that might prove valuable. This is what Dewey and Ambedkar see as being done with the nonresistance of individuals such as Tolstoy. Russell, Ambedkar worries, might be read in this fashion by his Indian readers and might be used to buttress a certain unnamed "Indian philosophy" that encourages passivism and quietism in the face of oppression.

At this point in 1918, Ambedkar is less concerned with the conceptual simplifications in force that lead to the use of *violent* force than he is with the reduction of all force to evil and the resulting backing away from activity that it entails. Ambedkar wants reconstruction and social progress, not a hopeless inactivity. But he does not want the use of force that forecloses too many other ends that an individual or other individuals might also value. This is the path of the *fanatic*, one who overvalues one end in a way that results in conceptually or pragmatically deprioritizing other ends. What Ambedkar wants is an *intelligent* force. This would become an enduring theme for Ambedkar over the years, as he continued to call for acts of intelligence or reflection among moral agents (such as those who would have heard his *Annihilation of Caste* as a speech). Ambedkar would always be committed to the pursuit of progress, and he firmly believed that he (or any individual so motivated) had a role to play in that development. Later in his life, Ambedkar would engage Tolstoy's philosophy once again, acquiring a copy of the Russian's works "A Confession" and "What I Believe" in July 1936.[113] Tolstoy's inclinations toward nonresistance developed in concert with a distrust of the state, as well as skepticism about the prospects of real progress through individual or collective efforts. Ambedkar read and thought through Tolstoy's engagement with his own pessimism, marking with his pencil one of Tolstoy's claims about the general pointlessness of ideals in most of life: "Development and progress in infinity can have no aim or direction." In an instance that both displayed his intellectual commitments to the promise of reflection *and* performed such agency, Ambedkar wrote his response to that line in his own hand in the margin: "That is where human intelligence comes in."[114] This marking was most likely made only a year or so after the crushing death of his wife Ramabai, in May 1935. Ambedkar's belief in the power of intelligence, a central term in Dewey's psychology and meliorism, continued to shine in his darkest personal moments.

At the time of his 1918 review, possibly penned during or after his frantic search for the merest shelter while attempting to work in Baroda, his hope still emanated forth in his belief that the reformer could best muster the sort of force that can be effective yet not fanatical; with intelligence, a reformer could reshape society and not destroy important parts of that community that he or she wanted to reconstruct. Engaging his review in the context of the Dewey lectures that we are certain he was exposed to, it is easy to see his unease with the supposed middle ground of coercive linguistic force that operated on fear and hope to maintain and enforce group customs. For Ambedkar, these self-enforcing customs are what required improvement. Dewey surely allowed room for such reconstruction—his lectures feature many instances of his extolling progress and the room that individualism as a philosophy makes for the critique and improvement of a community—but his sociological manner of describing the workings of groups and nations did not foreground paths of meliorism the way that other Deweyan works not engaged by Ambedkar did. Russell became the goad for Ambedkar to extract or augment the themes of meliorism in Dewey's account of the individual-community dialectic. Like Dewey, he saw language as holding a power over members of the group; spurred on by Russell, Ambedkar saw *his own rhetorical activity* as wielding that power, whether it was on the Indian audience of the economics journal or, eventually, the masses that would hear him speak and that would avidly read his books.

The Russell-Dewey interaction that Ambedkar created in the course of his 1918 review allows us to see him replacing *coercive force* with something more akin to *persuasive force*. This is a helpful term for what reformers are doing as they educate and reform individuals and collections of individuals in an effort to reconstruct society. They are shaping and reshaping individuals and institutions through words chosen for their efficacy. This sense of advocacy and rhetoric is evident in Ambedkar the speaker, the politician, the philosopher, and the activist, but it is easy to overlook. The Russell review, once one sees the linkages that Ambedkar is making between reform, education, and reconstruction, forces us to recognize persuasion as theoretically and practically important. While shame, boycott, and excommunication all represent pernicious uses of force that did more harm than good, for Ambedkar's reading of the Indian social context, persuasion held out the hope that it could reconstruct society in a progressive fashion. As we shall see in the following chapters, as Ambedkar increasingly stepped onto the public stage, he explicitly calculated his rhetoric to have different effects on different audiences. For non-Hindu observers, such as British and international audiences, he intended to forcefully place caste issues on their agendas. For his "upper caste" Hindu audiences who may or may not have been sympathetic to his cause, he intended to jar them into intelligent reflection on the problems of caste. For his Dalit followers, beaten down by centuries of habits and customs, he intended to convince them of their agency and power in the pursuit of their own emancipation. Persuasion and rhetoric became central parts of Ambedkar's ever-evolving program of reform and reconstruction as soon as his first sojourn in the West concluded and his reimmersion in Hindu culture began.

# Reconstructive Rhetoric, Appropriation, and the Strategic Use of Reference

Putting one's words in print for present and unknown future generations to read and react to takes a certain kind of courage. Standing in front of foreign rulers and an audience of high-caste individuals and telling them that fundamental injustices are going unaddressed takes another kind of bravery. Ambedkar's development as a pragmatist critic of the Indian caste system developed in both of these venues before the 1920s. His 1918 review of Bertrand Russell's book on social reconstruction gave him a forum for testing out a range of ideas through synthetically combining pragmatism, European thought, and Indian concerns in a new meliorative amalgam. In 1919, he utilized another modality of communication to hone his message and rhetorical method. After returning from England in 1917 at the behest of his royal benefactor in Baroda, Ambedkar struggled to find employment as a tutor and college teacher due to his caste status as an "untouchable." Even though he was appointed as a professor of political economy at Sydenham College in November 1918, he found that he could not effectively execute his duties as a teacher due to the lack of respect students and fellow faculty showed him; some faculty even objected to his drinking water reserved for the teachers.[1] While his Russell review talked of social reform, he now seemed ready to push for specific, concrete changes to meliorate the social situation in which Dalits found themselves.

His chance to advocate for specific political reforms came in early 1919. The Montagu-Chelmsford Report of 1918 recommended that the British parliament extend some type of franchise to the Indian people. Lord Southborough was tasked with leading the Franchise Committee—commonly referred to as the Southborough Committee—to gather information on how the franchise ought to be given to the Indian people. Ambedkar seized this opportunity to speak in front of British (and some Indian) power brokers and submitted testimony to this committee. He was also examined by the committee on the arguments contained in his testimony on January 27, 1919.[2] This action differs from his review of Russell's book in two major ways: he was advocating for specific reforms and much of his advocacy took the form of oral argument. While he was not the only Dalit testifying in front of this committee, he was unique in a variety of ways. First, he was the only Dalit present who was not affiliated with any reform group. Others represented some organization, such as G. A Gawai, who spoke on behalf of the Depressed India Association.[3] Ambedkar stood alone. Second, he also excelled by virtue of his eloquence and educational accomplishments. He was one of the few Dalits in the country with a decent education, let alone the four years of graduate training he had acquired at Columbia University and in London. He wrote and spoke in eloquent English, a fact that was surely noted by the largely British committee. Eleanor Zelliot comments on this striking feature of his testimony: "He was entirely his own man. . . . This quality of independence gave Ambedkar an aura of strength and dominance and a reputation for representing Untouchables single-mindedly, without subtle pressures from collaborators."[4] This event, in many ways, set the tone for the remainder of his reform efforts in the next three decades.

Ambedkar was impassioned, and he argued as he was trained. Educated in philosophy and acclimated in the law, he stood out as a lawyer arguing for strengthening democracy through democratic means. He ultimately asked the committee to reserve nine seats of the one-hundred-person Bombay Legislative Council for Dalit candidates. These efforts seemed to be for naught, as the committee ultimately awarded only one reserved seat for the Dalit constituency in Bombay.[5] Usually, the Southborough Testimony is viewed as important for what it portended: an increasing interest in activism in Ambedkar and a newfound respect for him by Dalits as well as the British. Indeed, the British were so taken by Ambedkar's performance in his 1919 testimony and elsewhere that they invited him as one of two Dalit representatives to the London Round Table Conferences in 1930–32.[6] What this chapter argues, however, is that the Southborough Committee testimony is important in its own right as the earliest instance of Ambedkar's reconstructive pragmatist rhetoric being applied to a specific situation of caste-based social injustice. Upon examination, we shall see how his arguments extend the Russell-Dewey synthesis highlighted in the previous chapter that institutions and individual habits matter for the full functioning of democracy. One committee member, the lawyer K. Natarajan, was recorded as ending the oral examination of Ambedkar by summing up the reformer's position: "His view was that British rule in India was meant to provide equal opportunities for all, and that in transferring a large share of the power to popular assemblies, arrangements should be made whereby the hardships and disabilities entailed by the social system should not be reproduced and perpetuated in political institutions."[7] Ambedkar was applying the meliorist ideal of a reformer fixing social problems through a calculated persuasive intervention into the institution-individual relationship.

The conflict over the extension of the franchise was not, however, simply a chance to get his anticaste message across. His testimony to the committee also contains the almost fully developed form of his reconstructive rhetoric. In it he begins to make explicit *and* implicit use of the words and ideas of Dewey as resources in his efforts to push for social reform and an end to caste injustice. Whereas the last chapter explored the *themes* and *commitments* of the reconstructive rhetoric that he developed from his pragmatist training in the West, the present chapter emphasizes the *form* or *method* of how such a pragmatist rhetoric operated in the hands of Ambedkar. In order to fully explore the contours of this early instantiation of his pragmatist rhetoric, we must take seriously matters of rhetorical style and argument. As we discovered in the previous chapter, one can reconstruct Ambedkar's engagement with Deweyan pragmatism by exploring the presence of Deweyan sources in and among his various works. It would be a mistake to see Ambedkar as *simply* reiterating a Deweyan pragmatism in India, but it would also be ill-advised to see him as *completely disconnected* from Dewey's influence, given the intriguing and sustained use of Dewey's texts and ideas in many of Ambedkar's appeals. Finally, the chapter concludes by trying to make sense of what Ambedkar is doing with his unusual use of Dewey's texts. Why are some quotations noted as such, whereas others are directly appropriated into his arguments and messages? What rhetorical *purpose* could be served by this tactic of argument? My claim is that in 1918 and 1919 Ambedkar is slowly discovering his voice. This voice merges pragmatic reconstruction with the needs of an Indian people controlled by the British and differentially affected by an age-old caste system. It is the voice of a meliorist pragmatism, one attuned both to Dalit oppression and the creative power of rhetoric.

## The Southborough Committee Hears Ambedkar *and* Dewey

This experience of caste discrimination at the hands of the Brahminical system that consolidated its power around Sanskrit texts came to a head for

Ambedkar in 1919. He realized that this system of caste oppression must be addressed if one wanted the sort of integrated, flourishing democracy talked of by his teacher, Dewey. On January 27, 1919, Ambedkar seized his first chance to take a very public stand against caste. It was then that he eloquently testified (in English) to the Southborough Committee. We must not overlook the role language played in Ambedkar's *ethos*. For Dalits like Ambedkar, a Sanskrit education was forbidden by Hindu tradition. Learning English, the language of the colonial oppressors, and then employing it masterfully in one's own liberatory actions highlighted a new source of agency that was not authorized by the Vedic tradition and its Brahmin guardians. As S. Anand describes the use of English in twentieth-century India, "English, however, has no notion of sacredness attached to it. It is something a person may aspire to, irrespective of one's varna [caste], religion or gender."[8] Gandhi's popularity overcame his tendency to use the vernacular Gujarati as his language of choice, but Ambedkar strategically chose to address many of his audiences in English: "Had he not written in English, he would certainly not have become a pan-Indian figure."[9] It is no wonder that in a 1920 issue of his newspaper, *Mook Nayak*, Ambedkar praised the English-language instruction of the British: "English education means the milk of [the] Tigress. Those who got the opportunity to drink it in them it generates a new alacrity, a new awakening and a new light."[10]

Besides being his first public appearance, this testimony is interesting because it reveals two things about young Ambedkar's commitment to reform. First, it highlights that at this early point he saw promise in political reforms as a way to help the depressed classes. This differed from the policies of the Indian National Congress, which emphasized political independence as a way to eventually eradicate the causes of unequal representation, and of moderate Hindu reformers, who wanted a minimal number of reserved seats for Dalits.[11] Ambedkar desired a more significant number of reserved seats, but he also wanted an acknowledgment that something was deeply problematic within the Hindu social system. Ambedkar objected to positions implicating more moderate reforms in his testimony, arguing that they did not truly address the evil that was caste in India.[12] According to Ambedkar, the Congress followed the line "that the social and the political are two different things having no bearing on each other." This leading party of Indian reform was "by design political Radicals and social Tories."[13] Ambedkar perceived that they couldn't see the dependence of political reform on fundamental social problems such as caste. Hindu high-caste reformers, well-intentioned as they may have been, still made the fundamental mistake of depending on the vast majority of caste Hindu representatives to look out for the interests of the Dalit community. For Ambedkar, Dalits should be integrally involved in shaping their future. Reserved electoral seats were a prime way that he saw in 1919 to preserve the chance of achieving such an outcome.[14]

The second notable aspect to his testimony to the Southborough Committee concerns the *form* of this reasoning and speaking, namely how he made his democratic arguments against the caste system. How he made these appeals illustrates his extension and augmentation of Dewey's pragmatist way of thinking about political and social reform and evinces a unique style of arguing and presenting ideas and supporting evidence. As Arun Mukherjee has noticed, Ambedkar had a penchant for weaving Deweyan terminology and Dewey's own way of putting things into his own texts addressing the Indian context.[15] Another way of articulating this point is that Ambedkar was practicing a *reconstructive* method that foregrounded appropriation. Appropriation is a difficult and complex topic; it both describes and prescribes certain uses of the materials of others. But by going through this early—and often overlooked—text produced by Ambedkar's written and oral testimony in 1919, we can begin to augment the constitutive notions adduced in the previous chapter about the theoretical commitments of reconstructive rhetoric with a notion of how such a style of argument might operate in practice. Let us pick the starting point, however temporary, of appropriation. When one appropriates something, it often implies the *use*, unauthorized or authorized, of some technique, concept, string of words or ideas, or other materials from some originating person or group for some new purpose. Appropriation can be general or specific in the content used, and it can be attributed or nonattributed in terms of noting the source from which the appropriated material stems. I can borrow a specific idea or phrase or a general theme. My novel use of such materials can either be accompanied by an acknowledgment that they stem from another source, or they can lack this acknowledgment or citation. In intercultural settings, the ethics of appropriation becomes difficult.[16] The specific communicators, intentions, power relations, and actual effects involved must be attended to before judgments are reached. Appropriation is also a rhetorical process insofar as it occurs in practices of language use and persuasion. A rhetor or speaker who appropriates material from other sources will use those resources in some new fashion suited for their own ends in that situation.

If we take the notion of appropriation as a complex rhetorical practice, two functions of the appropriation of pragmatist thought become evident in Ambedkar's rhetoric: practices of argument that employ Dewey's texts as useful objects and practices of argument that extend or use general concepts and themes from pragmatism. Ambedkar uses both senses of appropriation in important parts of his writings and speeches. Like the young Indian student Adlerblum recounts as convincingly reciting Dewey's lectures in the distinctive style of the American thinker, Ambedkar's synthetic appropriation of Dewey's thought and style often appears naturally in his arguments and is left unmarked. As Mukherjee puts it, "So deeply embedded is Dewey's thought in Ambedkar's consciousness that quite often his words flow through Ambedkar's discourse without quotation marks. . . . Ambedkar not only borrowed concepts and ideas from Dewey, his methodological approach and ways of argumentation also show Dewey's influence."[17] The former type of appropriative activity occurs when Ambedkar speaks lines that are virtually identical to Dewey's text. Ambedkar sometimes cites Dewey and at other places explicitly quotes him word for word. These discursive moves constitute the more overt sense of translation through appropriation. They would also seem to mitigate concerns that he sought to profit from Dewey's effort and work. Ambedkar is not simply taking Dewey's argument and philosophy and pretending it is his own. His use is much more selective and strategic than that. He is using, changing, and resisting parts of Dewey's philosophy in an effort to construct his own version of pragmatism. Perhaps Ambedkar saw a certain justice to this: the West, after all, had taken so much from India. Beyond such motives, however, it's more likely that Ambedkar simply *embodied* the Deweyan *ethos of bending texts and theories toward practical life*: he began to *think* and *argue* like Dewey would have, given the unique contexts he found himself in when pushing for practical change and reform. In a related way, Keya Maitra implores us to see Ambedkar's pragmatism as resident in his words *and* in his general spirit; by detailing the ways that both types of appropriative activity occur in Ambedkar's rhetorical activity, we can see how Ambedkar argues and thinks like a pragmatist in the Indian context.[18]

Appropriation is an integral part of reconstruction. How do these various ways of appropriating the words and ideas of Dewey function in the method of reconstructive rhetoric Ambedkar tentatively explores in 1919? Let us look at some of the important passages in which this technique takes place to ascertain the contours of this communicative strategy. Ambedkar's testimony quickly focuses on whether India is fit for representative government. He argues a nuanced position: If America has a range of social divisions but still is fit for representative government, why isn't India also immediately ready? Of course, Ambedkar wants a democracy, but not in a form in which existing social divisions will immediately exclude the under-educated and socially disempowered Dalits from its machinations. In the fourth passage of the testimony, we see Ambedkar's thesis: "In my opinion their contention cannot be granted[,] for the social divisions of India do matter in politics."[19] The tenor of much of his later political advocacy and social reform efforts is set with this simple statement. In the decades that followed, Ambedkar would preach the gospel that political reform both affects and necessitates some type of social reform. This is a reconstructed view of Russell's form of meliorism, of course, as it does not simply focus on political institutions first as a way to affect individual mindsets or habits. Instead, we see Ambedkar acknowledging that the social must be addressed in some fashion parallel to a focus on the political, as well as the individual along with the social.

How Ambedkar supports this point is most unusual. Right after putting his argument in this straightforward matter, he begins to outline how social divisions affect democracy. Specifically, he focuses on the circumstances in which social groups coexist in an ideal fashion. He then makes the following argument:

> Men live in a community by virtue of the things they have in common. What they must have in common in order to form a community are aims, beliefs, aspirations, knowledge, a common understanding; or to use the language of the Sociologists, they must be like-minded. But how do they come to have these things in common or how do they become like-minded? Certainly, not by sharing with another, as one would do in the case of a piece of cake. To cultivate an attitude similar to others or to be like-minded with others is to be in communication with them or to participate in their activity. Persons do not become like-minded by merely living in physical proximity, any more than they cease to be like-minded by being distant from each other.[20]

This passage in 1919 is important, as its content highlights the theoretical dimensions of the Deweyan-Russellian form of social reconstruction that Ambedkar wants to advance. Communal harmony is vital, and it can be actualized only by the holding of the right individual attitudes toward other individuals. One can live close to others ("in physical proximity") but can be worlds apart. Surely in Ambedkar's mind is his caste experience, wherein he wandered and worked among high-caste individuals yet was treated as if he were an interloper from a polluted foreign realm.[21] I want to focus on the choice he makes in using language and argument to convey this point, however. If one looks closely, many of these words are not Ambedkar's. They are Dewey's words, appropriated, reframed, and retasked. Highlighting the appropriated words, one can see the original source of the initial lines in Dewey's 1916 *Democracy and Education*:

> *Men live in a community in virtue of the things which they have in common;* and communication is the way in which *they come to possess things in common. What they must have in common in order to form a community or society are aims, beliefs, aspirations, knowledge—a common understanding—like-mindedness* as the *sociologists* say.[22]

Ambedkar uses many of the words here in his own point about caste oppression and democracy, but at points he rearranges the order or makes contextual changes. He rephrases the clause after the semicolon as a question: "But how do *they come to possess things in common?*" and places this after its original occurrence in Dewey's phrasing.

Ambedkar's stated answer to this question also involves echoes of Dewey's 1916 book, albeit less directly appropriated. Compare the passage about sharing a piece of cake to Dewey's way of making this same point:

> Such things cannot be passed physically from one to another, like bricks; they cannot be *shared* as persons would share a pie by dividing it into physical pieces. The *communication* which insures *participation* in a common understanding is one which secures *similar emotional* and *intellectual dispositions—* like ways of responding to expectations and requirements.[23]

Ambedkar adds the language of "sharing" physical objects and mindsets. He changes Dewey's mentions of "emotional and intellectual dispositions" to the more general concept of "attitude," but the argument connects to Dewey's points: like-mindedness or harmony among groups and individuals stems from a harmony among individually possessed attitudes or orientations. Dewey makes a similar claim about physical proximity after this point about common dispositions: "*Persons do not become* a society *by living in physical proximity, any more than* a man *ceases to be* socially influenced by being so many feet or miles removed from others."[24] Notice that Ambedkar alters this passage: what they become changes from "a society" to "likeminded," an important part of the context of his new argument. He is concerned with emphasizing to the Southborough Committee that Hindu society is divided, so the Deweyan phraseology is altered to focus on the lack of like-mindedness among groups in Hindu society. He simplifies the last clause, bluntly pointing out that "being distant from each other" does not make individuals differently minded. He is most likely altering this because of the similarity in caste mindsets that he sees across the vast expanse of the Indian subcontinent. Ambedkar perceives a like-mindedness among higher castes that divides them from the lower castes and Dalits. In the fourth passage of Ambedkar's testimony, he talks of the state that overcomes this partial like-mindedness:

> And so long as the groups remain isolated the conflict is bound to continue and prevent the harmony of action. It is the isolation of the groups that is the chief evil. Where the groups allow of endosmosis they cease to be evil. For endosmosis among the groups makes possible a resocialization of once socialized attitudes. In place of the old, it creates a new like-mindedness, which is representative of the interests, aims, and aspirations of all the various groups concerned.[25]

This statement, while mostly Ambedkar's original phrasing, continues a conversation with Dewey's teachings and writings. If one looks at a part of *Democracy and Education* some eighty pages later than the previously appropriated sections, one sees Dewey putting his point this way: "A separation into a privileged and a subject-class prevents social *endosmosis*. The *evils* thereby affecting the superior class are less material and less perceptible, but equally real."[26] Dewey, like Ambedkar, describes the lack of a free flow of ideas and interests among groups—a lack of endosmosis, in other words—as an "evil."[27] The lack of communicative intercourse among individuals is what is being castigated, and Ambedkar echoes and reconstructs it in his own argument for reserved seats as a way of battling this lack of like-mindedness among a caste-separated society.

Further into Ambedkar's argument to the committee he begins talking of government as potentially "by the people" or "for the people," referencing the American context. Condemning the latter option on its own terms, he explains his reasoning:

> It will be granted that each kind of association, as it is an educative environment, exercises a formative influence on the active dispositions of its members. Consequently, what one is as a person is what one is as associated with others. A Government for the people, but not by the people, is sure to educate some into masters and others into subjects; because it is by the reflex effects of association that one can feel and measure the growth of personality.[28]

In this passage, Ambedkar uses the ideals of growth, personality, and the individual-community dialectic in a novel line of argument to critique caste oppression. This text also appropriates a variety of Dewey's points from *Democracy and Education*. For instance, the first sentence builds on this passage:

> Each household with its immediate extension of friends makes a society; the village or street group of playmates is a community; each business group, each club, is another. Passing beyond these more intimate groups, there is in a country like our own a variety of races, religious affiliations, economic divisions. Inside the modern city, in spite of its nominal political unity, there are probably more communities, more differing customs, traditions, aspirations, and forms of government or control, than existed in an entire continent at an earlier epoch. *Each* such group *exercises a formative influence on the active dispositions of its members.*[29]

Ambedkar takes Dewey's phrasing about groups and extends it into the context of a critique of two major approaches to government. A descriptive point about groups and their formation becomes, in Ambedkar's hands, a normative critique of government that replicates caste-based oppression *and* paternalism. The following sentence is also echoed from Dewey: "*What one is as a person is what one is as associated with others*, in a free give and take of intercourse."[30] Notice that this passage occurs over a hundred pages later in *Democracy and Education*. Through his memory or preparatory reading, Ambedkar is selectively pulling from parts of Dewey's work, creating new constellations of ideas that can be used in arguments about Indian politics that Dewey could not have anticipated. This echo segues in Ambedkar's passage to a point about masters and slaves. Dewey's discussion of Plato in *Democracy and Education* occurred in yet a different location and read as follows: "There must be a large variety of shared undertakings and experiences. Otherwise, the influences which *educate some into masters*, educate *others into slaves*."[31] Again, we see Ambedkar taking various descriptive points as inspiration from Dewey and forming them into a fully normative basis of critique. Government institutions are educative, according to Ambedkar's synthesis in his testimony, and we ought to take care that they do not form or educate vast swathes of society into slaves or outcasts.

The point that follows this about "growth of personality" is synthetic and creative in Ambedkar's hands. It seems to merge Dewey's later fixation on growth (from *Democracy and Education* onward) with his very early emphasis on personality. The latter occurs in texts such as his early essay, "The Ethics of Democracy," from 1888, a text we shall see again in Ambedkar's rhetoric in the 1930s. In this early text, Dewey talks not of growth, but of personality, as the key feature in democratic functioning, noting that "from this central position of personality result the other notes of democracy, liberty, equality, fraternity." Personality enshrines these three values, "symbols of the highest ethical idea which humanity has yet reached—the idea that personality is the one thing of permanent and abiding worth, and that in every human individual there lies personality."[32] Ambedkar seems interested in combining the rather static idea of personality from Dewey's idealist writings with the sort of emphasis on "growth" we see in Dewey's later pragmatism. Indeed, following the passages noted previously in his testimony, Ambedkar writes:

> The growth of personality is the highest aim of society. Social arrangement must secure free initiative and opportunity to every individual to assume any role he is capable of assuming provided it is socially desirable. A new [role] is a renewal and growth of personality. But when an association—and a Government is after all an association—*is* such that in it every role cannot be assumed by all, it tends to develop the personality of the few at the cost of the many—a result scrupulously to be avoided in the interest of Democracy. To be specific, it is not enough to be electors only. It is necessary to be lawmakers; otherwise who can be lawmakers will be masters of those who can only be electors.[33]

Ambedkar's rhetoric is in conversation with Dewey's pragmatism. The first line, clearly a synthetic prioritizing of growth *and* personality, goes beyond Dewey's way of putting things in his 1920 text *Reconstruction in Philosophy*, in which he bluntly states that "growth itself is the only moral 'end.'"[34] Ambedkar makes a related point but retains the individual focus provided by the use of "personality" from Dewey's early work on ethics. This seems to presage the emphasis of Ambedkar in his later works on individual mental habits and their relation to the caste system. As we will see in the following chapter, caste is informed by social arrangements, but ultimately, according to Ambedkar, caste is a state of mind or attitude.

Ambedkar's invocation of the growth of personality as ideal also can be seen as a creative addition to Dewey's philosophy. In *Democracy and Education*, we see Dewey making the following point about occupations and democracy:

An occupation is the only thing which balances the distinctive capacity of an individual with his social service. To find out what one is fitted to do and to secure an opportunity to do it is the key to happiness. Nothing is more tragic than failure to discover one's true business in life, or to find that one has drifted or been forced by circumstance into an uncongenial calling. A right occupation means simply that the aptitudes of a person are in adequate play, working with the minimum of friction and the maximum of satisfaction.[35]

The point both Ambedkar and Dewey are committed to is simple: individuals flourish when a government allows them to thrive according to their capacities and in line with "social service" or societal benefit. The individual *and* the group flourish in the best scheme of government. This growth in personality is not simply a private affair, of course. Ambedkar merges individual flourishing into the Deweyan concepts of association and government by the people to make his normative point: we only see individual flourishing or growth of personality when individuals have a say in the direction of their group. This voice is enabled by participatory governmental institutions. In his testimony, we witness Ambedkar weaving these separate Deweyan points into an argument for the desirability of reserved seats for Dalit lawmakers. This rhetorical style of appropriative argument adds to the story of Ambedkar's own form of pragmatism, as it begins to develop starting with his Russell review in 1918.

## Rhetorical Reconstruction, Appropriation, and the Uses of Quotation

Ambedkar's 1919 testimony reveals his multilevel synthesis of this Deweyan *ethos* with his emerging critique of the caste system. One way of conceptualizing its relation to pragmatism is through seeing Dewey's thought as informing a framework *for* reconstruction and a path *of* reconstruction in Ambedkar's battles against the caste system. These appropriative moves do not fade as Ambedkar's voice evolves in the 1930s. As the following chapters will explore, the Deweyan echoes continue to grow in Ambedkar as he fights more fiercely for reform in the following decades. But it is useful to ruminate on the *method* of rhetorical reconstruction we see emerging in his 1919 testimony. His 1918 book review gestures toward the usefulness of parts of Dewey's thought in its synthesis of Deweyan pragmatism and Russellian institution-critique, but something new is added in his testimony: a distinctive *way* of making his points to a given audience. His discourse in English is one feature of his address that builds his *ethos* as a reformer who was an "untouchable." His explicit and implicit use of Deweyan phrases, passages, and concepts is another feature of his rhetorical activity in 1919. I will call the rhetorical technique of appropriating the text of Dewey in novel arguments "echoing," since it purposefully repeats some of what was uttered previously in a new context; slight changes or entropic degradations are introduced in a process of revision, and the echoed text is not often announced *as* echoed; it simply uses a selection of previous material in the new context of advocacy.

The question remains: Why does Ambedkar echo the words and passages of Dewey in these creative ways? He undoubtedly understands the systems of citation prevalent in scholarly sources, as he displays in his various academic theses that lack any instances of such echoing. There must be a deeper reason that we can postulate, one that we can access if we think of Ambedkar as a *rhetor*. Such an approach takes him as an individual committed to using various means of communication and persuasion in an end-directed and audience-sensitive fashion, not simply a thinker variously enunciating parts of a seamless, consistent, and homogenous theory or doctrine that stands behind all of his texts and speeches. Ambedkar was many things, but one thing that gets lost is that he was a powerful and creative orator. He knew how to argue (he was, after all, trained as a scholar and as a barrister) and how to adapt arguments to specific situations and audiences. Indeed, this process of constant adaptation is one characteristic of rhetoric as a concept. Thinking about the rhetorical value of echoing will shed light on *how* Ambedkar argues as a pragmatist to different audiences and in different strategic contexts; in other words, this approach will illustrate the pragmatist aspects of his method of communicating and arguing across various situations of action.[36] This will constitute one distinctive aspect of the form or *means* of rhetorical reconstruction when coupled with the meliorative *ends* noted in the previous chapter.

Why did Ambedkar so often not use overt mechanisms of quotation or reference in employing the words of Dewey in his own speeches or texts? This brings up a more general question: Why does any speaker or arguer quote anything at all? Put another way, what is the rhetorical value of *not* quoting sources of information? In academic contexts, some might try to take the ideas of others and get credit for them as their own creation. This is not the case with Ambedkar, as his academic theses and writings play the game of citation perfectly. And his speeches that echo do not "steal" Dewey's ideas, as they are substantively distinct from anything the American philosopher was doing in his texts and chapters. There is a precedent for such a practice in situations of advocacy. The civil rights leader Martin

Luther King Jr. also used passages from previous preachers and theologians in many of his sermons and speeches, a rhetorical technique that Keith Miller describes as "voice-merging."[37]

Scholars have studied quotational practices in general and provide us with a range of reasons a speaker or writer might quote material or might be reticent to set off the words of others as a quotation. Let us review a range of these explanations to understand why Ambedkar's rhetoric would foreground the practice of echoing at important points. To start with, the absence of overt quotation might be intended to signal in-group status. As Gary Saul Morson puts it, "Some quotations are meant to be heard precisely *as* unmarked: they are spoken or written with no clear clue to their status so that most will miss them and only the properly educated will recognize them for what they are. The speaker or writer shares a secret with one part of his or her audience at the expense of the rest."[38] But this cannot be the case for Ambedkar, whose audiences ranged from British committee members to various parts of the Indian populace. It is unlikely that any of these individuals would recognize a line or two from John Dewey, or that there would be any strategic purpose in getting them to this recognition in the moment of persuasion. Unlike using lines from the *Mahabharata* or Shakespeare's plays, deploying subtle allusions from Dewey would not impress many in India; put simply, Dewey was not an important figure in the political circles in colonial India. If Dewey were more popular in India, one might slip into such allusions or ways of talking unconsciously, but the context, detail, and purposiveness of Ambedkar's echoes mitigate against this explanation.[39]

Ambedkar, a trained and eloquent speaker and arguer, is being strategic in how he makes his arguments in specific speeches and texts. His rhetorical employment—and adaptation—of parts of Dewey's body of work is too specific and ranges over too many pages in a source text to be merely the result of memorization or unconscious imitation. The purposiveness of their use also reveals their persuasive intent. In parts of his Southborough testimony, Ambedkar changes Dewey's lines and passages to fit his argument; he is not accidentally talking like Dewey at points and at others explicitly citing Dewey as an academic writer might. He is *using* and *reconstructing* Dewey's material thought in this way because it seems to promise the most persuasive force given that specific context. To build this case, however, we must investigate the rhetorical practice of quotation further, as well as what it enables and disables in terms of audience persuasion. First, what is a quotation? This is a deceptively simple question, as quotations can be demarcated in various verbal and nonverbal ways, and they can be of varying lengths.[40] Even aspects of quotation taken for granted in the West—such as double quotation marks—have a historical contingency.[41] We can and must brave a starting definition of quotation, however, one that covers most of the phenomena we want to analyze. Morson provides such a starting point by defining *quotation*, positing that it "repeats the words (or actions or other defining features) of another *as* the words of another."[42] Thus, when I quote another person, it is evident that those words come from *that* other speaker. There is an explicit reference to the words of another, as well as an implicit differentiation of those words from my words. In written communication, this is usually set off by quotation marks, although one could dispense with this notation by saying something like "Taylor said" or "Paul claimed." This ability of quoted text to be translated and stated in different ways generates various debates in philosophy.[43] Regardless of the philosophical disputes over the nature of quotation, we can discern a rhetorical aspect of quotation use: it "doubles" the voices involved from one side of the communicative encounter. Instead of me addressing you, there is now me, you, and a person or character that I bring into the discussion through the act of quotation. As Morson describes it, "Quotationality confers upon phrases a degree of otherness."[44] This distance between a speaker and the quoted material allows the speaker to do a variety of things with that summoned text. The speaker can employ it (and its speaker) as expert evidence in support of their original point. Or they can ironically or sarcastically negate the evoked words, since their ultimate point is not necessarily the point of *that* phrase or speaker. A speaker could also bring forth quoted, distanced text in a neutral manner, as a scientist or even Aristotle might do in surveying the range of views of others before them.

Quotational practice plays with the distance between my voice and another's voice. It is rhetorical insofar as this variable distance is part of an utterance or speech act directed at another party in the interaction. As a rhetorical technique, quotation constitutes a means of persuasive force oriented at and toward another subject hearing or reading a text or speech. We can give some clarity to the variance of distance involved here by assigning different practices locations on what can be called the *quotational force spectrum*. At one extreme, there is no voice present but one's own. This is the condition that Morson describes as "just saying what one means: speaking directly with no attempt to invoke anyone else's utterances."[45] This extreme represents simply the utterance of your thoughts and words. No one else can take the blame, or the credit, for these words or ideas. This is a situation that lacks quotational force; the only force present is the claim that your utterance makes on your hearers. At the other extreme would be the phenomenon of mediumship: the voice and personality of another agent totally taking over one's self and using it as communicative means. This is a situation of total quotation. You speak many things, but none are yours. These utterances and ideas are directly attributable to that other person or spirit. There is no self as author here, just self as transmitter of other-authored words. In the middle of this spectrum lies most of our everyday quotational practices. Here is where the phenomenon of clearly quoting resides, as Morson puts it, as sometimes "unambiguously citing another's words *as* another's words."[46] The voice of another person exists in communication alongside your voice. All of this is involved in addressing some interlocutor who also has a voice, and who can direct it at you, the speaker, in acts of agreement or of rebuttal.

It is in this middle ground of double-voiced quotation that a range of illocutionary forces can be marshaled to act on some listener. In service to the goal of persuasion, one can summon the voice of the quoted author as proof of one's own point, effectively saying, "See, expert X supports what I want you to believe." Or one can simply observe what person X said by presenting the quoted material for you and the listener to observe. This is rhetorically distinguished from the two ends of the quotational force spectrum. At the first extreme—that of no quotation of others—there is but one voice, your own, and no one else is responsible for the message save you. It is *your* point, and the listener must decide to accept your take or not. The case of mediumship takes away all illocutionary force from your hands; it is the spirit or other entity speaking through you that attempts to persuade. You cannot be held accountable for discursive moves you seem to make in the presence of a listener. Quotation gives us new options and tactics, but it also necessarily removes our voices from a text and places some distance between our points and the range of positions taken by others.

This analysis of the multivocality and distance that quotation introduces to the persuasive encounter gives us a way to understand why Ambedkar does what he does with Dewey's words in 1919 and beyond, as well as a way to explain how such a technique functions rhetorically. Put simply, Ambedkar strategically adopts, adapts, and uses portions of Dewey's texts without quotation because this best leverages the persuasive force they exert on an audience far removed from Dewey's literary circles. Quotation presents Dewey as something distant, even if he is given the label of "expert." Even if he is made to fit the rhetorical situation Ambedkar faces, summoning Dewey as evidence still exudes a sense of indirection. As Finnegan puts it, "A speaker can choose to set the words quoted at arms' length, presented as a kind of autonomous text or, alternatively, as closely associated with or endorsed by themselves."[47] Even in this last employment, however, there is still a distance making the closeness not identity. Retasking another's words in Ambedkar's own voice, however, offers the promise of maximizing their impact on an audience, since such a usage synthesizes and portrays a range of voices as integral parts of his empowered voice. He quotes experts and texts from the West, but not when it matters most for the goal of persuasion. When he is most impassioned in making his points, as he does in the 1919 testimony that serves as his entrance to Indian politics, he often relies on *direct address*. There is a rhetorical function behind this; without the distancing provided by quotation practices, it is *Ambedkar* making the important points about caste, like-mindedness, and endosmosis, not an American philosopher who must be effortfully bent to fit the demands of the Indian social and rhetorical situation. Ambedkar's appropriative tactics, rhetorically considered, allowed for the most forceful and direct critique of Indian culture and politics possible in his speaking situation in 1919.

This appropriation of the words and ideas of Dewey in Ambedkar's testimony has related antecedents in both the Indian tradition and the West. In Western contexts, one can see why a speaker might shy away from quoting in some cases; issuing one's own thoughts in one's original words is taken as a sign of greatness or genius. We typically do not quote others quoting others. We quote others when they are the source of a specific thought, phrase, or text that serves as a way of linguistically capturing wit or wisdom. Thus, assertiveness combines with insight in a dominant Western way of approaching rhetoric, that of the unique genius creating words worth listening to and repeating. We see a precedent for what can be called *echoing*—the unannounced use of past important phrases in a present text—in the Indian tradition. As Wilhelm Halbfass explicates in his work, the Indian tradition has a curious relation to the resources and thought of the past.[48] On the one hand, the Hindu tradition (for instance) evinces a great respect for the philosophical and religious texts of the past. The *vedas* are a constant concern for the philosophical systems that seek to move beyond them; even in changing key elements (such as the use of violence), later Hindu philosophers still maintain the sacredness of the *vedas* and Vedic tradition. The past is not thrown away or abandoned, even when present changes depart radically from what should be infallible revelation. Echoing of the past occurs in specific forms in this tradition in the form of *mahāvākyas*, or "great sayings."[49] These are lines from earlier texts that are judged to be especially powerful and enlightening, such as the famous phrases describing the relation between self and ultimate reality, *tat tvam asi* ("That thou art") from the *Chandogya Upanishad* and *neti, neti* ("Not this, not this") from the *Brihadaranyaka Upanishad*. Similar phrases are repeated throughout the Vedic tradition, appearing in the *Upanishads*, the *Bhagavad Gita*, and other texts. The source of such phrases is typically not explicitly cited, since it is assumed that either they will be recognized or their power will be effective in any case on an attentive listener. In some strands of Vedanta, concentration on these phrases—regardless of their context and history—is said to be efficacious in procuring enlightenment.[50] In various parts of the Indian tradition that Ambedkar was situated in and reacted to, there was an established practice of echoing wise and effective phrases of the past without noting their original context. Ambedkar's form of pragmatism parallels this tendency with his performance of this tactic in his reform efforts aimed at the target of caste oppression.

Ambedkar's appropriation of Dewey's words and ideas can be best seen as a rhetorical method of *reconstruction*. He practices this tactic in his 1919 testimony, but he does not publicly explore or reflect upon the reconstructive nature of this method until his planned 1936 speech, ultimately published as *Annihilation of Caste*.[51] This speech—composed in English and undelivered due to its controversial message—will be analyzed further in the next chapter, as it grounds Ambedkar's use of conversion as a tactic of social melioration. Here we can engage portions of it as a way to explain what Ambedkar is doing when he echoes Dewey's texts, in 1919 or in his later speeches. In this speech, Ambedkar explicitly discusses his reconstructive method and clearly links it to Dewey. His echoes and uses of Dewey are purposive and selective, and they alter the original text for his present goals of reform. Amid Ambedkar's passionate argument in 1936 painting the Hindu religion as a source of the mental notions of caste that infect the Indian people, he evokes Dewey and the idea of reconstruction of the past in light of the present:

> Prof. John Dewey, who was my teacher and to whom I owe so much, has said: "Every society gets encumbered with what is trivial, with dead wood from the past, and with what is positively perverse. . . . As a society becomes more enlightened, it realizes that it is responsible not to conserve and transmit, the whole of its existing achievements, but only such as make for a better future society."[52]

This is a remarkable passage, given its overt reference to Dewey. Let us pause for a moment and remain curious about the matters to which our rhetorical focus directs our attention. Ambedkar is not simply relaying Dewey's passage here; he is using and sculpting that text to fit his needs and context. One may note the ellipsis and wonder: How does the original text read? What revision does the ellipsis represent? We can identify the full quotation, along with the parts excised, in Dewey's *Democracy and Education*:

> *Every society gets encumbered with what is trivial, with dead wood from the past, and with what is positively perverse.* The school has the duty of omitting such things from the environment which it supplies, and thereby doing what it can to counteract their influence in the ordinary social environment. By selecting the best for its exclusive use, it strives to reenforce the power of this best. *As a society becomes more enlightened, it realizes that it is responsible not to transmit and conserve the whole of its existing achievements, but only such as make for a better future society.* The school is its chief agency for the accomplishment of this end.[53]

In his activity as a synthetic rhetor, Ambedkar is extending Dewey's point about thinking of the past: it matters for the present, but only insofar as we can *make* it matter given our present needs and interests. We should not, however, revere or preserve the past blindly. Reconstruction, in this reading, becomes an active sloughing off of "dead wood" or useless past commitments in light of our present challenges. This method does not leave Ambedkar, as he enunciates the method of reconstruction again in the 1950s when he is describing the virtues of Buddhism as a pragmatic religious doctrine. In an English-language article in the Buddhist journal of the Mahabodhi Society in May 1950, Ambedkar talks of the Buddha and how "He wished, His religion not to be encumbered with the dead wood of the past. He wanted that it should remain evergreen and serviceable at all times. That is why He gave liberty to his followers to chip and chop as the necessities of the case required."[54] The same reconstructive engagement with the resources provided by a tradition are present there as are found in his earlier echoes of Dewey's texts in a new Indian context.

In the explicitly quoted passage taken from *Democracy and Education*, we see Ambedkar "chip and chop" at Dewey's thought as the necessities of the battle against caste oppression dictate. By excluding the lines discussing the duties of "the school" in Dewey's original text, Ambedkar makes the passage and phrases used speak less about educational reform in the classroom and more about social reform in the context of abandoning Hindu holy texts and practices. Dewey's concern in the context of this passage was the relation between schools and an increasingly industrial society that aspired to be a democracy, a different motivation from Ambedkar's situation of rhetorical action.[55] The Indian reformer leaves aside some "dead wood" from Dewey's past pursuits in his 1916 book to kindle his reform efforts against the religious traditions underwriting caste oppression. Ambedkar reconstructs Dewey's passages on reconstruction to make his own point about caste oppression. The focus on schools is optional. Reconstruction is a rhetorical method, or a way of arguing, that goes beyond one context—it is instead a method of selectively using and excluding past resources, both textual and traditional, in its pursuit of goals that empowered individuals choose to seek in the present.

Another passage from Ambedkar's *Annihilation of Caste* address in 1936 sheds light on this reconstructive method that is present in his earliest rhetorical activity. In discussing why Hindus should refuse to follow the promptings of their holy books, such as the *shastras* and the *Manusmṛti*, he again explicitly quotes Dewey:

> The Hindus must consider whether they must not cease to worship the past as supplying its ideals. The beautiful effect of this worship of the past are best summed up by Prof. Dewey when he says: "An individual can live only in the present. The present is not just something which comes after the past; much less something produced by it. It is what life is in leaving the past behind it. The study of past products will not help us to understand the present. A knowledge of the past and its heritage is of great significance when it enters into the present, but not otherwise. And the mistake of making the records and remains of the past the main material of education is that it tends to make the past a rival of the present and the present a more or less futile imitation of the past." The principle, which makes little of the present act of living and growing, naturally looks upon the present as empty and upon the future as remote. Such a principle is inimical to progress and is an hindrance to a strong and a steady current of life.[56]

This lengthy reference to Dewey in 1936 is enlightening insofar as it shows Ambedkar merging a Deweyan reading of the value of the present with a methodological point of how we talk about and use the resources of our past. In other words, Ambedkar is opining about how to use the past and present in a future-oriented program of reconstruction. This passage occurs shortly after the overt reference to Dewey on the "dead wood" of the past in Ambedkar's printed speech text, but it comes from a more distant part of Dewey's *Democracy and Education*. The original passage is framed by and connected to Dewey's analysis of educational subject matter:

The theory that the proper subject matter of instruction is found in the culture-products of past ages (either in general, or more specifically in the particular literatures which were produced in the culture epoch which is supposed to correspond with the stage of development of those taught) affords another instance of that divorce between the process and product of growth which has been criticized.[57]

Immediately following this contextualization, we can note the passages and phrases that Ambedkar appropriates for his 1936 appeal to Hindu reformers in their original context in Dewey's *Democracy and Education*:

To keep the process alive, to keep it alive in ways which make it easier to keep it alive in the future, is the function of educational subject matter. But *an individual can live only in the present. The present is not just something which comes after the past; much less something produced by it. It is what life is in leaving the past behind it. The study of past products will not help us understand the present,* because the present is not due to the products, but to the life of which they were the products. *A knowledge of the past and its heritage is of great significance when it enters into the present, but not otherwise. And the mistake of making the records and remains of the past the main material of education is that it* cuts the vital connection of present and past, and *tends to make the past a rival of the present and the present a more or less futile imitation of the past.* Under such circumstances, culture becomes an ornament and solace; a refuge and an asylum. Men escape from the crudities of the present to live in its imagined refinements, instead of using what the past offers as an agency for ripening these crudities. The present, in short, generates the problems which lead us to search the past for suggestion, and supplies meaning to what we find when we search.[58]

Seeing the amount of selectivity displayed by Ambedkar in engaging Dewey's passage, one realizes that Ambedkar is remaining true to Dewey's reconstructive orientation toward the past *in* the present. We must use the materials of the past selectively in solving the problems generated in our present situation. Our "searching" and "using" is the activity denoted by the term *reconstruction*. Ambedkar's practice, however, emphasizes the fact that our *rhetorical* activity—our speaking and persuading of others to think or act differently—is itself an action that can be a site of reconstruction. In other words, Ambedkar's use of Deweyan text in his appeal not only *describes* reconstructive method to his audience, it *performs* reconstruction insofar as his quotational practice selectively adapts and adopts Dewey's ideas to fit a program of caste reform in India. Upon inspection of the original passage from *Democracy and Education,* published twenty years earlier, one sees that Ambedkar has left out Dewey's focus on educational subject matter and the schools to make his point about social reform through a selective appropriation of the past. His battle was with social custom, not merely practices of formal education.

Reconstruction essentially involves some reliance on and use of the resources of a past tradition. Much of this past survives—in both India and America—in the form of textual products, so Ambedkar is keen to sustain Dewey's emphasis on how we reconstructively engage with texts that our tradition has preserved. Arun Mukherjee is one of the few commenters on Ambedkar who has noticed what Ambedkar leaves out in his 1936 rephrasing of Dewey's analysis of present experience and past tradition—namely, the phrase "because the present is not due to the products, but to the life of which they were the products."[59] Mukherjee notes that "by deleting part of the sentence and dropping the italicization [on 'products'], Ambedkar makes an important change in Dewey's meaning. In the Indian context, Ambedkar can be read as saying that 'the present *is* due to the products.' The past is, he suggests, what is written in the texts, and it is this textual past that is being used to shore up the present system of inequality to prevent people from making progress."[60]

Mukherjee's point is insightful, and it does explain why Ambedkar would take care to remove that phrase from his reconstructed utterance in 1936. We can extend this analysis, however, with a sustained focus on rhetoric and persuasive force. Like the mentions of "schools" or "educational subject matter," it was a trace of past texts (Dewey's) that did not serve the needs of Ambedkar's present rhetorical situation in seeking caste reform. One can also notice another phrase that Ambedkar deletes from his quotation of Dewey, a line on how an emphasis on past texts and records "cuts the vital connection of present and past." Why would Ambedkar leave out this phrase? It seems to dilute the force of the message that he wants to convey to the higher-caste Hindu reformers who were his speech's intended recipients. He wanted to persuade them to renounce the past, not to preserve connections unworthy of the label "vital." While the next chapter will analyze this famous 1936 speech in further detail, we can see from this selective examination that Ambedkar is both talking about and performing a reconstructive rhetoric that can be revolutionary in form and effect, if one changes or appropriates the matter of the past in an *intelligent* fashion. The past does not disappear from the present, but portions of it can be selectively employed in shaping a radically new future.

## Ambedkar's Reconstructive Rhetoric

What emerges from this chapter and the former chapter's interrogation of two texts infrequently engaged—the 1918 review of Russell's book and the 1919 testimony to the Southborough Committee—is a conception of Ambedkar as an evolving pragmatist in spirit, goal, and method. Starting from his return to India in 1917, he began to develop and practice his own version of pragmatism that emerged in the crucible of social injustice he and his fellow Dalits knew so well. As we shall see throughout this book, Ambedkar's reconstruction of pragmatism responded to and used the resources of both the West and the East in operating as a way of meliorating the problems he faced as a Dalit and that millions of other Dalits faced in India. Synthesis and strategic hybridity, not tradition-bound purity, was his motto in practice. Combining the lessons and themes extracted from this chapter and the previous chapter, we can conclude by clearly demarcating some of the major aspects of what we can call Ambedkar's *reconstructive rhetoric*. The method of much of his speaking and writing on behalf of the oppressed is inflected by his engagement with American pragmatists like Dewey, and it is committed to seven entailments. This reconstructive rhetoric can also be taken as representing Ambedkar's *meliorism*, since it covers so much of the scope of his efforts to understand and improve the lived experiences of caste-bound individuals suffering in India.

1. *Society and tradition can and must be optimized or reconstructed.* This is the first and foundational commitment to a reconstructive rhetoric. Society—a collection of people, institutions, and practices with a history—grounds where individuals find themselves, but it should not inherently limit their capacities or happiness. Individuals and communities must always strive to change and reform the features bequeathed to them by shared cultural customs and habits, but only when they can be optimized or further improved. Change for change's sake has no place in a pragmatist system. But doing things in one set way for a long time does not justify continuing in that manner. Ambedkar acknowledged these commitments, and the full examination of his rhetorical practices and activities will highlight his fight for reform of deep cultural habits when it is beneficial. For instance, in the 1920s he fought for the full inclusion of the Dalits within the Hindu fold by leading a variety of temple entry movements and

*satyagraha* actions to gain access to communal water supplies. By the period covered in the next chapter (the 1930s), Ambedkar came to the realization that the Dalits would be best served by leaving the Hindu religion. In no case did he advocate destroying or ignoring the Hindu tradition wholesale during this period; all of his reform and conversion moves were in relation to specific goals that could be attained if the then current situation of religious community were improved. A reconstructive rhetoric starts with a melioristic commitment to improve problematic situations in one's own community and one's own lived experience and to seek just solutions to maladjustments among individuals and communities.

2. *The growth of individual personality is closely tied to the reform of social groups and institutions.* As noted in the previous chapter, Ambedkar merges Dewey and Russell in making a vital point: there is a dialectical relationship between institutions at the systemic level and individual habits at the specific level. We must remember that Ambedkar praises the social reformer, Bertrand Russell, at the end of his review by attributing to Russell the fundamental recognition of the "psychic basis of social life." Ambedkar combines this with a Deweyan reading of individual personality and the benefits of organic growth in light of a natural or social environment to ground his new reconstructive rhetoric. Individual habits and mindsets affect and condition situations identifiable as happy, just, and so forth. In line with Russell's point, Ambedkar acknowledges that institutions such as government or economic practices alter individual mindsets, allowing one to foresee individual change and improvement if specific institutions are suitably meliorated. Ambedkar's reconstructive program goes beyond this, however, through its inclusion of an individual focus. As I discuss in future chapters, Ambedkar often looked back at the Deweyan ideal of personality and its growth as a central part of the notion of democratic citizenship. If the individual-institution dialectic is truly a bidirectional relationship, one can alter or reform institutional or systemic realities by meliorating enough individual mindsets. Ambedkar's form of reconstructive rhetoric seeks reform or improvement of society on a variety of levels: that of individual attitude or orientation toward self and others and that of the systemic level of legal and political institutions that so often encourages the presence of certain attitudes or habits among large swathes of the population.

In this way, Ambedkar's developing method of reconstruction delivers on a promise that Dewey made in a text on his idealistic ethics from 1891, the year that Ambedkar was born: "In the realization of individuality there is found also the needed realization of some community of persons of which the individual is a member; and conversely, the agent who duly satisfies the community in which he shares, by that same conduct satisfies himself."[61] Ambedkar's rhetorical strategies aim to demonstrate that the community can improve the lives and flourishing of individuals, and that individual change and improvement can similarly improve the overall community. The individual-community dialectic theorized in Dewey's lectures and texts thereby gained a meliorative hue in Ambedkar's pragmatist approach as it evolved back in India.

3. *The process of improving these habits or mindsets is education; rhetorical activity can be educative.* Ambedkar's reconstructive rhetoric is committed to the notion of societal reform and to habit as vital in this pursuit. Expanding on Dewey and Russell, Ambedkar sees the reform or optimization of habits as an instance of education. Ambedkar goes beyond Dewey in operationalizing the various ways in which this education can take place. Dewey made a point in *Democracy and Education* to say that all experience was educative to some extent, but formal education clearly was the emphasis of his melioriative program given the intelligent control administrators and teachers can exert over the effective environments.[62] Given the Indian context and the crushing burdens of untouchability, Ambedkar could not singularly emphasize formal education. Ambedkar was a firm believer in education, of course, but the risk he faced was that any increase in access to formal schooling would most likely be grounded in or dependent on the Sanskrit tradition, thereby amplifying and continuing the oppressive tendencies inherent in the Indian past.

To seek true reform and reconstruction of the tradition that framed Dalit life, Ambedkar would have to appeal directly to those affected by and implicated in this system. As the following chapters will demonstrate, this would mean speaking directly to high-caste Hindu reformers as well as his Dalit followers. As the present chapter has illustrated, it might also mean appealing directly to the British rulers of India regarding improvements they could bring to the lives of Dalits. Combining Russell's emphasis on reform with Dewey's reading of education as vital to democracy, Ambedkar reconceptualizes the reformer as educator. The reformer's rhetorical activity can be both educative and a force for reform. If Ambedkar could pick the right enlightening and liberatory words, then he could effect reconstructive changes in the habits and mindsets of those listening to him. And these changes, in turn, could lead toward better treatment of the oppressed and a more just community. All of these commitments and aspirations will be seen as operative at various levels in the way that Ambedkar's rhetorical activities are analyzed in the following chapters.

4. *Force is both essential to and worrisome for efforts at reconstruction.*

Ambedkar's review of Russell's book in 1918 sounds a note that would reverberate throughout his work focused on political and social reform over the next four decades, that of the dangers and necessities of force. For Ambedkar, force is necessary to effect change; one cannot be intelligent, effective, or pragmatic without employing some sort of means to change the world to one's desires. Our ends necessitate the application of force to see them actualized. But as Ambedkar observes when reading Russell's book, force too quickly plays into a destructive cycle of mutual self-assertion. The individual wishes to reform social institutions, be they working conditions of the shop or governmental procedures that foster exclusion; they identify enemies to this desired change and then apply force to them and the institution to bend the world to their will. Perhaps they will "win." Yet the point that Russell pushes—and that Ambedkar extends with his revisions to Dewey's variegated idea of force—is that in applying force to one's discursive or political enemies, one creates the conditions for the use of counterforce. One's enemies do not sit idly by and abandon their commitments. One's force can affect various directions of forethought and reaction in the target of the employed forces. Your enemies may react in such a way as to reassert their vision of the world and an optimized society and employ new forces at their disposal in confounding you and your efforts at reform.

Force is a double-edged sword. It is how we actualize the changes needed to improve communities, but it also can evoke the worst in communities through aggravating and magnifying conflict. Perhaps we could even say that absolute force corrupts absolutely; as Russell worried about in his book, the oppressed can quickly become the oppressors in forcing their vision of justice and retribution upon the former oppressors. The tightrope of force is an undeniable part of Ambedkar's reconstructive rhetoric, and it is one of the reasons that he never abandons the use of rhetorical activity. Through speaking and writing, Ambedkar often hoped to use the "soft force" of persuasion to get his opponents to willingly see his side of things. At times he missed his mark, but he never gave in to the temptation to use or encourage violence or destructive force to remake the world in his image. He always endeavored through his rhetorical activity to achieve an intelligent reconstruction of the world, one that still held a place for his opponents in an enriched community.

5. *Selectivity is both necessary for and worrisome to reconstructive activities.* When we think, talk, or act, there is a radical contingency to our actions. Our choices and our planning make a certain possible line of activity real, but other choices could have been made. The same goes for how pragmatists say we think about the world. Our analyses are saturated with human

purpose, and humans can have a stunning array of different purposes and meanings behind their activities. We are purpose-driven creatures, and our actions—including our reflective acts of thought and communicative choices—are beholden to and conditioned by the contingent purposes that animate us in that present moment. Selectivity is contingent in its details but necessary as a general feature of human activity. For Ambedkar the ever-developing rhetor, this theme was present as early as 1918. We recall that in his published review, he criticizes Russell for unimaginatively collapsing all possible motives, purposes, or uses behind economic activity to one: the love of profit and property.[63] Characterizing the pursuit of riches as simple greed or acquisitiveness denies the other laudatory motives and uses that could animate monetary gain. In Ambedkar's case, he could clearly envision the beneficial uses to which the Dalits could put financial gain, a financial progress that was largely precluded by the oppressive religious system that underwrote the caste system and its division of people and occupations.[64] In the 1918 review, Ambedkar also decries the Marxist oversimplification of societal problems to class conflict centering on economic power. Like Russell, Ambedkar does not deny there is a truth in these readings, but he simply worries about the cost of making these readings into some all-important, unchangeable truth. We must always watch out for emphasizing *the* end at the exclusion of other ends and the agents who pursue them, a point he notes for the Southborough Committee in 1919. Our reconstructive activities are always selective, and we must remain aware of the costs and benefits of this contingency in our guiding ideals or narratives.

6. *Reconstruction takes place both in discourse and through discourse.* As we have seen, Ambedkar believed that speaking and writing in the right way could help both individuals and communities. Persuasion was the force that intrigued Ambedkar as a means conducive to the ends of democratic community building. In his later, more religiously focused activity, we see this commitment amplified. All of this rhetorical activity aims at the reconstruction of individuals and communities through the means of discourse. He spoke and wrote in the hopes of changing his audiences and their surrounding communities. But he seems to have stopped short of using the types of force that could destroy others and permanently break apart communal bounds. What the present chapter has added, however, is the entailment that reconstruction often happens *in* and *through* discourse. Ambedkar's appropriation of Dewey occurs in the planning and execution of his review of Russell and his testimony to the Southborough Committee. He does not point to the whole of Dewey's thought; he picks out

pieces of it that fit the Indian situation, changes parts that almost work, and connects these with his own argumentative ligatures. All of these creative uses—explicit or implicit—are employed in such a way as to maximize their discursive force. When immediacy of address is needed, we often see Ambedkar reconstruct Dewey's thought into a seamless, one-author argument; when some distance in appeals to expertise are allowable, we see Ambedkar quote his beloved "Professor Dewey." Each of these uses is an instance of reconstruction in and through discursive means of argument, strategies we will see amplified and adapted in the following decades of Ambedkar's political activism.

One can observe this dual-natured sense of reconstructive rhetoric in his reply to Mohandas Gandhi appended to later editions of his *Annihilation of Caste*. Gandhi became an obstacle to Ambedkar's message and reforms given the Mahatma's resistance to concessions given to Dalit constituencies by the British in the early 1930s. He embarked on a fast until death to force Ambedkar to give back these concessions, a use of coercive force that Ambedkar would never forgive the symbol of Indian *swaraj* for in the following decades.[65] Gandhi continued his struggle with Ambedkar for the symbolic and literal leadership of the Dalit movement and objected to Ambedkar's call for renunciation and conversion in 1936. Ambedkar, responding to Gandhi's objections to the original publication of *Annihilation of Caste* in the second edition of the controversial text, problematized a mindless adherence to the past with reconstructed Deweyan echoes:

> The Mahatma appears not to believe in thinking[.] He prefers to follow the saints. Like a conservative with his reverence for consecrated notions he is afraid that if he once starts thinking, many ideals and institutions to which he clings will be doomed. One must sympathize with him. For every act of independent thinking puts some portion of an apparently stable world in peril.[66]

This response to Gandhi illustrates both the end-focused nature of reconstruction and the means that it often entails. Ambedkar wants his readers and listeners to challenge the past and its ideals and to reflect on how they may constrain us. This reexamination should issue forth in reconstructed selves, habits, and institutions. But to make this point as directly as possible, Ambedkar uses the Deweyan vocabulary and texts he is most familiar with and uses the strategy of rhetorical echoing to push his point. Dewey's original passage, with appropriated parts italicized, is taken from a book that we know Ambedkar owned, read, and annotated, Dewey's *Experience and Nature*:

Let us admit the case of the conservative; if we *once start thinking* no one can guarantee where we shall come out, except that *many* objects, ends and *institutions* are surely *doomed*. Every thinker *puts some portion of* an *apparently stable world in peril* and no one can wholly predict what will emerge in its place.[67]

The general reference of "conservative" is changed to a specific target—Gandhi—and "objects, ends" are translated into ideals, a more religiously tinged word adapted to Ambedkar's context. Cutting around terms and phrases that did not matter for his reconstructive efforts in Indian society, Ambedkar uses those parts of Dewey's work that could function as criticisms of Gandhi, whom Ambedkar sees as all too complacent in challenging the deep religious basis for caste discrimination. Tentative phrases such as "no one can guarantee where we shall come out" are abandoned, since Ambedkar has a specific goal for his reconstructive rhetoric. We no longer have a general paean to the value of reflective thinking; in Ambedkar's hands, Dewey's words become merged with his very specific criticism of Gandhi as an unreflective and reform-stymying religious traditionalist. Reconstructive rhetoric can imply a reconstruction in the texts that one uses to argue, as well as in the social goals one wishes to achieve as an effect of this rhetorical activity.

7. *Reconstructive activity is tentative and impermanent.* At these points in 1918 and 1919, Ambedkar is beginning to pursue his reform program with passion and forethought; we can gather from his evocations of Deweyan ideas and text concerning the ever-changing present and the selectivity involved in end-based intelligent activity, however, that he was also sensitive to the temporal situatedness of reconstruction. One attempts to optimize through reconstruction *this* society or *these* individuals, all with a specific historical path leading up to and constituting their specific dimensions. After one's reform efforts—successful or not—the community or group of individuals will be changed from how they were before one's rhetorical activity. Such is the history of effect in rhetorical efforts at reconstruction. The challenges of the present—any present—must be minded in their concrete detail, and the past must be used selectively but intelligently, with an eye toward what this present situation demands as resources for reconstruction. There is not always one path to reconstructing the present, as the range of past experiences and future-oriented purposes is contingent and diverse.

As the following chapters will illustrate, Ambedkar's experiences and purposes evolved throughout his career as a reformer, such that his efforts at social reconstruction in the 1920s look radically different from his efforts in the 1930s or 1950s. Instead of trying to integrate Dalits into Hinduism, the latter decades feature him using his powers of speech to find respect for Dalits by convincing them to convert from Hinduism to a reconstructed notion of Buddhism present in such texts as his magisterial *The Buddha and His Dhamma* (1957). A reconstructive rhetoric takes its present activities very seriously but still maintains a sense of temporal fallibilism that acknowledges and respects others, both in present conflicts and in future presents of importance. Much more must be said beyond these general contours of the reconstructive rhetoric that Ambedkar developed in his Indian context, but this task will best be exemplified in the progression of the following chapters that analyze the complexities of this important Indian pragmatist's life and activity.

# FOUR

# Pragmatism, Reflection, and the Annihilation of Caste

Philosophers as complex as John Dewey and Bhimrao Ambedkar mature and change over time; complexity and evolution is part of their deep engagement with ideas and ideals. As the previous chapters have demonstrated, young Ambedkar engaged the ideas, texts, and meliorist methods of Dewey. These points of contact with Dewey's thought pushed him to inflect his quest for social justice—pursued in oral and written testimony to the Southborough Committee and through publications in economic journals—in certain recognizably pragmatist ways. But Ambedkar continued to evolve as a thinker throughout the 1920s, fighting for Dalit rights through *satyagraha* efforts aimed at gaining access for Dalits to communal water tanks and Hindu temples.[1] All of these events and activities helped clarify Ambedkar's commitment to reform and resistance to caste oppression, and they also helped determine the directions he would take at the Round Table Conferences and beyond in the 1930s. Acrimony between Ambedkar and caste Hindus would ultimately lead to insurmountable tensions in the 1930s. The centrifugal forces culminated in his monumental break with Hinduism, made publicly in his speech at Yeola in October 1935, in which he exclaimed that even though he was born a Hindu, "I solemnly assure you that I will not die a Hindu."[2] Until this period, Ambedkar seemed committed to reforming Hinduism from within its ranks.

The 1930s serve as a crystallizing moment for Ambedkar as pragmatist thinker and anticaste activist. As we shall see, he employed the reconstructive technique of "echoing" in his speeches and texts most frequently during this period, and his commitment as an individual reformer and rhetor to being an educator of the masses achieved full instantiation and visibility. The decade brought together Ambedkar's various performances as activist, democratic theorist, anticaste thinker, and political speaker in a series of high-profile texts. It is in these material traces of Ambedkar's thought and philosophy that we find his clearest engagement with Dewey's thought, as well as the aspects of pragmatism that Ambedkar was unsatisfied with or that he saw fit to change and adapt to his own anticaste purposes. Given the rhetorical angle that this project has foregrounded—the aspect of Ambedkar adapting messages to specific audiences, as well as trying to persuasively change those audiences with his specific appeals—this chapter explores arguably his most important work: his 1936 undelivered speech, *Annihilation of Caste*. This text was crafted to serve as a persuasive appeal to a specific audience, and examining its rhetorical functioning can help us work out the various ways that Ambedkar forged his own pragmatism through a reconstruction of parts of Dewey's philosophy. As I demonstrate in this chapter, Ambedkar's engagement with Dewey mattered for both his *method* of arguing and persuading, as well as for the *ideals* that animated his push for caste justice and democracy in India.

This chapter will expand what we see in Ambedkar's activities and works in the 1930s—as well as deepen our understanding of him as an original pragmatist thinker in the Indian context—by revealing themes and specific points of contact between his developing thought and pragmatist resources that he drew upon in making his arguments. The background provided by his Philosophy 231 course with Dewey will be shown to be an important vector for the psychology of human action that underlies many of his vital appeals and arguments in his 1936 text. Beyond these classroom experiences with Dewey lies the preparation Ambedkar as a thinker experienced before he penned the powerful speeches, delivered and undelivered, that remain in our memory of the anticaste thinker from the 1930s. As many know, Ambedkar loved reading and loved his books. What can his book collecting—and habits of annotating—tell us about the developing lines of argument we see concretized in his speeches and writings? I start with an analysis of Ambedkar's engagement with two Deweyan texts that assumed prominence in his *Annihilation of Caste* text, then transition to an analysis of this work as enunciating Ambedkar's pragmatism and theory of conversion in the 1930s.

## Reading Dewey, Seeing Caste

The concretized form that we receive Ambedkar's texts in, as well as the normative aura they often possess, tempts us to see them as springing forth from his mind as unique moments of argument. But they have roots as much as they have effects, and they can be placed in the timeline of

Ambedkar's changing and developing thought over his decades of activism and writing. How can we *see* these roots? How can we go beyond—or better yet, how can we augment—the meaning resident in the published texts that we have received from Ambedkar? One way of doing this is by tracing out the lines of contact, resistance, and influence from his works to the theories, ideas, lectures, and texts of figures like Dewey. The previous chapters have used this approach. I also employ the method of tracing textual indicators of pragmatism's specific influence later in the next chapter, as his conversion speeches in the 1930s and beyond to fellow Dalits display an undeniable engagement with central parts of Dewey's pragmatism—at least as Ambedkar heard and read parts of it. But there is another way to flesh out and expand our understanding of what Ambedkar saw in and took from pragmatism. We know that Ambedkar was a dedicated collector of books, amassing a library that numbered close to fifty thousand books by the time of his death in 1956. We also know that he was a voracious consumer of books, as his personal assistants such as Nanak Rattu, Shankranand Shastri, and Devi Dayal attest in their recollections of Ambedkar's constant practice of reading.[3] Ambedkar was not a passive reader; he often marked or annotated his books with his distinctive red or blue (or sometimes gray) colored pencils as he read through them.

Ambedkar's reading habits were very finely honed and selective. He rarely read an entire book to simply hear its author out. He engaged texts and ideas like a pragmatist, with a purpose and with forethought as to how they might be usable in his own endeavors or struggles. If a book did not look worth his time, or if reading it in its entirety offered diminishing intellectual returns compared to the time he would have to invest, Ambedkar was not afraid to cut his losses. And Ambedkar's time was extremely valuable. He once told U. R. Rao, an India-based manager for one of Ambedkar's main publishers, Thacker & Company, that reading an entire book is

> seldom my style of reading. There are only a few books which call for deep study, from cover to cover. When I see a new title on a subject I am interested in, say socialism, I glance through the blurb, the introduction, the contents, decide which chapters would probably offer me some new thoughts and ideas on the subject. And then I read only those pages, for the rest is familiar ground. And when I have done that, you may say I have read the book.[4]

The surviving collections of Ambedkar's personal books bear out this claim; in many there are annotations only in a chapter or two that interested him.[5] Many of his books are unmarked and possibly untouched. If

Ambedkar's reading habits involved selection with a purpose, there is very good reason to take his annotations and marking habits while reading seriously. Discussing the general nature of reader engagement with texts as material objects, H. J. Jackson argues that markings and "marginalia are the product of an interaction between text and reader carried on—since books are durable objects—in the presence of silent witnesses."[6] Ambedkar served as one of those silent witnesses in future readings when he relied on his markings to jog his memory or to save him time in identifying key points and arguments; we are also those quiet but purposeful observers who may turn to the marks as unnecessary, but meaningful, breaks in the reading process of authors qua readers that channels their energy into creating new material traces of their thinking process that will outlive them. These interruptions in Ambedkar's silent reading process are important in helping him both remember ideas and text and prepare for their future use in his own writings and speeches. They are also vital for us in striving to understand Ambedkar, since such markings and marginalia can be studied "for clues to the identity of the writer" or something akin to "'access to the inner life'" of the author.[7]

If one peruses the thousands of books from Ambedkar's personal library that survive today in various locations—including collections at Siddharth College in Mumbai, the Symbiosis Institute in Pune, Milind College in Aurangabad, Rajgraha in Mumbai, and various private collections—one quickly becomes familiar with Ambedkar's distinctive styles of annotating and marking texts with his gray, blue, or red pencils. Ambedkar's published works are only part of his story as a thinker. His reading and study habits are a vital way to see what material conversations Ambedkar took seriously, before and beyond writing his works. For instance, Christopher Queen notes that "Ambedkar's habit of marking and annotating the texts he wished to consider most deeply offers us a rare opportunity to witness his way of entering into dialogue with the great thinkers of the past."[8] Queen makes an astute observation: the marks in texts such as Dewey's *Democracy and Education* not only provide evidence that Ambedkar read it thoroughly (one could own a book that hasn't been read, and Ambedkar also admitted that he rarely read entire works), they also serve as physical manifestations of Ambedkar engaging with the pragmatist thought of Dewey through this text. Since not every part of a book can be emphasized, we can take such selective marks as signaling ideas that Ambedkar judged at that formative time of reading and intellectually digesting important enough to note for future reflection.[9] Devi Dayal, a personal assistant to Ambedkar from 1943 to 1951 (as well as the caretaker of his beloved book collection), sheds light on what these material traces of textual engagement mean: he remembers Ambedkar telling him, "It is my childhood habit. I must have a pen or pencil in my hand while reading a book. When I come across an important para[graph], sentence, or phrase, I note it down." Dayal recalls that "besides writing on the notebooks, he marked or underlined an important para[graph] or sentence in a book with a pencil. . . . It was in Babasaheb's habit to read the para[graph]s marked, or written on the notebooks in his leisure time. Thus, he refreshed his extraordinary intelligence. It was his childhood habit, inculcated to remember something."[10] Ambedkar's markings are a sure sign of what he read, what he took as important when he read, and what he most likely returned to in future reading sessions.

What Ambedkar meant, if anything, by using different color pencils is unknown. They do not seem to reveal a complex system of different sorts of annotational meaning.[11] Beyond the point aired by Dayal about Ambedkar's strategic reviewing of marked sections, the various styles of annotating his texts also reveal something about the *frequency* of his sustained engagement with certain books; the texts marked with various styles and colors of pencil very likely indicate that Ambedkar read or reread these works, or at least certain parts of them, at different times.[12] All of this combined allows for a rich spectrum of evidence to emerge for those charting Ambedkar's influences and the evolution of his thought: there are books he most likely didn't own or read; books he owned but didn't read; books that did not engage him enough to make any markings in them, if he read them at all; books he annotated in one style in the course of one read through; books that show the signs of multiple engaged readings; and books he owned whose text is quoted or implicitly echoed in his published works. It is by operating in this complex web of quotational practices, reading habits, and a synthetic rhetorical habit of reconstruction that we can add to what we know simply from Ambedkar's published writings.

Turning toward the use of these sources of evidence drawn from Ambedkar as *reader* and Ambedkar as *writer*, we can fill in our picture of Ambedkar as *rhetor*, as one creating meaning through persuasive communication that synthetically engages and uses traditions inside and outside of India to challenge caste injustice. I will turn to Ambedkar's speaking and writing activities shortly, but it is important first to flesh out Ambedkar's pragmatism of the 1930s by exploring what themes or ideas appear to have captivated Ambedkar as a reader of two books by Dewey vital for his discussions of democracy, caste, and religion in the 1930s: Dewey's *Democracy and Educa-*

*tion* (1916) and Dewey and James Hayden Tufts's *Ethics* (1908). Ambedkar owned multiple copies of these books and annotated most of them to a significant extent, from beginning to end.[13]

## Ideas Worth Emphasizing in *Democracy and Education*

Ambedkar's most used, and earliest, copy of *Democracy and Education* contains more than eighty pages with penciled annotations.[14] Ambedkar signed the book and indicated that he bought it in January 1917 during his stay in London, after his time in Dewey's classrooms. The book shows signs not only that he read all of it, but also that he was energized or engaged by many passages and ideas. Many of these passages start appearing as echoes as early as his 1919 Southborough testimony, as I revealed in the previous chapter. This book also informs his epochal moves in his speeches during the 1930s, so it is useful to identify the themes in *Democracy and Education* that seem to have captivated Ambedkar as reader. In my analysis of the array of markings and annotations in his 1916 copy of Dewey's *Democracy and Education*, a constellation of three emergent thematic points arises that further expands what we know about his pragmatic meliorism: the idea of education as serving the needs of society as a means of transmission, the relation of past to present in the idea of reconstruction, and the interrelation of communities and individual dispositions.

### Education as Transmission

When he turned to the pages of *Democracy and Education*, Ambedkar did not miss one of Dewey's major themes. Dewey was concerned in this book with recrafting what we think of life, experience, and the role of education. It is clear that Ambedkar picked up on the central theme of grounding education in the notion of experience: he marks in red pencil the opening line of *Democracy and Education*, "The most notable distinction between living and inanimate beings is that the former maintain themselves by renewal,"[15] then continues on the next page to highlight Dewey's recasting of the organism as caught between past and present. Ambedkar saw Dewey's sense of "experience" in all of this, as he boldly marks in red pencil Dewey's statement, "We employ the word 'experience' in the same pregnant sense. And to it, as well as to life in the bare physiological sense, the principle of continuity through renewal applies."[16] This, of course, occurs after Dewey's insistence that his example, the "Life of Lincoln," is not simply a physiological account; Ambedkar marks that example, as well as the following line, in recognition of Dewey's idea that experience goes beyond the biological into the realm of the cultural. And culture would be vital for Ambedkar, given that the thousands of years of Hindu tradition were exactly the experiential force that he, as a Dalit, had to resist and reform to remove present stigma and social injustice. The descriptive recognition behind this normative stance shines through when Ambedkar highlights one of Dewey's most important phrases in *Democracy and Education*: "Society exists through a process of transmission quite as much as biological life."[17] Ambedkar also underlines in red pencil Dewey's implication about this claim: such a process "makes possible through transmission of ideas and practices the constant reweaving of the social fabric."[18] Communication was central to education and democracy for Dewey, and it's important that Ambedkar noticed this, as it speaks to his focus on persuasive force. He also marks Dewey's connection of communication to such a process of transmission, noting through a marginal check mark Dewey's famous line, "Society not only continues to exist *by* transmission, *by* communication, but it may fairly be said to exist *in* transmission, *in* communication."[19]

Dewey was concerned in the early chapters of *Democracy and Education* to make the case that schools are one of the most important means of societal continuity we have, and that schools accomplish this not through the transmission of memorized and concretized knowledge, but through the purposive manipulation of a student's environment. Ambedkar the reader focuses on both of these themes, highlighting Dewey's presentation of the value of indirect effects in education. For instance, Ambedkar notes the important role of communication and education, highlighting through a marginal line in red Dewey's phrase, "Schools are, indeed, one important method of the transmission which forms the dispositions of the immature."[20] Ambedkar also appears interested in Dewey's nuanced distinctions concerning this position, however, noting in gray pencil Dewey's distinctions between formal and informal education, as well as training and educative teaching.[21] Ambedkar notices the theme that education is a vital part to social continuation, and that it occurs in explicit *and* implicit contexts, points we saw Ambedkar the writer tease out in his 1918 engagement with Russell. Schools are unique insofar as they are formal instances of educative experience, a point that Ambedkar underlines in gray pencil: "We never educate directly, but indirectly by means of the environment. Whether we permit chance environments to do the work, or whether we design environments for the purpose makes a great difference."[22] Whether we are trying to educate or not, social experience has a certain inertia and a specific educative force among its members. This would be a vital motivating factor later when Ambedkar attempted to meliorate caste oppression through the creation of educational institutions such as Siddharth College in 1946, as well as his early reform efforts to recraft social environments through caste integration of temples, water source usage, and situations of intercaste dining in the 1920s and early 1930s.[23]

### *The Relation of Past and Present in Reconstructive Efforts*

A central characteristic of Dewey's philosophy, as well as any notion of his pragmatism, is the idea and method of *reconstruction*. While Dewey would write and speak more about reconstructive activity in philosophy later (in places and texts that we are unsure Ambedkar knew of), this idea was only tangentially approached in his Columbia courses. This theme of reconstruction was present in *Democracy and Education*, and it was clearly noticed by Ambedkar as reader. Ambedkar highlights the passage on purposive reconstruction that he would later trim and reconstruct for his own anticaste purposes in his *Annihilation of Caste*, as we saw in the previous chapter. Expanding the significance of the truncated echo in his 1936 speech, we see different factors featured in Dewey's text that so engaged the Indian reformer. Ambedkar the reader was excited by the concept of reconstruction, marking the entire section with that theme in *Democracy and Education*, which then gave Ambedkar the rhetor the basis from which to alter this passage enough to get what he wanted: a notion of reconstruction that goes beyond or does not emphasize the instrument of formal education. Rhetorical action, such as his 1936 speech, can be educative insofar as it serves as an instance of and means toward reconstruction. Of course, Ambedkar did not slight formal education; he wanted to pursue the reconstruction of society through schools as well as through political means such as mass organizing and political speeches. In a real sense, his recalibrated emphasis on schooling represents his reconstruction of a wider notion of Dewey's idea of reconstruction in *Democracy and Education*, one calculated to fit with the political and social realities of caste-based oppression in an India often preoccupied with achieving political independence from its colonizers.

Ambedkar's sense of reconstruction was Deweyan in its history of development and its general themes, but it evolved in a unique manner given Ambedkar's battles with a millennia-old caste system and a purposefully selective reading of Dewey's work on education. What can we say about Ambedkar's notion of reconstruction based on what he read and marked in his copy of *Democracy and Education*? A pattern of four features emerges from what he marked as notable in Dewey's text. First, reconstruction not only involves the means of the school; it can also involve other means of addressing the dead wood of society's past, such as political advocacy and persuasive oratory. Second, reconstruction involves a sense of charity or situational context in how we evaluate skills, capacities, and uses of intelligence. We see Ambedkar noting this point early on in his copy of *Democracy and Education* when he highlights with both gray and blue marginal lines Dewey's warning against judging "primitive people," along with their different habits and dispositions, as less capable: "We incline to account for it by attributing congenital stupidity to our forerunners and by assuming superior native intelligence on our own part. But the explanation is that their modes of life did not call for attention to such facts, but held their minds riveted to other things."[24] We can assume that for Ambedkar the student in America and London, most likely treated by some as "primitive," this phrase had particular relevance. Beyond matters of biography, we see Ambedkar noting the adaptive sense of reconstruction and intelligence in action: people's ways of adjusting past to present are not to be ranked, but instead must always be approached as contingent ways to adapt to changing and often problematic present situations. Any moralized approach to such matters beyond this represents, in all likelihood, a privileging of one's own contingent ways of doing things. Ambedkar's notion of reconstruction is optimized for effectiveness, not simply a parochial maintenance of the traditional value of certain ways of doing things.

A third characteristic of Ambedkar's notion of reconstruction evident in his engagement with *Democracy and Education* is the connection of past and future in the reconstructive present. For Dewey, reconstruction is an activity that intensely connects one with the problems of the here and now. While it is not fixated on the past or future, it surely is funded by the past and/or oriented toward the future. Ambedkar notices this when he reads *Democracy and Education*. Dewey is concerned that emphasis on biological factors such as heredity will overcome intelligent attempts to inculcate skills and capacities in all students. Ambedkar, the reformer who would rebel against the birth-based fixity the caste system postulates about its members, hears a related, but slightly different, point when he highlights the lines in *Democracy and Education* that speak to this problem: "It is assumed that heredity means that past life has somehow predetermined the main traits of an individual, and that they are so fixed that little serious change can be introduced into them."[25] For the Indian context, "past life" may mean something more than what Dewey is implying, yet the implications are similar; any related approach would limit one's focus now on the distant past and the events that it held. For Dewey in *Democracy and Education*, reconstruction operates best when it fuses the past into the rich present. Ambedkar seems attentive to this position, as he highlights with a gray marginal line the passage preceding this reference to past lives: "Literatures produced in the past are, so far as men are now in possession and use of them, a part of the *present* environment of individuals; but there is an enormous difference between availing ourselves of them as *present* resources and taking them as standards and patterns in their retrospective character."[26] This is a significant passage, as its theme underwrites Ambedkar's later critique of the holy texts (*shastras*) that define Hindu traditions, law, and customs.

What Ambedkar is sensing as he reads and engages *Democracy and Education* is the idea that reconstruction will use the past in service of the present and not merely default to honoring the past by blindly maintaining it in the present. The past is to be used as a resource for present activity, or not at all. This segues into another aspect of reconstruction that we see Ambedkar extract from Dewey's *Democracy and Education*. Dewey is perpetually concerned about things that tradition has left out. In the Western philosophical tradition so enamored with logic and epistemology, "imagination" is often just such a remainder. While this is not emphasized by Dewey in every part of *Democracy and Education*, Ambedkar takes note of it when it is broached. For instance, at Dewey's discussion of how "the past is a great resource for the imagination," Ambedkar underlines Dewey's explanation—only when the past is seen as "the past *of* the present."[27] The resources of the past are useful in *imaginatively* engaging the present; one should not mindlessly default to honoring the past no matter what social consequences it has now, nor should one appropriate without imagination the same elements of the past if they do not truly help one in the present situation. This nonimaginative continuation, of course, is what Ambedkar would later impugn as the harm of those continuing the caste system through a mindless extension of the supposedly *sanatan* or eternal Hindu tradition into the social matters of the present.

The fourth and final characteristic we can identify in Ambedkar's reading of reconstruction in *Democracy and Education* concerns the standards or criteria of effect or normativity. One cannot establish *the* way that society or relationships should be based on past patterns or customs, as any specific strategy may not help adjust us in the best way to our present environment and social demands. We see Ambedkar highlight in blue pencil this passage in *Democracy and Education* concerning the locus of our ideals for moral judgment and behavior:

We cannot set up, out of our heads, something we regard as an ideal society. We must base our conception upon societies which actually exist, in order to have any assurance that our ideal is a practicable one. But, as we have just seen, the ideal cannot simply repeat the traits which are actually found. The problem is to extract the desirable traits of forms of community life which actually exist, and employ them to criticize undesirable features and suggest improvement.[28]

Reformers must not fool themselves into thinking that one resource the past provides is a timeless standard or ideal. We must extract, with an appropriate sense of fallibility, provisional standards from our communities that seem to be working, both in the past and in more recent times. This point was of value to Ambedkar the reformer once he returned to India and pursued efforts to bring respect and equal rights to his fellow Dalits, as early as 1919 and in the period in the 1930s that we will analyze in this chapter. Hindu society, and those that constitute it, in this reading of reconstruction, cannot simply do things the way they've always been done, as this is mere question begging in terms of *why* they should construct communities in this fashion. Instead, Ambedkar the pragmatist will demand that all involved in society be treated in a way that usefully protects their interests and respect, not in a way that simply bows to tradition-based biases among caste groups.

### *The Dialectic between Community Ideal and Individual Disposition*

This general, method-focused reading of reconstruction taken from *Democracy and Education* by Ambedkar leaves out arguably the most important dividend the Indian thinker appropriated from this pragmatist book. The biggest conceptual boon that Dewey bestowed upon Ambedkar was the idea that democracy entailed a certain ideal drawn from its successful instantiations. We know that Ambedkar literally searched *Democracy and Education* for such an ideal, a goal for which his and others' reform efforts should aim. Only three of his marks are evident in the index to his copy of *Democracy and Education*; one is a gray pencil check mark next to "Human association, implications of." Perusing these pages in his 1916 edition, one sees extensive engagement with the core of Dewey's view of democratic community. One sees Ambedkar, in both red and blue pencil marks (likely indicating multiple readings), taking note of the ideal community animated by free and shared interests among its members:

This is equivalent to saying that there is no extensive number of common interests; there is no free play back and forth among the members of the social group. Stimulation and response are exceedingly one-sided. In order to have a large number of values in common, all the members of the group must have an equable opportunity to receive and to take from others. There must be a large variety of shared undertakings and experiences. Otherwise, the influences which educate some into masters, educate others into slaves. And the experience of each party loses in meaning, when the free interchange of varying modes of life-experience is arrested.[29]

A passage highlighted with blue pencil on the following page makes a similar point: lack of shared interest correlates with truncated patterns of communication, and all of this adds up to a nonegalitarian and nondemocratic community among individuals. Ambedkar was clearly taken by Dewey's emphasis on shared interests among the members of a true democratic community. Indian community, as structured by Hinduism and its graded caste system, prevented free communication among individuals and relegated some to the status of masters and others (viz. Dalits) to slaves. It resulted, in Dewey's words highlighted by Ambedkar in blue pencil, in "a separation into a privileged and a subject-class" that "prevents social endosmosis."[30] Ambedkar saw in Dewey's reading of community an explanation of why the experience of Dalits was not only oppressive but without the sort of meaning that a fulfilled life should possess.

Ambedkar as reader also notes Dewey's reference to the "Democratic Ideal" in *Democracy and Education*, highlighting in blue pencil one of Dewey's clearest explanations of what characteristics the ideal community will possess:

> The two elements in our criterion both point to democracy. The first signifies not only more numerous and more varied points of shared common interest, but greater reliance upon the recognition of mutual interests as a factor in social control. The second means not only freer interaction between social groups (once isolated so far as intention could keep up a separation) but change in social habit—its continuous readjustment through meeting the new situations produced by varied intercourse. And these two traits are precisely what characterize the democratically constituted society.[31]

This is a crucial passage, as it spells out the ideal of community as Dewey saw it in 1916: it will be present when a group has numerous shared interests *and* enables free interaction among various other subgroups. A famous line on the following page, one that we shall see again in Ambedkar's *Annihilation of Caste*, is highlighted in red underlining, along with blue and gray marginal lines: "A democracy is more than a form of government; it is primarily a mode of associated living, of conjoint communicated experience."[32] What all of these annotations demonstrate is that Ambedkar was well aware of the end point Dewey sketched out in his *Democracy and Education:* democracy is a way of life (though Dewey did not use that exact phrase in 1916), a way of interacting with others that allows each a role in the group's activities and that does not oppress or crush any individual or group of individuals. Ambedkar highlights Dewey's critique of a structured and unequal Platonic society not because he objected to the Greek view, but instead because he saw in Dewey's objections to Plato's account reasons that his own tradition was in need of radical reconstruction.[33]

What must be emphasized is that Dewey's ideal of the democratic community or association is nothing without a strong dialectic between community reality and individual habit or disposition. This point was a central focus of the Philosophy 131–132 lectures that Ambedkar heard from Dewey in 1915–16. Just as our school communities form individual dispositions that will together create larger democratic communities, Ambedkar senses in Dewey's conception of the democratic ideal a similar attitudinal emphasis. A passage that Ambedkar highlights in red pencil in his copy of *Democracy and Education* illustrates Dewey's point about individual orientation in an ideal community:

> Persons do not become a society by living in physical proximity, any more than a man ceases to be socially influenced by being so many feet or miles removed from others. A book or a letter may institute a more intimate association between human beings separated thousands of miles from each other than exists between dwellers under the same roof. Individuals do not even compose a social group because they all work for a common end. The parts of a machine work with a maximum of cooperativeness for a common result, but they do not form a community. If, however, they were all cognizant of the common end and all interested in it so that they regulated their specific activity in view of it, then they would form a community.[34]

Ambedkar echoes this exact passage in both his 1919 testimony to the Southborough Committee considering the franchise for Dalits and, as we shall see, his infamous canceled address in 1936 targeting Hindu tradition.[35] It encapsulates an important idea for Ambedkar concerning the locus of caste oppression and the means for its eradication. Individuals are habitually disposed toward what they value or are interested in, and this personal variable affects how they relate to and value other people and interests. If one can habituate a shared end or interest among a range of agents, then one has taken a step toward instantiating a democratic way of life or sense of community.[36]

## The 1908 *Ethics* and the Individual Mandate of Reflective Morality

Another text of Dewey's stands out as influential and important, based on the indicators of annotations and the echoes in later works of Ambedkar: John Dewey and James H. Tufts's 1908 edition of *Ethics*. Ambedkar owned two copies of this book; while both are marked, one bears extensive annotations.[37] This book was divided by Dewey and Tufts into three main parts: "The Beginnings and Growth of Morality," "Theory of the Moral Life," and "The World of Action." According to the preface, Tufts (a former colleague of Dewey's at Chicago) authored the entire first section and all but the first two chapters of the third section; Dewey authored the entire second part and the first two chapters of the third part. Both authors are said to have contributed "suggestions and criticisms to the work of the other in sufficient degree to make the book throughout a joint work."[38] This book is of interest to us not only insofar as it was a work that Ambedkar engaged with as a reader *and* as a rhetor in his *Annihilation of Caste* address, but also in that the book itself represents an intermediate step from Dewey's early, idealistic accounts of ethics in the 1880s and 1890s to his more mature ethics that began to emerge around the time that Ambedkar was taking Dewey's courses at Columbia University. *Democracy and Education* is also part of this evolution from an idealist ethics to a fully social ethics in Dewey's later thought, culminating in the publication of the revised 1932 *Ethics*.[39]

The 1908 *Ethics*, however, is important for us because it offered to Ambedkar an account of ethics that reinforces and develops the theme of individual reformers and activists being vectors of educative force in social matters that I have explored in earlier chapters. But an important question arises here: When did Ambedkar read or think through the 1908 *Ethics*? It is not signed and dated in the same fashion as his copy of *Democracy and Education*. Both copies owned by Ambedkar have a copyright date of 1908. Confining my analysis to the heavily annotated copy, I see by further examination of its title page that it was the British edition, which was actually printed as a reissue in late 1910.[40] How did Ambedkar acquire this book? When did he acquire—and read—it? Another clue that might prove valuable appears on the title page of the heavily annotated copy of *Ethics:* in handwriting at the top is "K. A. Keluskar," indicating that it was most likely part of the library of Krishna Arjun Keluskar, a Maharashtra-based reformer and teacher at Wilson High School in Bombay who befriended young Ambedkar while he was studying at Elphinstone High School. Christopher Queen has also noticed this signature and infers that it means the book was given to Ambedkar by Keluskar.[41] It could also have been acquired by Ambedkar from the remains of Keluskar's library after his death in 1934.[42]

Beyond the timing of when he engaged its ideas, we can also ask: What constellation of ideas did the 1908 *Ethics* reveal to Ambedkar as reader? The first edition of the *Ethics*, published in 1908, is significantly different from the 1932 revision undertaken by Dewey and Tufts. The 1908 edition centers on Dewey's moral theory in part II, which, as Abraham Edel puts it, "at this period still remains fixed on the individual agent rather than the transactional field, although he is perfectly clear about what such a field requires."[43] The transactional view of societies and individuals being cocreated inhabits Dewey's later works and is even present in an early form in the focus of the dialectic between communities and habits in *Democracy and Education* and his lectures in 1915–16. In 1908, however, Dewey still seems enamored with pursuing an analysis of society and ethics through the lens of the individual, a continuation in emphasis from his earlier idealistic ethics and partially enshrined in Dewey's Philosophy 231 course in spirit, if not in every detail. As we shall see when we trace Dewey's echoes in some of Ambedkar's important works of the 1930s, the individual focus of the *Ethics* sustains the weight Dewey placed in his early ethics on the ideals of personality and self-realization; the focus on individual psychology in his idealistic ethics has been tempered but not replaced in any significant measure in 1908. The individualistic notes of the *Ethics* surely resonated with Ambedkar, with his explorations in works of 1918 and 1919 of the role of the individual reformer. What does this book add to or reinforce in this focus on the individual as vital to forceful, effective, and moral reform efforts?

One central emphasis in the 1908 *Ethics* is the idea that societies historically develop in the same general pattern as individuals do. In its pages, anthropology and moral philosophy combine in just the sort of scientifically backed philosophy that Dewey had been pining for since his early idealistic efforts led him to reconcile philosophy with any insights that psychology would hold in the late nineteenth century in works such as his *Psychology* from 1887. Tufts's analysis of the evolution of groups and societies in part I dovetailed with Dewey's theory of the moral life (and its development) in part II. Ambedkar was surely taken by the parallelism between the social progress of groups and the moral development (or "realization" as Dewey would put it in his earlier works) of the individual moral agent. Social groups and communities became an important part of the story presented in the *Ethics* based on this individual progression, slightly jarring with the dialectical pairings of habit-custom and individual-collective as presented in Dewey's Columbia courses from 1914 to 1916.

Ambedkar realized the importance of social groups, as he wrote on caste and its relation to social formations as early as 1916 in his seminar paper "Castes in India." But one sees from his engagement as reader with specific parts of *Ethics* that his anthropological interest in familial and societal groups gains an added dimension by being connected to the moral progress of groups *and* individuals. This is vital, as this reading of parallel moral development of groups and individuals will be a unique theme that is not emphasized in Dewey's classes or later works that Ambedkar read. Ambedkar's engagement with *Ethics* opens up Deweyan pragmatism filtered through the anthropological emphasis of Tufts's perspective and Dewey's evolving early idealism. This scientific approach would remain normative in important regards. From the beginning of *Ethics*, we see Ambedkar highlighting the following lines: "Ethics is the science that deals with conduct, in so far as this is considered as right or wrong, good or bad. . . . Ethics aims to give a systematic account of our judgments about conduct."[44] Ambedkar saw the evaluative aspect to morality, with its focus on choice, justification, and values. *Ethics* as a whole was not simply an account of how societies and individuals develop; it offered a powerful account of how groups and agents *should* develop and change. As Ambedkar would underline in red pencil, in such a scheme ethics is not only about a choice of values that guide action, it is also about the formation of one's self: "I am to 'choose' it [the good] and identify myself with it, rather than to control myself by it. It is an 'ideal.'"[45] Thus, ethics was seen as the choice of action, as well as a determination of the sort of self that we create through that action. But *Ethics* goes beyond Dewey's early focus in his idealistic ethics on self-realization and begins to foreground a focus on the self-as-related-to-other-selves. Ambedkar notices this in the introduction and highlights the passage: "To study choice and purpose is psychology; to study choice as affected by the rights of others and to judge it as right or wrong by this standard is ethics."[46]

Part I of *Ethics* quickly ensconces this normative choice of ideals (and self) within an empirical account of the development of ethics. It analyzes the importance of kinship groups and religious units for the development of morality. Our groups shape our actions and attitudes through their influence. This can and does change given development and moral progress. Ambedkar surely saw the leverage provided by a term that would assume increasing prominence in Dewey's "mature" ethics: the idea of "growth." Ambedkar highlights one of the first invocations of this flexible end point (growth, of course, is a process and only a temporary end-in-view) where Tufts writes that moral growth "may be described as a process in which man becomes more *rational*, more *social*, and finally more *moral*."[47] What is important for our present inquiry is the unique and sustained employment of this pattern of development in *Ethics*, a version of the Deweyan story of reconstruction and moral progress that differs from his explanations elsewhere. In the portion of part I that applies this idea to the progression of stages in individual moral reasoning within historical groups, Ambedkar marks with red pencil the three levels of conduct: "1. Conduct arising from instincts and fundamental needs . . . 2. Conduct regulated by *standards of society* . . . 3. Conduct regulated by a standard which is both social and rational, which is examined and criticized."[48]

The related argument is complex, but this general structural claim is sustained throughout all the parts of *Ethics*: societies form and shape their individual members, sometimes even providing them with motives for action and standards for what is ethical. This fact, however, is not the conclusion of moral activity. Individuals and groups attempt to rise to the third level, one that involves conscience and reflective consideration of *why* agents act in that way or encourage others to act in a certain way. The second, and more sociological, level is vital for morality, as it contains and enunciates the scientific analysis of habits, force, and control; it denotes a group-based way of forming selves and actions that is grounded in social custom. As Ambedkar notices and underlines, "Inasmuch as the agencies by which the group controls its members are largely those of custom, the morality may be called also 'customary morality.'"[49] Groups train their members to act in certain ways, forming and enforcing desired habits in those individuals through shared experience.

Ambedkar continues to read and annotate Dewey and Tufts's analysis of the force of group customs in this edition of the *Ethics*, but he also notes the contrasting third level: the notion or stage of reflective morality. The Indian reformer underlines what might be the clearest explanation of this point in the 1908 *Ethics*: "Complete morality is reached only when the individual recognizes the right or chooses the good freely, devotes himself heartily to its fulfillment, and seeks a progressive social development in which every member of society shall share."[50] Habits and customs are conservative;

they are forced, formed and reformed, and enforced by the group. They maintain the group as it is and as it was. Moral progress demands more, according to Dewey and Tufts in the 1908 *Ethics*. Ambedkar sees Dewey's emphasis in part II of *Ethics* on the role of reason—or reflection, as Dewey puts it elsewhere—in moral progress. Ambedkar marks Dewey's analysis of moral progress as a personal quest to reshape one's self:

> Which shall he decide for, and why? The appeal is to himself; what does *he* really think [is] the desirable end? What makes the supreme appeal to him? What sort of an agent, of a person, shall he be? This is the question finally at stake in any genuinely moral situation: What shall the agent *be*? What sort of a character shall he assume? On its face, the question is what he shall *do*, shall he act for this or that end.[51]

In Dewey's section, we see a continuing emphasis on morality as integrally involving the active individual. The agent has a vital role to play in the transition from a merely customary, group-based morality to the stage of reflective morality. The way individuals do this is by instantiating the capacity for reasoning through means and ends, a point that Ambedkar marks with his red pencil: "But the incompatibility of the ends forces the issue back into the question of the kinds of selfhood, of agency, involved in the respective ends."[52] Such a conflict among valued ends, perhaps created by habits or impulses coming to an impasse, evokes reasoning and reflection from the individual to address the situation. If this demand for inquiry is heeded, the habit of reflective morality is inculcated in an agent's *attitude* toward both present and future actions.

Ambedkar notes this progression toward reflective morality in the first chapter of part III, where he annotates Dewey's passage concerning "the transformation of customary into reflective morals," which concerns the changing of one's orientation "from 'Do those things which our kin, class, or city do' to 'Be a person with certain habits of desire and deliberation.'"[53] After this statement of reflective morality at the level of individual habits and attitudes, Ambedkar notes Dewey's utterance that "while the agent has been learning that it is his personal attitude which counts in his deeds, he has also learnt that there is no attitude which is exclusively private in scope, none which does not need to be socially valued or judged. Theoretic analysis enforces the same lesson as history. It tells us that moral quality *resides in* the habitual dispositions of an agent; and that it *consists of* the tendency of these dispositions to secure (or hinder) values which are sociably shared or sharable."[54] Individuals are the locus of moral analysis and progress, but even then groups are implicated as that which must be overcome or re-formed to instantiate moral development in historical timelines. Similar to the parts of descriptive psychology presented in Dewey's Philosophy 231 course, attitudes as complexes of socially formed and group-directed habits hold the key to an individual's merely following customary morality or practicing reflective morality. While Dewey's *Democracy and Education* gave Ambedkar a theoretical vocabulary for the transformative power of experience in group settings, such as that proffered by formal education and settlement houses like those created by Mary Simkhovitch and Jane Addams, the 1908 *Ethics* gave him the framework necessary to describe how groups enforce habitual patterns of activity on individuals and what ideally ought to lie beyond such a state should the individuals that comprise a group be led to moral progress beyond customs and set ways of thinking and acting.

Another theme noted by Ambedkar in his engagement with the 1908 *Ethics* focuses on the role of the individual agent in moral progress. *Democracy and Education* included individuals as important parts of the group processes of habit formation, but the 1908 *Ethics* went even further in emphasizing the role that *individual* reflective thinking about the problematics of morality played. As Ambedkar read in the previous section of *Ethics*, getting all individuals to reason and reflect on values and ends is a vital part of escaping custom-based group morality. But "reason" is no abstract capacity of the human mind; it is really shorthand for certain useful ways of thinking through concrete problems. What can be said about these more or less abstract guides to the range of specific actions? In Dewey's portion of *Ethics*, we are introduced to an important distinction for Ambedkar's pragmatism, that between rules and principles. Dewey castigates set rules of past moral theories as unresponsive to the demands of particular situations. Ambedkar highlights (in both of his copies) Dewey's clearest statement of these mental shortcuts to moral judgment with two gray marginal lines: "Rules *are practical; they are habitual ways of doing things. But principles are intellectual; they are useful methods of judging things.*"[55] Habits and customs, concretized into rules, become problematic when they are fixated on the past and unresponsive to any given present situation. How can one rectify or improve on these remnants from a group's past experience? One cannot be without any habit or custom, nor can one totally escape tradition. Through the application of principles, or *"useful methods"* of moral judgment, our habits and past inheritance of custom can be meliorated; this indicates a transition to the level of reflective morality. This extends the sociological claims broached in Tufts's first section of *Ethics*, in which he argues that reflective morality is denoted by the presence of principle-based activity. There, Ambedkar notes that reflective morality "involves power to see *why* certain habits are to be followed, what *makes* a thing good or bad. *Conscience* is thus substituted for *custom*; principles take the place of external *rules*."[56]

The 1908 *Ethics* emphasizes that the individual is the center of moral activity, including the optimal case of principle-based judgment. The individual agent reevaluates problematic habits and customs instilled in them by the forces of group membership. Societies become reflective because the accumulated behavior of individuals is reflective; these societies also are built around institutions that encourage or enable this reflectivity at the individual level. All of this surely struck Ambedkar while he was reading this text, as his entire life was defined by the paralyzing strictures placed on him by the antiquated social customs of caste morality in Hinduism. Rules, stated or unstated, enslaved him, all with the sanction of the divine. While reading the *Ethics*, he highlights a passage that examines the forces that operate when specific rules of conduct are grounded in religion and God. This foundationalism, according to Dewey and Tufts, deprives rules of usefulness in an ever-changing world: "The moral life is finally reduced by them to an elaborate formalism and legalism."[57] Reading through *Ethics*, Ambedkar most likely was driven to the thought that many of the Indian religions of his day precluded reflective principles vital to a flexible approach to the world and action.

How does an individual agent use these powers of reflection to affect self and others? Dewey, in his chapters in part III of *Ethics*, outlines an answer: one can alter the habits and activities of others through speech and persuasion. Ambedkar sees this claim about persuasive force and underlines in his gray pencil Dewey's argument that "liberty of thought and expression is the most successful device ever hit upon for reconciling tranquility with progress, so that peace is not sacrificed to reform nor improvement to stagnant conservatism."[58] Social reformers must depend on such persuasive methods to attain two goals: to alter society for the better and to maintain the group at some stage without the application of violent force. Thinking beyond the current habits of one's self and talking of such ideas beyond the customary paths of action are both ways to create the impasses that push for reflection by self and others. This reflection is central to the account of moral progress in the 1908 *Ethics*. Individual agency is not merely a *means* to moral end points of progress but also serves as the normative *ideal* or *end* itself. Ambedkar perceived this point, as his copy of *Ethics* contains marks around a passage where Dewey explicates the moral ideal, at least as far as his ethical thought had progressed in 1908:

The moral criterion by which to try social institutions and political measures may be summed up as follows: The test is whether a given custom or law sets free individual capacities in such a way as to make them available for the development of the general happiness or the common good. This formula states the test with the emphasis falling upon the side of the individual. It may be stated from the side of associated life as follows: The test is whether the general, the public, organization and order are promoted in such a way as to equalize opportunity for all.[59]

The focus in this work is still on the individual agent in this way of putting the ideals of moral progress, although precursors of the individual-collective dialectic, as evident in Dewey's notion of "effective freedom" in his 1916 lectures, shine through in this earlier text. Associated life, a vital focus on *Democracy and Education*, also appears, but it remains to some extent subservient to the ultimate goal of setting free individual capacities. These aspects of human personality or agency—desires, talents, projects, and so forth—will contribute to group happiness, but there is still an element of tension within this account between the individual agent and the social group, which extends beyond and encompasses any given individual personality. As we shall see when we turn to the effects Dewey's moral theory had on specific emphases and parts of Ambedkar's rhetorical activity in the 1930s, tensions within Dewey's texts and among his developing moral thought planted the seeds for tensions and new syntheses within Ambedkar's critique of Hinduism, caste, and the sorts of ideals he aspired to reach with the help of his fellow Dalits.

## Rhetoric, Reconstruction, and Conversion in *Annihilation of Caste*

Ambedkar voiced the developed form of his unique form of pragmatism in the 1930s, using and appropriating some of Dewey's ideas, texts, and methods in a synthetic fashion to attack the injustice perpetrated by the caste hierarchy. Pragmatist works such as the 1908 *Ethics* and *Democracy and Education* form an important part of the background that supplied these later speeches, essays, books, and political campaigns with their melioristic meaning. To illustrate Ambedkar's pragmatist approach and lineage in both ideas and rhetorical methods, let us examine his most important and well-known work, the 1936 *Annihilation of Caste*. In the 1910s and 1920s, Ambedkar largely conceived of the Dalits as members of the Hindu fold who could regain rights that were lost ages before. By the 1930s, the political landscape had changed considerably for Ambedkar and his project of reform. Ambedkar's rhetorical activity also extended to political negotiations in London and India with the likes of Gandhi. The relationship between these two great figures of Indian politics soured in 1930 and 1931 in the context of the Round Table Conferences in London concerning the political franchise and the fates of various segments of the Indian population. After Ambedkar had secured concessions from the British for separate electorates for the Dalits in 1931, Gandhi embarked on a rare "fast until death" until Ambedkar gave back these protections.[60] Ambedkar was stunned by Gandhi's extreme methods of resisting separate electorates for the depressed classes (Dalits, largely), stating in September 1932, "It passes my comprehension why Mr. Gandhi should stake his life on an issue arising out of the communal question which he, at the Round Table Conference, said was one of comparative small importance."[61] Ambedkar was even reported as trying to assuage the worries that Gandhi had about the divisive nature of the demands for separate electorates, claiming that the Dalits "mean no harm to the Hindu society, when we demand separate electorates."[62] Ambedkar worried in 1932 about the violent forces that the Mahatma was potentially releasing among his—and Ambedkar's—followers through such a suicidal fast, noting that Gandhi was "fostering the spirit of hatred between the Hindu community and the Depressed Classes" and "thereby widening the gulf between the two."[63] Rather than be responsible for the death of the symbol of *swaraj*, Ambedkar ultimately relented and gave up most of his gains for the considerations now known as the "Poona Pact." But he would never forgive Gandhi for the forceful tactic of wagering his life against the political gains of Dalits.

Gandhi supported the Dalits, but he wanted such support to be firmly entrenched within the Hindu social system. Gandhi thought that "untouchability was a sin, whereas caste was a mere social distinction."[64] Caste (as *varna*) was fine and need not be eradicated; untouchability and the impurity it imputed to individuals and groups, however, was worthy of eliminating. Unlike Ambedkar, Gandhi did not see an intrinsic connection between the concept of caste and that of untouchability. Gandhi even went so far as to affirm the social separations common among castes as nonharmful: "Interdrinking, interdining, intermarrying, I hold, are not essential for the promotion of the spirit of democracy. I do not contemplate under a most democratic constitution a universality of manners and customs about eating, drinking and marrying. We shall ever have to seek unity in diversity."[65] Gandhi, like many high-caste Hindu reformers, was firmly committed to the basic idea of the castes in Vedic thought: that society was divinely and best organized when animated by a set number of hereditary castes.[66] All of this resistance among Hindus supposedly committed to social reform seemed too much for Ambedkar; in early 1933, we see Ambedkar changing his demands from temple entry for Dalits to more demanding charges laid upon higher-caste Hindu reformers. According to a report in the *Times of India* from February 6, 1933, Ambedkar indicated that "his community will not be satisfied with mere entry into the temples." To Ambedkar, this was "a secondary consideration," as the "moral and social uplift of his people and their education were of far more importance." Thus, Ambedkar was reported as now insisting that Hindu reformers make more extreme efforts against the caste system: "He now demands that Mr. Gandhi and his reformist friends shall attack the whole caste system, wipe it out and admit the *Harijans* to Hindu society without any restrictions."[67] Ambedkar's demands of the sympathetic—or apparently sympathetic—elements within the Hindu fold were steadily increasing, up until the monumental apex represented by the actions of 1935.

By 1935, Ambedkar's life and career had undergone momentous change. He announced his retirement from politics and political offices, perhaps as a sign that he was satisfied with the political gains he had eked out for his fellow Dalits, or perhaps out of concern for the civil service requirements for his new appointment as principal of the Government Law College or his hopes for a judicial appointment to the High Court.[68] Personal tragedies also shook Ambedkar's political world. His wife, Ramabai Ambedkar, who had sacrificed so much while Ambedkar was pursuing his education in foreign lands, died on May 27, 1935. Despite the pull of personal loss and the allure of keeping away from the dust and heat of political activity, Ambedkar could not leave the arena of controversy. On October 13, 1935, he made one of the most epochal utterances of his life, one that would provide a foundation of meaning for much of what followed in his life and the liberation movement of the Dalits. Knowing what he had experienced with Gandhi and other Hindu reformers, Ambedkar had moved to the certainty that respect—beyond the issue of political safeguards—could not be gained for him and his millions of Dalit followers from within the bounds of Hinduism. Thus, he delivered a bombshell address at Yeola in October 1935 to ten thousand followers, exclaiming that even though he was born as a Hindu, "I solemnly assure you that I will not die a Hindu."[69] Other reports indicate that Ambedkar stated that "we shall cease our fight for equality where we have been denied it. Because we have the misfortune to call ourselves Hindus we are treated thus. If we were members of another faith none dare to treat us so. We shall repair our mistake now. I had the misfortune of being born with the stigma of an untouchable. But it is not my fault and I will not die a Hindu for this is in my power."[70]

This announcement of leaving the Hindu fold immediately caused a stir across India, as Ambedkar was the undisputed leader of the millions of "untouchables" and outcastes throughout the colony; he would inevitably take millions out of the Hindu fold with him.[71] Gandhi was reported as stating that the speech "seemed unbelievable," and that it was missing the mark, since "untouchability," according to Gandhi, was "on its last legs."[72] Ambedkar responded the next day to such reactions by issuing a statement that "the Hindu religion is not good for us" and that "inequality is the very basis of it, and its ethics is such that the Depressed Classes can never acquire their full manhood."[73] Muslims, Sikhs, Christians, and other delegations visited with him in an attempt to acquire this mass of converts. Ambedkar spent twenty years before he formally announced that Buddhism was to be the religion of his, and his people's, conversion. If the subject of the provocative Adlerblum recollection examined earlier is Ambedkar, this process is of a piece with his searching examination for a bridge between Buddhism and pragmatism that began at Columbia University in his earlier days.

Hindu elements committed to independence—and sometimes to social reform—did not stand still as Ambedkar threatened to leave the Hindu fold. By the end of November 1935, the *Times of India* was reporting that Ambedkar had been presented with a resolution adopted by the Nasik Hindu Progressive Citizens Conference, with the Shri Shankaracharya (otherwise known as Dr. Kurtakoti or Vidyashankar Bharati) presiding over its activities, concerning the pace of social reform. While the resolution supported such demands as temple entry, it recognized them as "extremely controversial and outside the sphere of immediate practical achievement" and promised merely that "every possible effort should be made to bring about a change of public opinion with regard to that question."[74] The conference also promised continued employment of "propaganda" and other "constructive work" to secure rights for *Harijans* or children of God, as Gandhi called Dalits, to attend schools and other institutions alongside "touchables."[75] Ambedkar was not convinced to change his new course of conversion. He sensed that these were placating moves, ones that did not reach the root cause of the phenomenon of caste oppression, nor ones that would be vigorously pursued. Ambedkar's response in 1935 was telling, and to the point: he affirmed his belief that "the foundation of religion" is "essential to the life and practices of society," and that the basis of contemporary Hinduism was codified in the notion of caste-inflected dharma or duty "as prescribed in the '*Manusmriti.*'"[76] He responded with pessimism to the gestures toward reform offered by the Hindu reformers, noting, "I do not think it possible to abolish inequality in the Hindu society unless the existing foundation of the '*Smriti*' religion is removed and a better one laid in its place." At the end of 1935, Ambedkar the pragmatist, however, "despair[ed] of the Hindu society being able to reconstruct on such a better foundation."[77]

All of this forms the background for the events that would happen in 1936. In that year, Ambedkar was invited to give the presidential address for the Jat-Pat-Todak Mandal of Lahore, a group of upper-caste Hindus dedicated to erasing caste discrimination. This organization was an off-shoot of the Arya Samaj movement, a monotheistic group dedicated to reforming Hinduism and reasserting the primacy of the vedas over later accretions to the religious tradition of Hinduism. The Jat-Pat-Todak Mandal was fairly small, comprised of only twenty-two men and women who had paid a membership fee and vowed to marry themselves, or their off-spring, to members of a different caste. But its initiatives made a splash in the reform circles of preindependence India. As a result of its focus on caste reform, the group was alienated from the larger factions of the Arya Samaj, which did not seem interested in focusing on or resolving the social issues of caste.[78] As Ambedkar's biographer Keer documents, the Mandal's leaders eventually got wind of Ambedkar's address and demurred at his mention of destroying the vedas, along with other Hindu holy texts, as the only way to eradicate caste.[79] In the prologue to the published version of the address, Ambedkar reprinted the letters from one official of the Mandal, Sant Ram, who worried: "I am now very anxious to read the exposition of your new formula—'It is not possible to break Caste without annihilating the religious notions on which it, the Caste system, is founded.'"[80] The Mandal, still aligned generally with many prevailing commitments of the Arya Samaj, saw this path of eliminating the scriptural basis of Hinduism as too great a threat to the version of Hinduism they sought to preserve and correct; it probably also perturbed them that the month before the conference was to be held, Ambedkar was meeting with Sikhs in Amritsar, a possible target for Dalit conversion.[81] The Mandal decided to postpone the conference indefinitely so as to prevent Ambedkar's delivery of his incendiary speech. Ambedkar, having already printed up fifteen hundred copies of *Annihilation of Caste*, sold them all within two months in 1936. It would soon be reprinted, in 1937 (and in 1944), with the addition of Gandhi's reply to the speech and Ambedkar's subsequent response. This English-language speech manuscript has an interesting rhetorical history of its own, seeing that it was read by others at subsequent Dalit conferences as a stand-in for the great leader, Ambedkar.[82]

Many have turned to *Annihilation of Caste* over the years as a manifesto of disgust with caste oppression, a statement of the Ambedkarite creed, and the most important document in forming the resistance to caste discrimination. It is a work that holds the answers to many different lines of questioning. In this chapter, however, I want to engage the text as a site in which the themes of pragmatism, rhetoric, and individual political activism are worked out in Ambedkar's life. I engage this text as a rhetorical artifact, one that must be thought of as a text for a specific audience created by Ambedkar, not simply as a discursive container of abstract arguments and positions. Thus, the rhetorical emphasis of this project will continue in the present chapter by highlighting Ambedkar as a rhetor, one who creatively shapes a message for certain situational purposes and for a specific audience or type of audience. Also of vital interest is the fact that central parts of this text continue Ambedkar's conversation with Deweyan pragmatism. As I will demonstrate, this undelivered speech is full of undeniable echoes of Dewey's works, especially *Democracy and Education*, the 1908 *Ethics*, and *Experience and Nature*.[83] If we approach it as part of the story of pragmatism's appropriation and evolution in India, we can also see Ambedkar developing his own melioristic method through the practice of reconstructive rhetoric. This analysis will build upon and extend Arun Mukherjee's pioneering study of the influence of *Democracy and Education* on *Annihilation of Caste* by exhaustively exhuming all identifiable echoes of Dewey employed in this 1936 text as well as bringing in the concept of rhetoric as a way to shed further light on what Ambedkar is doing in this address. There are many ideas and arguments in this undelivered speech, but in what follows I emphasize the parts in dialogue with Dewey's pragmatism, as these are vital markers in the working out of Ambedkar's own lived and performed pragmatist rhetoric and philosophy.

*Annihilation of Caste* is straightforward in its critique of those in the South Asian context who, like elements of the Arya Samaj and the Indian National Congress, refuse to see full-throated social reform as vital for India's political independence and advancement. Ambedkar comes out swinging against those in the Congress who insist on political reform (including self-rule) before any sort of social reform and those influenced by Marxist socialism who demand economic reform before or instead of social reform. All of these, Ambedkar maintains, miss the fundamental decay that lies inside of the Indian proto-nation struggling toward self-rule: the caste system that divides and devalues vast groups within the millions of people that would make up a free India. After setting aside these putatively unhelpful rejections of pushes for social reform, Ambedkar begins his relentless assault on caste, the invidious system that divides groups of individuals based on hereditary and religious concepts. Answering those who would defend caste based on its being a useful societal division of labor, Ambedkar counters, "It is also a division of labourers . . . it is a hierarchy in which the divisions of labourers are graded one above the other."[84] Ambedkar fleshes out this claim in the following passage:

> This division of labour is not spontaneous; it is not based on natural aptitudes. Social and individual efficiency requires us to develop the capacity of an individual to the point of competency to choose and to make his own career. This principle is violated in the Caste System in so far as it involves an attempt to appoint tasks to individuals in advance, selected not on the basis of trained original capacities, but on that of the social status of the parents. . . . Industry is never static. It undergoes rapid and abrupt changes. With such changes an individual must be free to change his occupation. Without such freedom to adjust himself to changing circumstances it would be impossible for him to gain his livelihood.[85]

This is a pointed argument that caste divides workers based on a metaphysics of karma, writing unjust social exclusion and servitude into the nature of the world. But looking closer at this text next to a book that we know Ambedkar read and annotated, Dewey's 1916 *Democracy and Education*, we begin to see its further resonances. Ambedkar is echoing and reconstructing Dewey's phrases and passages in this novel argument against the Indian caste system. Dewey's original passage from *Democracy and Education*, with the words echoed by Ambedkar italicized, focuses on the American context:

> A democratic criterion requires us to *develop capacity to the point of competency to choose and make its own career. This principle is violated* when the attempt is made to fit individuals in advance for definite industrial callings, *selected not on the basis of trained original capacities, but on that of the* wealth or *social status of parents.* As a matter of fact, *industry* at the present time *undergoes rapid and abrupt changes through the evolution of new inventions.* . . . When the occupation changes its methods, such individuals are left behind with even less ability to *readjust themselves* than if they had a less definite training.[86]

This point is originally situated in Dewey's critique of methods of education biased toward tracking individuals into menial jobs in increasingly larger and more impersonal corporations. It is clearly not about caste or religious pollution due to karma, yet Ambedkar takes it and echoes parts of it—with his reconstructive changes—to transform it into a vigorous critique of the inflexibility of the caste system.

This echoing of Dewey's *Democracy and Education* continues as Ambedkar implicates the caste system in the creation of unjust conditions of existence for Dalit and lower-caste individuals. On the next page, one sees a similar echoing in Ambedkar's text:

> Considerations of social efficiency would compel us to recognize that the greatest evil in the industrial system is not so much poverty and the suffering that it involves as the fact that so many persons have callings which make no appeal to those who are engaged in them. Such callings constantly provoke one to aversion, ill will and the desire to evade. There are many occupations in India which on account of the fact that they are regarded as degraded by the Hindus provoke those who are engaged in them to aversion. There is a constant desire to evade and escape from such occupations which arises solely because of the blighting effect which they produce upon those who follow them owing to the slight and stigma cast upon them by the Hindu religion. What efficiency can there be in a system under which neither men's hearts nor their minds are in their work? As an economic organization Caste is therefore a harmful institution, inasmuch as, it involves the subordination of man's natural powers and inclinations to the exigencies of social rules.[87]

The caste system assigned occupations to individuals based on family birth. This is not an optimal way to set up society, Ambedkar argues, using an incipient pragmatist criterion of organizing economies based on the maximum value or meaning added to individuals with a diverse range of capacities and interests. This argument echoes and reconstructs Dewey's critique of industrialized education in *Democracy and Education*:

> Sentimentally, it may seem harsh to say *that the greatest evil of the* present régime *is not* found in *poverty and* in *the suffering* which it entails, but in *the fact that so many persons have callings which make no appeal to* them, which are pursued simply for the money reward that accrues. For *such callings constantly provoke one to aversion, ill will, and a desire to* slight *and evade. Neither men's hearts nor their minds are in their work.* On the other hand, those who are not only much better off in worldly goods, but who are in excessive, if not

monopolistic, control of the activities of the many are shut off from equality and generality of social intercourse.[88]

Dewey's point about acquisitiveness and greed in capitalist schemes of work—and the consequent meaninglessness they so often give to occupational activity—is taken by Ambedkar and changed into a critique of caste-based occupational sorting. Ambedkar leaves out the phrases concerning the rich or the focus on monetary reward by workers, topics dealt with partially in his 1918 review, as aspects that do not intersect in the same way with the context of caste oppression. In their place, he emphasizes the meaninglessness of occupations forced upon individuals by caste placement underwritten by the doctrine of *karma*. Dalits, forced into particularly unsavory occupations from which they cannot escape, offer the worst case of occupations not flexibly matching up with an individual's capacities or interests.

After arguing that caste is not defensible on economic grounds or a racial basis, Ambedkar turns toward the core of his argument: caste must be resisted because it fragments and devalues entire communities of individuals. Throughout this argument one also finds Ambedkar echoing and reconstructing parts of Dewey's thought in an attack on caste ideology. For instance, Ambedkar writes:

> The Hindus often complain of the isolation and exclusiveness of a gang or a clique and blame them for anti-social spirit. But they conveniently forget that this anti-social spirit is the worst feature of their own Caste System. . . . An anti-social spirit is found wherever one group has "interests of its own" which shut it out from full interaction with other groups, so that its prevailing purpose is protection of what it has got. This anti-social spirit, this spirit of protecting its own interests is as much a marked feature of the different castes in their isolation from one another as it is of nations in their isolation.[89]

While his target is unique, Ambedkar extends and alters Dewey's ideas of democratic community. Compare this passage to Dewey's argument about the nature of democracy in *Democracy and Education*, with overlapping phrases italicized:

> *The isolation and exclusiveness of a gang or clique* brings its *antisocial spirit* into relief. But this same *spirit is found wherever one group has interests "of its own" which shut it out from full interaction with other groups, so that its prevailing pur-

*pose is the protection of what it has got,* instead of reorganization and progress through wider relationships. It *marks nations in their isolation* from one another; families which seclude their domestic concerns as if they had no connection with a larger life; schools when separated from the interest of home and community; the divisions of rich and poor; learned and unlearned.[90]

The argument in *Annihilation of Caste* parallels Dewey with its focus on what makes democratic communities ideally democratic, yet Ambedkar molds the critique to target caste deformations in group interactions.

For Ambedkar, castes are animated by an antisocial spirit that does not contribute shared interests and meanings to all in the community; instead, the concept and practice of caste orients each subgroup against all other subgroups. The idea of interests and how they affect activity is a recognizable Deweyan point, but we see its altered application to a society fragmented by caste a few pages later in Ambedkar's text:

> The assertion by the individual of his own opinions and beliefs, his own independence and interest as over against group standards, group authority and group interests is the beginning of all reform. . . . It is true that man cannot get on with his fellows. But it is also true that he cannot do without them. He would like to have the society of his fellows on his terms. If he cannot get it on his terms then he will be ready to have it on any terms even amounting to complete surrender. This is because he cannot do without society.[91]

Some of the ideas and concepts in these lines represent echoes of Dewey and Tufts's much different work, *Ethics*, from 1908. In the first section, authored by Tufts, we find material (with the echoed portion italicized) that must have been in the mind of Ambedkar the rhetor as he penned the previous passage in *Annihilation of Caste*:

> They constitute what Kant calls the unsocial sociableness of man. *"Man cannot get on with his fellows* and *he cannot do without them." Individualism.—The assertion by the individual of his own opinions and beliefs, his own independence and interests, as over against group standards, authority, and interests, is* known as individualism.[92]

We see here the rhetorical technique of echoing, along with the insertion of important changes; the order in *Annihilation of Caste* is different than it is the original text, and Ambedkar breaks the quotations about Kant's notion of unsocial sociability into two parts, deleting the reference to the Prussian philosopher along the way. The reconstructed argument becomes Ambedkar's own, but one can see the emphasized *individualism* of the 1908 *Ethics* clinging to Ambedkar's arguments, foregrounding what caste oppression does to the individual, and what the individual reformer can do about it. Extending and applying the emphases he read in the *Ethics*, Ambedkar highlights the role of individual reformers and their reflective critique of social customs as central to reform in his 1936 text.

What do individual reformers aim for in their reconstructive efforts? Turning our attention to one of the most crucial passages in *Annihilation of Caste*, we see Ambedkar use this rhetorical technique of echoing alongside an evocation of Enlightenment values to manifest a particular critique of caste. He turns to the "constructive side of the problem" and inquires what the "ideal society" will be based on: "If you ask me, my ideal would be a society based on *Liberty, Equality* and *Fraternity*."[93] Even though Ambedkar most likely first heard these values in Dewey's 1916 lectures, the way he uses them resists part of the American pragmatist's thought; Ambedkar often emphasizes or inflects these concepts as an almost transcendental way to ground critique outside of Hindu tradition and its ideals, versus other parts of Dewey that highlight ideals residing within shared community experience. In *Annihilation of Caste*, Ambedkar defends and deploys these values, especially fraternity or fellow feeling:

An ideal society should be mobile, should be full of channels for conveying a change taking place in one part to other parts. In an ideal society there should be many interests consciously communicated and shared. There should be varied and free points of contact with other modes of association. In other words there must be social endosmosis. This is fraternity, which is only another name for democracy. Democracy is not merely a form of Government. It is primarily a mode of associated living, of conjoint communicated experience. It is essentially an attitude of respect and reverence towards fellowmen.[94]

This passage shows the extensive reach of Ambedkar's grasp of Dewey's distinctive formulations of democracy and the democratic ideal. For instance, Dewey describes the democratic ideal in *Democracy and Education* as follows: "In short, *there are many interests consciously communicated and shared; and there are varied and free points of contact with other modes of association.*"[95] Ambedkar echoes the highlighted portions of this passage in a different part of his argument against caste. He also appropriates and deploys the core of Dewey's position on democracy from *Democracy and Education,* which the American put as follows: "*A democracy is more than a form of government; it is primarily a mode of associated living, of conjoint communicated experience.*"[96]

The concept of "social endosmosis" marked by Ambedkar the reader and referenced by Ambedkar the writer further displays his pragmatist dialogue with Dewey. As Mukherjee notes, "the term 'social endosmosis' was used by [Dewey] only once," but it became "a major heuristic tool that [Ambedkar] used repeatedly in his writings."[97] Mukherjee explains the meaning behind Ambedkar's use of this term: "When a society has groups that are separated into 'a privileged and a subject class,' social endosmosis—free circulation of individuals, with various points of contact—cannot take place." This leads to "a sort of atherosclerosis of the social body. . . . Ambedkar's frequent use of metaphors of disease and pathology to describe Indian society is thus an extension of the metaphorical possibilities of endosmosis."[98] In Ambedkar's reconstructive use of Deweyan terms, caste is the malady that destroys the fellow feeling that is so vital in creating and sustaining a free interchange or communication between various groups in a society. Democracy demands such a free interchange exist, regardless of the status of voting rights or constitutions. Like Dewey, Ambedkar sees democracy as a deep habit of interaction among individuals and groups, not merely as a matter of institutions.

For Ambedkar, caste divisions destroyed or precluded the unity that real community entailed. Elsewhere in *Annihilation of Caste,* he offers an extended rumination on this point. Do Hindus themselves constitute a society? He replies in the negative, drawing upon a style of pragmatist reasoning to buttress his assertions about Hinduism. Thinking that Hinduism points at a unified group, even if it is oppressive toward other groups, "misunderstand[s] the essentials which go to make up a society. Men do not become a society by living in physical proximity any more than a man ceases to be a member of his society by living so many miles away from other men. Secondly similarity in habits and customs, beliefs and thoughts is not enough to constitute men into society. Things may be passed physically from one to another like bricks. In the same way habits and customs, beliefs and thoughts of one group may be taken over by another group and there may thus appear a similarity between the two."[99] Ambedkar's argument echoes and retasks passages from *Democracy and Education* in which Dewey claims that "persons *do not become a society by living in physical proximity, any more than a man ceases to be* socially influenced by being *so many* feet or *miles* removed from others," and that "like-mindedness" entails that "such *things* cannot *be passed physically from one to another, like bricks.*"[100] Ambedkar, however, adds a cultural context to Dewey's point on community and education, following these passages with the claim: "Culture spreads by diffusion and that is why one finds similarity between various primitive tribes in the matter of their habits and customs, beliefs and thoughts, although they do not live in proximity. But no one could say that because there was this similarity the primitive tribes constituted one society."[101]

As Ambedkar perceived in the 1908 *Ethics*, customs and social habits tended to define groupings of individuals. But as Dewey evolved—and Ambedkar the student and reader followed his changing thought through the progression of his courses and works—*Democracy and Education* added complexity to the situation by highlighting that even groups adapted to their environment and common struggle might not instantiate the ideals of *community*. In his 1916 book, Dewey expands this ideal to constitute the truly democratic, self-organized grouping of individuals with adaptive habits oriented toward growth. This explains why in *Annihilation of Caste* Ambedkar combines elements of these two approaches to ethics and criticizes Hindu society as not being a society, with its hierarchy of groups; it lacks the fundamental unity of purpose that characterizes a democratic society. "Society," for Dewey and Ambedkar, becomes a normative concept. As Ambedkar phrases it, "Men constitute a society because they have things which they possess in common. To have similar thing[s] is totally different from possessing things in common. And the only way by which men can come to possess things in common with one another is by being in communication with one another. This is merely another way of saying that Society continues to exist by communication indeed in communication."[102] This passage echoes and reconstructs part of Dewey's *Democracy and Education*, in which the American writes:

> *Society* not only continues *to exist by* transmission, *by communication*, but it may fairly be said to exist in transmission, *in communication*. There is more than a verbal tie between the words common, community, and communication. *Men* live in a community in virtue of the *things which they* have in common; and *communication* is *the way* in which they *come to possess things in common*. What they must have in common in order to form a community or society are aims, beliefs, aspirations, knowledge—a common understanding—like-mindedness as the sociologists say.[103]

Ambedkar was taken by Dewey's diagnosis of the problems that could beset a nondemocratic group, but his problematic was different. His primary target of using this approach of society-focused analysis was the structured hierarchy of caste, one that rendered the seemingly unified society of "Hindu religion" not unified in the domains that matter: communication patterns and interests rendered habitual. Adopting *Democracy and Education*'s approach, Ambedkar diagnosed the problem of Hinduism in pragmatic terms: caste precluded deep communication and sharing of interests, vital characteristics of a *like-minded* society. As we saw in the previous chapter, Ambedkar draws on this same passage—and includes Dewey's mention of "like-mindedness"—in his 1919 testimony to the Southborough Commission. The problems of caste, society, and community are rendered in terms of communication and sharing, and these augment different points explored in Dewey's *Democracy and Education*. As Ambedkar continues in *Annihilation of Caste*:

> What is necessary is for a man to share and participate in a common activity so that the same emotions are aroused in him that animate the others. Making the individual a sharer or partner in the associated activity so that he feels its success as his success, its failure as his failure is the real thing that binds men and makes a society of them. The Caste System prevents common activity and by preventing common activity it has prevented the Hindus from becoming a society with a unified life and a consciousness of its own being.[104]

This passage extends Dewey's analysis in the early chapter of *Democracy and Education*, "Education as a Necessity of Life," to encompass a critique of a seemingly united, but oppressive, society dominated by the upper castes (especially Brahmins, for Ambedkar's analysis). It's illuminating to look at Dewey's original passage to see the resonances and divergences:

> *Making the individual a sharer or partner in the associated activity so that he feels its success* as his success, *its failure as his failure, is the* completing step. As soon as he is possessed by the emotional attitude of the group, he will be alert to recognize the special ends at which it aims and the means employed to secure success. His beliefs and ideas, in other words, will take a form similar to those of others in the group. He will also achieve pretty much the same stock of knowledge since that knowledge is an ingredient of his habitual pursuits.[105]

Dewey is talking about the fact, insofar as his *Democracy and Education* account goes, that social environments—encompassing social customs as discussed in his earlier *Ethics* and his Columbia courses—create shared meanings and the process of individual habit formation: through the meanings attached to actions, and their social consequences, the young member of society finds their "mental habitudes are gradually assimilated to those of [their] group."[106] Ambedkar as rhetor combines—and sometimes resists—the different emphases in Dewey's texts to form a unique critique of caste as destroying the ability of individuals to develop the habits needed to instantiate true community with others.

One can see a related point, made again in conversation with Dewey's various works, at another place in Ambedkar's 1936 assault on caste. Making the point that "nowhere is human society *one* single thing. It is always plural," Ambedkar appears to draw upon a claim by Dewey, highlighted by Ambedkar in his 1916 copy of *Democracy and Education*, that "society is one word, but many things."[107] Ambedkar then continues with his critique of Hinduism, while acknowledging the pragmatist idea of a spectrum of types of groups occurring in nature: "In the world of action, the individual is one limit and society the other. Between them lie all sorts of associative arrangements of lesser and larger scope, families, friendship, co-operative associations, business combines, political parties, bands of thieves and robbers. These small groups are usually firmly welded together and are often as exclusive as castes. They have a narrow and intensive code, which is often anti-social."[108] Ambedkar adds new ideas to Dewey's claim in his part of the final section of the 1908 *Ethics* that *"the world of action* is a world of which *the individual is one limit, and* humanity *the other; between them lie all sorts of associative arrangements of lesser and larger scope, families, friendships,* schools, clubs, organizations for making or distributing goods, for gathering and supplying commodities; activities politically organized by parishes, wards, villages, cities, counties, states, nations."[109] One sees Ambedkar transform parts of Dewey's text, and combine distinct passages and works, to make his own arguments against *caste*. In doing so, Dewey's emphases on schools and cities and so on evaporate, and in their place arise organizations and groups that make more sense given the social context in which Ambedkar and his audiences are located.

Ambedkar's criterion has recognizable antecedents in Dewey, but his application of it is unique to the context of caste oppression. For instance, combined with this partial echoing of Dewey's thoughts as of 1908 are his 1916 indications of the "ideal society." Ambedkar continues his critique of

Hindu caste hierarchy as antisocial by stating his standard: "The questions to be asked in determining what is an ideal society are: How numerous and varied are the interests which are consciously shared by the groups? How full and free is the interplay with other forms of associations? Are the forces that separate groups and classes more numerous than the forces that unite? What social significance is attached to this group life? Is its exclusiveness a matter of custom and convenience or is it a matter of religion?"[110] Ambedkar the reader underlines this passage, and Ambedkar the rhetor echoes Dewey's account of the social idea in *Annihilation of Caste*. Dewey's own statement in *Democracy and Education* claims that the standard is: "*How numerous and varied are the interests which are consciously shared? How full and free is the interplay with other forms of association?*"[111] Ambedkar adapts these criteria to question the unique aspects of caste in Hinduism, versus similar manifestations in other South Asian communities:

> It is in the light of these questions that one must decide whether caste among Non-Hindus is the same as caste among Hindus. If we apply these considerations to castes among Mohammedans, Sikhs and Christians on the one hand and to castes among Hindus on the other, you will find that caste among Non-Hindus is fundamentally different from caste among Hindus. First, the ties, which consciously make the Hindus hold together, are non-existent, while among Non-Hindus there are many that hold them together.[112]

This passage serves as an extension of Dewey's standard for the ideal community, which he spells out in terms of criminal associations in the American context. Speaking in *Democracy and Education*, Dewey put it as follows: "*If we apply these considerations to*, say, a criminal band, we *find that* the *ties which consciously hold* the members *together are* few in number, reducible almost to a common interest in plunder; and that they are of such a nature as to isolate the group from other groups with respect to give and take of the values of life."[113]

The sharing of interests implicates a certain personal autonomy that inhabits citizens in some relatively equal amount. This autonomy serves as a sort of liberty, or freedom and capacity for individualized self-direction. It is related to the idea of "effective freedom" that Dewey spoke of in his 1915–16 courses. We choose to share interests and have the ability to choose our own unique individual inflections in life and in the projects that we will be devoted to over the course of our existence. In other words, Ambedkar's evocation of fraternity is integrally connected to liberty and equality and reveals the state that is to be avoided: that of slavery or servitude. As Ambedkar was painfully aware, such slavery could be formal or informal, institutionalized or rendered culturally present through unspoken customs. In enunciating the value of liberty in his community ideal, Ambedkar again echoes Dewey in *Annihilation of Caste* and brings the concept of slavery into his analysis:

> But to object to this kind of liberty is to perpetuate slavery. For slavery does not merely mean a legalized form of subjection. It means a state of society in which some men are forced to accept from others the purposes which control their conduct. This condition obtains even where there is no slavery in the legal sense. It is found where, as in the Caste System, some persons are compelled to carry on certain prescribed callings which are not of their choice.[114]

Part of this passage adapts Dewey's discussion of Plato in *Democracy and Education*:

> Plato defined a slave as one who accepts from another the purposes which control his conduct. *This condition obtains even where there is no slavery in the legal sense*. It is found wherever men are engaged in activity which is socially serviceable, but whose service they do not understand and have no personal interest in.[115]

Ambedkar builds his conceptual structure using part of Dewey's argument; he reconstructs and uses these conceptual tools for a purpose that Dewey did not seem cognizant of: the critique of caste as inherently harmful for freedom and liberty.

Free citizens ought to be equal citizens. The exact nature of equality, however, is complex, as are the challenges in instantiating it while not creating new problems. This vital concept gets a pragmatist treatment in *Annihilation of Caste*:

> Equality may be a fiction but nonetheless one must accept it as the governing principle. A man's power is dependent upon (1) physical heredity, (2) social inheritance or endowment in the form of parental care, education, accumulation of scientific knowledge, everything which enables him to be more efficient than the savage, and finally, (3) on his own efforts. In all these three respects men are undoubtedly unequal. But the question is, shall we treat them as unequal because they are unequal? This is a question which the

opponents of equality must answer. From the standpoint of the individualist it may be just to treat men unequally so far as their efforts are unequal. It
may be desirable to give as much incentive as possible to the full development of every one's powers. . . . On the other hand it can be urged that if it is
good for the social body to get the most out of its members, it can get most
out of them only by making them equal as far as possible at the very start of
the race.[116]

Equality implicates and extends personal will, effort, and agency. In other
words, equality preserves the agential *force* or effective freedom of an individual living and acting among other forceful individuals.

In making this point, Ambedkar is engaging part of Tufts's final section in *Ethics* to create his argument against caste, identified here with the
echoed parts italicized:

> *A man's power is due (1) to physical heredity; (2) to social heredity, including*
> *care, education, and the stock of inventions, information, and institutions which*
> *enables him to be more efficient than the savage; and finally (3) to his own efforts.*
> Individualism may properly claim this third factor. It is just to treat men
> unequally so far as their efforts are unequal. It is socially desirable to give as
> much incentive as possible to the full development of every one's powers.
> But the very same reason demands that in the first two respects we treat men
> as equally as possible. For it is for the *good of the social body to get the most out*
> *of its members,* and *it can get the most out of them only* by giving them the best
> start possible.[117]

We see Ambedkar engaging another Deweyan text—this time, the 1908
*Ethics*—and using echoed portions as part of a novel argument against
caste. Ambedkar, dealing with the structural and religious inequalities bequeathed to India from a millennia-old religious framework, emphasizes
the inequalities among people in his context. He couples this emphasis
with a stronger reading of equality as a moral ideal. Even though caste
members are unequal now, that does not mean it is ideal or virtuous for
our future actions to continue to reinforce this inequality. The seemingly
naturalized inequality in Hindu culture may be one reason Ambedkar is
attracted to the three general values of equality, liberty, and fraternity as
a counterweight to the Sanskrit concepts (e.g., *dharma, moksha*) he could
have used as ideals. They allow him to show how his received tradition is
fundamentally at odds with the ideals of democratic community, without
lapsing into a new metaphysical essentialism.

In the following portions of *Annihilation of Caste*, Ambedkar seemingly advises the destruction of the current form of Hinduism that created this state of injustice—including its *shastras* and holy *vedas*. This was uttered by the same Ambedkar who burned a copy of the most famous *shastra* or law book, the *Manusmrti*, in 1927 during a protest for Dalit rights to communal water sources.[118] His Mandal audience would surely have been horrified had he uttered these solutions in a presidential address. But as the printed copy of his speech reveals, he was ultimately a *pragmatist* about such matters. He did not seek to destroy religion—or even Hinduism *per se*—simply to be free of all religious guidance. Even in the 1930s, a period of time identified with his rejection of Hinduism, he strives to clear up what he means "by destruction of religion." Acknowledging that "some may find the idea revolting to them and some may find it revolutionary," he explains his position by drawing a distinction between "principles and rules."[119] He then explains this distinction as follows:

> Rules are practical; they are habitual ways of doing things according to prescription. But principles are intellectual; they are useful methods of judging things. Rules seek to tell an agent just what course of action to pursue. Principles do not prescribe a specific course of action. Rules, like cooking recipes, do tell just what to do and how to do it. A principle, such as that of justice, supplies a main head by reference to which he is to consider the bearings of his desires and purposes, it guides him in his thinking by suggesting to him the important consideration which he should bear in mind. This difference between rules and principles makes the acts done in pursuit of them different in quality and in content.[120]

This builds upon the distinction that Ambedkar as reader highlighted in both of his copies of Dewey's (and Tufts's) *Ethics*. Here is how Dewey and Tufts put the distinction in the 1908 *Ethics*, with echoed passages italicized:

> *Rules are practical; they are habitual ways of doing things. But principles are intellectual; they are useful methods of judging things.* The fundamental error of the intuitionalist and of the utilitarian (represented in the quotation from Mill) is that they are on the lookout for rules which will of themselves *tell agents just what course of action to pursue;* whereas the object of moral principles is to supply standpoints and methods which will enable the individual to make for himself an analysis of the elements of good and evil in the particular situation in which he finds himself. No genuine moral *principle prescribes a specific course of action; rules, like cooking recipes, may tell just what to do and*

*how to do it. A moral principle, such as that* of chastity, of *justice*, of the golden rule, gives the agent a basis for looking at and examining a particular question that comes up. It holds before him certain possible aspects of the act; it warns him against taking a short or partial view of the act.[121]

Ambedkar appropriates the point from Dewey and Tufts's vision of ethics as an evolution from customary morality to reflective morality and applies it to the caste system.

In Ambedkar's new argument, caste is a harmful habit, based on rules, that needs reflective attention and melioration from a forceful individual. What is needed is the use of principles to sort through this complex, problematic social situation in India; Ambedkar wants to destroy Hinduism as a set of rules and replace it with "religion in the sense of spiritual principles."[122] This would be a type of religious orientation that would be "truly universal, applicable to all races, to all countries, to all times."[123] Whereas Dewey and Tufts's critique applied to overly sedimented habits of moral judgment in a social environment and within a group setting, Ambedkar adapts their normative framework to communities bound and conditioned by religion: "Religion must mainly be matter of principles only. It cannot be a matter of rules."[124] Might this be the bridge between Buddhism and pragmatism that Adlerblum recalled from the "Indian student" she so vividly remembered from her time at Columbia? Perhaps it was. In any case, Buddhism became the religion of principle that Ambedkar was searching for by the 1950s. Hinduism, in the form of a religion of rules, promulgates caste and results in a situation that Deweyan pragmatists would abhor: "[It] tends to deprive moral life of freedom and spontaneity and to reduce it (for the conscientious at any rate) to a *more* or less anxious and servile conformity to externally imposed rules."[125] The conclusion is clear. Even though his thought is clearly distinct from Dewey's pragmatism, Ambedkar chooses to make certain points using ideas and ideals from *Ethics* and *Democracy and Education* as material to appropriate, reconstruct, and even palpably resist. It is in this rhetorical engagement with Dewey and his texts that Ambedkar works out and performs important parts of his anticaste pragmatism.

## Reflective Morality, Orientation, and Pragmatic Reform

Emerging from this close analysis of the textual traces of Ambedkar's engagement with Dewey's pragmatism in his *Annihilation of Caste*, one can start to see the commitments of Ambedkar's own form of pragmatism as it was developing in the 1930s. A vital part of this pragmatist philosophy was its forum of development: Ambedkar worked it out in books, essays, and speeches that anticipated specific and unique audiences. He surely saw no value in abstract academic tomes on his theory of pragmatism. The value of pragmatism was in its *use* for his causes. The *Annihilation of Caste* was a perfect example of the rhetorical characteristic of Ambedkar's thought. As originally planned and formulated, Ambedkar's message was aimed at Hindu higher-caste reformers. Yet it occurred right after his announcements and appeals to his fellow Dalits to convert away from Hinduism. His appeals in the Mandal speech were not calibrated to strike the ears of an oppressed people considering conversion as a way out of caste oppression. He was talking to sympathetic, but all-too-Hindu, reformers. He selected his words and made his arguments with this audience in mind, one that was interested in reforming the caste structure so as to remove the most egregious instances of oppression of Dalits, but one that was also committed to a deep respect for the *vedas* and the *shastras*. Ambedkar's speech was constructed to persuade these individuals—committed to Hinduism as they were—that solving the problematic situation of caste involved radical measures, not piecemeal change. Ambedkar knew this was a tall order given the rhetorical situation. Why would Ambedkar plan on giving such a jarring and, most likely, ineffective address? Perhaps he had hopes of persuading—or converting—the reformers to his views on what anchored the caste system. Or perhaps he knew how much of a shock his message would be for these high-caste reformers—and others, once the shock to his audience reverberated beyond the specific (anticipated) performance at the Jat-Pat-Todak Mandal conference. There is, however, a way to read his response in this rhetorical situation that makes sense of the jarring mismatch between his message and his audience.[126]

Ambedkar bluntly asks his anticipated audience to destroy the *vedas* and *shastras*, texts that they seem committed to at all costs. Why would he ask something of a sympathetic audience that he knows they could not acquiesce to in meeting his communicative demands? Perhaps he overreached and misjudged the effectiveness of his persuasive abilities. This explanation would mean that the reformer pursued a path of reform that was not, and could not, be effective, at least to the anticipated audience of the Mandal's conference. This also assumes a rather straightforward model of persuasion and public address, one in which a rhetor asks his audiences for belief and/or action change, then succeeds or fails at getting compliance. Another reading of this situation is available, however, if we remember the formative themes of *reflective morality* that we saw Ambedkar underline in his copies of Dewey and Tufts's 1908 *Ethics*. One vital emphasis in that book is the idea that questioning or reexamining social mores and customs is essential to the highest stage of morality, *reflective morality*. This is an activity that, at least insofar as the 1908 *Ethics* puts it, is instantiated at the individual level. Societies made up of, and encouraging of, such individuals become *reflective societies*, but we should make no mistake about it—Dewey and Tufts conceptualize *principles* as cognitive instruments for an individual to practice reflective thinking and to gain more purchase on the intelligent ordering of values bequeathed to them by their surrounding social environment.

Ambedkar saw these emphases in his reading of *Ethics*, and he even revised an obscure line in the ethics that effectively defined *individualism* to read as a central commitment of his concerning *reform*: "The assertion by the individual of his own opinions and beliefs, his own independence and interest as over against group standards, group authority and group interests is the beginning of all reform."[127] We have already examined some of the surrounding context to this line (viz. its connection to the discussion of a Kantian form of individualism in *Ethics*), but here it is enough to emphasize that this altered line resists and changes the meaning in the original context in *Ethics*. For Ambedkar's pragmatist orientation, it stemmed from the fact that reform begins when *individuals* realize that the value and worth of social expectations, roles, and customs should be thought about and evaluated as they impact the individual's autonomy or liberty, their interests and capacities. Things do not gain normative import simply from being old or, as he put it in his review of Russell's book, simply by surviving. Moral value is not eternal, but it can be accessed by the reason-based thought of individuals. Individuals who do such an intelligent reevaluation of their place vis-à-vis their surrounding society are *reflective* and are reformers within Ambedkar's notion of reform. Ambedkar was one such individual, evincing his reconsideration of much of what his Hindu tradition and even Hindu myths told him about his place in the world. Ambedkar instantiated the pragmatist idea of the reflective thinker, the thinker irritated by some doubt or problematic aspect of experience and who attempted to meet their needs through an intelligent engagement with the materials provided by the situation and environment. In Ambedkar's case, this was coming to terms with and attempting to reform the *problematic situation* represented in and through social experience in a culture saturated with Hindu texts, concepts, customs, and traditions. He was questioning and challenging what society demanded he do, and a certain kind of sense can be made of the planned address by reading his message as an attempt to inculcate in his audience the same sort of reflective questioning.

Ambedkar's goal in the *Annihilation of Caste* need not be limited to convincing his anticipated audience of reform-minded Hindus to give up what they might think defines them as Hindus. His strong and sometimes shocking appeals to jettison central parts of the Hinduism of his day seem calculated to succeed with a variety of audiences committed to Hinduism precisely because they are unreasonable and jarring. This shock can be seen as a way to render the ordinary status quo of Hinduism as *problematic* in the Deweyan sense. Ambedkar read and annotated Dewey's *Experience and Nature* (the British version of the second edition issued in 1929), so he was well aware of the pragmatist commitment (from Peirce through James, Dewey, and Addams) to an uncertain, changing world of experience made palatable—and sometimes too concretized—through the intervention of human habits. At the social level, habits gained the nomenclature of "custom" or "mores," a point Ambedkar heard in Dewey's 131–132 courses. The emphasis on reflective morality that he saw and appropriated from the 1908 *Ethics* sat in an uneasy tension with the world made predictable by habit. Yet these habits and self-created certainties eventually run into conflicts generated by other habits, other agents, or the world that pushes back in the form of pain and thwarted desires. As Ambedkar puts it in his planned address, "Man's life is generally habitual and unreflective," a point that he surely saw as applying to his audience of higher-caste reformers affiliated with the Arya Samaj movement. He continues in a way that resonates with Dewey's idea of reflection in both *Ethics* and the educational contexts of *Democracy and Education*: "Reflective thought, in the sense of active, persistent and careful consideration of any belief or supposed form or knowledge in the light of the grounds that support it and further conclusions to which it tends, is quite rare and arises only in a situation which presents a dilemma—a crisis."[128] Ambedkar, through his rhetorical activities of crafting a shocking message in light of the needs and expectations of a specific audience, was oratorically creating a problematic situation for these auditors. Perhaps he created a problematic situation with too much exigency; after all, his talk was never given because of its provocative content. But the Mandal saw it in print, and many more read or heard his words through its three editions and its use as a text that was read at Dalit conferences Ambedkar was unable to attend in person.[129]

Ambedkar wanted to create in his audience the shock that would produce the irritation of doubt, the itch that needed rational and independent thought to satisfy. What would be the focus of this reflective reevaluation of Hindu society, if things went well for Ambedkar as rhetor? For his Mandal audience, it was a reflective consideration of the *habitual* roots of caste. As we saw in chapter 1's account of the Deweyan psychology that Ambedkar was exposed to in his Philosophy 231 course in fall 1914, a central tension is evident between individually located habits and attitudes and the formative forces at play in their social environment. Attitude was an important habit for individuals, since it conditioned their reactions to specific stimuli. Indeed, it did more than orient a passive organism to react in certain ways; as Dewey noted in his early critiques of dominant behaviorist tendencies in psychology, our mental habits send us out into the world looking for and anticipating certain stimuli.[130] In Dewey's psychology from the turn of the twentieth century onward, the organism was active at its deepest levels. In his thought as it appeared in the 1910s, these active and anticipatory characteristics were conditioned, shaped, and formed by societies and languages. Our societies tell us what objects are hated, dangerous, or to be desired; we internalize these anticipations, then act and react in accord with them.

In such essays as his seminar paper "Castes in India" from 1916, Ambedkar takes a more sociological approach to caste and its dysfunctions. By the 1930s, however, we see a clear and distinct emphasis on caste as integrally related to individual *attitudes* in addition to abstract entities like *systems* or *societies*. This is most likely due to his synthetic merging of the psychology he heard in 1914 and read in Dewey's 1916 *Democracy and Education* with the project of individual reflective morality proffered by the 1908 *Ethics*, along with other influences. Societies do affect individuals' habits of thinking and acting, but the primacy in *Annihilation of Caste* comes down ultimately to what habits or attitudes individuals possess or reject. As he puts it in 1936, "Caste is a notion, it is a state of the mind. The destruction of Caste does not therefore mean the destruction of a physical barrier. It means a *notional* change."[131] Hindus who practice caste are not inhuman or "wrong headed," Ambedkar claims. They simply are following and internalizing social customs that govern their communicative activities and their normative reactions in a way that is not reflected upon or examined. In other words, they are "deeply religious," to such an extent that reflective examination of the implications and harms of their habits escape them. They are not practicing reflective morality when they need to most.

This was all well and good for a high-caste audience, had they heard this speech. The shocking part, at least for the reformers of the Mandal, comes from Ambedkar's diagnosis of the cause of the problem. The revolution he wanted in society would not come from altering the statutes of a given municipality, or as the socialists claim, revolution for the oppressed economic classes. Caste indicated a deep-seated social problem that had its roots in a "mental attitude" or orientation of caste members toward other castes.[132] Reorganize the material and economic matter of society, and the socialist will still face the mental attitude that is caste: "Turn in any direction you like, caste is the monster that crosses your path. You cannot have political reform, you cannot have economic reform, unless you kill this monster."[133] This monster of caste is not physical; it is very similar to the mental habits and attitudes Dewey talks of in his work on ethics and education from the 1910s and 1920s. Ambedkar remarks that "in every Hindu the consciousness that exists is the consciousness of his caste."[134] Ambedkar was shifting the focus from a revolution against the external force of an overtly oppressive political system to one of an epochal reorientation within each member of society. To revolt against the monster of caste, then, is to address these mental habits that condition the consciousness of those who comprise various social groups in Indian society. What Ambedkar sought first was a mental revolution within Indians implicated in the caste system, both among those oppressing and those who are oppressed. How to achieve this mental revolution—in self and in others—became the problematic of his pragmatism in various contexts of application from the 1930s onward.

Ambedkar's response to solving caste oppression is complex and multifaceted. As Dewey told Ambedkar's class, habits interact with the abstracted category of group custom, and custom affects and can be affected by institutions. Part of Ambedkar's advocacy is aimed at institutional or legal change, a facet amply explored and emphasized in the literature on Ambedkar.[135] What the focus on pragmatism and rhetoric brings to the forefront are the often-overlooked aspects of force, psychology, and the dialectic between individual-collective that enables various nonexclusive paths of rhetorical meliorism. In texts like *Annihilation of Caste*, such an approach allows us to appreciate Ambedkar's emphasis on adjusting or meliorating habits of caste as reified in individual habits of thinking, judgment, and communicating. Shortly after claiming that "all reform consists in a change in the notions, sentiment and mental attitudes of the people towards men and things," Ambedkar relates his reading of caste as attitude to language. Words and labels, as Dewey pointed out in his Philosophy 231 lectures in 1914, can become sedimented as objects of experience holding certain valences and values. We can fool ourselves into thinking that words means only *this*, and that objects that bear that label also mean only *this*. Ambedkar seems particularly concerned with applying this psychology of attitude and language to caste since caste (*varna*) is so integrally connected to distinct terms, labels, and categories. The language of caste, it seems, maps perfectly onto the reality and essential values of actual individuals and groups.[136] As Ambedkar puts this psychology in his planned 1936 address to the Mandal:

> It is common experience that certain names become associated with certain notions and sentiments, which determine a person's attitude towards men and things. The names, Brahmin, Kshatriya, Vaishya and Shudra, are names which are associated with a definite and fixed notion in the mind of every Hindu. That notion is that of a hierarchy based on birth. So long as these names continue, Hindus will continue to think of the Brahmin, Kshatriya, Vaishya and Shudra as hierarchical divisions of high and low, based on birth, and act accordingly.[137]

Caste is a notion, a state of mind, and such attitudinal habits get sedimented and connected to linguistic bearers of meaning such as caste labels. Our labels and terms can evoke and strengthen these attitudes.

Reflective thinking, a key term in the 1908 *Ethics*, is merged in Ambedkar's pragmatism with the idea that environments can be intentionally or unintentionally educative—including the social environment largely comprised of other individuals communicating with and about each other in specific, contingent, and ultimately changeable ways. Groups socialize individuals with the religious and caste-based concepts and rhetoric that shape their future actions and reactions to self and others. Ambedkar remarks in *Annihilation of Caste* that "the Hindu must be made to unlearn all this. But how can this happen if the old labels remain and continue to recall to his mind old notions?"[138] In a manuscript that was assembled sometime after 1951, Ambedkar includes a chapter titled "Away from the Hindus." In this chapter, we see a continued emphasis on caste names being correlated with an internalized caste psychology:

> Unfortunately, names serve a very important purpose. They play a great part in social economy. Names are symbols. Each name represents association of certain ideas and notions about a certain object. It is a label. From the label people know what it is. It saves them the trouble of examining each case individually and determine for themselves whether the ideas and notions commonly associated with the object are true. People in society have to deal with so many objects that it would be impossible for them to examine each

case. They must go by the name that is why all advertisers are keen in finding a good name. If the name is not attractive the article does not go down with the people.[139]

Names and labels are concretizations of habits of action, reaction, and judgment. They are normative, in other words. In the caste matrix, caste labels become associated with the extreme valuing and devaluing that grounds the harmful actions and reactions of caste individuals to each other, or of policies and institutions to members of a certain group or class. As Ambedkar puts the point in this later essay, "The name 'Untouchable' is a bad name. It repels, forbids, and stinks. The social attitude of the Hindu towards the Untouchable is determined by the very name 'Untouchable.' There is a fixed attitude towards 'Untouchables' which is determined by the stink which is imbedded in the name."[140] The central idea of caste as a problematic and deep-seated mental attitude or habit stuck with Ambedkar long after the dust settled from the *Annihilation of Caste* controversy.

Ambedkar's solution, as we will explore in his addresses to his Dalit followers in the next chapter, will foreground conversion and the donning of new labels of identity. This movement was hinted at in *Annihilation of Caste*, even to the anticipated audience of higher-caste individuals, as he claims that "if new notions are to be inculcated in the minds of people it is necessary to give them new names. To continue the old name is to make the reform futile. To allow this Chaturvarnya, based on worth to be designated by such stinking labels of Brahmin, Kshatriya, Vaishya, Shudra, indicative of social divisions based on birth, is a snare."[141] As he was to tell his fellow Dalits in another speech in 1936, changing religions is integrally connected to changing the names one is known by. According to the Deweyan psychology Ambedkar is extending, our concepts and labels send us out into the world looking for certain things as bearers of value, and also as objects of attraction, fear, or disgust.

This diagnosis of caste as mindset or orientation is vital for Ambedkar's rhetoric of reorientation: it is what persuasion will target, what conversion will attack, and it is what the forceful agent will change. But here we see a stage of induced *reflection* followed by a stage of *renunciation* emerging in his religious rhetoric. For his high-caste audience, Ambedkar focuses primarily on persuading them to reflectively examine and abandon key parts of their religious heritage. Speaking of the attitudes constitutive of a Hindu individual, Ambedkar claims that "religion compels the Hindus to treat isolation and segregation of caste as a virtue. Religion does not compel the Non-Hindu to take the same attitude toward caste. If Hindus wish to break caste, their religion will come in their way."[142] Combine this deep critique of the customs rendered habitual with his criticism of smaller reforms that might be supported by the Mandal, and one sees the inevitable shocking conclusion. Intercaste dinners, a move often debated in social reform circles targeting caste, are physical and outer activities that do not necessarily kill "the spirit of Caste and the consciousness of Caste"; they do not affect the *orientation* of those dining.[143] Ambedkar agrees with the Mandal's thematic of intercaste marriage, claiming at one point that "the real remedy for breaking Caste is inter-marriage. Nothing else will serve as the solvent of Caste."[144]

Ambedkar's Deweyan *ethos*, however, goes deeper than advocating changes in a few external activities. One could marry another and still see them as lesser in value or as not deserving the same rights to equality and liberty as one receives. In addition, to fully implement sustainable schemes of intercaste marriage, we must remove the orientational causes resisting it, and to do this we must address the root cause of these orientations: religion or Hindu society, for Ambedkar. By building upon aspects of social reform that are familiar and palatable to the members of the Mandal, Ambedkar uses shared spaces of agreement to incline his caste audience toward the more radical and shocking program represented by his rhetoric of religious reorientation. He and the Mandal agree on one putative solution, intercaste marriage. But this solution's implementation is precluded by existing caste structures, and those structures are not physical but mental. The only way to truly affect these mental attitudes is to "apply the dynamite to the *Vedas* and the *Shastras*, which deny any part to reason, to *Vedas* and *Shastras*, which deny any part to morality. You must destroy the Religion of the *Shrutis* and the *Smritis*. Nothing else will avail. This is my considered view of the matter."[145]

The solution that follows from this shocking conclusion, for Ambedkar, will involve reflective thought. Ambedkar claims that the "two most powerful weapons in the armoury of a reformer" are "reason and morality."[146] The latter concept, morality, is integrally related to the notion of reflective morality in its Deweyan senses. Ambedkar explicitly combines the need for reflection with the instruments represented by conceptual overlays labeled by Dewey and Tufts as "principles." Assuming his audience will balk at his suggestion to destroy their religion, Ambedkar clarifies his claim: he instead asks his audience to destroy a *religion of rules* and leaves open the option of reconstructing Hinduism as a *religion of principle*. Reflection and principles are closely related. Reason seems to be connected to the ability to form, apply, and reform *principles* that govern activity and thought.

Rules are synonymous with closed and set social customs that clearly incline the individual to act and react in certain ways. Caste is just this sort of attitude, one that makes Hindus recoil from certain caste-marked individuals. Ambedkar wants his Hindu audience to seek a religion that is "a matter of principles only," preferably universal spiritual principles; perhaps it can be derived from the *Upanishads*, but in all likelihood it will involve the rejection of sacred texts like the *shastras* in a way, as the Buddha and Guru Nanak evinced.[147] The "finality and fixity" of a rule-based religion of Hinduism ought to be abandoned, Ambedkar argues. Employing the language of a pragmatist inspired by a desire to engage a world without set categories, Ambedkar points out that "happiness notoriously varies with conditions and circumstances of a person, as well as with the conditions of different people and epochs. That being the case, how can humanity endure this code of eternal laws, without being cramped and without being crippled?"[148] Here we see Ambedkar deploying the vocabulary of an antifoundationalist pragmatism to question the most foundational matter of his high-caste Hindu audience's lives: their religious orientation and its entailed rules of behavior and caste. Religious reorientation, reflective thinking, or reconstruction begins with his audience (or readers) moving away *from* an orientation or attitude they have unreflectively held so dear. It therefore represents an *intelligent* use of persuasive force as one primary way to change or meliorate habits in line with the democratic ideals and ends that Dewey and Ambedkar shared.

# FIVE

# Education, Force, and the Will to Convert

Throughout all the phases of his career as a public advocate for Dalits, Ambedkar evinced a belief that *oratory* or *rhetoric* in public speech can change people and thereby change society for the better. Ambedkar obviously put weight on systemic changes—he was the chief architect of India's constitution, after all, and he seemed to always be vying for political office. But public address and persuasion is a thread weaving its way through much of his various activities and political life. Ambedkar was a master of using newspaper publications and large conference events to reach his audiences, both literate and illiterate. In his later years, he redoubled his commitment to the art of speaking as a way to free the Dalits from the chains of caste oppression. At an award ceremony for a speaking contest held on the grounds of Siddharth College on January 14, 1948, he argued for the importance of cultivating the art of speaking, citing famous Indian orators (Gopal Krishna Gokhale, Pherozeshah Mehta) and non-Indian orators (Winston Churchill) as examples of the hard work such cultivation entailed.[1] The art of speaking is not solely about achieving a speaker's desired result. Ambedkar explains this qualification in his address to the student parliament of Siddharth College on September 25, 1947. There he notes a subtle distinction between *force* that cuts off community and *eloquence* that persuades others. Autocracies involve laws being made by the dictates of a tyrant or monarch; such a dictator

> need not pay any attention to eloquence because his will is law. But in a parliament where laws are made, no doubt by the wishes of the people, the man who succeeds in winning our opposition is the man who possesses the art to persuade his opponent. You cannot win over a majority in this House

by giving a black eye to your opponent. . . . You will have to carry a proposi-
tion only by the art of speaking, by persuading [your] opponent, by winning
him over his side by argument, either gentle or strong, but always logically
and instructively.[2]

This is a vital point in Ambedkar's theory of social change: persuasion represents a "soft force," even in vigorous argument and agitation, because it
upholds the value of the target of persuasive activity. Unlike the habits of
caste, it allows for a mutuality of interaction *and* value, even in situations
of critique and argument. Solving a social problem with such an approach
not only includes getting your way, it also insists on not creating more enemies among your conversational partners. Drawing on his decades of vic-
tory and defeats in the forums of policy deliberation, Ambedkar tells the
student leaders that "although Parliamentary Democracy for the purpose
accepted the principle of a majority rule do not think that you can by any
way you like ill-treat or put to a disadvantage a minority. You will create
a great deal of trouble for yourself in this very House. The minority must
always be won over. It must never be dictated to."[3] Persuasion succeeds in
light of a specific audience, and it ought to create the conditions among
that audience for success in future interactions.

Persuasion, education, and reform all combined in Ambedkar's two-
decade-long campaign of oratory among his followers, the oppressed
Dalits whom he wanted to convince that conversion was vital to their
emancipation and self-respect. In many ways, Ambedkar's pragmatist philosophy reached its culmination in the conversion movement, an absolutely unique event in the philosophical evolution of pragmatism around
the world. This chapter explores Ambedkar's persuasive activity directed at
his fellow Dalits from the 1930s and beyond in service to this conversion
movement. The following questions that emerge synthesize Ambedkar's
concerns as a pragmatist thinker with his skill as a persuasive rhetor: Why
did Ambedkar employ the rhetoric of conversion as a sustained strategy in
speaking to his audiences of fellow Dalits? How does conversion extend
or reimagine the Deweyan pragmatism that Ambedkar encountered during his education at Columbia and in the pages of the beloved books that
he counted as his constant companions? How might his rhetoric of conversion reveal lines of influence that both *echo* and *resist* Dewey's conceptual moves regarding political philosophy and the individual? What might
this complex relationship with Dewey's evolving thought reveal about
Ambedkar's evolving form of pragmatism?

## Self-Realization, Dewey's Early Psychology, and the Power of Conversion

Ambedkar's pragmatist commitments—and, as we shall see, his resistance to certain aspects of Dewey's early thought—forced him to consider the sorts of habits his audience might have and ideally should cultivate. These intellectual commitments shaped and formed his rhetoric of conversion, which in turn gave body to his attempts to shape and reform his audience by advocating the act of conversion. In 1936, he not only spoke about the need to annihilate caste—and potentially crucial parts of Hinduism—to individuals who were almost unchangeably tied to some version of Hindu identity, he also initiated what would become a decades-long campaign of advocating for the conversion of his fellow Dalits as a means of emancipation from caste oppression. For his Dalit audiences, his goal was to rhetorically affect this reorientation toward self, other, and community in the world. The frustration that grounded these appeals had come to a head in the 1930s, as Keer puts it, since "for the past ten years Ambedkar had tried in vain to create an opening for his people into Hindu society. He had to fight to secure for his people the right of drinking water from public places, the liberty of wearing good dress and of using metal utensils, and the right of receiving education."[4] At Yeola in 1935, he declared his urge to leave the folds of Hinduism through conversion. After the controversy surrounding *Annihilation of Caste*, he became convinced that higher-caste reformers were not willing to make the sacrifices needed to lift the Dalits out of their social predicament. Shortly after that address was supposed to occur, Ambedkar delivered a speech in Marathi known as "What Way Emancipation?" to an exclusively Mahar audience of approximately thirty-five thousand people attending the All-Bombay District Mahar Conference on May 30–31, 1936.[5] These audience members, like Ambedkar, had all personally experienced the oppression, humiliation, and harm that being labeled as a Dalit entailed. This personal connection between the rhetor and his topic most likely explains why this audience sat in rapt attention through all fifty pages of Ambedkar's oration.[6]

What we shall see in examining his appeals to his fellow Dalits in 1936 is a theme deeply embedded in his engagement with pragmatism: the importance of personal effort and will in developing one's individuality, especially in the face of social sanctions and customs that would seek to crush such a spirit of assertion. But it helps to pause for a moment and consider the relative incredulity some must have felt when Ambedkar proposed conversion as a solution to their oppression. Was this not a way of foisting the problem of caste prejudice onto those affected in an unjust fashion by the actions of others? Would it even be successful? How could one's own conversion solve something that we are tempted to label now as systematic oppression, an injustice that meets each and every one born to certain classes of parents? In other words, conversion seems to be an *individual* strategy of action that hopes to alleviate problems with *systems* and among *classes.* Ambedkar seems to have sensed these tensions, as he early on indicates in his 1936 speech that "the matter of conversion" should be approached from "two aspects": "Social as well as Religious; Material as well as Spiritual."[7] This is a rather curious way of putting his point, since he effectively identifies *four* aspects on two continuums: social, religious, material, and spiritual. From his following explanation, however, it seems that the social *is* the material, and religion *is* the spiritual, at least in this speech's manner of cutting up the matter of conversion. Dalits suffer from deprivation, assault, and want in the Hindu system that defines them as "untouchables." This entails and enables a corresponding lack of self-respect and dignity through their having to assume a religious or spiritual system that defines them as without value. Thus, social power is related to spiritual or religious matters. Paradoxically, Ambedkar's invocation of the rhetoric of conversion hopes to invert this relationship; instead of material oppression leading to spiritual depression, the idea is to use a change in religion to affect the material fortunes of Dalits.

Conversion and the problematic situation of caste-based oppression that evokes it therefore serve as arenas for religious and ideological forces to play out on the bodies and minds of Indians. There is a clear power dynamic to this situation, but Ambedkar also realizes there is a *class*-based dimension to it. As he puts it to his Mahar audience, "the problem of untouchability is a matter of class struggle" between "Caste-Hindus and the Untouchables."[8] But Ambedkar's appeal is to *each* "untouchable" audience member, holding in tension an important commitment of his pragmatism: *individuals* must be conceptualized as empowered to solve problems that can be analyzed also as *group* or *class* phenomena. This stems partially from Ambedkar's exposure to Dewey's psychology of habit and impulse, which inhabits the "psychological standpoint" and gets altered with Dewey's accounts of community and education after the 1908 *Ethics,* which further emphasizes the social dimensions of experience.

But one thing has not changed: Ambedkar's engagement with the dynamics of force and reform. How can his audience reform themselves and their oppressive situations, if that is indeed the right path, and where can this force come from that will create their effective freedom? How can

*Ambedkar* spur them to take such a path? Ambedkar's rhetoric of reorientation and its engagement with the problematics of force becomes prominent in this 1936 address when he foregrounds the sources of power available to his Mahar audience yearning for justice and dignity. Ambedkar canvasses three sources of power and first claims that their effective power does not lie in numbers or "man-power," since there is the chance that other Dalit groups will not show solidarity with the Mahars. Ambedkar admits that Dalits in the Bombay Presidency are only one-eighth of the population. Does their strength lie in money or financial sources of power to effect changes? The Mahars, like other Dalit groups, tended to lack financial means due to their systematic exclusion from the mainstream economy of India. Ambedkar postulates one final area that power can stem from in social matters: the realm of psychological resilience, or mental strength. He is initially pessimistic about this source of power, since "for centuries, you have not only served the higher caste but also tolerated their insults and tyranny without grudge and complaint, which has killed the sense to retort and revolt."[9] The Dalits have become habituated to being societal slaves. This is the orientational reality of the caste system as a form of mental slavery. Ambedkar's rhetoric of reorientation is promised as a way to remove the weakness and lack of self-respect entailed in this mental slavery, but Ambedkar is no fool; habits and attitudes established over a lifetime cannot be undone immediately. Yet conversion seems to promise to do just this in some manner. How can it hope to be this efficacious? Or put in a way that foregrounds the *spiritual* aspect of the solution to this religious problem, why should one have *faith* that conversion out of Hinduism will solve each individual Dalit's oppression?

Ambedkar has faith in conversion because he thinks so highly of religion as a way of structuring and shaping interactions, communities, and experience. In this manner, he differs from Dewey's mature pragmatism of the 1920s and 1930s, which did not place religion at the center of its approaches.[10] For Ambedkar, religion was central to diagnosing the problems of India and to identifying their solutions. But his notion of religion was unique. There was not one true religion, nor were all religions really the same; there were religions in the plural, each with its own way of orienting an individual toward society and nature. Like habits, religions could be changed or meliorated. Conversion, viewed through this approach, became an important program of rehabituation of the living organisms that comprised a society. Unlike quotidian habits, however, religion was noteworthy because it entailed habits that had a wide focus and because it exhibited a binding and shaping force over individuals, classes, and groups.

Interestingly, Ambedkar states that he takes this strong notion of religion from Bal Gangadhar Tilak (also known as Lokmanya Tilak; 1856–1920), an Indian nationalist and "the foremost leader of the *Sanatani* Hindus."[11] Even though he disagreed with Tilak on the *sanatan* or timeless nature of the Sanskrit tradition and the priority of political reform, Ambedkar shared with him the idea that religion is "that which governs" or holds people. The binding force that holds or governs people could be conceptualized as an external force, as caste oppression of the "lower" castes might seem to those bearing the brunt of the religious rules of purity and impurity. But these rules only work insofar as people—the individual organisms that bear habits and attitudes that make religion a flesh and blood reality— operate on and within their conceptual strictures. The paradox appears that religions *bind* or *hold* individuals, but individuals play an important role in instantiating or enabling this governance. In an important way, humans choose the religion that holds them to a certain course in experience. If re- ligion is a self-chosen, or self-instantiated, binding of activity and possibil- ity, might we possess, or at least hope we possess, the strength to alter these bindings by instituting another way of forming ourselves and our world?

These are questions about the nature of religion, a query that Ambedkar asserts is very relevant to the worldly concerns of many in his audience. Re- vealing the practical tendencies at the center of his pragmatism, he quickly links this discussion in his speech to another way of asking this question about the ideal binding of human life and how it might be changed: "What should be the relation between a man and society?"[12] In this speech to oppressed—and most likely, illiterate and uneducated—Mahars, Ambed- kar makes a curious digression into the "answers" to this query about the relations between individual and society given by "modern social philoso- phers."[13] While this surely could not have had a strong resonance with his audience, it does reveal the thought process behind his appeals for con- version. Thinking out loud about positions he would soon reject in the speech, he indicates that these unnamed social philosophers postulated three different relationships possible between the individual and the state. "Some," perhaps those political thinkers following in the social contract tradition growing out of Locke and Hobbes, "have said that the ultimate goal of society is to achieve happiness for the individual."[14] In this case, laws are a coercive necessity, with trade-offs with individual freedom, but all having the larger goal of securing a peaceful and happy existence for citizens. A second group, perhaps denoting neo-Kantian idealists like T. H. Green, a philosopher that Ambedkar encountered in Dewey's 131–132 courses, is said to have argued that "society exists for the development of the inherent qualities and energies of man and [to] help him to develop his self."[15] And a third group of philosophers asserted that "the chief object of social organization is not the development or happiness of the individual but the creation of an ideal society," a nod perhaps to the Platonic view of the ideally just state involving a precise balance among its constituent elements and classes.[16] Ambedkar does not name any of these thinkers, but it's clear that he is disagreeing with ideas and ideals of the state that in some way reduce individuality to elevate the powers of the group. Hinduism goes beyond the flaws of these approaches with its graded hierarchy, leading Ambedkar to quickly claim that "Hindu religion is, however, very different from all these concepts" and that it has "no place for an individual."[17] In his 1936 *Annihilation of Caste*, Ambedkar echoes Dewey's exact criticism of Plato as "lumping of individuals into a few sharply marked-off classes," resulting in a problematic and "very superficial view of man and his powers. It is purely constructed about a 'class-concept.'"[18] In the present speech discussing conversion, Ambedkar makes it clear that a satisfactory account of religion, as well as society, must foreground what is left out of many philosophies (including Hinduism and Platonism): a recognition of the individual. As he puts it in criticizing both Hinduism *and* these "modern social philosophers," "mere social welfare cannot be the ultimate goal of religion," and presumably, society.

What is Ambedkar's ideal relation of individual and society? After criticizing these other approaches (and Hinduism), he argues that his ideal prioritizes the individual and their development: "Man's life is independent. He is born not for the service of the society but for his self development." Shortly after this point, Ambedkar reaffirms this faith in the individual as ideal, stating that "the basic idea underlying a religion is to create an atmosphere for the spiritual development of an individual."[19] Ambedkar seems to be agreeing with the second answer that unnamed philosophers posited, namely, the idea that society exists to "help him to develop his self." Yet he explicitly disagreed with this option, as well as the other two readings of the relationship between the individual and society. What explains this tension in Ambedkar's analysis of the individual and their development in social settings? If one is sensitive and attentive to Ambedkar's constant, even if implicit, reference to Dewey's thought when it comes to matters of social and political philosophy, and one is sensitive to the development and detours that Dewey's thought evinced, one can answer this question. Ambedkar's tensions over individual and society are connected to his engagement with an early idealist essay of Dewey's, "The Ethics of Democracy" (1888), and illustrate how his pragmatism both extended and resisted certain doctrines of his American professor.

Why should we think that "The Ethics of Democracy" informs Ambedkar's appeals in 1936? First, as we shall see, Dewey's early idealist reading of individuality and its organic relation to society both fit into Ambedkar's preferred answer, as well as the second option that extends the idealist views prevalent in England and America concerning Hegel, self-development, and the role of the state. Second, Ambedkar follows Dewey's 1888 essay in connecting self-development and human personality as a political and moral ideal with three values that reappear throughout Ambedkar's work: sympathy (fraternity, effectively), equality, and liberty. In his "Ethics of Democracy" essay, Dewey ties the central ethical ideal of personality "with the other notes of democracy, liberty, equality, fraternity," which form the "highest ethical ideal."[20] But there is more evidence to highlight Ambedkar's sustained interest in this early text of Dewey's idealist period. In 1954, Ambedkar corresponded with a Dalit student in London, V. B. Kadam, about a range of topics. Included were Ambedkar's requests for Kadam to purchase books that were needed for Ambedkar's various writing projects. One work that he requested was "a very valuable book called 'Democracy' by John Dewey," which is eventually revealed in following correspondence to be Dewey's 1888 essay, "The Ethics of Democracy." In these letters from August and September 1954, Ambedkar notes that he had the essay—and had parts of it committed to memory—but that he had recently lost it. Even in his final years, Ambedkar saw the importance of Dewey's early idealist thought for his own democratic projects. "I am writing a book on Democracy in India," Ambedkar tells Kadam in a letter in August 1954, "for this I need very much Dewey's book." Kadam eventually copied and sent this essay, after first mistakenly sending Dewey's 1939 "Creative Democracy— The Task Before Us" speech, to Ambedkar on September 17, 1954.[21] "The Ethics of Democracy" was so important that he sought another copy in his final years, but the question remains: Did Ambedkar have access to this 1888 essay—one of Dewey's first works on political and social matters—in the 1930s?

From the available textual evidence, we can be certain he had it in his possession in the early 1930s. In a speech delivered to the All India Depressed Classes Congress conference held in Nagpur on August 8, 1930, Ambedkar engaged the political and social problems of India by answering the central question, "How can a heterogeneous mass of humanity function as a self-governing community?"[22] His speech was lengthy, but at a crucial point he appealed to his oppressed class fellows:

Gentlemen, you must be on guard against being led away by such a mechanical notion of human conduct. If you will beware of such abstraction you will realize that men cannot be reduced for political purposes any more than for any other, to bare figures, marks to be placed in rows over against one another. A man when he comes to vote—taking that to be the embodiment of politics—does not put off from him, like a suit of old clothes, his outlook, his interests and his opinions and become a naked unit. He carries with him in his voting all that which goes to make his personality and determine his attitude towards life.[23]

This passage shows Ambedkar's commitment to a form of political and social organization that uplifts individuals and groups and that resists sacrificing or mechanically crushing any given subset of the social unit. It also is an echo of a passage in Dewey's "The Ethics of Democracy" that evaluates elitist critiques of democracy as purely a numerical matter of governing, issued by thinkers such as Sir Henry Maine. This passage in Dewey follows, with the parts echoed by Ambedkar in 1930 italicized:

But the student of society has constantly to be *on* his *guard against* the abstract and purely *mechanical notions* introduced from the physical sciences. *If he will beware of such abstractions, he will* remember *that men cannot be reduced for political purposes, any more than for any other, to bare figure* ones, *marks to be placed in rows* set *over against one another. A man when he comes to vote does not put off from him, like a suit of old clothes, his* character, his wealth, his social influence, his devotion to political *interests, and become a naked unit. He carries with him in his voting all* the influence *that* he should have, and if he deserves twice as much as another man, it is safe to say that he decides twice as many votes as that other man.[24]

Ambedkar clearly had the 1888 essay in his possession or memory as of 1930 and saw it as a source of valuable inspiration for argument reconstruction. But like the echoes in *Annihilation of Caste*, Ambedkar appropriates Dewey's phrases and ideas only to make a new and creative use of them. For instance, we see Ambedkar graft on a crucial addition at the end of this passage: instead of political voting bringing a person's *influence* with it, Ambedkar argues that voting carries "all that which goes to make his personality and determine his attitude towards life." Ambedkar brings the concept of *personality* to the foreground in sustaining a notion of democracy that uplifts individuals and communities.

This is not an isolated evocation of this central term in the philosophy of self-development, however. Individual *personality* is a recurring theme in Ambedkar's philosophy and activist endeavors. His 1918 review of Russell's book makes reference to certain industrial systems "dwarfing the personality" of workers, and in his 1919 Southborough testimony, Ambedkar refers to the "growth of personality" being hampered by forms of government that "develop the personality of the few at the cost of the many—a result scrupulously to be avoided in the interest of Democracy."[25] Later in his arguments to the Southborough committee, he claims that "not only has untouchability arrested the growth of their personality but also it comes in the way of their material well-being."[26] In a speech to the All India Depressed Classes Conference held at Nagpur on July 18–20, 1942, Ambedkar casts his appeals to his followers in the rhetoric of combat, claiming that their struggle is "a battle for the reclamation of human personality which has been suppressed and mutilated by the Hindu Social System."[27] Ambedkar seems struck by the usefulness of this concept so central to Dewey's early reading of democracy; Dewey indeed claims in his 1888 essay that "democracy means that *personality* is the first and final reality."

To ascertain the import of Ambedkar's revising of Dewey's way of formulating the relationship between the individual and society, we must dive deeper into Dewey's early idealist reading of the interrelations among the individual, the group, and the state resident in his thought around 1888. "The Ethics of Democracy" was notable because it was one of his first forays into political thought in his neo-Hegelian phase, a period in his intellectual development that spanned most of his time teaching at the University of Michigan and the University of Chicago, the major appointments that preceded Dewey's move to Columbia University in 1904. In the 1880s, Dewey was entranced with neo-idealism, a way of engaging central topics in philosophy such as epistemology and metaphysics firmly rooted in a Hegelian approach. Dewey's education at Johns Hopkins University in the nation's first secular philosophy graduate program during the early 1880s was formative because it exposed him to two diametrically opposed intellectual lights, George S. Morris and G. Stanley Hall. As Dewey's biographers illustrate, these two thinkers exerted contrary pulls on Dewey toward neo-idealism and empirical psychology.[28] Morris represented the former vector of force, giving Dewey an intriguing reading of Hegelian idealism that emphasized the development of self and the correspondence of self with a Hegelian Absolute. For Morris's religiously inspired idealism, the self was both the center of experience and the crux of the objective world: "We must regard self as not only individual, but also universal or participating in— organically one with—the universal."[29] As Jennifer Welchman points out in her study of Dewey's early ethics, for idealists like Morris (and Dewey), all knowledge was self-knowledge, since it involved and implicated objects as known by some self or locus of consciousness.[30] This line of argument extended similar claims made by F. H. Bradley that impugned empiricist lines of thought in British philosophy that seemed to make all knowledge a matter of knowing material things and hence as excluding any vital sense of consciousness or self. Thinkers like Morris did not oppose theories such as evolution and the developing scientific tradition they entailed; they simply resisted a scientific reductionism that eliminated self, and philosophy and religion, from the world of what comprises truth and knowledge.

Resisting these lines of critique was surely Dewey's other influence, G. Stanley Hall, who studied under Wilhelm Wundt and imbibed that period's vision of empirical psychology.[31] Dewey appreciated the scientific advances that were (and would be) made using such novel approaches; he also seemed taken by Wundt's volunteerism, or the idea that the central part of human psychology was integrally connected to will or mental-physical activity. Dewey would never abandon the ideas stemming from Wundt (and Hall) that the human mind was not a concrete entity or independent thing, but instead represented merely a conceptual shorthand for the activities and engagement of the human organism with its natural and social environment.[32] For Morris, the world was integrally connected to a self or consciousness that knew of it as both object and subject; for Hall, the world implicated organisms driven by contingent and distinct purposes in specific environments.

Dewey's early thought, enshrined in the 1880s in such works as his *Psychology* (1887) and "The Ethics of Democracy" (1888), echoed both of these lines of influence. These works are situated in Dewey's years at the University of Michigan, where he worked out the implications of the new physiological psychology that Wundt, Hall, and others were bringing to the forefront of academic study. Yet at this time he was also deeply committed to a Christian version of neo-Hegelian idealism as an interpretative framework for both that new psychology and his turn toward the social and practical. His *Psychology* gave a thoroughgoing account of psychology and insisted on all psychological matters being ultimately grounded on what he—following early accounts from James Seth and James Ward in separate works in 1883—dubbed the "psychological standpoint."[33] This approach tethered epistemology and actually any scientific endeavor to matters of individual consciousness, or experience. In this way, Dewey (and his fellow neo-idealists) saw themselves as extending the insights of earlier British empiricists in grounding knowledge on individual perception, but with the important (idealist) caveat that this individualized perception occurred in an experiential framework saturated by a subjective consciousness.

For Dewey and his fellow travelers in the 1880s, there were no such things as facts observed, known, or operative without some consciousness beholding them. The individual consciousness was but a part of consciousness per se, or the Absolute as the neo-Hegelians were wont to call the consciousness that encompasses and knows all things. Individual consciousnesses (or selves) participated in the ongoing process of actively coming to know, or "idealize," the world in regard and response to that self's impulses and desires. According to the account in *Psychology*, the individual consciousness becomes more *self*-conscious insofar as it comes to know what impulses push it to action and what these mean in terms of consequences and effects achieved in the world. The concept of "desire" becomes important in Dewey's early psychology precisely because it represents an individual gaining self-knowledge about impulses as idealized (or meaningful) parts of their consciously known world.[34] As habit would function in Dewey's later work in psychology and ethics, which Ambedkar would grapple with both during and after his time at Columbia, the early psychology that informs essays like "The Ethics of Democracy" offers a similar story about an organism coming to know—and intelligently engage—its environment. The main difference is that Dewey embeds this account of an active organism in the philosophical vocabulary of idealism: the creature was an individual spark of consciousness coming to know the Absolute totality of consciousness through an act of individual self-realization. As it came to know what its impulses and desires meant in the world of action, it came to know and express its true self; knowing this individual self was, according to the neo-Hegelians, coming to know the Absolute. Thus, Dewey's early psychology of the 1880s dovetailed with an ethical position that posits *self-realization* as a normative endpoint.

"The Ethics of Democracy" represents one of Dewey's earliest forays into political philosophy, and it too was steeped in both the neo-Hegelian framework and an ongoing commitment to a Christian worldview. As Steven C. Rockefeller recounts, Dewey delivered countless lectures to and wrote a significant number of short essays on Christian thought and doctrine for the Students' Christian Association at the University of Michigan in the 1880s, all with the goal of delivering a Hegelianized Christianity that posited the salvation of human individuals as constituted by coming to realize their unity with God, or the Absolute consciousness.[35] In this short essay spurred on by Henry Maine's critique of democracy as fragmenting individual power and force in political matters, Dewey takes steps to spiritualize democracy in an idealist manner. Presaging the accounts of democracy as a form of association that so moved Ambedkar in the passages he read and echoed from *Democracy and Education,* Dewey uses Maine in this 1888 essay as a foil to produce an earlier version of this theme— namely, "whether democracy is adequately decided as only a form of government."[36] Maine adopted an individualistic or atomic view of political association, with societies merely being a summation of individual agents and their aggregated force. Democracy in this account is problematic because it represents an infinite splintering of the force of any given agent in the political mass, which typically results in disorganized anarchy.

The essay that Dewey wrote in response to Maine's critique—and that Ambedkar read and valued—rebuts this "atomistic" conception of political society with a Hegelian "theory of the 'social organism.'"[37] Dewey refuses Maine's starting point, that "the ultimate reality is an individual unit," and instead argues that "man is essentially a social being," which means the atomic or "non-social individual is an abstraction."[38] As Dewey puts it, it is the "unity of will" that renders democracy an organism. Of course, he recognizes that no society is wholly unified or without strife, but he notes that, ideally, "a state presents men so far as they have become organically related to one another, or are possessed of unity of purpose and interest."[39] He leaves open the question of whether or not a particular form of government multiplies the strife between "classes within society, circles within the classes and cliques within the circles," but he maintains that this is an empirical question that can't be settled by Maine's *a priori* method of defining democracy as effectively the fragmentation of force beyond all useful parameters.[40] Democracy best instantiates or realizes this ideal of society as a thriving organism, or in the terms of his psychology, one in which each individual is a fully realized, conscious part of the Absolute consciousness.

Underlying this argument for democracy is an appropriation of the concept of "organism" that animated Dewey through such sources as Hall and Morris, as well as through his reading of Thomas Henry Huxley and Charles Darwin from his early education.[41] These sources, combined with Hegel's distinctive dialectic form of analyzing problems and phenomena of consciousness, which he imbibed from Morris, led Dewey to make organic relations central to not only human psychology but also social matters. In "The Ethics of Democracy," he compared the individual to society not as atom to larger structure, but instead as organ to composite organism. "Human society" for Dewey represents the most ideal organic relation because it is thoroughly reciprocal in ways the relationship between a kidney and an animal, say, is not. In the social organism, "the whole lives truly in every member, and there is no longer the appearance of physical aggregation, or continuity. The organism manifests itself as what it truly is, an ideal or spiritual life, a unity of *will*."[42] As there is this unity of will, each individual more and more represents or realizes this "common purpose and spirit" and knows itself as "its vital embodiment."[43] Other forms of government lack this sort of unity and exclude members of the polis "outside of the political society in which they live." As Dewey puts it, "Not participating in the formation or expression of the common will, they do not embody it in themselves."[44]

Democracy goes the farthest toward eliminating the two classes that Dewey sees in every social setting: "one of governors, one of governed." This value-based hierarchy fails in the perfected organism of democratic community, since each part has its adjusted function in and for the whole society—and is not valued as less than the whole, given that it embodies valuable functions in its individuality. Government, says Dewey, "does not mean one class or side of society set over against the other."[45] These two groups are not separate classes, but instead are "but two aspects of the same fact—the fact of the possession of society of a unified and articulate will."[46] Translating this point into concrete details that Ambedkar surely recognized in his Indian context, Dewey argues that "wherever government is a matter of birth, of heredity, of wealth, of superior 'social' standing, in a word, of privilege, society is still unorganized, and in so far, chaotic. There are two wills; the governors and the governed are two separate classes. . . . There is a condition of unstable equilibrium."[47] Contra Maine, democracy promises the most harmonious and sustainable political structure precisely because it best realizes the *spiritual* dimensions of association. Presaging his 1916 exposition, Dewey argues in this early essay that "democracy, in a word, is a social, that is to say, an ethical conception, and upon its ethical significance is based its significance as governmental. Democracy is a form of government only because it is a form of moral and spiritual association."[48]

Aristocracy, Dewey recognizes, also attempts to realize some instantiation of a stable and unified community like the more-perfect form of democracy. What is the difference? It comes down in this essay to an issue of ends and means, or the types of force employed to create or reach certain end points. The question is "how this unity of the individual and the universe, this perfect man in the perfect state, is to be brought about."[49] In the case of aristocracy—or rule by and through the force of a concretized and separate class of rulers—the "multitude is incapable of forming such an ideal and of attempting to reach it."[50] Such aristocratic states seek harmony and individual self-development, but they do not empower the majority of selves to pursue this process of self-realization or the development of personality on their own. It is external and not truly organic or self-driven. It is the force of the ruler or intellectual class that will propel the others toward their proper place and good: "The aristocratic idea implies that the mass of men are to be inserted by wisdom, or, if necessary, thrust by force, into their proper positions in the social organism."[51] The problem is that there is no room in such a scheme for the forces of the individual to work out their own salvation or their own self-realization. "It is true," Dewey answers aristocrats like Maine, "that when an individual has found that place in society for which he is best fitted and is exercising the function proper to that place, he has obtained his completest development, but it is also true (and this is the truth omitted by aristocracy, emphasized by democracy) that he must find this place and assume this work in the main for himself." The *means* employed by democracy ideally leverage the force of the agent and their personality and "must begin in the man himself, however much the good and the wise of society contribute. Personal responsibility, individual initiation, these are the notes of democracy."[52]

For democracy, the force and the ideal—the means and the end, in other words—come from within the community insofar as it already exists in each member: "Democracy holds that the ideal is already at work in every personality, and must be trusted to care for itself."[53] This individualism inherent in democracy is not of the aggregative type assumed by Maine and others, but instead is of the sort that uplifts and relies upon the *personality* of each individual part of society. Dewey's notion of personality emphasizes a socialized agent that mediates and creates ideals in social experience; it is thoroughly saturated with his Hegelian commitments. From Dewey's vantage, developing the personality of each individual in a community not only completes that community, it realizes the ideal of the Kingdom of God here on Earth in actual communities that matter to individual experience.[54]

"The Ethics of Democracy" represents one of Dewey's earliest attempts to sell such a democratic community as spiritualized ideal on the egalitarian lines of his readings of Christianity and Hegelian idealism. This view of democracy recognizes the primacy of the individual, gives them a role in actuating its ideal in the world, *and* attempts to recognize the individual as already social in nature. "Democracy," in this reading,

> means that *personality* is the first and final reality. It admits that the full significance of personality can be learned by the individual only as it is already

presented to him in objective form in society; it admits that the chief stimuli and encouragements to the realization of personality come from society; but it holds, none the less, to the fact that personality cannot be procured for any one, however degraded and feeble, by any one else, however wise and strong.[55]

Agency, will, and idealized meaning are pulled from Dewey's idealist psychology and applied to the political realm; political action becomes a way to realize one's self, or to develop and display one's personality as a unique agent.

What lies behind this important concept of "personality" in Dewey's essay on democracy? His 1887 *Psychology* informs it with its themes of coming to self-knowledge or realization through the increasing mediation—or idealization—of our impulses as desires. Each individual has a unique set of impulses that psychological theory cannot exhaustively categorize. The task of the individual in self-realization in this early work is to come to know the potentialities of these impulses in specific environments; they become desires as they are laden with meaning and consequences, which are then anticipated by the knowing agent. In other words, as the self comes to know the meaning and effects of its desires, it can begin to consciously choose among competing desires and thereby choose or realize its self. As Jennifer Welchman puts it in her account of Dewey's early ethics, the goal here is not determining "what I ought to do," but instead is a matter of coming to realize whether "I am the sort of self that I ought to be."[56] Coming to realize the nature and meaning of our impulses in natural and social environments is a vital part of attaining this knowledge of self. This realization involves choice, which in turn involves the idealization of desires that are chosen as motive for certain actions and projects. As Dewey puts it in *Psychology*, "Choice, in fact, is the declaration of self that a certain ideal shall be realized. The motive is another word for the ideal."[57] This decision to realize—in the sense of declaring through our action and value judgments—our self implicates a central part to one's personality: the notion of *will*.

An individual has not only impulses but also the power to do something with or about these impulses. This is what Dewey claims is "an ultimate fact in the psychological constitution of man": "*He has the power of determining himself*. He has the power of setting up an ideal of what he would have himself be, and this ideal in form depends only upon himself."[58] Dewey describes this complex concept of personality as follows in *Psychology*, closely connecting it to self-realization:

This ideal of self-realization depends *for its form* upon the self and upon that alone. For its content, for its specific and concrete filling up it depends, as previously shown, upon his education, surroundings, etc. But the man's own will, the core of his personality, decides what he would have himself be, and this decision decides what he is. Man determines himself by setting up either good or evil as a motive to himself, and he sets up either as he *will* have himself be.[59]

The individual personality is a mixture of *consciousness* in its general form, *specific characteristics* about an individual organism and its placement in an environment, and the sheer and ever-available ability to *will* or choose what will be realized in and through individual action. The last feature represents for Deweyan psychology a vital sense of force at the individual level; this will evolve as Dewey's ethics move toward the psychology that Ambedkar heard in 1914, the account that places much of its weight on "habit" and impulse, but it still contains the sense of individual agency that attracted Ambedkar to the idea of reflective thought in the 1908 *Ethics*, which featured so prominently in the previous chapter. In "The Ethics of Democracy" and the psychology that it implicates, Ambedkar also saw a sense of willfulness and individual force that would fit perfectly into his push for Dalit conversion.

Dewey in the 1880s linked individual will and force to religion; Ambedkar's rhetorical activity in India during the 1930s also prominently featured this connection. Dewey's emphasis was a continuation of the Christianized Hegelianism he saw in his teacher and friend, George S. Morris, who similarly emphasized the role of effort and willfulness in individual self-realization:

He is as yet only the bare possibility of a man, and in order to be a man in fact, in order to have in him the reality of true human substance, he must be up and doing. He must act. He, I say, and not another, must act. By his own self-conscious, self-determining, purposeful activity, he must redeem and realize the divine possibility that resides in him. In order to be himself, he must create himself. Thus is man in the image of God and like God. But only like God, not equal with him.[60]

The individual consciousness was part of the Absolute (God) but did not exhaust it. It did, however, entail God-like aspirations that individual action and force would make a difference in determining who that individual truly is. Action and will were central to self-realization of one's unique personality in a social environment. Likewise, at the end of *Psychology* Dewey places religion in a sort of unifying role, one that implicates and idealizes individual will and forceful efforts. The "religious will" that emerges in the individual undergoing self-realization involves knowing the "perfect ideal"; such a self finally "performs the act of identification once for all. . . . Religious will declares that the perfect will is the only source of activity and of reality, and that it is in itself perfect activity and perfect reality. It is the completely self-determined. In it realization and the ideal are one."[61] Dewey's meaning here is difficult to discern with precision, but one gets the general idea: at the highest levels of realization, the individual realizes or experiences the fundamental linkage between individual consciousness and absolute consciousness: "The religious will declares that God, as the perfect Personality or Will, is the only Reality, and the Source of all activity."[62] Thus, will "is the man, psychologically speaking," and this individual knows self as part of a larger whole or consciousness. But the sense of agency does not evaporate, even if Dewey does not subscribe to a transcendent soul or self that possesses this consciousness: "The unity of the self is the will" in the stream of experience.[63]

What attracted Ambedkar to this idea and ideal of personality, and what prevented him from adopting the surrounding theoretical framework of neo-idealist organicism that accompanied it in "The Ethics of Democracy"? Ambedkar clearly liked the notion of uniqueness and will that was linked to the idea of personality. Part of his reason for resisting the complete idealist ethics in "The Ethics of Democracy" lies in the imbalance Ambedkar surely sensed in it between the individual and society. Dewey's individual expresses, in a clear or less fully realized fashion, the spirit of the society that surrounds them. As Dewey puts it, "society and the individual are really organic to each other," which means that "the individual is society concentrated."[64] In a true democracy, there is a sense that the individual expresses and contains this spirit fully, without compromising their personality and agency. Dewey allows for other systems—aristocracy, for instance—to less than fully include (and hence not fully express) the individual in the group, but the tension is real: Where is individuality in a strong sense in Dewey's idealism? Where is the path for individuals to make a melioriative difference in a society that is not truly unified in terms of common will and spirit? Committed as he was to Hegelian lines of thought, Dewey explicitly lays his cards out in the 1888 essay: the individual is thoroughly social and does not exist as an atomic unit before the advent of a surrounding social context. Dewey thereby seems to disable a strong sense of hope in individual efforts to will and enact reform. Society and the state

condition and constitute the agency of the individual; the individual's personality is closely bound with the nature of the state that surrounds them.
Knowing and realizing this seems be the factor that is emphasized in 1888,
not any sense of appreciating a situation for what it proffers in terms of
intelligent control and reform.[65]

The commitment to the Absolute—and the individual's task of knowing it and becoming a self-conscious realization of it—jarred with Ambedkar's reading of the role of Hindu religion in Indian society, especially as it
related to the caste-based oppression of his fellow Dalits. Advaitin monis-
tic strains that emphasized the oneness of all being, without distinction,
and that collapsed empirical selves into one universal Self, surely struck
Ambedkar as similar to Dewey's Hegelian project in such early works.
This approach would never do, as Ambedkar hints in his 1936 "What Way
Emancipation" address when he tells those he is urging to convert to value
individual progress. "Unlike the drop of water that merges its existence
with the ocean in which it drops," says Ambedkar, evoking a common metaphor in Vedantic forms of Hindu philosophy, "man does not lose his entity in the society in which he lives. Man's life is independent."[66] Ambedkar
then quickly affirms his commitment, however, to a notion of individual
self-realization that is parallel to Dewey's version in the 1888 essay: "He
is born not for the service of the society but for his self development."[67]
The relationship between the individual and the Absolute (or some sort of
self or self-consciousness that extends beyond and absorbs the individual)
even vexed Dewey; as John Shook discusses, Dewey slowly drifted away
from the concept over the course of the 1890s.[68] James A. Good attributes
some of the impetus to Dewey's own abandonment of the Absolute to his
relationship with Thomas Davidson, an entrepreneurial but eccentric Scot-
tish American philosopher who conversed with Fabian socialists such as
Sidney and Beatrice Webb, H. G. Wells, and George Bernard Shaw in London during the 1880s. In 1887, Davidson moved to New York, where he
established the first of a series of programs designed to educate individuals outside of the elite confines of university contexts. In 1889 and 1890,
Dewey lectured in Davidson's summer program in Farmington, Connecti-
cut, and he owned a cabin next to Davidson when Dewey taught in his
new summer school when it moved to Mt. Hurricane.[69]

Davidson was important not only because he introduced Dewey to a
network of Fabian socialists—many of whom would serve as Ambedkar's
teachers after 1916—and intellectuals involved in the Ethical Culture Society, but also because Davidson both knew Hegel's philosophy and was
opposed to this approach that Dewey cared so much about at the time.

Davidson had been a member of the St. Louis Philosophical Society, the same group that contained William T. Harris, a Hegelian thinker who encouraged a young Dewey to attend graduate school in the early 1880s. Even though he was around those committed to Hegelian approaches, Davidson was "convinced that it absorbed the individual into the absolute and was therefore unsuitable as a basis of ethical and practical action."[70] Formal education, like Hegelian philosophy, was also critiqued by Davidson since it "stops with knowing and does not go on to living and doing."[71] Davidson's love of communities of debate and inquiry, combined with his skepticism of German-influenced systems of higher education in America, would lead him to eschew any formal association with established universities and colleges; instead, he sought to put his own ideas into practice in informal, but highly discursive, institutions of education of his own design.[72]

Even as Dewey realized this point about the Absolute—and the lackluster melioriative value of simply "knowing" it—his idealistic ethics still held little room for the individual in light of the emphasis placed on a larger social whole. One can see this in his next major work in ethics after "The Ethics of Democracy," a book titled *Outlines of a Critical Theory of Ethics* (1891). This book largely eschews talk of the Absolute or consciousness in general, but the same structure of an individual coming to know or realize their self *in a social environment* is still central. Expanding on the notion of personality and what makes it unique, Dewey extends the reading given in *Psychology* to a view of self-realization that sees the self as a "function," or as an "active relation established between the power of doing, on one side, and something to be done on the other."[73] The self is a function between individual elements of consciousness and an environment; in the *Outlines* vision of this relationship, Dewey indicates that self-realization involves a "progressive adjustment" or balancing between a "specific capacity" of the individual personality and a "specific environment," or "station, situation, limitations, surroundings, opportunities, etc."[74] Gone is an appeal to the Absolute or self-consciousness in general, but still remaining is the realization of what is at stake, and how to balance it, in the mediated relationship between self and social environment. The individual personality plays a role in achieving the adjustment or balance implicated in this function between impulsive self and social context, but its meliorative potential still seems limited by aspects determined by social setting, such as role and "stations" in that social hierarchy.

This appeal to social context as it is would still not please Ambedkar's meliorative goals and would not assuage concerns with Dewey's idealistic view of the self-realization of human personality. Indeed, one sees the

integration—perhaps to the denigration of individual willfulness in reform—in how Dewey spells out the fundamental "ethical postulate" in his
1891 *Outlines*: "In the realization of individuality there is found also the
needed realization of some community of persons of which the individual
is a member; and conversely, the agent who duly satisfies the community
in which he shares, by that same conduct satisfies himself."[75] Such a view
of an increasingly naturalized Deweyan idealist ethics was still too much
for Ambedkar; satisfying the Hindu community and the demands of tradition, for Ambedkar, was tantamount to surrendering to caste oppression. It
was the organic approach gone too far. As he tells his fellow Dalits in his
1936 speech, "According to me, individual welfare and progress (individual development) should be the real aim of the religion. Although the individual is part of society, the relation with society is not like the body and
its organs, or the cart and its wheels."[76] This was an embrace of the value
of individual personality and self-development, but alongside a rejection
of an organic reading of society that subordinates the individual to a larger
or more absolute consciousness or organism. Ambedkar would not abide
the idea that developing the individual as society specifies through its roles
and stations would also involve the improvement of the whole. Individual
melioration, like reflective thinking that he takes from Dewey's later ethics,
must be allowed to challenge and shake the received and common spirits
that course through society's veins.

The concept of personality—that which is unique to each individual
and that which ought to be developed through social relationships—is
central to Ambedkar's 1936 appeals for conversion. This concept of the
fundamental equality and capacity of each unique individual grounds
Ambedkar's critiques of Hinduism and the caste system. In "Away from
the Hindus," an unpublished essay written sometime after his "What Way
Emancipation" speech, Ambedkar talks extensively about the relationship of religion and the development of human personality, drawing on
Charles A. Ellwood's 1922 book *The Religious Reconstruction*.[77] Ellwood was
a devoted student of Dewey during the pragmatist's idealist period at the
University of Michigan. Dewey was so impressed by Ellwood's engagement
with his (and others') philosophical thought that he wrote in his recommendation letters in 1899 for Ellwood that the young student was an able
philosopher and that he could serve as a teacher in any social science disci-
pline.[78] Ellwood is well-known for extending many aspects of Dewey's ethical theory of self-realization into his analysis of sociology in the 1910s. The
concept of personality, with this Deweyan genealogy, appears in a more
central usage in Ambedkar's 1936 address to his fellow Mahars. There he

also indicates that the "basic idea underlying a religion is to create an atmosphere for the spiritual development of an individual."[79]

How Ambedkar explicates the development of the individual in his 1936 speech is vital, however, because it involves his drawing on how Dewey explicates personality in his 1888 essay. Ambedkar indicates that "three factors are required for the uplift of an individual. They are: Sympathy, Equality, and Liberty."[80] Regardless of his disagreements with Dewey on the role of the Absolute vis-à-vis an existing society, this element of his appeal clearly engages Dewey's idea that democracy "holds that the spirit of personality indwells in every individual and that the choice to develop it must proceed from that individual." As we shall see in the remainder of his 1936 speech, Ambedkar values both personality in its uniqueness and the potential strength resident in the will of each oppressed Dalit individual he is speaking to in his address. "From this central position of personality," Dewey continues in his 1888 essay, "result the other notes of democracy, liberty, equality, fraternity,—words which are not mere words to catch the mob, but symbols of the highest ethical idea which humanity has yet reached—the idea that personality is the one thing of permanent and abiding worth, and that in every human individual there lies personality."[81] Ambedkar had heard these three values—the motto of the French Revolution—in his Philosophy 131–132 courses with Dewey at Columbia in 1915–16, and would continue to use these three touchstones in enunciating and applying his critical notion of social democracy. Here, in a Marathi-language address to his fellow Mahars, we see a functional equivalent to these three values emerge in his explication of what is required for self-development of personality. Ambedkar uses the Marathi word *sahanubhuti* to refer to the part of the triumvirate usually occupied by "fraternity." This term is composed of *sah* ("with") and *anubhuti* ("feeling"), connoting a sense of empathetic feeling with others, a connotation not far removed from that usually associated with "fraternity." Why did Ambedkar choose this term to translate "fraternity" or fellow feeling to his audience? Ambedkar might have selected *sahanubhuti* over, say, *badhutva* (which conveys brotherhood) as a translation of the concept of fraternity in this trio of values because he wanted to emphasize the aspect of suffering that could be similarly felt and experienced or that could be objectified and ignored by others.[82] Indeed, Ambedkar offers "fellow-*feeling*" as a stand-in for "fraternity" in his 1936 *Annihilation of Caste*, as well as in his "Riddles in Hinduism" manuscript from the 1950s; in *The Buddha and His Dhamma*, Ambedkar talks of *metta* as the feeling or state of compassion for beings. *Sahanubhuti* clearly conveys the sympathetic feeling for the suffering of self and others, a meaning not far removed from the Deweyan psychology that Ambedkar seems intent to draw upon in this 1936 speech, with its focus on self-development: in the pages of *Psychology*, Dewey foregrounds the social implications of the feeling of sympathy, noting that "sympathy, in short, is the reproduction of the experience of another, *accompanied by the recognition of the fact that it is his experience*."[83] Sympathy, as a translation of *sahanubhuti*, captures the functional concept that Ambedkar wants to convey to his audience: Does Hinduism as a religion create a context in which other Indians *feel* the experiences of the oppressed as the novel but important experiences *of those other agents?* Ambedkar's answer, surely shared by his Mahar audience, is that Hinduism does not facilitate such sympathy toward and feeling-with the oppressed.

Lest we think that this appeal to personality is a mere aberration, it is helpful to consider a similar constellation of appeals appearing across Ambedkar's work, all of which extend the sort of conceptual structure resident in Dewey's 1888 "The Ethics of Democracy" essay. He was enamored of the critical possibilities related to caste oppression that were revealed by the concept of personality. Ambedkar's 1943 text, "Ranade, Gandhi and Jinnah," criticizes Hinduism as "a religion which is not intended to establish liberty, equality and fraternity. It is a gospel which proclaims the worship of the superman," and as one that results in Dalits having "no life of their own to live, and no right to develop their own personality."[84] In Ambedkar's unpublished work, "Philosophy of Hinduism," composed most likely in the final decade of his life, we see an even more obvious example that similarly draws upon Dewey's early idealist thought. The *Laws of Manu*, a consistent target of Ambedkar's rage, is said to "not stop with the non-recognition of human personality. He advocates a deliberate debasement of human personality."[85] Recognizing the unique value and fundamental equality of personality in each agent means for Ambedkar what it meant for Dewey: a democratic egalitarianism that rose above certain ideological ways of making some into rulers and others into slaves or servants. This is similar to how Ambedkar puts it in another later, and unpublished, work, "Hindu Social Order: Its Essential Principles," intended as part of a planned work called "India and the Pre-requisites of Communism." Like his 1936 speech and his unpublished "Philosophy of Hinduism," this work foregrounds personality as the fundamental value for his evaluation of religions and possible meliorative paths, and he reduces it to the same trio of values that Dewey held as far back as his 1888 essay: "Once the sacredness of human personality is admitted the necessity of liberty, equality and fraternity must also be admitted as the proper climate for the development of personality."[86]

Across these works and others, Ambedkar is not always consistent in how he relates or subordinates these three values, but we can be certain that each is vital in some manner for personality and its development. In "Philosophy of Hinduism," Ambedkar emphasizes equality: "Fraternity and liberty are really derivative notions. The basic and fundamental conceptions are equality and respect for human personality. Fraternity and liberty take their roots in these two fundamental conceptions. Digging further down it may be said that equality is the original notion and respect for human personality is a reflexion of it."[87] In other works, Ambedkar emphasizes other values as higher in priority, but here we can resolve such tensions by indicating that at the least equality may occupy the status as something of a prerequisite for these other vital and important values to be instantiated in society, even if it is not more important in a larger sense. "Philosophy of Hinduism" seems to suggest this sort of compromise, arguing that "where equality is denied, everything else may be taken to be denied."[88] Even though personality was a stable topic in much of his discourse, the rhetorical nature of his appeals often meant he was flexible in how he argued for these values to specific audiences.

In his 1936 speech arguing for conversion, Ambedkar employs this same structure of values to highlight what is lacking should the Dalits stay within the caste-determined folds of Hinduism. In terms of "sympathy," Ambedkar sees no fraternity with and among Hindus and Dalits. Caste Hindus do not respect, or feel in a sympathetic manner, what the religious overlay of caste does to the experience or the personality of those affected negatively by it. The negative evaluation inherent in caste is based on what Ambedkar sees as a fundamental inequality at the heart of Hinduism. Speaking to his fellow Mahars, he exclaims, "Can anybody believe that there exists an animal called man by whose touch man becomes impure, water is polluted, and God becomes unworthy for worship?"[89] Like lepers, Dalits are despised. But Ambedkar emphasizes something his Mahar audience surely can identify with: lepers often get the sympathy of those avoiding them, whereas Dalits are loathed because of a polluting nature bequeathed to them through past deeds and the law of *karma*. Lepers suffer from a medical condition; Ambedkar and his fellow Dalits suffer from a judgment of their innermost personality foisted on them by a religion that others—and sometimes, they themselves—hold dear.

The narrative of conversion that Ambedkar is constructing in this speech is closely tethered to this ideal of human personality. Caste oppression destroys the ability of the individual to will courses of action that lets their capacities, impulses, and desires flower in the unique way that they would should they be granted the liberty to do so. In other words, as Ambedkar tells his audience, "You have ceased to be respected."[90] But what does it mean to be respected? Part of the answer lies in another concept that Ambedkar often wrestled with, the idea of "dignity." This term, along with the trio of fraternity, equality, and liberty, appears in another document whose origin integrally involved Ambedkar in the 1940s: the preamble to the Indian constitution. Dignity, as respect due to each human individual, is foregrounded along with fraternity in this document. As Aakash Singh Rathore has shown, Ambedkar's influence on the drafting of the preamble was extensive, and it was Ambedkar who inserted and defended the phrase "*fraternity* assuring the dignity of the individual and the unity and integrity of the Nation." Others wanted to reverse the order of its elements, leaving the dignity of the individual seemingly as a mere afterthought or to eliminate dignity altogether. Ambedkar, maintaining the idea of dignity as a notion of the fundamental value of *each* human personality (versus other common meanings that rank humans as more or less dignified) insisted on it remaining closest to the idea of "fraternity" in the preamble. As Rathore notes, Ambedkar would not allow moving the "dignity of the individual" phrase to the end of the sentence, as "he would not see individual dignity lose its pole position, and take a back seat to the nation."[91] Self-respect and dignity, in Rathore's analysis, are integrally connected. According to one philosophically minded observer of Ambedkar's drafting of the preamble, K. M. Munshi,

> The incorporation of the phrase "dignity of the individual," therefore, was an express rejection of the Hegelian theory on which modern totalitarianism is based; namely, that the State is a metaphysical entity, independent of and overshadowing the individual whose only aim was to secure its existence. It is also an explicit repudiation of the hereditary, social or feudal distinctions which we had inherited from the past.[92]

As we can now see from Ambedkar's sustained evocation of personality and associated concepts such as fraternity or sympathy across his intellectual development, his later insistence on dignity was a resistance not only to a Hegelian notion of the state, but also a specific disagreement with Dewey's early idealist ethics and its emphasis on an organicism of the state that threatened the efficacy of and respect due to human personality. In

Ambedkar's 1936 effort to implore his fellow Mahars to follow him in converting first away from Hinduism—and eventually toward some religion that would foster respect for their personality—we see a similar appeal to courses of meliorative action to uphold personality and individual dignity. Groups, societies, and communities fall out of focus in such an approach, as the uniqueness inherent in what is denoted by individual personality becomes that which is to be valued and held as an end point.

In Deweyan fashion, however, personality is not simply a remote end. It is also the means to achieving this status of dignity that humans *qua* agents deserve. In "What Way Emancipation," Ambedkar deploys a rhetoric of willfulness that reconstructs Dewey's notion of personality. Dewey's concept was not only ambiguous, it was constantly threatened with evaporating into the nation-state or Absolute in his early works. Ambedkar was surely sensitive to these tendencies, as this was precisely the problem with Hinduism: it swallowed up the initiative, value, and dignity of each individual Dalit by virtue of a systematic overlay that made them, in the eyes of self and others, "untouchable." The "external conditions of a slave" that Dalits lived under were clearly a harm, but material progress was not the only end or means to Dalit emancipation. Ambedkar tells his audience that Hinduism is particularly pernicious insofar as it "has sacked your mental freedom and made you slaves."[93] Eschewing external means of improvement—Ambedkar states that "castes cannot be abolished by inter-caste dinners or stray instances of inter-caste marriages"—he warns his audience of the same point that he extracted from Dewey's psychology and educational thought from 1914 to 1916 in his *Annihilation of Caste* text: "Caste is a state of mind. It is a disease of the mind. The teaching[s] of the Hindu religion are the cause of this disease."[94] He and his fellow Dalits are just as implicated in the cause of their condition as their oppressors, since "we practice the casteism, [and] we observe the Untouchability, because we are asked to do so by the Hindu religion in which we live."[95] In shaping individual and group experience in such ways, religion becomes a "display of force."[96] The only antidote to such a state, according to Ambedkar, is the reclamation of human personality not only as an end but also as a means to achieve this end point of dignity and equality.

What does it mean to use or instantiate human personality? It means, for Ambedkar, going beyond Dewey's strictures in his 1888 essay and asserting one's self as agent, as a personality. As we have seen, there is an undercurrent to the self-realization ethics of Morris and Dewey that values the will and effort as a vital part of individual personality. This is a theme that has always intrigued the gregarious Ambedkar, at least in matters of politics and thought that interested him. He was never one to shy away from a fight, whether it was with Gandhi or the communist organizers in Bombay in the 1930s, or with orthodox Hindus whose religion he constantly lambasted. Devi Dayal, a daily associate of Ambedkar as his assistant from 1943 to 1951, recalls (with the help of his diary entries from September 1944) Ambedkar opining about the importance of will and effort: "The will has infinite power. A man who wills to do something big and good, measures through his sheer will its main limitations and hurdles, and he naturally feels that the difficulties are dissipating, and the means are coming forth. He is empowering them himself."[97] Ambedkar clearly valorized effort and will power, whatever our contemporary sensibilities may tell us about systems and agency, and he saw in his own initiative and willfulness a power that transcended the strictures that had held him and his family back for too long. This focus on personal agency was more than a personality trait of Ambedkar's, however, as it extended into the realm of the intellectual commitments that his rhetoric would evince throughout his life. It is there in his reading of "personality" as an ethical ideal in various works, and we can also see it in his engagement with the Buddhist tradition he worked so hard to recover and reconstruct for his own emancipatory purposes in the final years of his life.

Even before his public advocacy of Buddhism as a target for conversion, we can see traces of this commitment in the annotations that Ambedkar the reader added to various books. For instance, in an otherwise unremarkable—and basically unmarked—book by T. Christmas Humphreys, *Karma and Rebirth* (1948 edition), we feel and see Ambedkar's worries over doctrines that disable personal initiative and will in efforts to improve self and others. Ambedkar writes with his own hand on the page bearing the book's table of contents the query, "What place has will and effort in the law of karma?"[98] Karma and rebirth are problematic for Ambedkar, as they seem to justify one's empowered or disempowered social position (viz. caste status). They are also worrisome insofar as they represent a religiously justified conceptual scheme that evaporates any sense of agency or hope for effective change in this lifetime that the agent might desire. In Ambedkar's view, personality implies a strong sense of unique drives and desires, as well as a commitment of one's own to the possession of the will and means to enact such projects in the common world.

In his "What Way Emancipation" speech, Ambedkar leverages the rhetoric of slavery not only to highlight the deprivation that the personality of his fellow Dalits has felt at the hands of caste oppressors, but also (paradoxically) to enable the personal effort needed to do something about this state of oppression. Equality is compromised, in part, because Dalits lack liberty. But the liberty or ability to freely act goes beyond mere matters of what is granted through statutes: "The Untouchables are in more need of social liberty than that which is guaranteed by law. So long as you do not achieve social liberty, whatever freedom is provided by law to you, is of no avail."[99] What is missing, Ambedkar indicates, is "freedom of the mind," the absence of which makes an ostensibly free individual really a "slave," "prisoner," or "dead" man.[100] Real, meaningful, and lasting freedom— "effective freedom," as in Dewey's final lecture of spring 1916—must, Ambedkar argues, start with the possession of freeing mental habits. His speech to his fellow Dalits paints the caste system as grounded in a habitualized way of thinking of self and others that places some groups and individuals in a subservient position, thereby destroying their freedom, agency, and hopes for developing their personalities. Even if laws are passed that guarantee a certain level of treatment, there is no guarantee that the mindsets or attitudes that devalue others will be meliorated. But his "Emancipation" address is aimed at those oppressed by caste and its concepts, so Ambedkar's message is recalibrated to serve as a rhetorical appeal to each person in his audience to reclaim their own personality, and with it, their own dignity. Ambedkar urges his Mahar audience to aspire to the level of being "a man who is his own master" or "a free man."[101]

What is such a person, and what constitutes this personalized ethical ideal? Ambedkar explains that it features an individual holding an emancipated *orientation* toward self, other, and the value of activity:

> I call him free, who with an awakened consciousness, realises his rights, responsibilities and duties, he who is not a slave of circumstances, and is always bent upon changing them in his favor. . . . One who is not a slave of usage, customs and traditions, or of teachings because they have come down from his ancestors, whose flame of reason is not extinguished, I call him a free man.[102]

Part of the power of the ethical ideal of personality, whether it is in Dewey's hands or Ambedkar's speech, is that it places the needed emphasis on the point that each of us should control the path of our lives, since such projects implicate a unique set of values and interests that we each know best for ourselves. One ought to be the master of their own destiny, all things being equal among agents, since this is most in line with the idea that each is valuable because they possess a unique personality. Each agent's personality is different and unique in content and makeup, given their "specific capacities" and "specific environment," as Dewey put it in his *Outlines of a Critical Theory of Ethics*, but the fact that each agent possesses such a thing as a personality is a general ethical truth. Personality is both particular and universal in its meaning. Ambedkar's appeal to his Dalit audience represents an attempt to get them to realize the specific nature of their agency in regard to taking control of the amount of respect and dignity they attribute to themselves, and that will surely condition the respect meted out by others. The individual's mental attitude toward self and society is not the only aspect relevant to social melioration, of course, but it is a vital element that conditions, enables, and transforms other factors. External, political, or material changes matter little if one's internal orientation stays the same.

It is at this point in his speech on conversion that Ambedkar wrestles with the efficacy of religious conversion. Ambedkar was well aware of demurs from those like Gandhi, who thought of religious conversion at will as an impossibility, or those Dalits who would worry that change in religion would entail no improvement in treatment from Hindus *or* the community of the target religion. But the question still remains: If conversion was a matter of asserting one's unique and respect-worthy *personality* in an act of changing religions, how did it bear these psychological fruits for the converting individual? Ambedkar's story is deceptively simple, and eminently rhetorical insofar as it invokes the power of language. In "What Way Emancipation," he indicates that "change of religion is the only antidote" for caste oppression for Dalits, and that it involves not simply changing doctrinal commitments, but also the taking on of a new *name*.[103]

What is in a name for Ambedkar? Few have emphasized Ambedkar's reliance on the *name* or *label* aspect that inevitably comes along with changing one's religion. Perhaps the importance of language is all too easy to miss. Ambedkar saw the import of rhetoric, however, and perceived the connection between language, attitude, and habit. If one subscribes to Christian doctrine and is baptized, one is not merely acting like a Christian; one becomes the bearer of the name or label "Christian," both for themselves and from the perspective of others. They will refer to themselves as such, and others might address or describe them as "Christian." Beyond this, however, are the concerns with kinship and language use that arise in this speech, and even more so in the accompanying unpublished essay, "Away from the Hindus," in which Ambedkar relates conversion and its entailed renaming to the gaining of a family or kin of religious fellows. Thus, names are significant in how they orient us toward others and how they influence our judgments and anticipations of how we (and others) ought to act. In other words, names have a *rhetorical force* insofar as they channel action, thought, and judgments of communal import.

Soumyabrata Choudhury is one of the few commentators on Ambedkar who has noticed the rhetorical aspect of his conversion speeches. Choudhury notes Ambedkar's "so-called 'pragmatic' philosophical temperament, apparently transmitted to him by his American teacher John Dewey" as "a temperament acutely sensitive to the *pragmatics of language.*"[104] Choudhury's account focuses on pragmatics as "extracted from the *being* of language," but as the analysis in this book has shown, it can also be found as a reimagining of Dewey's mature and early psychology.[105] Notions such as "idealization" in Dewey's idealist phase play a similar role as "reflection" and "intelligent habit" in his later thought—both indicate contingent patterns of self-conscious habituation or educative growth that give meaning to one's experience and environment and set up more fulfilling future experiences. Names fit into such a scheme as they implicate *linguistic habits*. They incline us to act and react, to judge and ignore, in certain meaningful patterns that can be more or less consciously controlled or monitored. We can now add a detailed pragmatist story to the ontological and materialistic implications that Choudhury sees in Ambedkar's reconstruction of conceptual labels through religious conversion. Given the contours of human psychology, desire, and habit, reconstructing names offers a way to rethink the value and content of our personality *through* an act of willful agency. This is not only ontologically and materially important, it is also ethically meaningful, as it reveals and shapes what we see as the value of our personality and what we expect of others vis-à-vis our dignity.

Ambedkar's appeal to conversion in 1936 is strategically ambiguous. "To call oneself Muslim, a Christian, a Buddhist or a Sikh" he advises his fellow Mahars, "is not merely a change of religion but is also a change in name."[106] Is it the name that changes one's status, or is it the change in religion? In truth, it is both, as they are integrally connected. One could "fake" being a Muslim, say, but such a shallow use of a name—as "protective discoloration" in Choudhury's analysis—would not be sustainable or continually meaningful in future experiences with members of that religious group. But even if one adopts the conceptual structure that gives meaning to that religious name and acts in ways that others will attach to those bearing that name, there is still the chance that the conversion will be for naught, at least in terms of respect from others being given. Ambedkar acknowledges this, all while stating some rather flat-footed arguments implying that Dalits will be seen as simply equal "outsiders" once outside the

Hindu fold. But the realist side of Ambedkar also surfaces when he points out that Hindus do not let Muslims and Christians "enter their temples, like you," and they have few intermarriages with these groups; nonetheless, Ambedkar claims, conversion outside of Hinduism must occur with a realization of "the affinity and love which these people have," which "is not in between you and the Hindu."[107] In other words, Ambedkar is maintaining that even if conversion outside of Hinduism does not change the views of Hindus toward former "untouchables," it stands a good chance of putting the converts in a *new* communal relationship that would develop their personality and self-respect. Converts and Hindus would be equal *in the eyes of the convert*, at least, which matters greatly if a central part of personality is how agents conceive of their value, their projects, and their agency in relation to others.

Central to this willful realization of personality is the inner emphasis on one's own acts mattering. Whether or not one's own conversion—or the conversion of others—will matter years later is beside the point when considered from the vantage point of Dewey's ethics of self-realization, which Ambedkar retasks and greatly revises in his 1936 conversion appeals to his fellow Mahars. Consider the divergence between Ambedkar's proposed conversion and Gandhi's renaming of the Dalits as *harijan*, or "God's children." Gandhi's suggested change of name comes from a source *external* to the affected person and therefore cannot serve as a self-realized act of their inner personality. The implications of such a rhetorical label for self and others does not cut as deep, Ambedkar's pragmatism maintains, as a *self-chosen* name or label. Deciding to don a new label that sets anticipations for oneself and others serves as an instance of one's own mental freedom and of the power of one's will to create more desirable and desired future experiences. And as Ambedkar puts it in 1936, "The freedom of the mind is the real freedom. A person whose mind is not free, though not in chains, is a slave. One whose mind is not free, though not in prison, is a prisoner. One whose mind is not free though alive, is dead."[108] Ambedkar merges Dewey's later emphasis on nonreflective customs (in his 1908 *Ethics*) with the earlier connection of personality to will: "One who is not a slave of usage, customs and traditions, or of teaching because they have come down from his ancestors, whose flame of reason is not extinguished, I call him a free man." The connections to reflective thinking are emphasized further in the following lines: "He, who has not surrendered himself, who does not act on the teachings of others, who does not believe in anything unless it is examined critically in the light of the cause and effect theory, is a free man."[109] All of this is connected to the psychological focal point of the individual agent implicated in the concept of personality when Ambedkar concludes, "In short, a man who is his own master, him alone, I consider a free man."[110] Regardless of whether the reflective thinking enshrined in the rejection of Hinduism that Ambedkar proffered will be materially beneficial, it will at least involve a willful act of *not* acquiescing to the power and evaluative rhetoric of others, and it will represent an attempt to direct one's own life, dignity, and value.

In short, conversion not only promotes the conditions wherein one's personality can further develop, it *is* an act of the strong personality that Ambedkar wants his audience to realize in their own experience. As Ambedkar closes his lengthy but captivating speech, he emphasizes the momentous occasion that this conference on the viability of conversion represents: "You have to keep in mind that this is, therefore, a crucial occasion. . . . If you decide today to get liberated, your future generations will definitely be liberated. If you decide to remain slaves, your future generations will also be slaves. Hence yours is the most difficult task."[111] While he has not publicly indicated what religion to convert to, he clearly wants to aim his persuasive appeals toward achieving *reflection* on and *renunciation* of the Hindu religion by his fellow Dalits in order to serve as the means and end of strengthening their personalities as valuable agents.

## Reconstruction and Reform in Ambedkar's Later Appeals for Conversion

Ambedkar's appeals for conversion began in earnest after 1935, but his rhetorical activity changed in significant ways in his final years. Eventually, Buddhism was announced as his preferred religion—one that would safeguard the personality of each oppressed Dalit. By 1950, some in the Indian press had tired of his attacks on Hinduism and did not believe the justification behind the anticipated conversion. For instance, the *Free Press Journal* of May 18, 1950, included a short but scathing note on Ambedkar's recent moves toward Buddhist conversion, demanding, "Let him make up his mind once for all. . . . Dr. Ambedkar should make it clear why the Hindus should embrace *Buddhism* and what is wrong with the Hindu religion at present." The unsigned commentary even echoed Gandhi's critical comments on conversion from the 1930s, incredulously asking, "Does he imagine that changing one's religion is as easy as changing one's walking stick?"[112] Ambedkar's speeches to his followers in the 1950s served as his way of directly or indirectly answering such skeptical questions about the planned conversion to Buddhism. The frequency of these discussions of religion and conversion increased during his final years. Emphasizing his calculated uses of communication as a way to effectively change agents and the socially problematic situations they inhabit is a vital part of understanding Ambedkar *as a pragmatist*. If a central part of rhetoric, or the art of speech aiming to persuade, is attention to the particularities of self and audience in such problematic situations, it follows that understanding Ambedkar *as a rhetor* means attending to the specifics of how he attempted to move his various audiences through his speeches and texts, given their specific concerns.

When Ambedkar addressed his followers in the 1950s, he typically spoke in Marathi, the tongue of his stronghold of Maharashtra. Keer tells us about the power of his speaking style: "Ambedkar was a powerful speaker both on the platform and in Parliament. Galvanic and embarrassingly brutal to a fault in his speech, he showered a fusillade of pistol shots at his opponents. . . . Simple, direct and trenchant, his speech had a charm of its own. Its fearlessness was sharpened by a vast confidence and experience which he had attained by his ceaseless study."[113] This directness was altered in his speeches to friendly audiences, however, and augmented by his personal ethos as a successful Dalit in modern India. Instead of addressing confrontational arguments to his followers, Ambedkar was direct and clear about the need for *his* audience to convert to Buddhism. In a Marathi speech entitled "I Shall Devote Rest of My Life to the Revival and Spread of Buddhism" and delivered to an audience at Bombay's Buddha Vihar on September 29, 1950, Ambedkar extends his earlier point (made in *Annihilation of Caste* and elsewhere) that the problems of India were not merely political; they were primarily those of religious orientation. The *Sunday News* reports Ambedkar claiming to his audience that "as long as there is no purity of mind, wrong doing and utter disregard of morals would continue in every day life; and as long as man does not know how to behave with man and creates barriers between man and man, India can never be prosperous."[114] The problem with India, still reeling from the pains of independence and violent partition with Pakistan, is cast in terms of purity and impurity. Instead of Dalits being a source of impurity, it is the mental habits associated with Hinduism that bring impurity and division into a society that otherwise could be whole. This habit-spurred division among social groups is anathema to Ambedkar's reconstructed notion of Deweyan democracy. In the 1930s, in texts like *Annihilation of Caste* and "What Way Emancipation?," Ambedkar calls for consciousness of this problem and a renunciation of the problematic orientation. Now, in 1950, he tells the audience what orientation to convert to: "To end all of these troubles, India must embrace Buddhism. Buddhism is the only religion based upon ethical principles and [that] teaches how to work for the good and well-being of the common man."[115]

Ambedkar's rhetorical activity with his Dalit audiences continued to gain in strength. On January 14, 1951, he delivered a Marathi address to a meeting of the Buddha Doot Society in Bombay known as "Buddhism Will Once Again Be the Religion of This Country." In the heart of his most favorable constituency in his native state of Maharashtra, Ambedkar puts more detail into the orientational solution of Buddhism. One of the reasons Ambedkar was drawn to Buddhism was that it, unlike Christianity, both prized equality *and* was native to the Indian subcontinent. He attempts to establish this point by noting that "Buddha lived in this country in blood and flesh for 80 years. He spent 45 years of his life counseling the people of this country."[116] Yet this person who traveled by walking to help relieve individuals of their suffering "is not even remembered in this country! Nowhere his name is even uttered. I am very puzzled."[117] Of course, Ambedkar is betting that those hearing this utterance will also be puzzled and be pushed to reflect on why this state of affairs is unjustified. Buddha's views are portrayed as the truth, and "the truth always prevails. Today, that time has come. Buddhism will be again the religion of this country, I am sure about it."[118]

His enthusiasm is matched with a dichotomous way of approaching Buddhism, buried in Ambedkar's way of parsing the complexity of Indian history. He follows this personal exclamation with a matter-of-fact reading of the Hindu religion being like a stream formed from two other rivulets, "one of clean water and the other one of dirty water." The former is "that of clean Buddhism and another rivulet was that of dirty Brahminism," the interpretation of the Vedic tradition that placed Brahmins as the superior caste, much to the disadvantage of the lowest castes.[119] The resulting third stream is dirty and impure; the audience must see Buddhism as retaining a lost sense of purity that must come with the entropy of its merger in ancient times with Vedic Hinduism. What is the audience to do? Ambedkar follows out his own evocation of the rhetoric of purity and claims, "We must clean it by removing the dirty customs imposed by Brahminism, so that the Hindu religion becomes clean and pure."[120] Cleansing modern Hinduism of Brahminism arguably returns it to Buddhism, a fact revealed by his advocacy of Buddhism as a replacement for Hindu habits of mind. This is why he claims that once his listeners join the Buddhist fold, "you will not be allowed to carry the Gods, customs or rites of Hinduism along with you. *Khandoba* (Hindu god) inside your hearts and Buddha on the front of your house will not be allowed."[121] The return to pure Buddhism—of habit and observable practice—also means leaving behind the concept and practice of caste.

Ambedkar senses that this path will be difficult, so he exhorts his audience to "take time off to come here [to the Vihar or temple], learn it and then only if keen, [they] should adopt it."[122] He also states that he and others must assist would-be converts by formulating "some rules" for converts to Buddhism.[123] He concludes his appeal to his followers by evoking guiding principles and values that echo his early appeals for self-respect among Dalits: "The principles of equality, compassion, fraternity and brotherhood which are essential for the welfare of humanity are found only in Buddhism." Harkening back to his initial pronouncement to leave Hinduism at Yeola in 1935, he completes the circle of conversion by indicating, "I have studied all the religions of the world for the last twenty years. And only after that it is my firm belief that everybody should adopt Buddhism."[124] The stages of *reflection* and *renunciation* happened long before for his followers in regard to their original religion of Hinduism, but now he was certain enough to advocate a positive path of orientational reconstruction: all Dalits should choose to convert to Buddhism, as it is more useful and meaningful for their need for equality, freedom, and dignity. In short, it fulfills the conditions needed for the flourishing of personality of individuals that he sought in the 1930s.

Ambedkar's appeals to his followers to convert to Buddhism began to grow in detail and strength in his final years. In a Marathi speech titled "The Tide of Buddhism Would Never Recede in India" (given on May 24, 1956), Ambedkar speaks to around seventy-five thousand followers at the celebration of the 2500th Buddha Jayanti in Bombay.[125] There he links Hinduism to a belief in the caste system, thereby emphasizing his concerns that the mental orientation connected with this religious tradition divides individuals and ranks them in a pain-producing hierarchy. Buddhism, however, as a mindset or religious orientation "has no place for the Caste System and *Chaturvarnya*."[126] Buddhism foregrounds equality among all humans. Reports of the speech highlight that during his address he compares himself to Moses, most likely because of his status as positive lawgiver in the form of the Indian constitution and in terms of advancing the spiritual law of Buddhism to an Indian people that had long forgotten it.[127] He also indicates three causes for the decline of a religion, presumably Buddhism in India: "Lack of abiding principles in it; lack of versatile and conquering orators; and lack of easily understandable principles."[128] The first cause is important, as it establishes continuity with his appeals in the

1930s to reflect on and then renounce Hinduism. Ambedkar evokes the Deweyan distinction between set "rules" and flexible "principles" in criticizing the Hindu mindset in *Annihilation of Caste*, in which he expresses longing for a religion of principle, not of rules. What he wants his audience to do in 1936 is to abandon Hinduism, since it is a religious orientation that is fixated on *rules*, not on general guiding principles that allow for an adaptive engagement with changing social situations. By 1956, at the very end of Ambedkar's life, Buddhism had become the orientation to convert *to* because it holds the possibility of being such an adaptable religion of principle. Even if its past instantiations suffer from being too rigid, Ambedkar implies that this isn't inherent in it in the same way that caste is integrated into the Vedic worldview. We simply need creative and brave lawgivers—strong reformers with will and an emboldened personality—who also serve an *oratorical* function as a spur to further Buddhism's renewed growth. These willful agents and individual reformers will be the "versatile and conquering orators" who will spread the understandable principles of Buddhism, just as Ambedkar demonstrates in his own example in his address. *Reflection* and *renunciation* now achieve their promised culmination in the act of *conversion to* Buddhism, a tradition reimagined for his audience as a religion of principle.

## Conversion to a Religion of Principle

The full extent of conversion, however, is often left out of these later addresses to Ambedkar's oppressed Dalit audiences. He speaks their language and appeals to religious reorientation as a way to bolster their self-respect and equality vis-à-vis other citizens of an independent India, but he still has not delivered on the promissory note he advanced concerning the specifics of the principle(s) animating his reconstructed Buddhism or the specific rituals that aspiring Buddhists need access to in order to render their religion a living faith. The first of these—specification of Buddhism as a religion of principle—is revealed most fully in *The Buddha and His Dhamma*. Ambedkar completed a draft of this work around 1951 (then titled *The Buddha and His Gospel*), but the revised and final version was only completed shortly before his death on December 6, 1956; it would not be published until 1957. Many of his English-language speeches and publications in the 1950s, however, would also spell out parts of Buddhism as a religion of principle. In terms of ritual for his reconstructed religion, Ambedkar did manage to enact his promise of giving important rites to his would-be Buddhist converts in the form of his own conversion ceremony.

Ambedkar had wanted to make a grand public conversion to Buddhism, perhaps as early as his Columbia University days, as the Adlerblum recollection seems to imply, but he seemed to always have something else demanding his time. Keer reports that it was finally in May 1956 that he decided the Buddha Jayanti celebrations in October would be the time of his conversion. But he was confined to his Delhi abode from June to October 1956 during his fight with diabetes and old age. His legs could not hold him up without a cane anymore, and his eyes were failing. His declining health seemed to spark a new sense of urgency, energizing him to make October 14 in Nagpur the date of his conversion. He invited his followers to come with him if they wanted, or to remain away if they felt differently about his act of conversion to Buddhism.[129] This individual act of will in changing one's religion (and one's descriptive label) was at once an intensely private and overtly public act of orientational change. He arranged for the oldest Buddhist monk in India, Bhikku Chandramani, to officiate at the ceremony, but the design of the ceremony was all under Ambedkar's control.

The conversion ceremony had two notable parts, at least for my account of Ambedkar as pragmatist rhetor: the actual conversion of Ambedkar (and his wife, Savita) to Buddhism on Sunday morning, October 14, and his public address to the crowd on Monday morning, October 15, 1956. These events were framed by a "magic lantern" image presentation on the life of the Buddha, occurring on the evenings of Saturday and Monday.[130] The entire duration was to be a grand event, not only focused on the conversion of Ambedkar and his wife but also involving the conversion of the masses of loyal followers in his audience. What if only a few attended and converted? Such an outcome would be disastrous, given that it would indicate the failure of his attempts at persuasion. Some of Ambedkar's loyal followers suggested he delay the conversion until after the coming elections, to minimize the risk to Dalits and their political pursuits. Ambedkar, sensing his life was growing short, pushed forward regardless of these risks. Fortunately, early signs pointed toward a grand turnout. Thousands of men, women, and children poured into Nagpur in preparation for the conversion ceremony; some came as early as a week beforehand.[131]

The anticipation of his public conversion brought not only support from his followers but also public concern about the pragmatic value of such an act. Many outside of Ambedkar's circles did not understand or appreciate conversion as a response to systemic or cultural forms of caste oppression. Following his public pronouncements in May 1950 that all Hindus, and not merely Dalits or oppressed castes, should adopt Buddhism, parts of the public and media reacted with incredulity; the *National Standard* from May 12, 1950, argued that "the scholarly Law Minister's solution is naïve. It is one thing to leave a religion and quite another to seek to end social tyranny by dyeing a whole community in another religious colour." Pointing at "the existence of caste spirit among some converted Christians of South India," the newspaper concluded "that if all Hindus became *Buddhists*, *Brahmin-Buddhists* would still look down on *Harijan-Buddhists*."[132] Another individual, writing in the *Indian Express* on January 8, 1955, saw Ambedkar's push for conversion as a useless decision; instead, "the right approach is to campaign for the eradication of the caste system and not to hate Hinduism." The author concludes that Ambedkar's ineffectual desire for conversion was not motivated by "the desire for spiritual attainment" but "by a hatred for *Hinduism*."[133] The theme of ineffectiveness in conversion was also apparent in the *Times of India* on January 2, 1955, which bluntly laid out the *realpolitik* of the situation as the editors saw it: "As a so-called untouchable leader, Ambedkar has political value. As a *Buddhist* he will have none. By liquidating his religion, he will liquidate his political stature."[134]

After the conversion took place, the news reported concerns about the conversion taking away reservations and protections for scheduled castes now that many had become Buddhists.[135] More serious, perhaps, were those fears about Ambedkar and his mishandling of the best means for effectively reconstructing Hindu society and tradition. A pseudonymous writer, "Caliban," mused in the *Times of India* on October 21, 1956, that Ambedkar's conversion was a withdrawal from the world, and that the conversation over rebirth bared too much of Ambedkar's soul; "it is not good to denude one's soul in public any more than it is desirable to undress in the market place."[136] As a nod toward the rhetorical functioning of the conversion event, Caliban also chided Ambedkar for having a more celebrated and grand conversion to Buddhism than that of the Buddha himself. Why did Ambedkar's conversion encumber all of these reactions? What might our approach of rhetoric and persuasion bring to how we understand this contested and complex event?

Seeing the conversion as a rhetorical event—one surrounded by the aura of such ideas as personality, agency, persuasion, and force in pursuit of the ideal community—will allow us to see meanings that extend beyond its impact on caste and reservations, say, or even the political influence of Ambedkar pre- and postconversion. What it will show us is how he designed and executed a series of rhetorically meaningful actions to create an image, and a persuasive power, for him and his followers. Our rhetorical approach to Ambedkar and his conversion will give due attention to the staging and framing of this momentous event. As for any speaking occasion, the time and place matter. The October 14 date possessed great rhetorical meaning. It was supposedly the day that the great Indian emperor, Ashoka, converted to Buddhism.[137] Ashoka was one of the most important Buddhist figures in Indian history, and he illustrated the power and political success that Buddhism could possess as an active, practical orientation toward life. Ambedkar was simply following in his footsteps, this framing suggested, given his previous political victories and status as a Moses-like lawgiver.

The location also held great meaning. As Ambedkar would explain in his speech on October 15, Nagpur was the site of the Nag people. They are characterized by Ambedkar as an ancient native population who resisted the invading Aryans; only one of their number survived, and then only by magical intervention by a sage, Agasti.[138] The descendants of this lone Naga became the worshippers of Buddha and assisted him in spreading his teachings throughout India. While elements of this story are mythical, this fact by no means lessens the symbolic importance of this location. Ambedkar, in his quest to become a Buddhist, returned to an important birthplace of the Buddhist faith in India (as well as within his stronghold of Maharashtra). Like the Nagas, he was to be reborn through the fortuitous intervention of conversion to Buddhism. Of any spot to embrace Buddhism, this one had a *public* significance because it perfectly indicated group commitment to the doctrines of the Buddha. When Ambedkar discussed the one surviving Naga in his narrative and claimed "we are the descendants of him," he could have meant various things. The Dalits could be historically related to these brave but subdued people, and like the Nagas they could rise again through a collective embrace of Buddhism. Or he could mean, in a metaphoric sense, the people converting at the event were embarking on a new path animated by the orientation of the Buddhist *dhamma* or teaching. Either meaning, of course, gives the physical space a grand significance befitting a historic event that had been decades in coming.

As an act of will and agential effort, the conversion ceremony was important because it was an observable and repeatable example of a voluntary conversion to the Buddhist way of approaching the world. It also gave a performative, embodied meaning to Ambedkar's own praise of Buddhism; instead of simply *speaking about* its doctrines, he was in an important sense *living* them through his perlocutionary utterances. One can see these aspects in how the event unfolded on October 14. Ambedkar arrived in the morning, leaning on a staff and his trusted aide, Nanak Chand Rattu.[139] He walked out on the stage set up in an otherwise ordinary field in Nagpur to observe the sea of white-clad audience members ready for conversion, estimated variously at 300,000 to 600,000 followers. Most, but not all, of these attendees were Dalits.[140] On the stage were a few Buddhist monks, along with Ambedkar and his second wife, Savita.[141] Ambedkar and Savita were the first to convert to Buddhism, repeating the Pali oaths administered by Bhikku Chandramani in Marathi, the language best understood by many in the audience. They repeated three times the Buddhist tributes to the Buddha, the *dhamma* (the Buddha's teaching), and the *sangh* (the community of Buddhists monks). They were then administered the *Pancha Sila*, a moral code from the Buddhist tradition whereby they vowed to abstain "from killing living beings," "from taking things not given," "from sexual misconduct," "from false speech," and "from intoxicating drinks and drugs."[142] Ambedkar and Savita then bowed three times with clasped hands to the Buddha statue on the stage and placed an offering of white lotuses in front of it. After the recitation of a set of twenty-two vows that Ambedkar had composed in Marathi for the conversion to Buddhism, the entry into Buddhism was complete. Ambedkar and his wife received waves of applause and shouts of support from the massive audience.[143] Ambedkar's conversion had culminated in something more than his speeches and writings ever intimated: it was the affective living out of what he had preached and argued for in so many previous ways.

Thinking about this epochal event from a more conceptual level, the notion of conversion becomes more complex than we might have originally thought. Conversion could be seen as a voluntary, private affair of the heart. As common as this view might be, it was clearly not the case in Ambedkar's conversion ceremony. While it was voluntary, it was by no means private. His conversion was publicly observable, and he repeatedly proclaimed "I renounce Hinduism" at its conclusion. It was also not limited to him as a subject of conversion. His own performance of conversion was immediately followed by his focusing on his audience; he then invited all those in the audience who wanted to convert to Buddhism. Nearly the entire audience stood up to convert, a number that Keer places at 300,000.[144] Ambedkar led them through the three refuges (the Buddha, the *dhamma*, and the *sangh*) as well as the *Pancha Sila*, along with the administration of the twenty-two vows he had created.

It is useful to spell out these vows, since they are of Ambedkar's own design and answer his own demand for the construction of Buddhist rituals and moral principles. They will also reveal something more about his pragmatism. They include the following public commitments:

1. I shall have no faith in Brahma, Vishnu[,] and Mahesh, nor shall I worship them.
2. I shall have no faith in Rama and Krishna, nor shall I worship them.
3. I shall have no faith in "Gouri," "Ganpati[,]" and other Gods and God-desses of Hindu religion, nor shall I worship them.
4. I do not believe in the theory of incarnation of Gods.
5. I do not and shall not believe that Lord Buddha was the incarnation of Vishnu. I believe this to be sheer madness and false propaganda.
6. I shall not perform "Shraaddha" nor shall I give "pind-dan."
7. I shall not act in a manner contrary to the principles and teachings of the Buddha.
8. I shall not perform any ceremony through Brahmins.
9. I shall believe in the equality of mankind.
10. I shall endeavor to establish equality.
11. I shall follow the Eightfold Path taught by the Buddha.
12. I shall follow the *Ten Paramitas* enunciated by the Buddha.
13. I shall be compassionate to all living beings and nurture them with care.
14. I shall not steal.
15. I shall not lie.
16. I shall not commit carnal sins.
17. I shall not consume liquor.
18. I shall strive to lead my life in conformity with the three principles of Buddhism, i.e., *Pradnya* (wisdom), *Sheel* (character)[,] and *Karuna* (compassion).
19. I hereby embrace Buddhism by renouncing my old Hindu religion, which is detrimental to the prosperity [of] humankind and discriminates [against] human beings and treats them low.
20. I firmly believe that the Buddha Dhamma is the *Saddhamma*.
21. I believe I am entering the new life.
22. Hereafter I pledge to conduct myself in accordance with the teachings of the Buddha.[145]

Much can be said about these oaths or vows administered to the thousands of dedicated audience members. Part of their importance was their compact and ritualized accounting of what it meant to become and to function as a Buddhist. They clearly call for a practical renunciation of Hinduism, namely through the commitments to stay away from the theological baggage that is entailed by Hinduism (vows 1–4). The pernicious claim that the Buddha was an avatar of the Hindu God Vishnu to attract and lead astray evil doers is also rejected (vow 5), along with a refusal of Hindu rituals (vows 6 and 8). These are all more limited guides for action; they tell one exactly what they are not to do or believe.

In the Deweyan parlance that Ambedkar echoed in *Annihilation of Caste*, such vows (e.g., 1-8) function as mere *rules*. Rules have a value in their specificity, but they are not the core to a sustained and adaptive reflective morality. The most vital component for a living ethics or religion—*principles*—can be found in the later vows created by Ambedkar, many of which capture in general terms the egalitarian and compassionate nature of Ambedkar's humanistic Buddhism. The convert utters that they will follow the Buddha's eightfold path governing the right attitudes behind acting and being in the world amid others (vow 11), along with the affirmations contained in the *Pancha Sila* (vows 13-17). The convert also vows to cultivate the three virtues of character, wisdom, and compassion (vow 18); all of these vows represent flexible principles that can inform or guide our reflection on and activities in the world of uncertainty, not specific actions to be done or forbidden. They trade simplicity and concreteness for flexibility and imaginative potential. Ambedkar's social reading of Buddhism is also apparent in vows 9 and 10 concerning the equality of all humans, a claim that Ambedkar saw as perhaps the most desirable doctrinal feature of Buddhism and as a central implication of the concept of personality drawn from Dewey's early idealist ethics.

The importance of these vows is easy to overlook if one is focused on arguments and positions, however. They also entail paradoxes if one is attentive to their functioning. If one reflects on the nature of vows, a question may arise: Aren't vows a voluntary limitation on one's future freedom? One vows to do something in the future, and they should not diverge from that commitment no matter what the conditions are later in their life. Vows are paradoxically an act of freedom in the present that seems to limit one's freedom in the future. How can they enhance the sort of respect and autonomy that Ambedkar sought in his escape from caste strictures? How do they conduce to what we've called "effective freedom"? This is where the exploration of the Deweyan background that Ambedkar appropriates, changes, or resists proves so useful. Rules have the benefit of being concrete and specific, but therein lies their weakness in the face of an uncertain future. They also represent the sort of truncated freedom that vows offer in their binding force on future action. But principles, taken in the pragmatist sense, do not bind specifically or concretely; they guide action in a range of specific situations with certain values and methods of inquiry. Thus, the many vows that Ambedkar creates and commits to are binding, but most do not constrict his future freedom; operating as principles, many of the vows will constructively channel the use of future freedom and reflection in unknown contexts yet to be engaged.

Taken as a set, Ambedkar's list of vows is noteworthy because it is composed of both *rules* (vows 1–8, 13–17) and *principles* (vows 9–12, 18–22). While many might think of it as a mere ritualization of more important positions and themes, I argue that this set of vows can be taken to be a vital part of Ambedkar's *Navayana* or "new vehicle" Buddhism. This conversion ritual and its rhetorical positioning illustrate the meliorative turn to Ambedkar's efforts to persuade his audience about his vision of Buddhism; they not only are to *believe* in the equality of all, they are to always attempt to *establish* it through positive action. Much more could be said about the content of these vows, but we must note their rhetorical functioning as a *performance* of Buddhism: the audience member, repeating Ambedkar's vows, not only aspires to be a Buddhist but *becomes* a Buddhist through the speech act of *diksha* or conversion. Ambedkar, of course, has displayed his status as a "conquering orator" here not only in the words he utters, but in the words he makes others live through and utter in the act of beginning a "new life" through the adoption of the *principles* of Buddhism. In this way, his performance unites the themes of individual reformers mattering, speech as educative to those who hear it, rhetoric as reconstructive, and the value of an agent's willfulness.

Ambedkar's rhetorical activity on this momentous occasion did not stop with his conversion to Buddhism or the conversion of hundreds of thousands of others immediately after his conversion. The next morning, October 15, 1956, he addresses the eager (and now largely Buddhist) crowd in his native tongue of Marathi. While he had been involved in writing the complex set of vows performed on the previous day, this speech showcases his uncommon strength as an orator producing a message calculated to move his audience toward orientational change. Whereas the vows could be replicated in future conversion ceremonies, this message is for this newly minted Buddhist audience alone. After explaining why he has chosen Nagpur as the spot of this historic event, he rallies the crowd against higher-caste critiques of his conversion movement, which asserted that such a change would mean a loss of the "benefits" and accommodations accorded to the Dalits. Ambedkar's reply, surely cheered, is that the criticizing Brahmins are welcome to give up their status and gain the "benefits" of being a Mahar.[146] He then turns to his ultimate point and emphasizes why he and his followers are taking all of these measures: the act of conversion, building upon his appeals for reflection and renunciation in the 1930s, is calculated to gain a sense of self-respect and respect from others. He brushes aside the political concerns of the moment and continues his emphasis on the Deweyan philosophy of self-realization and respect, stating, "In reality self-respect is dearer to [a] human being and not material gain. . . . We are fighting for honor and self-respect."[147] Political rights should and hopefully will follow this gaining of self-respect, but respect as a foundation is vital.[148]

Even without material gain, self-respect instantiated through an act of will was still a monumental achievement. It took courage to say that one wouldn't be bound by the metaphysics entailed by caste. Referring to his performance of conversion the previous day, he recognizes that others may ask "why I embraced only this religion and not any other. This is the basic and important question in the [sic] any movement of a conversion."[149] He even echoes his own phrase from Yeola in 1935, stating that "though I am born as a Hindu I will not die as a Hindu." He notes that he "proved it yesterday."[150] One must remember that Ambedkar renounced the Hindu religious orientation in the 1930s and had explored a range of other faiths—including Sikhism, Islam, Christianity, and others—for the mass conversion of himself and the Dalits for over twenty years.[151] Reflection on and renunciation of a religious orientation are initial steps a willful agent can take to religious reorientation, but they are not coextensive with the gaining of a new orientation known as "conversion" in the Ambedkarite model. How does one determine a religious orientation to convert to? In line with the pragmatist *ethos* of theory and worldviews being valuable because of their usefulness in experience, Ambedkar looks at the practical value of religious orientations in everyday activity: What sort of religion enlivens you, gives meaning and value to your existence? Each person must examine this matter for themselves, just as each had to utter the vows of their own accord in the mass conversion the day before this talk. This is the charge of being an individual with personality and will, rendering one both equal to and unique from all other individuals. Comparing Buddhism to the anti-religious themes in Karl Marx's communism, Ambedkar takes a stand for the irreplaceable value of religious orientation. Religion is a matter of mind, going beyond our physical wants and desires. It grows out of and alters the Deweyan concerns of the previous chapters, as it includes the simultaneous realization of self in an individual functioning in a communal setting as well the meliorative shaping of shared habits and customs in a group. As such, reflection is integral to individual reform: "The mind should be developed. It should be made cultured."[152] Religion can give the mind a certain energy or "enthusiasm" that enables social progress, or it can rob an individual of any thoughts that they deserve self-respect, thereby stunting the realization of their full value, agency, and self-hood. Buddhism, for Ambedkar, embodies the sort of humanism that enables the former among the downtrodden Dalits.

Religion, Ambedkar argues, gives hope to the poor in a way that Marxist dogma cannot, and without this hope, progress in material matters important for the poor is likely to fail. One's self-respect is a vital part of their perceived self-efficacy; if we believe we are useless and worthless, surely we won't engage in full-bodied projects to accomplish great things or to increase our worth. Lack of self-respect confines an agent to a position that doesn't gain much respect from others. Ambedkar, emphasizing his reading of Buddhism as being without caste divisions, argues that adopting this egalitarian belief system extricates Dalits from the net of habits and customs that instantiate caste. The soft force of persuasion and personal performance becomes the keynote to his reconstructive project. Ambedkar and his wife, along with thousands of Dalits, converted voluntarily and evinced a willful agency that was both means and end to their activity. Never does one see Ambedkar appeal to the use of violent or strongly coercive force in the service of conversion. He gives voice to the attitude of respect for others that he sees in his social Buddhism:

> We will follow our path, you follow yours. We have found a new path. This
> is the day of hope. This is the path of elevation and progress. This is not the
> new path. This path has not been borrowed from any where. This path is
> from here, it is purely Indian. The Buddhist religion survived here for 2000
> years in India. Truly speaking, we feel regretted why we did not embrace
> the Buddhism earlier. The principles preached by the Lord Buddha are im-
> mortal. But the Lord Buddha did not make such [a] claim. There is a provi-
> sion for change with the change of time. Such generosity is not found in any
> religion.[153]

Ambedkar again ties the previous day's conversion ritual to *this* space, *this* historical land. It is also tied to the modern nation-state of India. All of these measures are designed to bolster the respect of these individuals for themselves—as individuals, they should proudly adopt the principles of Buddhism to confront the demands of acting in society because it is a scientific religion (viz. changeable and advancing with changing times) and since it holds out the egalitarian hope of seeing the world without caste divisions. This solves one of the perplexing mysteries in Ambedkar's reconstructive appeals, dating back to his calls for renunciation in the 1930s: if he sought unity and the free-flowing interactions among groups praised in *Democracy and Education*, why call for an exit from the dominant Hindu social system? This becomes understandable if one sees caste and society in the Deweyan terms enunciated earlier. If caste is a habit of how one sees and values self and others, then it has little to do with physical proximity or remoteness. It has everything to do with how much value is granted by individuals to their group's members and the members of other groups. Thus, the call for conversion to Buddhism is not a call to break away from interacting with others in Indian society; it is a call to break away from *thinking* about these individuals and one's self using the hierarchical categories of caste. The new orientation of Buddhism allows for social experience in and around others to have a new egalitarian meaning and potential. Labels, names, concepts, and reactions are all affected by this reconstruction.

Ambedkar concludes his speech with a reference to the important Buddhist dialogue between King Milinda and Nagsena, a story that also implicates persuasion and reflective conversion (Nagsena was formerly a Brahmin before his conversion to Buddhism). Ambedkar focuses his new Buddhist audience on Milinda's question, why do religions decline? He then paraphrases Nagsena's three responses in a way that echoes his speech on May 24, 1956. Religions are said to decline when they are "immature. The basic principles of that religion have no depth."[154] This is a restatement of his earlier critique of religious orientations as *unreflective*—as mechanical, unthinking, and maladaptive. Second, religions decline when "there are no learned preachers in that religion. . . . If the preachers of the religion are not prepared to hold debate with the opponents, then the religion declines."[155] This is another version of his appeal to develop (or to be) a willful and "conquering orator" for a chosen religion. The entailment of this statement about decline, of course, is that religions will grow *if* they have orators who embody and develop a forceful personality. Ambedkar does not hide the fact that he sees himself as such a figure: "It is my duty to give you in all respects the knowledge of this religion. By writing books, I will remove all your doubts and suspicions and will try to lead you to a stage of full knowledge. At least at present, you should have faith in me."[156] He is, in effect, priming them to have faith in what they will read about Buddhism through the more lasting texts that he leaves in his wake. The principles expressed through his enunciation of the Buddhist orientation, as well as in the ritual of conversion that he constructs, will avoid Nagsena's third reason for religious decline: the state of affairs that holds when a "religion and the religious principles are only for learned persons."[157] A religion of principle lives in its texts and rituals, as well as in the hands of strong personalities like Ambedkar himself.

Ambedkar's promise, not completely fulfilled in this speech, is that Buddhism is constituted by a set of principles for anyone to use in everyday life. This is vital for this audience, of course, because most of their self-respect and value lies shredded in their everyday experience at the hands of those acting and reacting within the mindset of caste. Buddhism is said to be expanding all over the world, and Ambedkar makes an appeal to the audience to realize their self-respect through this increasingly popular path: "If you feel, accept this religion. If this religion appeals to your reason, then accept it. Such generosity has not been allowed in any other religion."[158] Instead of focusing on otherworldly matters, Ambedkar highlights Buddhism's focus on the suffering in *this* world: "To emancipate those depressed and poor people from sorrow is the principal task of the Buddha's religion. What else did Karl Marx tell different from Lord Buddha's saying? Lord Buddha did not tell anything in a zigzag way."[159] Buddhism, at least in Ambedkar's reconstruction, is a straightforward way to improve or optimally realize self and society in this world. It simply depends on its being adopted as a guiding orientation to bring its effects into this world. As Ambedkar challenged his audience:

> Your responsibility is great too. Your behavior should be such that other people will honor and respect you. . . . We must resolve to follow Buddhist religion in the finest way. It should not happen that the Mahar people brought the Buddhism to disgrace, so we must have firm determination. If we accomplish this, then we will thrive ourselves, our nation, and not only that but the whole world also. Because the Buddhist religion only will be the savior of the world. Unless there is justice, there will be no peace in the world.[160]

The voluntary action of conversion helps the Buddhist religion through swelling its ranks, but more effort is needed from his audience; the more they see themselves as personalities, as living and acting in accord with and as animated by the Buddhist orientation, the more respect they will bring to that religious tradition among others in society. And the greater the *dhamma* grows in strength, the greater effect it will have on rendering social interactions democratic and egalitarian, in Ambedkar's pragmatism. He created a repeatable rite of conversion and administered it to hundreds of thousands of followers. Each of these reoriented individuals not only gained a new way of looking at their own value but now was encumbered with the duty of spreading this orientation among friends and opponents: Ambedkar's final line was "I proclaim that every Buddhist person has the right to *Deeksha*."[161] This was immediately followed by thunderous applause from his audience and was succeeded by mass conversions of large crowds to Buddhism in the following days. Buddhism had been reconstructed by Ambedkar into a performative rhetoric that bestowed a newfound sense of self-worth and respect for human personality through persuasion oriented toward others—and ultimately, toward one's self. If religious conversion affected the self at the deepest level of personality, Ambedkar was claiming *and* enacting the idea that every Buddhist person has the right to reconstruct their self. *Diksha* connoted the right to personal and social reconstruction.

## Conversion, Self-Emancipation, and Persuasive Force

Attending to what we can extrapolate from Ambedkar's translation and employment of pragmatism in his battles against social injustice, we can discern a meliorative emphasis on reforming certain wide-ranging mental habits in addition to his well-documented political and institutional reform efforts. This focus on habits and customs in particular can be conceptualized as a process of *rhetorical reorientation*. It is rhetorical insofar as it involves the use of communicative means to move audience members toward an end point. It involves reorientation insofar as its goal is not simply conversion, but a multiphase process of choosing a new orientation toward self, others, and the world. This rhetoric of reorientation reacts to what Dewey would call a felt *problematic situation*, or as Ambedkar puts it in *Annihilation of Caste*, "a crisis."[162]

The full process of reorientation uses communicative means to (1) reflectively *evaluate* held and potential orientations, (2) *renounce* a held orientation judged harmful, and (3) *convert* to a more beneficial orientation. In this general account, each of these stages is separate. One need not do all of them at once or appeal to an audience to undergo all immediately. For higher-caste audiences addressed by his *Annihilation of Caste*, Ambedkar mainly attempted to spur reflective thinking concerning the sources of harm in the religious orientations underlying the caste system. To the oppressed audiences addressed by his "What Way Emancipation?" address, the emphasis was on both reflective analysis of the causes of injustice and renunciation of the orientation enshrined in identifying as a Hindu. By the 1950s, Ambedkar publicly settled on Buddhism as the religion to which he and his followers should convert in their own acts of will. Ambedkar's rhetoric shows that religious orientations can be meliorated even without postulating a complete answer to a problem—without undergoing all three steps to reorientation. Regardless of the uncertain direction of his third step (*conversion to*), he still advocated reflecting on and renouncing Hinduism to both his higher-caste Hindu audiences and his oppressed Dalit listeners. This was a difficult pill for the former to swallow, but not so much for the latter audience, already conversant with the experiences of untouchability. His Dalit followers, however, did need a discursive push to see renunciation as meliorative and as a source of hope. It took courage to renounce a religion that foisted the labels and the metaphysics of caste on one's being. Renouncing one's "nature" seems, at first glance, both impossible and undesirable. But Ambedkar's pragmatism rebelled against such foundationalism and looked for possibility and potentiality in the contingency of the self and the world.

It was in the synthesis between malleable individuals and a modern approach to social psychology that Ambedkar saw a melioristic opening. His rhetoric of reorientation synthetically foregrounds the role agents can play in empowering themselves and others in seeking social justice, as well as the "reclamation of human personality." Conversion discourse, one type of rhetorical action used by Ambedkar, is thereby rendered a *persuasive*, other-focused attempt to enable communal change. Ambedkar was convinced of his need to convert, and in many of his speeches he tried to empower others to notice the reasons that had moved him to that decision. Ambedkar's attempts at reorientation did not assume a switch from nonbeliever to believer and thereby offer a stark contrast to the tenor of puritan conversion rhetoric discussed by Eugene White.[163] The pluralistic setting of the Indian subcontinent has long fostered some level of respect for argumentative exchanges among rival *darśanas* (literally, "ways of seeing") or philosophical systems.[164] The model that Ambedkar worked with is that of believers choosing from among a range of viable religious alternatives. Even though one has an orientation, one can reorient oneself through an act of will, initiated either by the agent or by a powerful rhetor like Ambedkar. Beyond the historical lines of influence, such a model is pragmatist in spirit as it foregrounds choice among options with an eye toward beneficial results; it is distinctively Indian in character since it assumes such a rich starting ground of religious diversity and potential intergroup argumentation.

The three steps of reorientation are based on the idea that religions have effects, and these orientations can be taken up or sloughed off at will. The individual will is vital in this process; it is both that which is conditioned by habits and that which could change or reform these habits. The individual conditions the social in a dialectical pragmatist sense; groups are made up of individuals bearing similar habits (e.g., customs), and these habits are influenced by group membership and the experience it channels for individuals. As Dewey stated in bringing his idealism to bear on education in 1887, the year before he published "The Ethics of Democracy," "Society is a society of individuals and the individual is always a social individual. He has no existence by himself. He lives in, for, and by society, just as society has no existence excepting in and through the individuals who constitute it."[165] Dewey's early ethical charge was to realize or know this relationship; Ambedkar's main theme, at least in the speeches he gave exploring and imploring conversion, is that individual effort can be an important point at which *intelligent* force can be applied in the maximally promising intervention. Such efforts must focus on meliorating the most fundamental individual orientations that lie at the root of social functioning.

## Conversion and the Right to Reconstruction

It is easy to overlook the importance of Ambedkar's conversion for his pragmatism, especially given his role in politics and our modern penchant for systems and structures. It is, however, an absolutely unique event in the evolution of pragmatism, and perhaps philosophy in general. Ambedkar's conversion at Nagpur represents an intersection of decades of his philosophical writings with his own meliorative attempts to do something with his person, his habits, and his mental orientation. In many ways, it was a lived and performed example that was the culmination of the quest of the "Indian student," recalled by Adlerblum, who was passionately "searching for a bridge between Dewey and Buddhism." Ambedkar's conversion merges abstract concepts like personality and effective freedom (autonomy created by balancing equality, liberty, and fraternity, in Dewey's complex sense) with a performance of self-change. Ambedkar ended his speech to the would-be converts at Nagpur by exclaiming that every individual has the right to *diksha* or conversion. Considered alongside his complex psychology of custom and habits, one realizes that Ambedkar just as easily could have exclaimed that every individual has the right to personal reconstruction. For conversion was an enacted and embodied reconstruction of self, habits, and, perhaps eventually, group and societal customs. Conversion was the reclamation of human personality through this act of personal reconstruction.

Conversion—or more concretely, *Ambedkar's* conversion—represented a bridge between an abstract pragmatist psychology and its associated philosophy of democracy and the living, breathing experience of self-respect. Such self-respect is not merely *self*-affecting, as Ambedkar knew that it was a precursor to demanding and attaining respect from other community members in line with the ideals of social democracy and its values of equality, liberty, and fraternity. What is intriguing about this grand event at Nagpur—perhaps the culmination of Ambedkar's *philosophy* as well as his *life*—was its merging of ideas, ideals, and actions. It is vital that the discussion of conversion as reconstruction be framed by *his* act of conversion, a personalization that philosophers are often reluctant to do with their focus on abstract systems, arguments imprisoned in all-encompassing language, and generalizations and summaries distanced from the messiness and inscrutability of everyday life. Ambedkar believed in *reconstructive rhetoric*, and he used this in reworking all sorts of ideas and texts, from those firmly ensconced in the Indian tradition to the passages of Dewey. The past was meant to be reconstructed in service of the future, and nothing was sacred or eternally secured. His act of conversion at Nagpur, however, shows that these general philosophical commitments and rhetorical practices also applied to his self, his body, and the ways that he was to act in the future.

*Ambedkar* reconstructed *himself* in the act of conversion. Seeing this action as part of his own pragmatist philosophy provides a way to place the conversion moment in Ambedkar's story other than the two prevailing ways that Gauri Viswanathan recounts: as either a "purely reactive" and symbolic move made in response to caste-based hostility or as "entirely a spiritual event connected to the discovery of moral truths that had the power to liberate oppressed dalits."[166] Viswanathan, following Christopher Queen, sees a middle path between these accounts, one that reads the conversion moment as an "exercise of individual choice based on reason, careful deliberation, and historical consciousness."[167] Queen's own analysis anchors this exercise of individual choice in the parts of Buddhism that Ambedkar valued and restated, and it reads Ambedkar's reconstruction of Buddhism as "an act of religious faith."[168] But where Queen grounds this in postmodern hermeneutics, I am more inclined to connect this act of conversion to Ambedkar's continuing revision of pragmatist themes of reconstruction, the psychology of habit, and the ideal of reflection-guided effective freedom at the individual and community levels. Ambedkar's Buddhist conversion did not point toward the *postmodern character* of his thought; it pointed to his enduring *pragmatism*.

This focus on pragmatism as the background to Ambedkar's reconstructive pragmatism allows us to see the connection between his personal act of conversion, his general concerns with force in reform efforts, and his own rhetorical practices. Ambedkar's oratory in the 1950s was aimed at persuading his fellow Dalits to take Buddhism seriously as *the* religion of principle that they should follow. He practiced the art of speaking to move his followers into this faith through the ritual act of *conversion*. This act was clearly separated from the phase of *reflection* on one's religious orientation and *renunciation* of problematic religious orientations, major themes of his public address in the 1930s. His own performed conversion to Buddhism instantiated this process that was advocated across many of his speeches and writings. This combination of rhetoric about conversion to Buddhism and his own conversion to Buddhism in a very public manner causes us to rethink the rhetorical potentials of conversion. Work on conversion tends to foreground narratives about one's own conversion, largely an inner or private affair.[169] Ambedkar's performed conversion emphasizes his own experience *and* the persuasive shaping of the experiences of other subjects. Ambedkar's own act of conversion becomes primarily *rhetorical* in that it implicates both self and others influenced by that self through constitutive religious discourse and ritual—it functions as a persuasive and meaningful appeal to those in the audience and those attending to the event.

How does Ambedkar's rich notion of conversion as orientational reconstruction use the personal experience of subjects? Why does it emphasize this feature, when so many other accounts would focus on material change in reforming society, as did those paths inspired by Marx that Ambedkar knew of and resisted in the 1950s? Ambedkar, of course, was integrally involved in organizing, activism, and policy change, but the enigma of his conversion still stands out. Does it matter to these philosophical questions about reform, justice, and social democracy? The answers to these questions surrounding his conversion implicate the ideas and conundrums of force that we have seen Ambedkar wrestling with since his days with Dewey at Columbia and since his review of Russell's book on reform and reconstruction. One concern remains across the years: How can one reform or alter an oppressive society using force without becoming oppressive to the agency and goals of self-realization evinced by other agents, or those with whom you must form a community? How can one be a reformer that does not create the new need in others to reform the oppression now instantiated in one's activities? Ambedkar saw conversion as one way around the attraction of the all-too-often revolutionary and violent forces available in political action, a path of constructive force that was compatible with the methods of intelligent speaking. Both speaking to his followers and enacting his own conversion became provisional answers to these questions of force—they were, effectively, experiments in finding the intelligent force of persuasion that did not coerce, shame, cajole, or damage self, others, or the hopes of community and fraternity. He spoke about and desired the emplacement of orientations or habits that allowed for intelligent, and sustainable, interaction with other members of one's community. His own act of conversion represented an observable and ritually replicable choice of self-reorientation.

How did his conversion function as a use of force in his efforts at personal and social melioration? Put simply, it preceded and enacted the exact sort of self-reconstruction he was asking his followers to enact. This revealing performance, combined with the rational force of his argumentative rhetoric, illustrates Ambedkar's commitment to intelligent and noncoercive means. In a sense, his performance of conversion not only highlighted the path he advocated, it *invited* his audience to imitate his example through their own performances. There is an intriguing scholarly literature on invitational rhetoric, a style of rhetoric informed by Western feminist theory and defined by its resistance to a putative "patriarchal bias" in rhetoric that pigeonholes rhetoric "as the conscious intent to change others."[170] Invitational rhetoric resists a notion of rhetoric as forceful, end-directed persuasion. Instead of focusing on the desire to force change in one's audience, invitational rhetoric represents "an invitation to understanding as a means to create a relationship rooted in equality, immanent value, and self-determination. Invitational rhetoric constitutes an invitation to the audience to enter the rhetor's world and to see it as the rhetor does."[171] It creates conditions for the audience's expression of their own views, along with the promotion of a nonhierarchical "offering" of the speaker's own perspective. Is Ambedkar's rhetoric of conversion—largely targeted at his Dalit followers—invitational in this sense? His forceful and direct arguments extolling conversion and its benefits seem very strong to be merely an invitation to his audience to consider his perspective. Yet his insistence on his own performance preceding any conversion of his audience members shows a related concern with persuasive force that does not cross the line into coercive or end-truncating force. Why is such a soft, intelligent force of verbal and performed persuasion morally good?

Ambedkar's combined use of forceful argument and his own performance of the advocated self-reconstruction that is conversion serves as the sort of force that respects the autonomy and agency of his audience. His words and actions might move his followers, but they do so in a way that respects their effective freedom. This point is nothing new in Ambedkar's thought and practice; he explicitly talks about such concerns in his speech honoring Ranade (and castigating Gandhi and Jinnah) in Pune on January 18, 1943. There, in discussing the reason for the demise of India's liberal party, Ambedkar concludes with this passage:

> All Liberals I know will say our duty is to follow the master. What else could be the attitude of a devout band of disciples? But can anything be more mistaken or more uncritical? Such an attitude implies two things. It means that a great man works by imposing his maxims on his disciples. It means that the disciples should not be wiser than the master. Both these conclusions are wrong.[172]

Forcing or cajoling one's followers into following what one says, without allowing for thought or reflection, does not constitute the end, or even the means, of democratic emancipation. What should a leader concerned with being effective in political organizing and social change strive for? Ambedkar's answer in 1943 foreshadows the convergence of his rhetoric and his own conversion at the end of his life: "No great man really does his work by crippling his disciple[s] by forcing on them his maxims or his conclusions. What a great man does is not to impose his maxims on his disciples. *What he does is to evoke them, to awaken them to a vigorous and various exertion of their faculties.*"[173]

It is this evocation of the powers of his followers that Ambedkar was trying to achieve with his appeals and his own performance of conversion on that grand stage in Nagpur. His reconstructive rhetoric operated in arguments, textual revisions, and meaningfully embodied actions, all with the goal of creating reflective agents who intelligently surveyed their habits and the customs of the society that affect the formation of more satisfying forms of community. Ambedkar's conversion was one way to show his followers how to invigorate themselves and how to reach for freedom and respect from others through an act of self-respect and personal change. As we have seen throughout this book, Ambedkar's pragmatism and Buddhism led him to develop a way of speaking that could enable equality, liberty, *and* community. He wanted each person to count in the democracy that India was becoming, and he wanted to form community through the reconstruction of problematic habits and customs. He wanted a social democracy animated by fraternity, and it was this concern that truncated the effective but end-destroying coercive and violent forces that he could have chosen. Conversion to Buddhism was an extremely visible example of the sort of force that hoped for—and that did not preclude—fraternity with friends and foes alike.

# The Vision of Ambedkar's Navayana Pragmatism

The chapters in this book represent only a start to answering the complex question of Ambedkar's reception of Dewey's thought. This reception was not complete, as Ambedkar only had access to parts of Dewey's enormous body of work. Nor was it one of mere imitation; while Ambedkar echoed some of the Deweyan texts he owned, he purposely selected and reconstructed those portions of Dewey's expansive thought that might prove useful for his own purposes, and he rejected or resisted other parts of Dewey's philosophy that he heard or read. Ambedkar combined parts of Dewey's ever-evolving thought in new ways and recovered parts of Dewey's idealist thought that the American had left behind by the time Ambedkar heard him in Morningside Heights. All of this demonstrates that Dewey's pragmatism mattered for Ambedkar's own highly original thought, much like Buddha's or Marx's philosophy mattered. Pragmatism's ideals, methods, themes, and texts all made specific and identifiable impacts on Ambedkar's development, and we can see them playing vital parts in his reconstruction of Buddhism, and his conversion to Buddhism, in the 1950s.

Let us step back from the intense focus on texts and arguments that has characterized this inquiry into Ambedkar's reception of Dewey's pragmatism and instead ask a more general question: What might the general contours of Ambedkar's pragmatism be, should we want to talk about his thought as part of the evolution of pragmatism around the globe? By this point, one should see the clear faults in objections that presuppose that labeling a thinker as part of the pragmatist tradition means that thinker replicates or adheres to all the commitments of, say, Dewey. William James and Charles S. Peirce clearly did not subscribe to everything Dewey wrote and in many cases differed from or disagreed with his philosophy. Ambedkar's classmate in his final seminar with Dewey, Hu Shih, also did not replicate all that he heard from Dewey, let alone all that Dewey asserted over his long career. Yet we still consider these figures part of the historical and philosophical story of pragmatism, one that emphasizes shared themes alongside many lacunae, resistances, divergences, and revisions. And considering figures as pragmatists does not exclude alternate framings or labels; James was also a psychologist, and Ambedkar was also a politician and a Buddhist. Outlining Ambedkar as a pragmatist does not erase other emphases applicable to his story. Instead, considering him as a pragmatist adds to these other stories and expands on what we know about the global development of pragmatist thought. Ambedkar, as this book has demonstrated, is part of the story of pragmatism in America. Along with the other roles he played in contemporary South Asian history, he is also the central figure in the evolution of pragmatism in India.

Ambedkar is one of the most original and influential anticaste thinkers. His texts, arguments, and activism all relate to the battle against a millennia-old oppression implicated in doctrines of *karma*, birth, and rebirth. But we must not let the fact that Ambedkar is an *anticaste* philosopher, and his status as a *Dalit* leader, blind us to the reality that he was also simultaneously a *philosopher* and a *leader*, taken in their more general senses. Telling the story of Ambedkar's pragmatism, both in its historical development and in its general commitments, allows room for readings to flower of this complex thinker as both an anticaste figure and a theorist of democracy. These concerns are interrelated, but they are also separable for certain uses. One must never forget that Ambedkar oriented much of his thought surrounding Buddhism toward international audiences, whom he addressed in English, that had no experience of caste oppression. Buddhism, for Ambedkar, was to be a universal religious orientation, not solely an escape for his fellow Dalits from their particular form of oppression; indeed, both versions of his "Buddhist Bible" were composed in English rather than Marathi or a language the oppressed of India might better understand. Many scholars have explored the dimensions of Ambedkar's thought as a philosophy oriented toward the injustices of India and a social system saturated with caste concerns; let us end this book by considering Ambedkar as philosopher of democracy and as a unique pragmatist figure, one who speaks to societies pursuing the democratic ideal in light of injustices that may or may not include caste division.

While Ambedkar's discussions of Buddhism did feature in the previous chapter, this book has to stop where Ambedkar's pragmatist thought gets most interesting: in the content of his reconstructed Buddhism displayed in works such as his monumental *The Buddha and His Dhamma* (1957). A comprehensive analysis of pragmatism's relationship with his "new vehicle" or Navayana Buddhism must wait for another occasion. It is enough to recognize the obvious: Ambedkar's pragmatism does not exclude or compete with his Buddhism, but in many ways they overlap and inform each other. Ambedkar's Navayana Buddhism is a vital part of his pragmatism, as it embodies the ideals and methods that he took from, or added to, a body of thought that so often brushed up against Dewey's texts, ideals, or concerns. In this conclusion, I sketch out the commitments to Ambedkar's pragmatism—what I will call his *Navayana Pragmatism* as a way of honoring its distinctiveness among the various philosophies and figures related to the streams of pragmatist thought.

One of the fascinating—and frustrating—aspects of detailing the philosophical thought of Ambedkar is the fact that he was committed to both rhetoric *and* philosophy. He reveled in ideas, but he always insisted that ideas spring from and land back in the world of practice. This relation to the integration of philosophy and life also entailed *meliorism,* or the commitment to orienting acts of theorizing toward the resolution of the problems of actual individuals and communities. The problem that assumed prominence in much of Ambedkar's thought was social inequality in the form of caste oppression. But his philosophy is not limited to this focus, an aspect revealed in his discussions of what democracy requires of its governments and citizens. Included within this focus on democratic melioration was Ambedkar's commitment to rhetoric, or the art of persuasion. This interest in persuasion as vital to social reform was related to concerns over the effectiveness—and effects—of force used to create a more ideal society. Ambedkar's status as a *rhetorical* figure complicates and enriches our account of him as a *philosophical* figure in various ways.

Beyond this, however, the lived rhetoric of Ambedkar as orator makes reconstructing his general philosophy more challenging. One assumption that is often made about intellectual figures is that there is a complete doctrine or philosophy in their minds; utterances in this speech or that text are shards of this whole picture. Consistency and systematicity is assumed, in other words, of anyone who is denoted as a philosopher. Rhetoric complicates this assumption, a fact that we readily see in Ambedkar's history of public arguments and acts of persuasion. When he spoke to his Dalit followers, he emphasized and asserted certain things; when he spoke to international audiences of non-Indians in the 1950s, he argued for and emphasized other things. His message was rhetorical in the deepest sense: he was engaged in trying to bend his audiences to his ideas, and his ideas to his audiences and their needs. No speech contained all of his ideas, nor were all of his ideas calculated to fit together as a seamless whole. Taking Ambedkar as a *philosophical* and *rhetorical* figure means reveling in his complex thought and acknowledging that parts of it reveal their greatest insight when one remembers the audience to whom each part was addressed.

If we outline the general contours of Ambedkar's Navayana Pragmatism, abstracted in a general and useful form for the purposes of drawing out some implications of this textual and historical study, what themes and commitments might emerge? As Pradeep Gokhale has argued, the notion of "philosopher" differs in Indian and European contexts. Given Ambedkar's hybrid status as imbibing from both Indian and Western traditions, texts, and philosophies, we can expect his own unique permutation of both of these senses. Gokhale points toward the systematicity and tradition that makes one a philosopher in the Indian sense, one who explains and defends a particular way of seeing the world or *darsana*. Western thinkers and their focus on the provision of rigorous argumentative accounts can also be fitted on Ambedkar, given his practices as a rhetor, but Gokhale's emphasis on *darsana* is a useful starting point.[1] A particular vision of the world, individuals, and the potentialities of action grounds Ambedkar's pragmatism. By focusing on this vision, we can construct an account of both what Ambedkar's pragmatism is committed to in terms of the sociology of community and the ethics of action in individual and social contexts.

This image of the world encompasses both guiding ideals as well as the range of means to realize them. I divide up this preliminary sketch of Ambedkar's Navayana Pragmatism into five themes, with the following caveats. First, there are other ways of characterizing his thought as a whole. But one must start somewhere, and no reading of Ambedkar will cover all potential ways of reading his thought or its importance. I refer to his pragmatism as Navayana Pragmatism to highlight its distinct character and commitments. Second, there is much more to say about his pragmatism, both at the conceptual level and at the level of its historical evolution. What follows is, in its generality, a necessarily abstract and arbitrary—but useful—concretization of a moving body of thought. Third, the fullest explanation of his pragmatism must occur next to an engagement with his Buddhist thought, which requires more space than remains in this already detailed exposition.

## Theme 1: Human Nature Is Contingent and Changeable

Ambedkar's Navayana Pragmatism is committed to the idea that the human is a live organism, a creature that is part of a species that is, in turn, part of the ever-changing natural world. Ambedkar is a naturalist, in other words, and eschews commitments to metaphysical or supernatural elements such as the soul (*atman*, in Hindu philosophy). His naturalism does not place much emphasis on evolution, as we have seen from his reluctance to use the sort of "survival of what's fit" rhetoric prevalent among those of his time—in America and in India—that was grounded in the exclusionary social Darwinism of Herbert Spencer. Not making much of the grander implications of species and evolution, however, still allows room for the basic point that naturalists like Dewey took from Darwin: the world (and its future progression) was not set in stone, and organisms and species have ways of adapting and changing to this environment. The naturalism of Navayana Pragmatism does not appeal to anything set in the nature of the world, be it revealed through divine texts or through evolutionary processes that supposedly issue in a culminating state or value. The human is part of this world of stability and flux, and it should find the best ways to adapt its capacities and desires to its natural and social environment. Survival and propagation is part of this story, but it's not the entirety of the tale. The flourishing of each individual assumes a vital role in the human-created environments offered by the state and the community.

For Ambedkar, it is the social environment that offers so many challenges and opportunities for the reshaping of individuals. Ambedkar paid attention to the ability of humans to take patterns of behavior and to change them. We are not born with innate ways of relating to others, but we learn such habits in the course of experience and social interaction. Once learned, they become second nature and are easy to act in accord with—and increasingly harder to abandon or remove. Mental capacities and patterns of acting and reacting are also habits; this was revealed in Ambedkar's insistence that caste *names* indicate something deeper and more pernicious: certain ways of valuing and reacting to individuals that fall under those concepts. This is the psychology of caste oppression that Ambedkar theorized, but it is important to understand that Ambedkar's reading of the individual psychology of caste can also help explain how habits are involved in systems of oppression involving race, gender, and more.[2]

The habits of caste have an experienced life in the actions of individuals who bear those habits, but one can capture an important part of social experience with the idea of customs as habits of the group. This was a point that Dewey made in his lectures early on in Ambedkar's development, and it was a point that Ambedkar continued to develop in his analysis of the customs of the Hindus and Brahminical philosophy in such texts as "Philosophy of Hinduism" and "Riddles in Hinduism." Ambedkar found it useful to identify problematic customs of the dominant Indian traditions of his time because they directly related to the habits of those who oppressed him—whether in the government offices in his early employment in Baroda or later in his life when he was a distinguished politician. Customs and habits are those moments of stability in the physical and mental orientations to a group and its specific members; they are a spot of temporary certainty in an inherently uncertain world. For Ambedkar's Navayana Pragmatism, experience is guided by these habits and customs, but the stream of experience also shapes these patterns of action and reaction. In some cases, it builds up the strength of these psychological acquisitions; in other cases it modifies, replaces, or eliminates them. This is why Ambedkar's philosophy commits him to valuing education in a broad sense; for those committed to pragmatic naturalism, experience itself is educative.

## Theme 2: The Whole Person Emerges out of the Dialectic between the Individual and the Collective

Even with its commitments to naturalism and a world of change and uncertainty, Ambedkar's Navayana Pragmatism still allows for stabilities—such as habit—and agencies amid the flux. As we have seen, Ambedkar placed the concept of *personality* at a prominent place in his complex philosophy. He did not always talk about it, but when he was raising the harms of age-old Hindu customs of caste, it frequently came into view as that which was disallowed or stunted by the oppression at hand. Ambedkar cared about groups and classes; some of his most incisive criticisms pointed out how the poor laboring classes and caste groups were oppressed by other groups in Indian society. We must never forget, however, in focusing on his diagnoses of systemic problems that the harm, and the experience of oppression, lay at the feet of actual individuals like him. This explains the very personal nature of his conversion appeals to his fellow Dalits, as well as the very personal path of conversion that he recommended in so many speeches in the final decades of his life. He railed against caste because it robbed the Dalits of the chance to fully develop as individuals, or as full *personalities*.

The term personality is one that Ambedkar saw in Dewey's early writings; there it served as a sort of moral ideal to Dewey's idealistic psychology. What was the individual? Dewey's answer was simple: it was a biological and spiritual personality that emerged out of the interplay between organic realities and communal constructions. If individuals choose wisely, and if society enables their choices to matter, then they might flourish as

the personalities they have been all along. Dewey's early neo-Hegelian idealism sought the revelation or realization of a personality that was already
there; his later thought looked for ways to grow or develop the personality
of an individual that was possible but not yet existent. In either approach,
the best society functioned in a similar fashion: it allowed for a harmonious operation of the forces of each individual's impulses and desires in
some social or natural environment with its limits and resources. The harm
of caste oppression, for Ambedkar, was that it stymied the development
and enjoyment of a range of meaningful pursuits and projects by all the
individual Dalits that the caste tradition crushed in different ways. Each
individual was a special mixture of drives, impulses, desires, and dreams,
and for Navayana Pragmatism, systems and states are ideally constituted
when they enhance the development of all these individual sets of capacities or characteristics. Each person's happiness and meaningfulness is different, but oppression is pernicious because it crushes the exploration of
such personal pursuits and enjoyments among too many members of the
community.

Underwriting all of the emphasis on the value of the individual personality is a psychology constructed by Ambedkar that built on some parts of
Dewey's later naturalism, as it developed beyond his idealistic psychology
pre-1904 and the early naturalism of the 1908 *Ethics*. Navayana Pragmatism agrees with Dewey's psychology of the 1910s insofar as it postulates
that the personality or individual self is an ever-changing entity, or perhaps
state of being, that emerges from the experienced dialectic between the realities of individual and collective experience. Ambedkar resisted themes
in Dewey's early idealist thought that held that the personality of each was
set and waiting to be known or realized. As we have seen in the analysis of the content of Dewey's Philosophy 131–132 course, the psychology
and social psychology that ultimately grabbed the Indian thinker posited a
dialectic between habit-bearing individuals and custom-enforcing groups.
The individual person and personality developed most of the powers and
abilities—means, in other words—through the intervention of culture and
custom. While their impulses issued forth from within them, agents were
clearly shaped and formed by their surrounding culture. This involved the
matters of force that Ambedkar wrestled with at so many points during
his life. Cultures force and enforce customs on individual members, and
they do this through individual members harming, shaming, training,
praising, and coercing other members. Culture and custom gain reality and
impact in the collections of the people and procedures that constitute historical communities. Such groups are self-sustaining, with their customs

enabling and inculcating patterns of survival and habitual continuance. The vital challenge, however, is to create the sort of reflective individuals who emerge from and reinvigorate a reflective society. This was a central idea in the 1908 *Ethics* that Ambedkar marked again and again. Individuals emerge from groups, but they also have some ability to criticize and reform those groups; this is what is meant when Ambedkar searches for a more rational or reflective society. It is one that is open to the melioriative efforts of reformers like himself or of groups of individuals committed to reform.

As a society or group becomes more reflective in its customs, possibilities exist for an increasing reflectivity among its individual reformers and agents. Dewey used the idea of "effective freedom" in his spring 1916 course with Ambedkar to explain the interplay between individuals and communitarianism in the European tradition. This was the discussion in which Dewey, rather nonchalantly, mentioned the ideals of the French Revolution: equality, liberty, and fraternity. Dewey employed these ideals there to show the collectivist addition to the individualist movement in the preceding century, using fraternity to link the empowered and protected individual to the group and its forces and fates. The idea of effective freedom eschewed metaphysical atomism or ideas of free will and instead highlighted the abilities of the collective to enable the ability of the individual. If customs and groups are formed in certain ways, they can enable a practical and effective agency among individuals. Ambedkar, through his philosophical writings and his own persuasive advocacy, highlighted an implication of the dialectical relationship: in these conditions, the individual can use their agency or autonomy—their practical and useful powers of freedom—to effect some amount of change to their society. Navayana Pragmatism takes seriously the societal and systemic customs that enable or disable practical individual agency, and it *also* takes seriously the ability of the individual to use this practical autonomy to affect the experiences of self and others. This practical autonomy is an important part of a fully flourishing personality among each member of the group, but it is not independent of or unrelated to group customs and societal tradition. Going beyond such reductionism, Ambedkar's Navayana Pragmatism allows for a pluralistic reading of the ways of explaining and employing human agency in social realities.

## Theme 3: Communication and Communicative Habits Matter for Individual and Group Flourishing

It is often tempting to paint pictures of our political and social utopias as silent scenes of bliss. Communication and interaction—including practices such as arguing, joking, criticizing, praising, and elaborating—fall out of the picture of the just and flourishing society. Ambedkar is a rare intellectual figure who valued the art of communication and made room for it in the picture of the ideal society that animated so many of his projects. Like Dewey, Ambedkar saw democracy as always entailing groups that interact; this interaction was often heated and a site of disagreement. Democracy at its best would preserve, or at least not seek an elimination of, this inevitable friction caused by communication, argument, and differing personalities and projects. The ideal of democracy encompassed a *way* of habitually interacting with others, whether they agreed or disagreed with you. Democracy also meant certain limits to communication—for instance, customs or habits that bent communication toward making more enemies, or more entrenched enemies, would be out of bounds. The ideal democracy meant groups interacting in certain broad and constructive ways.

Communication, meaning the free interaction among and between groups in a community, was both an end for Ambedkar's Navayana Pragmatism *and* a means. His efforts to instill democracy meant the pursuit of certain abilities among individuals and groups to interact and engage with other individuals and groups; caste destroyed this sort of interaction and equal engagement given its custom-based stratification of groups and individual worth. But his Navayana Pragmatism was also committed to the general idea that communication is valuable as a means to achieve such a goal. Our speech or rhetoric matters insofar as it expresses our self and its projects and insofar as it moves others toward agreement or away from us. Our agency and autonomy, our effective freedom, are effectively tied to our ability to communicate, as well as to the strictures and affordances the dominant group culture places on individual communication. Dalits, in Ambedkar's reading, were primarily disempowered because of the very limited range of ways they could express themselves or communicate with others; the ways they could interact, of course, were shadowed by the constant threat of social boycott, overt violence, or self-enforced shame. The customs and habits of caste were pernicious primarily because they destroyed the ability of Dalits to communicate in useful ways, both in terms of enjoying life and in terms of persuasive activity oriented toward improving their lot and the overall society. Beyond the import here to Ambedkar's caste critique, we see the value placed on communication as both means and end-in-view by Ambedkar's more general Navayana Pragmatism. Our communication can reveal, or create, closer levels of respect or connection, or it can disable or remove such possible connections that the general pragmatist reading of democracy prizes.

## Theme 4: The Ideal Community Is a Social Democracy That Balances the Values of Equality, Liberty, and Fraternity

Any philosophy must not only have an account of what flourishing or right living means for the individual; it also must contain and advance a guiding image of the optimal sort of arrangement and functioning of the overall community. For Ambedkar, as it was for so many in the pragmatist tradition, this goal was enunciated under the banner of democracy. If one had to pick one idea from Dewey that was of the most value to Ambedkar in all of his reconstructive endeavors, it would surely be that of democracy as a form of everyday life. As Ambedkar heard in Dewey's classes and read in Dewey's books, democracy was more than a decision-making procedure. It was more than a way of voting and then moving on with life. It denoted a *habit* of interacting with others, the others that made up one's community. Later in Dewey's life, in texts such as his famous essay "Creative Democracy—The Task Before Us" (1939), democracy was called a "way of life." This was a more personalized way of putting the tasks and demands of democracy, but it was of a piece with the focus on everyday individual and group habits that Dewey spelled out so eloquently in his 1916 *Democracy and Education*. As noted in chapter 4, it was in one of his copies of that book that Ambedkar underlined Dewey's clearest account of the "democratic ideal," an ideal that would drive important parts of Ambedkar's critique within *Annihilation of Caste*. In that passage, Ambedkar marks the two criteria: "How numerous and varied are the interests which are consciously shared? How full and free is the interplay with other forms of association?"[3] The former criterion means that individuals are aware of or recognize interests that animate their group, as well as other groups in the more general community or state. The latter criterion points to both habits and communication; as Dewey explains in a passage that Ambedkar marked, "The second means not only freer interaction between social groups (once isolated so far as intention could keep up a separation) but change in social habit—its continuous readjustment through meeting the new situations produced by varied intercourse."[4]

Ambedkar would continually return to these general touchstones in his critique of the caste customs of Hindu society, so much so that one could label him *the* philosopher of democracy in contemporary Indian history. Arguably, no one else used the ideal of democracy, filtered through its everyday implications, to critique everything from governmental policy to social mores. As Sukhadeo Thorat has made clear, there are many senses of democracy in Ambedkar, including political, social, economic, and religious versions.[5] Each of these is worth expounding on, but it seems that Ambedkar is particularly intrigued by the idea of *social democracy*. What does this term mean? It must mean something like the notion of democracy that Dewey was proffering, as evidenced by Ambedkar's sustained references over his career to the line in *Democracy and Education* that states, "Democracy is not merely a form of Government. It is primarily a mode of associated living, of conjoint communicated experience." Economic and political democracy are vital commitments of Ambedkar's thought, but they are based on the idea of social democracy, a notion that reaches beyond economic transactions and political power. The latter factors are important, but as Ambedkar puts it in his speech from the debates surrounding the proposed Indian constitution, they are not stopping points. He cautions his fellow lawgivers that they must "not be content with mere political democracy. We must make our political democracy a social democracy as well. Political democracy cannot last unless there lies at the base of it social democracy."[6]

This idea of social democracy lies beneath the surface of many of his texts criticizing the caste system and the Hindu tradition that he saw as supporting it. It often breaks into the open when he evokes the ideals of democracy. What can we say about the idea and ideal of social democracy beyond its use in the critique of caste oppression? In his 1949 speech to his fellow legislators, he explicitly defines social democracy as meaning "a way of life which recognizes liberty, equality and fraternity as the principles of life."[7] Here we see the famous three values mentioned by Dewey in discussing effective freedom, a concept he connected in 1916 to the individualist critique of collectivist overemphases in philosophy. Dewey used these values occasionally—for instance, in the 1888 "Ethics of Democracy" text that Ambedkar valued early on and returned to later in his life—but he did not make them the central ideals in his notion of democracy. Ambedkar, however, often referenced these three values as useful guides, or ideals in the pragmatist sense of a guiding but changeable "end-in-view," for those wanting to instantiate a democratic society.

Not only are these values or ideals flexible, they are fallible in their application and what they entail. They do not mandate one correct action, rule, or law, since they are *principles* in the pragmatist sense. They do not come with divine warrant or with the glow of issuing from pure reason. Ambedkar was a naturalist, a nonfoundationalist who resisted a reified metaphysics, so he was obviously inclined toward a realist reading of how societies evolve and adapt. But he wanted critique, and he wanted an end to oppression, so he needed guides or values by which he could, albeit temporarily or pragmatically, transcend his culture's dominant values and thereby critique and reform them. These three values became touchstones of his political thought and criteria that carried more weight than they ever did in Dewey's thought.

Toward the end of Ambedkar's life, he used them to describe what Buddhism had to offer for the social and political reconstruction of Indian life. In a short address that was broadcast on All-India Radio on October 2, 1954, Ambedkar explains that his "social philosophy" can be "said to be enshrined in three words—liberty, equality and fraternity. Let no one, however say that I have borrowed my philosophy from the French Revolution. I have not. My philosophy has roots in religion and not in political science. I have derived them from the teachings of my master, the Buddha."[8] In his posthumously published "Buddhist Bible," *The Buddha and His Dhamma*, Ambedkar also includes the three values as central questions that the Buddha had answers to in his philosophy. These are flexible, but useful, values that have traceable connections, historical or conceptual, to a range of traditions and contexts. The wrong question to ask is "where did Ambedkar *get* these values from?" I am confident that he heard them first from Dewey in 1916, but this isn't the most important detail concerning these values and Ambedkar's pragmatism. If we take his messages and texts not as parts that fit together in a seamless mental whole, but instead as rhetorical objects designed for persuading specific audiences with specific needs, we can see that the values' genealogy is of secondary importance. They can be used as effective ends in pushing the religious conversion movement in 1954 to would-be Buddhists, and they can also be used to hammer Hinduism as he did in his 1936 *Annihilation of Caste*. The better question to ask is "what do these three values mean for how we *act* and *reform* our society?"

It is clear that Ambedkar's Navayana Pragmatism is committed to the idea of social democracy, meaning a community with free interchange among and within groups by individuals who are allowed by custom and habit to flourish *as individuals*. Democracy, according to Ambedkar, pursues the "welfare of the people."[9] Its free social order, however, matters only insofar as it allows for the development of the *personality* of each individual. In an unpublished work written later in his life, "The Hindu Social Order: Its Principles," Ambedkar opines that there has been no dispute about "what constitutes a free social order" since "the days of the French Revolution." The first of two essential commitments of a free social order—a democracy, conceived of as freely communicating and interacting at all levels—is "that the individual is an end in himself and that the aim and object of society is the growth of the individual and the development of his personality."[10] In 1947's *States and Minorities*, Ambedkar also uses the language of Kant to describe the first premise of political democracy as that "the individual is an end in himself."[11] In his work from the 1950s, his Kantian verbiage becomes ensconced in the synergistic neo-Hegelian idealism of Dewey's early period, prizing the realization of individual *personality* as central to democratic or freely interacting societies. Either emphasis, however, puts to rest the idea that Ambedkar *only* focuses on the systemic or class-based realities in his philosophy; in "The Hindu Social Order," he bluntly states: "Society is not above the individual and if the individual has to subordinate himself to society, it is because such subordination is for his betterment and only to the extent necessary."[12] As we have seen, Ambedkar's Navayana Pragmatism rests on a pluralistic and dialectical reading of the individual *as* community member, one that does not make all social reality only about the individual or solely about what happens to more abstract entities like classes, groups, and systems. The second essential commitment to a free social order or democracy, according to this text, is "that the terms of associated life between members of society must be regarded by consideration founded on liberty, equality and fraternity."[13]

This trio of values is absolutely central to Ambedkar's philosophical conception of social democracy. It also contains many pathways for further questioning: What is the relationship among these values? Is one more central or foundational? Are these related to the philosophical commitments of the French Revolution, or are they integrally connected to an Indian tradition such as Buddhism? We do not have space here for a comprehensive examination of the evolution of Ambedkar's use of these terms, but others have gone an admirable distance in discussing them.[14] I have engaged some of these concerns in previous chapters, but here it will be enough to sketch out the general commitments of Navayana Pragmatism to social democracy and these three ideals. First, notice that these three items are *values*, not empirical claims. Ambedkar wrestled with the empirical claim that all humans are equal in power, capabilities, and resources, and was flummoxed by the factual realities of human inequality early in his writings, but he consistently turned toward a normative or pragmatic use of these terms. They do not describe how individuals and communities *are* now, but they are concepts that guide individuals and communities in deciding what they should do, what they ought to enable, encourage, or preserve. In Dewey's parlance, they are not *final ends* but flexible *ends-in-view*.

For Ambedkar, these three ends-in-view allowed him to criticize Indian society and posit ways to escape caste oppression. For a more general reading of Navayana Pragmatism, they can cover a range of oppressions, injustices, and problematic social situations, since they define social democracy in its *just* form. Justice, in other words, involves the balanced instantiation of equality, liberty, and fraternity. Equality is a complex term, but it entails that the value of and respect owed to each individual are the same, regardless of race, ethnicity, caste, or class. Human individuals—personalities— are ends in themselves, as Ambedkar puts it at vital points. Equality entails agents having the same opportunities and not being separated from others in their abilities to act, respect, or even communicate. These were all problems with the divided and isolated groups that he saw coming out of the habits and customs of caste, psychological tendencies that then replicated themselves in the institutions and systems of power and force.

Liberty is another core value, one that has been foregrounded in the West for many centuries. Philosophers such as Immanuel Kant made the ability to choose and direct one's life central to a metaphysically inflected notion of autonomy; even pragmatists like Dewey had a sense of effective freedom emerging from and informing groups and traditions. Ambedkar's Navayana Pragmatism similarly valued the freedom to act, choose, and plan one's life, including such mundane items as the choice of occupation. For Dalits, caste placed shackles on what they would spend the majority of their waking hours doing, what they would occupy their time with to secure the essentials of living. These occupations were forced upon the individual; most of this work was degrading and disgusting. As we have seen, Ambedkar saw resonances between Dewey's critique of capitalism and its estranged laborers and caste-based divisions of labor in India. For Navayana Pragmatism, autonomy—taken in the sense of effective freedom to do and act—is a central part of a flourishing and fully expressed personality. Individuals will differ as to their impulses, desires, needs, and skills, and social democracy ought to respect such personal inflections among its members as best it can in occupational choice and beyond. The lack of equality for Dalits is intrinsically linked to a limited liberty on their parts. As Ambedkar puts it in a manuscript—unpublished in his lifetime—from the 1950s, "Riddles in Hinduism," "Equality and liberty are no doubt the deepest concern of Democracy."[15]

The power of Ambedkar's conception of social democracy, however, is that it is so driven by a pragmatic desire to create sustainable and pluralistic communities of freely interacting groups that it demands consideration of the value of *fraternity*. This value is often overlooked by those engaging Ambedkar's conception of social democracy, since issues of equality seem the most pressing in a struggle for social justice against oppression. Equality is often something that can be measured and can be created through legislative means and incentives. It is a truth that equality is a vital concern, perhaps due to its felt absence in situations that are unjust. Yet there is more to the story. How are the equal members of society to view each other? Even if they treat, and see, each other as equals, something vital might be missing, something integral to the support and formation of deep community among disparate individuals. This is the value of fraternity. Taking it merely as an outcome of successfully pursuing the values of equality and liberty is incomplete. Ambedkar's Navayana Pragmatism posits fraternity as an important consideration for social democracy, both in terms of the means to achieve it and what it looks like once the end-in-view is realized in a specific political community.

Fraternity implies certain limitations on the means used to pursue the other values; it also indicates something about the end state that will be realized among individuals qua *community* members. How can it play such an integral role as means and end? It does this by specifying a certain individual habit or attitude that works opposite to those attitudes that Ambedkar identified in texts such as *Annihilation of Caste* that comprise the mental disposition of caste. If one doubts the mental importance of attitudes that individuals bear in the struggle for social democracy, we merely have to turn to one of the works authored during the final years of his life, "Riddles in Hinduism." There, Ambedkar underscores the often-overlooked connection of the individual and their habits to the battles of democracy: "Unfortunately to what extent the task of good Government depends upon the mental and moral disposition of its subjects has seldom been realized. Democracy is more than a political machine. It is even more than a social system. It is an attitude of mind or a philosophy of life."[16] In an earlier draft of this "riddle," Ambedkar experimented with connecting this focus on attitude to the idea of the person as ends in themselves, typing (and then crossing out) the words "the first tenet of democracy which is that no person shall treat another solely or even largely as a means but always as an end."[17] While the Kantian terminology was close to his mind in his final years, the focus on the person and their personality became filtered through a more pragmatic focus on attitude and habit.

The variable of habit and attitude of each agent toward others is vital for social democracy. Indeed, Ambedkar seems committed to the idea that fraternity as an attitude is what renders certain communities *social* and not merely in contact with each other. In the 1950s, Ambedkar valued this attitude of fraternity above even equality and liberty. Of course, this way of putting it seems like he is abandoning the latter values. This is incorrect, but it is accurate to say that his Navayana Pragmatism places the attitude of fraternity at the basis of a sustainable sense of equality and fraternity: "What sustains equality and liberty is fellow-feeling. What the French Revolutionists called fraternity." After showing his preference for the Buddhist concept equivalent to fraternity—*maitree* or *maitri*—Ambedkar then spells out his reasoning: "Without Fraternity Liberty would destroy equality and equality would destroy liberty. If in Democracy liberty does not destroy equality and equality does not destroy liberty, it is because at the basis of both there is fraternity. Fraternity is therefore the root of Democracy."[18]

What Ambedkar is realizing, especially in these later texts, is that part of the constructive energy from this threefold value structure is the tension that each holds with the others. They are not merely boxes to be checked in pursuit of social reform and justice. There are always trade-offs and costs, new oppressions to be created alongside freedoms regained. In an earlier draft of this "riddle," Ambedkar is blunt about these tensions: "Democracy would be impossible if it rested merely on liberty and equality. As has been said, liberty and equality are incompatible."[19] The draft manuscript of this text also includes another line, struck out in the final version, that nods to fraternity's vital and mediating role: "It is the attitude of fraternity which is at the basis of democracy and which makes liberty and equality possible. Democracy is the flowering of fraternity."[20] These lines show the importance of fraternity and fellow feeling in Ambedkar's Navayana Pragmatism, and they also reveal his continuing emphasis on the pragmatist ideals of free community interaction and unhindered communicative intercourse. But what does the value of fraternity add to this ethical and political position?

Fraternity is a desired end state, but we must not forget the common pragmatist commitment to *ends-in-view*, the reading of ends not as final but as temporary aiming points. They are ideal in the sense that they guide us toward something normatively better, but they also share functions with what we identify as means. They define *and* help us create a better society. Fraternity serves this complex role in Ambedkar's Navayana Pragmatism. It both tells us about the sort of community we ought to instantiate and informs us about the right sort of means we can employ to get to this end point. In other words, fraternity serves as both *end* (a state of mutual respect and compassion toward others) and *means* (as a way of feeling and acting toward others to achieve this transformed state of affairs). It is this dual-natured functioning of fraternity that makes Ambedkar's reading of social democracy so powerful and such a unique part of his Navayana Pragmatism. Understanding fraternity as means creates certain limitations on the ways we can pursue the creation of a state of equality and liberty. It also, I suggest, highlights an ultimately tragic sensibility in the powerful optimism of Ambedkar's political ethos. Put simply, fraternity as ends and means implies that we cannot solve the problems of inequality, say, while destroying the conditions for the realization of fellow feeling, compassion, and support among individuals. What this means in the abstract is clear: there may be cases in which rhetors or activists pursuing reform must hold back from achieving some desired state of equality because the means to achieve this goal will so anger, harm, or enrage their opponents that forming true community with them will be precluded. Political violence was one of those tempting, but worrisome, means that clashed with fraternity for Ambedkar.

Another place where this limiting feature of fraternity shines through in Ambedkar's works is in the speeches and texts during his final years in which he explicitly challenges Marx and communism with his pragmatic vision of Buddhism. We must recall that Ambedkar claimed that the Buddha was a pragmatist as early as an article penned in 1938, and that in the late 1940s he worried about his students trying to "win over" their parliamentary opponents by giving them a "black eye."[21] As we have seen, force had been a problematic for Ambedkar since his early review of Russell's book. All of these themes come together in the manuscript "Buddha or Karl Marx," which Ambedkar did not manage to publish during his lifetime. This text was authored around 1954, as it was listed as "in press" on an incomplete résumé Ambedkar most likely sent in the fall of 1954 to organizers of the third conference of the World Fellowship of Buddhists.[22] In this manuscript, Ambedkar compares Buddhism with Marx's communism and highlights various overlaps and differences. What makes Buddhism preferable to communism, he claims, is that it uses the most pragmatic sort of force. At the end of his life, Ambedkar once again harkens back to the distinction he heard in Dewey's classroom in 1916 and makes use of the "grounds against violence such as those urged by Prof. John Dewey."[23] He proceeds to evoke the same distinction that he attributed to Dewey in his 1918 review of Russell's book, that of force as energy and force as violence. This pragmatist distinction did not fade from Ambedkar's attention over his tumultuous life.[24]

In "Buddha or Karl Marx," he continues to use the distinction from 1918 wherein he described the harm of violence as truncating more ends, especially those held by others, in a fanatical and counterproductive fashion: "The achievement of an end involves the destruction of many other ends which are integral with the one that is sought to be destroyed. Use of force must be so regulated that it should save as many ends as possible in destroying the evil one."[25] All end-directed activity in a social environment, in other words, will affect and limit the pursuits, hopes, and projects of other individuals and groups. This is the messy reality of democracy, acknowledged by both Ambedkar's Navayana Pragmatism and Dewey's pragmatism. Violence simply means force that truncates or destroys too many other ends in pursuing one party's goals, a sort of short-term effectiveness that is ultimately destructive for the larger goal of forming a unified and supportive community. Communists, according to Ambedkar, use violence in such ways; as he puts it, dictatorship, violence, and the forcible taking of property might work in one sense, but in other senses they simply harden many community members into more resolved enemies and entrenched opponents. There are two objections to such uses of force as violence—too much force that precludes fraternal community, in other words—in Ambedkar's account. First, any achievement of community by violent or coercive force is not sustainable without more force. Once the force of dictatorship or the threat of violence is removed, people and groups will retreat to their old habits and customs again. Second, Ambedkar agrees with Edmund Burke that a reliance on this sort of force (violence) harms the object that one wants to secure with the application of force. In terms of Navayana Pragmatism's conception of social democracy, achieving some end in a forceful way that truncates or casts aside too many other values of other community members precludes the sustainable realization of a compassionate community of freely interacting and supportive members. One might win a specific battle, but in doing so one would lose the war that is democracy—they would create more enemies out of those with whom they are trying to create lasting community.

The differences between communists and Buddhists, according to Ambedkar's later thought, was primarily one of means.[26] Buddhism, and Ambedkar's Navayana Pragmatism on a more general level, advises the use of force as energy, not as violence, because the creation of community demands the integration and reconciliation of community members. Ambedkar's analysis of communism is complex and contested, but what is useful is the interplay between the three ideals of social democracy and the ideas of force that emerge. Ambedkar's general demur to communism is that it harms the liberty of some to attain their goals and desires out of a domineering concern for equality (especially in regard to economic means). This in turn precludes or destroys fraternity among these groups: "We welcome the Russian Revolution because it aims to produce equality. But it cannot be too much emphasized that in producing equality society cannot afford to sacrifice fraternity or liberty. Equality will be of no value without fraternity or liberty. It seems that the three can coexist only if one follows the way of the Buddha. Communism can give one but not all."[27]

Setting aside Ambedkar's emphasis on the means provided by Buddhism, as well as his reading of communism's specific tactics, we can see a fascinating general account of social democracy that includes, while extending beyond, the battle against caste oppression. Social democracy will be assisted by certain political structures, but the presence of such structures and even legislative protections such as political rights is not enough; we need a certain sort of habitual way of life enacted by all or most of the community members in interaction with each other. Inequality inhibits this free interaction, as well as the equal respect and value that all ought to give each other as community members. Legislative solutions, and even powers of public opinion such as collective shame, can be marshalled to level that which is unfairly tilted, but Ambedkar's Navayana Pragmatism issues a stern warning: we cannot achieve *justice* in the sense of a balance among the values of liberty, equality, and fraternity if we sacrifice one of these values. The difficult matter of fraternity, that which highlights its usefulness as informing and *limiting* the means we can employ, is so often what is sacrificed by maximizing or restoring powers of freedom (liberty), or the forceful and revolutionary instantiation of equality. The tragic hope of democracy, for Ambedkar's Navayana Pragmatism, is that the demand of fraternity conditions or limits the means that we can use in pursuing the creation of social democracy.

Nowhere does this impetus to fraternity as means *and* end become more evident than in Ambedkar's reconstructed Navayana Buddhism, a vital part of the complete picture of his Navayana Pragmatism. We do not have space to develop this analysis, but a few pragmatist starting points in Ambedkar's Buddhist texts can be noted. At the very end of his life, just as he was writing on Marx and Buddhism, Ambedkar was finalizing his Buddhist Bible—originally known in its 1951 version as *The Buddha and His Gospel*, and finally published in revised form in 1957 as *The Buddha and His Dhamma*.[28] This book showed the reconstructive and pragmatist spirit of his philosophical approach, as its controversial retelling of the Buddha's story and doctrine followed through on his claim in 1950 that the Buddha wished "His religion not to be encumbered with the dead wood of the past. He wanted that it should remain evergreen and serviceable at all times. That is why He gave liberty to his followers to chip and chop as the necessities of the case required."[29] This spirit of reconstruction creates effects in the world by textual appropriation, recontextualization, and revision, all themes we saw in Ambedkar as early as the echoes of Dewey in

1919 and most thoroughly in his 1936 *Annihilation of Caste*. In the 1950s, Ambedkar's Navayana Pragmatism enunciates its themes in the idiom of Buddhism, albeit a Buddhism that was socially engaged and attuned to the vicissitudes of violence and force, and that was posited as an alternative to the nondemocratic forces sweeping India and Asia. It also contains an individual aspect, however, one that acknowledges the primacy of individual reflection, emotion, and mental cultivation. Ambedkar's Buddhism, like his Navayana Pragmatism, is closely attuned to both individual and systemic aspects to experience because they are inherently intertwined.

Let us take one example of his constant negotiation of force, violence, and pragmatic effectiveness in *The Buddha and His Dhamma*. In doing so, we will catch a glimpse of how important fraternity as a *means* was for Ambedkar's pursuit of liberty and equality in his final years. The core to fraternity as means seems to be that we try to have compassion for our fellow community members, perhaps as groups, but certainly as individuals we encounter in the course of experience. What do we do when these individuals evince no compassion, fellow feeling, or even love for us? This, in a nutshell, is the riddle of democracy, and Ambedkar's emphasis on fraternity in all its complexity in his Navayana Pragmatism illustrates his appreciation for this challenge. Fraternity makes many appearances in *The Buddha and His Dhamma*, perhaps most notably among the other two values in a list of questions that Marx is said not to answer.[30] Ambedkar also talks of fraternity here and elsewhere as an imperfect version of the Buddhist concept of *maitri* (or *maitree*). *Maitri* is closely related to the other virtue of *karuna*, and Ambedkar defines both in *The Buddha and His Dhamma*: "*Karuna* is loving kindness to human beings. *Maitri* is extending fellow feeling to all beings, not only to one who is a friend but also to one who is a foe: not only to man but to all living beings."[31] Fraternity is translated into the Buddhist concept of equal compassion for all beings, including those who don't share such attitudes toward us. It is an attitude—something that directs and limits our active use of force in our own activities.

In the complex body of thought that is Ambedkar's explication of Buddhism, the connection between fraternity as *maitri* and compassion as love of all becomes an important part of social melioration. With this equation, he posits something that drives us that could replace the impulse provided by anger. At various places in *The Buddha and His Dhamma*, Ambedkar draws out a thread not often enunciated in his public rhetoric. He castigates the feelings of anger—even if warranted—in those who would follow his reconstruction of the Buddhist gospel. Like his earlier texts targeting caste as mindset, individual habits and attitudes hold a melioriative importance: "Man is what his mind makes him. The training of the mind to seek the good, is the first step in the path of Righteousness."[32] Resisting anger became a vital task for democracy. Ambedkar clearly had much cause to be angry with those who supported a system of Brahminical philosophy that oppressed him and his fellow Dalits. Anger is something that transcends his oppression, however. One feature in many societies, especially those divided by power and unjust states of affairs, will perhaps always be the real and justified anger against those judged to be oppressive or harmful. As Ambedkar read in his student days, Bertrand Russell talked of the anger the British felt toward the Germans, and vice versa. Ambedkar's Navayana Pragmatism, at a level that includes and extends beyond the battles against caste oppression, recognizes this power of individual habit and group custom and seeks ways to counterbalance its harmful instantiations in how it addresses anger. In *The Buddha and His Dhamma*, Ambedkar rejects anger, even against one's enemies or foes within one's community, and the harmful uses of force that anger justifies. He advises, "Cherish no anger. Forget your enmities. Win your enemies by love. This is the Buddhist Way of Life."[33] Lest a reader think that this focus on undoing the force of anger is a passing reference, Ambedkar continues in the following passages to make this point with even greater force:

> The fire of anger should be stilled. One who harbours the thought: "He reviled me, maltreated me, overpowered me, robbed me," in him anger is never stilled. He who harbours not such a thought, in him anger is stilled. Enemy works evil to enemy, hater to hater, but whose is the evil. Let a man overcome anger by love, let him overcome evil by good; let him overcome the greedy by liberality, the liar by truth. Speak the truth, do not yield to anger; give, if thou art asked for little. Let a man leave anger, let him forsake pride, let him overcome all bondage; no sufferings befall the man who is not attached to name and form, and who calls nothing his own.[34]

Anger is to be replaced by love, in our attitudes as well as in our actions, both of the individual and of social units such as groups and nation-states. Ambedkar in his later rhetoric is addressing *individuals*, a part of the social equation that will always matter in lived experience and felt emancipation, so he adds more emphasis on what one as an agent can immediately control. The idea is simple: when one feels anger toward another person or group, do not ask if that target *deserves* that anger. One should focus on how to win that other party over, or how to make them part of a community characterized by shared interests. In other words, fraternity as love limits and conditions what we do to a friend, or more importantly, to those labeled as an enemy, foe, or oppressor. Such is the rigorous demand of Ambedkar's ideal of social democracy when rendered into practical courses of action in his later Buddhist writings.

What sort of guide does Navayana Pragmatism give to group members seeking to overcome anger with love and to convert and persuade opponents to the right and just ways of thinking and acting? We see one answer in the pages of The Buddha and His Dhamma, but there are undoubtedly many others. In a new section added after he privately published The Buddha and His Gospel around 1951, Ambedkar discusses the important concept of ahimsa or nonviolence in relation to Buddhism. Ahimsa, of course, has a complex history within the Buddhist, Jaina, and Hindu traditions in South Asia, so Ambedkar is keen to give the term conceptual clarity. He also attempts to give it practical efficacy. It is, I submit, a central part of his Navayana Pragmatism beyond his Navayana Buddhism because it becomes another way of enunciating the ideal of fraternity as both means and end.

In The Buddha and His Dhamma, Ambedkar directly confronts the uniqueness of ahimsa for his Buddhism: "The question has been raised, however, whether His Ahimsa was absolute in its obligation, or only relative."[35] We continue to see Ambedkar using concepts and distinctions from the pragmatist tradition, albeit in his novel elucidation of social democracy and what it demands. Ambedkar asks of the Buddha's ahimsa: "Was it only a principle? Or was it a rule?"[36] Ambedkar acknowledges the variations of its definition but admits that if one defines it as a rule—a pronouncement such as "do not kill"—then "such a definition of Ahimsa involves the sacrifice of good for evil, the sacrifice of virtue for vice," since many problematic situations call for responses that involve harming some to save others.[37] Ambedkar then writes that the Buddha instead commands us to "'love all so that you may not wish to kill any.' This is a positive way of stating the principle of Ahimsa. From this it appears that the doctrine of Ahimsa does not say 'Kill not.' It says 'Love all.'"[38]

In this section of The Buddha and His Dhamma, Ambedkar is developing in his Buddhism what he desired in 1936: a religion of principle that is flexible and nonfoundationalist. Ahimsa is, in this reconstruction, a flexible guide to a range of situations, even those not involving killing: "It is quite clear that Buddha meant to make a distinction between will to kill and need to kill. He did not ban killing where there was need to kill. What he banned was killing where there was nothing but the will to kill."[39] This "will to kill" is connected to the attitude toward others that takes them as diametrically opposed, perhaps in their very existence, to us and our projects; this conceptualization necessarily entails our harming of or resistance to these targeted individuals. This stands in clear contrast to cases of self-defense, say, in which one's killing of another dangerous being is a clear existential necessity. When does a situation call for violence? Ambedkar leaves this determination to individual judgment: "No doubt he leaves it to every individual to decide whether the need to kill is there. But with whom else could it be left. Man has Pradnya [wisdom] and he must use it. A moral man may be trusted to draw the line at the right point."[40]

As we see in his 1950s analyses of communism, Ambedkar is very skeptical of force as violence simply because it cannot achieve or maintain the sort of fraternal community social democracy demands. Yet his Navayana Pragmatism cannot forbid *all* violence, because doing so would jar with his pragmatist sensibilities that universal and timeless pronouncements are usually covering up ignorance or false confidence. His Navayana Pragmatism values the habits of reflective thinking among individuals as an important part of achieving true community among disparate agents, and principles such as *ahimsa* become valuable as ways to instantiate fraternity as means: "To put it differently the Buddha made a distinction between Principle and Rule. He did not make Ahimsa a matter of Rule. He enunciated it as a matter of Principle or way of life. . . . A principle leaves you freedom to act. A rule does not. Rule either breaks you or you break the rule."[41] *Ahimsa* becomes a principle that focuses an agent on the active (and often difficult) love of others, not simply the violence-justifying love of one's self at the expense of others. It is both a way to be in community with others and a characteristic that all will share in once a just and democratic community life is fully realized.

## Theme 5: There Is a Plurality of Means to Reach the End of Social Democracy

Ambedkar's Navayana Pragmatism centers on an image of the just life and the ideal state and community, and it orbited around the flexible ideals of liberty, equality, and fraternity. Through his reading of the last value, for example, Ambedkar highlighted the melioriative vectors provided by individual psychology and attitude; group custom informs individual habit, but we can also affect group life through altering individual habits, including our own. This reading of a major theme in Ambedkar's life and work has been amply explored in this book, but one should not make the mistake of assuming it is the *only* way to rectify injustice and to enable social democracy. Ambedkar, like any pragmatist, was a pluralist who resisted foundationalism, confining certainty, and eternally unchanging answers. He was committed to a plurality of *means* in achieving the ideals of social democracy. The general types of means or ways to encourage or create social democracy can be labeled, at least provisionally, as *individual, social,* and *political.*

Each of these paths was traveled by Ambedkar, even if the present book does not have the space to canvas them. He clearly believed in the value of *political* means—including legislation that affected political rights and economic abilities—for the pursuit of Indian democracy. For instance, Ambedkar's role in the creation of the Indian constitution and his activities as a lawyer were driven by a belief that these sort of activities can further the causes of justice and community. *Social* means such as mass mobilization and large-scale conversion to Buddhism also have been noted as ways of using groups or classes of people as a means to change society for the better. Much scholarship that focuses on the class- or caste-based activism of Ambedkar's thought explicates these mechanisms of change.[42]

What has not been as emphasized enough, and what emerges clearly once we focus on Ambedkar as both a pragmatist *and* a rhetor are the *individual* ways to create social democracy. This valuing of the individual personality as something to be realized, cultivated, and used is an irreducible feature of both Ambedkar's Navayana Pragmatism and any story that talks of the influence of Dewey on Ambedkar's specific texts. Religion is a social means of melioration, as the conversion of an oppressed group to an emancipatory religion affects the community and its internal relations among groups. Religion was also an intensely personal matter for Ambedkar. He wrestled with his relationship to Hinduism and Buddhism beginning in his youth, and it seems that he wrestled with them when he was exposed to Dewey's pragmatism during his time at Columbia University. He spoke about these traditions to audiences of Dalits and non-Dalits throughout his life. Religion became a way of reshaping his fate and his life, and his own conversion was simultaneously an individual-focused reshaping of his caste-riven habits *and* a public appeal for others to likewise reconstruct their selves. His activism often took the form of advocacy that pushed to educate individuals who heard or read his words and that aimed to reform society.

Navayana Pragmatism orbited around the abstract ideals of social democracy, but it demanded the adaptable and ever-flexible intelligence of the reflective individual. This was the person that could notice and react to problematic situations, both recurring and novel. Ambedkar's Navayana Pragmatism placed much weight on the creation of—or education of—

reflective individuals who could act and think their way out of habits and group customs that oppressed self and others. Caste was clearly an emphasis for Ambedkar's rhetoric, but his Navayana Pragmatism is not limited to this form of injustice and oppression. Reflection is a general skill of adapting to and dealing with *any* situation; injustice and social discord is simply a very important type of problematic situation in social environments. Navayana Pragmatism sought to preserve effective and corrigible approaches to dealing with such problems and to form community with others who might or might not agree with one's diagnosis of the solution to such challenges. Reconstruction was the temporary solution proffered by reflective engagement with a problematic situation that created, hopefully, the conditions identified by the notion of social democracy: the balanced state of liberty, equality, and fraternity.

It is at this point that we can see more clearly the general connections among force, reconstruction, and the means of encouraging social democracy. Ambedkar saw that reconstruction was vital for society and was conceptually related to the reconstruction of communities. As implied by his psychology, individuals and their habits were important targets and means in this reconstructive activity. Yet one could not *force* or *coerce* individuals toward attitudes of fraternity. As we have seen in the course of this book, Ambedkar's pragmatism placed much emphasis on *persuasive force* as the way to address friends and opponents in the complex social settings of democratic communities. Persuasion implies attention to audiences and the ways to reach them given their specific needs and interests; it also necessitates minding what you think they need to become and the best ways to move them toward this state. It is in this way that Ambedkar's conversion rhetoric operates as a form of melioriative activity, one that focuses on reconstructing society through the reformation of individual habits and traditional customs. Buddhism was a social means of change, but it also was a living means of change and reconstruction. It became an idiom of intelligent reshaping of one's self—and hopefully of the selves of others. Ambedkar's Navayana Buddhism illustrates the larger, rhetorical point that we must make about Ambedkar's form of pragmatism. The sort of force as energy that is wisest to employ, mostly because it does not destroy the hope for fraternal community with allies and opponents, is one that values and respects the agency of those addressed. This theme, while not the only commitment in Ambedkar's complex thought, does make sense of the individual acts of persuasion he undertook in 1936 and beyond with both Dalit and non-Dalit audiences. Persuasion was one of the most important methods Ambedkar's Navayana Pragmatism possessed to try to achieve equality, liberty, *and* fraternity for Dalits and non-Dalits.

We can return once again to Ambedkar's discussions of communism and Buddhism in the 1950s to see the more general point about force and persuasion. This is a point that goes beyond Buddhism, at least in its conceptual parameters, and can thereby be attributed to Ambedkar's Navayana Pragmatism as a general philosophical commitment. In both his unpublished writings and public speeches placing Marx alongside Buddha, we see the full maturation of his pragmatist point: rhetorical means are some of the best ways possible of creating and sustaining social democracy with a just balance among its three values. In his unpublished manuscript, "Buddha or Karl Marx," Ambedkar highlights the difference between these two approaches: "The differences are about the means. The end is common to both."[43] Whereas Marxist approaches rely on creating equality through force, "the Buddha's method was different," opines Ambedkar in this late work. "His method," Ambedkar writes, "was to change the mind of man: to alter his disposition: so that whatever man does, he does it voluntarily without the use of force or compulsion." Rhetorical means—persuasively adapting ideas to audiences—was the Buddha's "main means to alter the disposition of men." This involved his persuading in and through "his Dhamma and the constant preaching of his Dhamma. The Buddha's way was not to force people to do what they did not like to do although it was good for them. His way was to alter the disposition of men so that they would do voluntarily what they would not otherwise do."[44] In his well-known speech that bears the same title, "Buddha or Karl Marx," delivered in November 1956 in Nepal a few weeks before his death, Ambedkar makes a similar point. "The means that the Communists wish to adopt in order to bring about Communism, by which I mean the recognition of *Dukkha*, and abolition of property, is violence and killing of the opposed," he tells an international conference on Buddhism attended by many representatives of Western nations, as well as a sizable contingent from the communist bloc. Drawing on the overlap, he claims that "there lies the fundamental difference between the Buddha and Karl Marx. The Buddha's means of persuading people to adopt the principles is by persuasion, by moral teaching, by love."[45] *Ahimsa* as love and as a force that does not foreclose too many ends of others comes together in the notion of persuasion; Ambedkar portrays the Buddha, and those following him, as seeking "to conquer the opponent by inculcating in him the doctrine that love, and not power can conquer anything."[46]

## Ambedkar's Pragmatism, Ambedkar's Buddhism

Ambedkar, like many thinkers in the Indian tradition, can be discussed in terms of the image of the ideal society that he posits, or that he dreams of achieving should the world break his way. As Gail Omvedt rightly points out, his Buddhism is a powerful part of what this picture contains.[47] But there is another way to position and contextualize his Buddhism, one that places it within the evolution of the pragmatist tradition in the Americas and beyond. This is the sense of Ambedkar I have attempted to sketch out in this book, one that places him as a pragmatist by virtue of his historical influences, his employment of a reconstructive method, and his touchstones of social democracy and its ideals. Others undoubtedly influenced Ambedkar, and undoubtedly more work remains to be done on all of the other figures and texts that inspired him, annoyed him, or otherwise motivated him in various ways. This book is a comprehensive start to unpacking one of the more important personal and philosophical influences on Ambedkar; it is, admittedly, only a start. Much more is left to be said on what Ambedkar liked or resisted in Dewey's pragmatism, or at least the parts of the American professor's thought that he was exposed to over many decades. And more must be said on what Ambedkar's Navayana Pragmatism means for his Navayana Buddhism. What should be beyond dispute are the claims that Ambedkar did engage Dewey and parts of his thoughts at various places and at various times throughout his life. This engagement mattered, both for the arguments he made and the goals he sought. Also beyond doubt should be the novelty and originality of Ambedkar's thought; even given its historical and textual connections to Dewey, it in no way looks identical to Dewey's thought, with its own foci and complex evolution. Perhaps Adlerblum is correct, and it is accurate to say that Ambedkar's meeting of Dewey "gave a new turn to his life." But the direction and distance that Ambedkar trod with his Navayana Pragmatism was all of his own doing.

It is unclear to me what Dewey thought of Ambedkar, the young student whom he most likely last saw in person in one of his seminars as the temperatures warmed in the New York spring of 1916. Despite all my searching in India and America, I have found no surviving letters or correspondence between the student and the teacher; despite searching and comparing texts, there are no clear instances of Dewey citing, echoing, or referring to the work of Ambedkar. Perhaps such a story is out there waiting to be told in detail.[48] But perhaps our expectations of a meaningful relationship between these two being reciprocal and personally immediate imports too much of our own desires. Ambedkar, as the leading figure in the story of pragmatism and its evolution in India, illustrates to us how relationships can be intellectual as well as personal, and that meaningful relationships can involve different patterns of appropriation, interaction, and refusal. Ambedkar's distanced, but respectful, relationship to Dewey was one of an intellectual nature and occurred mostly through the solitary activity of reading and marking books. The Indian leader and thinker, so great in his own accomplishments, still respected and loved his old professor on the other side of the globe for all of his wisdom, and despite all of his shortcomings, fumbling teaching style, and intellectual blind spots. Ambedkar knew Dewey as a mentor and as a memory and, in a deeply pragmatist spirit, as a thinker preserved in the pages of his cherished books who faithfully offered his own thought as a goad, as a source of imperfect ideals, and sometimes as a starting point for Ambedkar to pursue his own reconstructive endeavors. Perhaps Ambedkar owed Dewey a great intellectual debt. This seems true. But it is also evident that Dewey and those who follow in his wake owe Ambedkar so much more for his creativity and courage in pushing the tradition of pragmatism forward.

ACKNOWLEDGMENTS

This book project in many ways found me. In 2004, as a doctoral student, I was deeply focused on John Dewey's philosophy. When Martha Nussbaum asked me, in a conversation at a conference, what I knew of an Indian student of Dewey's—one Bhimrao Ambedkar—I mumbled "nothing much" and remained confident that the answers I sought from pragmatism lay in Dewey's thought. A decade later, when I should have been writing a book on Dewey and rhetoric during a fellowship at Princeton, I procrastinated by exploring more about this student of Dewey's who had so impressed Nussbaum. What I saw in Ambedkar from these cursory searches in many ways changed my scholarly trajectory, as well as my life. I saw in him a vision of Dewey's pragmatism that had been unexplored, one attuned to issues of justice and ways of community building in democracies that Dewey himself could not have anticipated. I also saw a cause—Ambedkar's fight against caste oppression—that deserved more space in our discussions of social justice than we had given it. And I found that no one had yet told a detailed story about how Ambedkar, Dewey, and the fight for Dalit rights all went together. I figured I might as well be the one to attempt to tell this story of pragmatism in India.

So many have helped me in telling this tale of Ambedkar's pragmatism. Larry Hickman, Thomas Alexander, and the staff at the Center for Dewey Studies at Southern Illinois University, Carbondale, must be thanked for assisting me even when their resources were strained. Jocelyn Wilk and Columbia University's Rare Book & Manuscript Library have been very helpful, as was the staff overseeing the Mary Kingsbury Simkhovitch papers at Harvard University and those who curate the Milton Friedman papers at the Hoover Institute, Stanford University.

My many trips to India were always a mix of excitement, discovery, and patience. Anjali Sandesh Kale and the librarians at the University of Mumbai kindly helped me access the Khairmode collection. Bhavana Bhupendra Bhalerao and her team, including the enthusiastic Jagannath Suresh Owhal, proved so helpful in my work at Maharashtra State Archives. S. B. Mujumdar and S. S. Mujumdar of the Symbiosis Institute in Pune must be thanked for graciously extending every hospitality to me and for opening their Ambedkar-related archives and artifacts for my research use. I also have spent many warm afternoons among the books once perused by Ambedkar at Siddharth College in Mumbai, helped by the dedicated and knowledgeable librarians Shrikant Talwatkar and Chaitali Shinde. I am also eternally grateful, and humbled, that Ramesh Shinde opened his private collection of books and letters to me, as well as his own recollections of the movement Babasaheb initiated.

Many scholars assisted in various ways with this project over the years. Foremost among the many is Christopher Queen, who so generously and earnestly helped me find the right people and the best resources for my project in India. This book would be lost without his early, and energetic, guidance. Pradeep Aglave, Sunaina Arya, Jennifer Breger, Matthew Butler, Isabelle Clark-Decès, Dennis Dalton, Robert Danisch, S. S. Dhaktode, Zachary Elkins, Jeremy Engels, Marilyn Fischer, V. Geeta, Kenneth Greene, Ramachandra Guha, Gopal Guru, Rod Hart, Stephen Heyman, Madhukar Kesare, Shanti Kumar, Kanchana Mahadevan, Mrudul Nile, Martha Nussbaum, Shailaja Paik, Danee Pye, Devika Rani, Anupama Rao, Aakash Singh Rathore, Kancha Ilaiah Shepherd, Laurence Simon, Peter Simonson, Paul Stob, John Stuhr, Suraj Yengde, Richard Fox Young, Dhananjay Wanjari, and many more all helped in their own ways to hone this work. Kyle Wagner, the late Doug Mitchell, and the staff at the University of Chicago Press must be thanked for being believers in this project from its earliest phases. Frances Pritchett is to be thanked for sharing her expansive knowledge of Ambedkar's life and thought. My students and research assistants are also to be thanked: Jaishikha Nautiyal, Anna Rose Isbell, Hannah Foltz, Justin Pehoski, Ileana Reese, Kat Williams, and Clayton Terry. I am also grateful for the institutional support provided by the Moody College of Communication and the provost at the University of Texas at Austin. Leaders such as Jay Bernhardt, Barry Brummett, and Craig Scott have ensured that I had the time and resources to execute this project to the level that Ambedkar's cause deserves. The South Asia Institute and Donald Davis must be thanked for supporting my project. The Office of the Vice President for Research, Scholarship and Creative Endeavors of the University of Texas at Austin is to be thanked for a subvention grant supporting this book. Princeton University's Center for the Study of Democratic Politics provided the perfect environment to incubate this project in 2014–15.

I must recognize the work that various organizations devoted to Ambedkar's mission are doing and thank them for including me as a part of their endeavors. Manoj Shambharkar and others at the Ambedkar International Center are to be thanked, as well as the late, but never forgotten, Rajkumar (Raju) Kamble of the Ambedkar International Mission. My friends at the Ambedkarite Buddhist Association of Texas, Jagdish Bankar, Yogesh Khankal, Kamlesh Nandagawali, and others, have long believed in this project. I also must thank Mahesh Wasnik, Chatak Dhakne, Pankaj Meshram, and other leaders of the Ambedkarite Association of North America for including Dewey in the stories we tell about Ambedkar's Buddhism. I am also grateful that the leaders and politicians carrying on Babasaheb's legacy in different ways—Anandraj Ambedkar, Bhimrao Ambedkar, Prakash Ambedkar, Vijay Mankar, and Nitin Raut—took the time to talk with me about Ambedkar's past and future in India.

Some arguments were tested in earlier forms in a range of scholarly journals. A portion of chapter 2 appeared in "Pragmatism, Persuasion, and Force in Bhimrao Ambedkar's Reconstruction of Buddhism," *Journal of Religion* 97, no. 2 (2017): 214–43. Some of the ideas contained in chapter 4 appeared in earlier forms in "Pragmatism and the Pursuit of Social Justice in India: Bhimrao Ambedkar and the Rhetoric of Religious Reorientation," *Rhetoric Society Quarterly* 46, no. 1 (2016): 5–27; "What Did Bhimrao Ambedkar Learn from John Dewey's *Democracy and Education*?," *The Pluralist* 12, no. 2 (2017): 78–103; and "Echoes of Pragmatism in India: Bhimrao Ambedkar and Reconstructive Rhetoric," in *Recovering Overlooked Pragmatists in Communication: Extending the Living Conversation about Pragmatism and Rhetoric*, ed. Robert Danisch (Cham: Palgrave Macmillan, 2019), 79–103. Part of chapter 5 appeared in "The Rhetoric of Conversion as Emancipatory Strategy in India: Bhimrao Ambedkar, Pragmatism, and the Turn to Buddhism," *Rhetorica: A Journal of the History of Rhetoric* 35, no. 3 (2017): 314–45. These publishers are to be thanked for their permission to allow the revised portions of these works to be used in this book.

I count some of the best friends I have among those individuals I have met in India. Vijay Khare has been kind and supportive of my endeavors, from working on this book to our joint venture in starting India's first Center for John Dewey Studies, in Pune. Pradeep Aglave and Niraj Bodhi showed me around Nagpur and introduced me to the living legacy of

Ambedkar's thought. Activists such as Mangesh Dahiwale and Lokamitra also selflessly showed me the extent of the Ambedkarite movement in the Nagaloka Centre in Nagpur and the Manuski Centre in Pune. Kishor Walanju trusted this random scholar who found him online and has helped me navigate Mumbai and the large network of Ambedkarite activists ever since. Manish Nagdeve and Sandeep Badole are exemplars of the Ambedkarite community, always making me smile with their insight and humor; they always made sure I met whomever I needed to meet while in India. Sukhadeo Thorat has helped me in my quest to know more about Ambedkar and Dewey, despite having much more important demands on his time; his generosity in helping me and so many other interested scholars will not be forgotten. Last, but certainly not least, is my dear friend Vijay Surwade. Surwade is a living encyclopedia of Ambedkarite knowledge, is an astute collector of photographs of Babasaheb, and has been my ever-present companion throughout this journey. From dusty archives to chai with legends like Ramesh Shinde, Surwade has given this project so much. I am forever indebted to him.

All of the archives and epicycles involved in this quest have taken me away from my own spot of community too often. I must thank my parents, Herman and Sandra Stroud, along with Pierre Jomini, Sandy Jomini, Paul Jomini, and Taylor Wilson, for support and encouragement that was so integral in completing this project. My intellectual companion and better half, Natalie (Talia) Stroud, deserves appreciation that I cannot put in words. My passion for Ambedkar's story has taken me away from her, Connor, and Clara too much. The love and support of my family has sustained me through this long but important project. Talia recognized early on what this project meant to me, and she supported it every step of the way. Our discussions, worries, and hopes about democracy lie under the surface of much of this account of pragmatism in India. Ambedkar's story is the most meaningful and powerful part of philosophy or rhetoric that I have come in contact with, and I am thankful that so many have been so willing to help me say a little more about the intersections between Bhimrao Ambedkar and pragmatism.

NOTES

INTRODUCTION

1.  Meenakshi Verma Ambwani, "Dr B.R. Ambedkar Voted as 'Greatest Indian,'" *Hindu*, August 14, 2012, https://www.thehindubusinessline.com/news/Dr-B.R.-Ambedkar -voted-as-%E2%80%98Greatest-Indian%E2%80%99/article20485049.ece.
2.  "'Untouchables' Represented by Ambedkar, '15AM, '28PhD," *Columbia Alumni News*, December 19, 1930, 12.
3.  The details of his correspondence and trip are taken from a June 4, 1952, letter Ambedkar wrote to Savita, preserved in the Dr. Ambedkar Papers Collection of Nanak Chand Rattu, New Delhi.
4.  Eleanor Zelliot, *Ambedkar's World: The Making of Babasaheb and the Dalit Movement* (New Delhi: Navayana, 2013), 69.
5.  Anand Teltumbde, *Republic of Caste* (Delhi: Navayana, 2018), 22.
6.  Teltumbde, *Republic of Caste*, 141.
7.  Meera Nanda, *Prophets Facing Backward: Postmodern Critiques of Science and Hindu Nationalism in India* (New Brunswick, NJ: Rutgers University Press, 2003), 182.
8.  Nanda, *Prophets Facing Backward*, 184.
9.  K. N. Kadam, *The Meaning of the Ambedkarite Conversion to Buddhism and Other Essays* (New Delhi: Popular Prakashanv, 1997), v.
10. Arun P. Mukherjee, "B.R. Ambedkar, John Dewey, and the Meaning of Democracy," *New Literary History* 40 (2009): 368.
11. Dhananjay Keer, *Dr. Ambedkar: Life and Mission* (Bombay: Popular Prakashan, 1990); and Narendra Jadhav, *Ambedkar: Awakening India's Social Conscience* (Delhi: Konark Publishers, 2014). See also L. R. Balley, *Dr. Ambedkar: Life and Mission* (Jalandhar: Bheem Patrika Publications, 2022).
12. Christophe Jaffrelot, *Dr. Ambedkar and Untouchability: Fighting the Indian Caste System* (New York: Columbia University Press, 2005); Gail Omvedt, *Ambedkar: Towards an Enlightened India* (New York: Penguin, 2004); Gail Omvedt, *Dalits and the Democratic Revolution* (New Delhi: Sage, 1994); and Eleanor Zelliot, *Ambedkar's World: The Making of Babasaheb and the Dalit Movement* (New Delhi: Navayana, 2013).
13. Anupama Rao, *The Caste Question: Dalits and the Politics of Modern India* (Berkeley: University of California Press, 2009).
14. Vijay Surwade and I stumbled across this document in May 2019 among various other letters and papers in the Maharashtra State Archives, confirming the infer-

ences in Scott R. Stroud, "Creative Democracy, Communication, and the Uncharted Sources of Bhimrao Ambedkar's Deweyan Pragmatism," *Education & Culture* 34, no. 1 (2018): 61–80.

15. Ambedkar's surviving books are preserved in various libraries at Siddharth College in Mumbai; at the Symbiosis Institute in Pune; in libraries at Milind College in Aurangabad; in the collection held at Ambedkar's residence, Rajgraha; and private collections in Mumbai.

16. "Nima Adlerblum, Philosopher, 92," *New York Times*, August 2, 1974, 30. For a detailed account of Adlerblum's life and writings, see Jennifer Breger, "Nima Adlerblum 1881–1974," in *The Shalvi/Hyman Encyclopedia of Jewish Women*, n.d., https://jwa.org/encyclopedia/article/adlerblum-nima.

17. Penina Peli, "Adlerblum, Nima," in *Encyclopaedia Judaica*, 2nd ed., ed. Fred Skolnik and Michael Berenbaum (New York: Thomson Gale, 2007), 409.

18. Nima H. Adlerblum, "On John Dewey," May 6, 1966, Center for Dewey Studies, recording.

19. Adlerblum, "On John Dewey," May 6, 1966.

20. Adlerblum, "On John Dewey," May 6, 1966.

21. Breger, "Nima Adlerblum 1881—1974."

22. Israel Adlerblum to Edwin Robert Anderson Seligman, May 19, 1915, Seligman Papers, Columbia University.

23. Israel Adlerblum to Elsie Simpson, January 28, 1915, Seligman Papers, Columbia University.

24. I have asked a range of prominent scholars of Dewey and pragmatism about any other known students of Dewey who hailed from India in the 1910s or 1920s. No other candidates have appeared, let alone any that fit so many of the details revealed by Adlerblum. Furthermore, my own searches through Dewey's vast correspondence fail to reveal him talking about any students (Ambedkar or others) from India or South Asia. One can find perfunctory correspondence between Benoy Kumar Sarkar (1887–1949) and Dewey in the 1920s, but there is no evidence that Sarkar took any classes from or had any established relationship with Dewey. Beyond not being a student of Dewey's, Sarkar did not foreground Dewey's conception of democracy, or the quest to eradicate untouchability or to recover Buddhism as the recollection indicates. Lala Lajpat Rai (1865–1928) visited New York around 1916, but there is no evidence that he had any interest in or connection to Dewey's courses, lectures, or even his philosophy. He also seemed much more interested in the cause of Indian independence than in ending untouchability, a fact evidenced by his establishment of the Indian Home Rule League in New York.

25. Eleanor Zelliot, *From Untouchable to Dalit: Essays on the Ambedkar Movement* (New Delhi: Manohar, 1996), 79.

26. Brant Moscovitch, "Harold Laski's Indian Students and the Power of Education, 1920–1950," *Contemporary South Asia* 20 (2012): 1, 36.

27. Eleanor Zelliot, "Dr. Ambedkar and America," 1991, http://www.columbia.edu/itc/mealac/pritchett/00ambedkar/timeline/graphics/txt_zelliot1991.html.

28. Kadam, *Meaning of the Ambedkarite Conversion to Buddhism and Other Essays*, 1.

29. There is good reason to believe that that young Ambedkar was interested in a teaching position; he had requested "professional work in the College" of Baroda sometime before June 1918, according to documents from the Gaikwad's administrators. See Bhimrao R. Ambedkar, "Appendix VIII," in *Dr. Babasaheb Ambedkar Writings and Speeches* (Bombay: Government of Maharashtra, 2003), 17:pt.1:473. Addition-

ally, an article in 1933 reports on a speech in which Ambedkar indicates that in his youth his "first wish was to take a job as a professor." See "I want to spend my Whole Life as a Student," *Janata*, April 22, 1933, translated by Sandeep Badole.

30.  There is no evidence that Adlerblum maintained any sort of correspondence with Ambedkar, that she read his work, or that she was particularly interested in Buddhism or India; no letters or mentions of Ambedkar survive.

31.  This brief, and uncorroborated, reference is noted in C. D. Naik, *Thoughts and Philosophy of Dr. B.R. Ambedkar* (Delhi: B. R. Publishing, 2015), 22, 176.

32.  "Diamond Jubilee of Dr. B.R. Ambedkar, Celebration of," police report, October 29, 1954, in *Source Material on Dr. Babasaheb Ambedkar and the Movement of Untouchables*, ed. B. G. Kunte (Bombay: Government of Maharashtra, 1982), 1:421–22.

33.  Bhimrao R. Ambedkar, "In Hindu Religion There Is Place for God and for the Soul but Where Is There Place for Human Life," in *Ambedkar Writings and Speeches*, ed. and trans. Narendra Jadhav (New Delhi: Konark, 2016), 4:297–302, 298.

34.  This is consistent with K. N. Kadam's cryptic and unexplained comment that Ambedkar was supposedly planning on writing a book to be entitled "The Philosophy of John Dewey." Kadam, *Meaning of the Ambedkarite Conversion to Buddhism and Other Essays*, v.

35.  Adlerblum, "On John Dewey," May 6, 1966.

36.  Donald C. Bryant, "Rhetoric: Its Function and Its Scope," *Quarterly Journal of Speech* 39 (1953): 401–24, 413.

37.  Ananya Vajpeyi, "BR Ambedkar: The Life of the Mind and a Life in Politics," *Indian Cultural Forum*, April 13, 2021, https://indianculturalforum.in/2021/04/13/br -ambedkar-the-life-of-the-mind-and-a-life-in-politics/.

38.  Aishwary Kumar, *Radical Equality: Ambedkar, Gandhi, and the Risk of Democracy* (Stanford, CA: Stanford University Press, 2015), 39.

CHAPTER ONE

1.  Bhimrao R. Ambedkar, "Waiting for a Visa," in *Dr. Babasaheb Ambedkar Writings and Speeches* (Bombay: Government of Maharashtra, 1993), 12:668.

2.  For detailed accounts of Ambedkar's life, see Dhananjay Keer, *Dr. Ambedkar: Life and Mission* (Bombay: Popular Prakashan, 1990); Gail Omvedt, *Ambedkar: Towards an Enlightened India* (New York: Penguin Books, 2004); Vijay Mankar, *Dr B.R. Ambedkar: An Intellectual Biography* (Nagpur: Blueworld Series, 2016); and Narendra Jadhav, *Ambedkar: Awakening India's Social Conscience* (New Delhi, Konark Publishers, 2014).

3.  Christopher S. Queen, "Dr. Ambedkar and the Hermeneutics of Buddhist Liberation," in *Engaged Buddhism: Buddhist Liberation Movements in Asia*, ed. Christopher S. Queen and Sallie B. King (Albany: State University of New York Press, 1996), 64.

4.  For Ambedkar's various theses and degrees, see J. Krishnamurty, "Ambedkar's Educational Odyssey, 1913–1927," *Journal of Social Inclusion Studies* 5, no. 2 (2019): 147–57.

5.  Christopher S. Queen, "A Pedagogy of the Dhamma: B. R. Ambedkar and John Dewey on Education," *International Journal of Buddhist Thought and Culture* 24 (2015): 9.

6.  See Robert Danisch, *Pragmatism, Democracy, and the Necessity of Rhetoric* (Columbia: University of South Carolina Press, 2007); and Scott R. Stroud, "Selling Democracy and the Rhetorical Habits of Synthetic Conflict: John Dewey as Pragmatic Rhetor in China," *Rhetoric and Public Affairs* 16, no. 1 (2013): 97–132.

7.  Sidney Hook, *Out of Step: An Unquiet Life in the 20th Century* (New York: Carroll and Graf, 1987), 82–83.

8.  Corliss Lamont, ed., *Dialogue on John Dewey* (New York: Horizon Press, 1959), 43.

9.  Lamont, *Dialogue on John Dewey*, 41.

10. Hook, *Out of Step*, 83.

11. The details of Ambedkar's educational record at Columbia are taken from a copy (issued March 24, 1965) of his transcript contained in the Khairmode Papers in the archives of the University of Mumbai.

12. This book can be found in the collection of Ambedkar's personal books at Siddharth College, Mumbai.

13. The works listed are *The Wit and Wisdom of John Dewey* (1949), which survives in the archives of Ambedkar's books held at Siddharth College, and *Knowing and the Known* (coauthor Arthur Bentley, 1949). This notecard is preserved in the Dr. Ambedkar Papers Collection of Nanak Chand Rattu, New Delhi.

14. Lamont, *Dialogue on John Dewey*, 40.

15. Lamont, *Dialogue on John Dewey*, 43.

16. Ambedkar did not take Philosophy 232 (spring semester, 1915). Instead, he enrolled in Economics 242, Radicalism and Social Reform as Reflected in the Literature of the Nineteenth Century, taught by Vladimir Simkhovitch in the same time period. I am tempted to speculate that the course on "interpretation of various types of modern radicalism, such as socialism, nihilism and anarchism, and of social and economic conditions on which they are based" grabbed Ambedkar's interest more than an additional semester of Dewey's psychology did; as we shall see in later chapters, Ambedkar absorbed enough of Dewey's psychology from the winter semester Philosophy 231 course in 1914 to make a noticeable difference in his works. Philosophy 131–132, with its emphasis on social and political philosophy, was a different story: it seemed intriguing enough to get Ambedkar to commit to the full year.

17. Lamont, *Dialogue on John Dewey*, 16.

18. Nima H. Adlerblum, "On John Dewey," May 6, 1966, Center for Dewey Studies recording.

19. Hu Shih, *The Reminiscences of Dr. Hu Shih* (New York: Columbia University, 1975), 103; see also 95. Hu indicates that he took Dewey's courses Types of Logical Thinking (Philosophy 201–202) and Moral and Political Philosophy (Philosophy 131–132) in 1915–16.

20. John Dewey, "Lecture Notes, Student and Steno: Philosophy 121–122, 1912," Special Collections, Morris Library, Southern Illinois University, Carbondale (hereafter cited as *References*).

21. Martin Jay, *The Education of John Dewey* (New York: Columbia University Press, 2003), 258–59; and John Dewey, "Lecture Notes, Dated: Psychological Ethics: Syllabus," Special Collections, Morris Library, Southern Illinois University, Carbondale (hereafter cited as *1917 Syllabus*).

22. According to the Columbia University *Bulletin of Information* from 1915 to 1917, Philosophy 231–232 was noted as "not given" in 1916–17, but it was listed as one of Dewey's courses for 1917–18. Dewey would leave for Japan, then China, in early 1919, and would not return to the United States until July 1921.

23. John Dewey, "Notes on Psychological Ethics: Historical," Special Collections, Morris Library, Southern Illinois University, Carbondale (hereafter cited as *Background Handout*).

24. John Dewey, "Lecture Notes, Student and Steno: Notes on Psychological Ethics," Special Collections, Morris Library, Southern Illinois University, Carbondale (hereafter cited as *Lecture Notes*).

25. Ambedkar did not enroll in Philosophy 232; it occupied the same time period as Simkhovitch's course. The fall term at Columbia University ran from September 23, 1914, to February 2, 1915; the spring term ran from February 3, 1915, to June 9, 1915.

26. John Dewey, "Lecture Notes, Student and Steno: Notes on Psychological Ethics," Special Collections, Morris Library, Southern Illinois University, Carbondale (hereafter cited as *Student Notes*). These may have been corrected or annotated by Dewey himself, a practice that W. W. Charters posits as possible in his recollection of Dewey's courses in Chicago around 1901: "It was already an established custom for some student in Dr. Dewey's classes to take copious notes (in shorthand, always, I think) on the lectures. . . . This student then had his notes duplicated, hectographed, in every case while I was there, and given to each of us who paid a small amount for this service to which we subscribed at the beginning of the course. . . . I am sure that Dr. Dewey would always have been consulted by the student who wanted to earn the small sums he would realize, probably Dr. Dewey might even select a reliable student to take case of this." For this account and others, see Reginald D. Archambault, preface to *Lectures in the Philosophy of Education, 1899, by John Dewey* (New York: Random House, 1966), vii.

27. John Dewey, "The Psychological Standpoint," in *The Early Works of John Dewey*, ed. Jo Ann Boydston (Carbondale: Southern Illinois University Press, 1969), 1:131.

28. *Lecture Notes*, 1.

29. *Lecture Notes*, 1.

30. *Student Notes*, 2.

31. *Lecture Notes*, 3.

32. *Lecture Notes*, 3.

33. John Dewey, "The Reflex Arc Concept in Psychology," in *The Early Works of John Dewey*, ed. Jo Ann Boydston (Carbondale: Southern Illinois University Press, 1972), 5:96–110.

34. *Student Notes*, 2.

35. *Student Notes*, 2.

36. *Student Notes*, 2–3.

37. *Student Notes*, 3.

38. *Student Notes*, 15.

39. *Student Notes*, 1.

40. *Student Notes*, 1.

41. *Student Notes*, 8.

42. *Lecture Notes*, 3. This is compatible with William James's famous account of habit in his 1890 *Principles of Psychology*, a text that is contained in the remnants of Ambedkar's personal library at Siddharth College.

43. *Student Notes*, 11.

44. *Student Notes*, 11–12.

45. *Student Notes*, 23.

46. *1917 Syllabus*, 24.

47. *Student Notes*, 4.

48. *Lecture Notes*, 25.

49. See Charles S. Peirce, "The Fixation of Belief," *Popular Science Monthly*, November

1877, 1–15. This article concludes with Peirce's fourfold account of how beliefs are settled or "fixed," which would reappear in the 1907 edition of P. Lakshmi Narasu's *The Essence of Buddhism*. Ambedkar respected this book so much that he would spearhead its third reprinting in 1948.

50. *Lecture Notes*, 22.
51. *Lecture Notes*, 7.
52. John Dewey, "Three Independent Factors in Morals," in *The Later Works of John Dewey*, ed. Jo Ann Boydston (Carbondale: Southern Illinois University Press, 1984), 5:279–88; and John Dewey and James Hayden Tufts, *Ethics*, vol. 7 of *The Later Works of John Dewey*, ed. Jo Ann Boydston (Carbondale: Southern Illinois University Press, 1986).
53. *1917 Syllabus*, 35.
54. *Lecture Notes*, 22.
55. *Lecture Notes*, 24.
56. *Lecture Notes*, 23.
57. *Lecture Notes*, 31.
58. *Lecture Notes*, 31.
59. *Lecture Notes*, 31.
60. *Lecture Notes*, 28.
61. *Lecture Notes*, 28.
62. *Student Notes*, 15.
63. *Student Notes*, 16 (emphasis in original).
64. *Student Notes*, 6.
65. *Student Notes*, 37.
66. *1917 Syllabus*, 31–32.
67. Bhimrao R. Ambedkar, "Castes in India," in *Dr. Babasaheb Ambedkar Writings and Speeches*, vol. 1 (Bombay: Government of Maharashtra, 1979).
68. *Student Notes*, 9.
69. See John Dewey, *Principles of Instrumental Logic: John Dewey's Lectures in Ethics and Political Ethics, 1895–1896*, ed. Donald F. Koch (Carbondale: Southern Illinois University Press, 1998); John Dewey, *Lectures on Psychological and Political Ethics: 1898*, ed. Donald F. Koch (New York: Hafner Press, 1976); and John Dewey, *Lectures on Ethics 1900–1901*, ed. Donald F. Koch (Carbondale: Southern Illinois University Press, 1991).
70. The original typed notes from Homer H. Dubs can be found at the Center for Dewey Studies at Southern Illinois University, Carbondale. The original handwritten notes taken by Robert Lee Hale are located in the Butler Library Rare Book and Manuscript Collection at Columbia University. Both sets of notes are transcribed and corrected in *Lectures by John Dewey: Moral and Political Philosophy*, ed. Warren J. Samuels and Donald F. Koch (London: JAI, 1990). Hereafter, page citations to these lectures refer to the Samuel and Koch edition, noting only whether the passage stems from the *Dubs* or *Hale* notes.
71. Luther Carrington Goodrich, "Homer Dubs (1892–1969)," *Journal of Asian Studies* 29 (1970): 889–91.
72. *Dubs*, 118 (emphasis in original).
73. *Hale*, 59.
74. *Hale*, 57.
75. *Hale*, 58.
76. *Hale*, 58.

77. *Hale*, 58.
78. Donald F. Koch, "Editor's Introduction: International Conflict and the Development of Dewey's Moral, Political, and Legal Philosophy," in Samuels and Koch, *Lectures by John Dewey*, 20–21.
79. *Dubs*, 122.
80. *Hale*, 59.
81. *Hale*, 59.
82. *Dubs*, 127.
83. *Hale*, 97–98.
84. *Hale*, 102.
85. *Hale*, 100.
86. *Hale*, 102.
87. *Hale*, 102.
88. Dewey referred his students to his 1915 book, *German Philosophy and Politics*, in his January 5, 1916, lecture. A 1915 edition of this book was owned—and annotated—by Ambedkar; his copy is held by Siddharth College.
89. *Dubs*, 162 (emphasis in original).
90. *Dubs*, 163 (emphasis in original).
91. *Dubs*, 163.
92. *Dubs*, 164.
93. *Dubs*, 164.
94. *Dubs*, 164 (emphasis in original).
95. *Dubs*, 165.
96. *Dubs*, 167.
97. *Hale*, 107.
98. *Dubs*, 167.
99. *Hale*, 108.
100. *Hale*, 112–13.
101. *Hale*, 109.
102. *Hale*, 114.
103. *Hale*, 114.
104. *Hale*, 115.
105. *Dubs*, 173–174.
106. *Dubs*, 174.
107. *Dubs*, 174.
108. *Dubs*, 174.
109. *Dubs*, 174.
110. *Dubs*, 174.
111. *Dubs*, 174.
112. *Dubs*, 196.
113. *Dubs*, 196.
114. *Dubs*, 196 (emphasis in original).
115. *Dubs*, 196.
116. *Dubs*, 196 (emphasis in original).
117. For the story of this preamble, see Aakash Singh Rathore, *Ambedkar's Preamble* (Haryana, India: Vintage, 2020).
118. *Dubs*, 196.
119. *Dubs*, 197 (emphasis in original).
120. *Dubs*, 197.

121. *Dubs,* 197.

122. *Hale,* 114.

123. *Dubs,* 216.

124. *Dubs,* 215 (emphasis in original).

125. *Dubs,* 218.

126. *Dubs,* 218.

127. *Dubs,* 218 (emphasis in original).

128. *Dubs,* 219–20.

129. *Dubs,* 216.

130. *Dubs,* 216.

131. *Dubs,* 227.

132. *Dubs,* 227.

133. *Dubs,* 227 (emphasis in original).

134. *Dubs,* 215.

135. *Dubs,* 222 (emphasis in original).

136. *Dubs,* 222.

137. *Dubs,* 222.

138. *Dubs,* 222 (emphasis in original).

139. *Dubs,* 222 (emphasis in original).

140. *Dubs,* 223 (emphasis in original).

141. Dewey invokes Franz Boas on revenge and various examples from anthropology to make this point. See *Dubs,* 229–32.

142. *Dubs,* 223.

143. *Dubs,* 223.

144. *Dubs,* 216.

145. *Dubs,* 126.

146. *Hale,* 75.

147. For mahars like Ambedkar, basic survival depended on the cooperation of upper castes, who influenced or controlled all sources of water and food.

148. *Dubs,* 235.

149. *Dubs,* 235.

150. *Dubs,* 235.

151. *Dubs,* 236.

152. *Dubs,* 237.

153. *Dubs,* 237 (emphasis in original).

154. *Dubs,* 237.

155. *Dubs,* 237.

156. *Dubs,* 237.

157. *Dubs,* 237


CHAPTER TWO

1. Dhananjay Keer, *Dr. Ambedkar: Life and Mission* (Bombay: Popular Prakashan, 1990), 32–33.

2. Dennis Dalton, *Mahatma Gandhi: Nonviolent Power in Action* (New York: Columbia University Press, 1993), 27.

3. Keer, *Dr. Ambedkar: Life and Mission,* 33.

4. Narendra Jadhav, *Ambedkar: Awakening India's Social Conscience* (New Delhi, Konark Publishers, 2014), 36.

5. For detailed annotations on this essay, see Sharmila Rege, *Against the Madness of*

*Manu: B. R. Ambedkar's Writings on Brahmanical Patriarchy* (New Delhi: Navayana 2013).

6. Ambedkar, incidentally, briefly referred to the work of Jevons—most likely William—in his review on Bertrand Russell, and most likely heard about his work in the summer 1914 course at Columbia, taught by Alvin S. Johnson of Cornell University, titled Economics 205 Modern Economic Theories.

7. H. Stanley Jevons to E.R.A. Seligman, September 9, 1917, Seligman Papers, Columbia University.

8. H. Stanley Jevons, editorial foreword, *Indian Journal of Economics* 1, no. 1 (1916): 1.

9. Jevons, editorial foreword, 1.

10. Jevons, editorial foreword, 2.

11. There remains the interesting question of *when* this review was actually written. The edition of the Russell book reviewed is noted as "1917" in the review; the 1917 British editions of this work (with a title distinct from the 1917 American edition) were issued in January and May 1917. We know that Ambedkar fled the harassment he faced in Baroda due to his untouchability in November 1917; it is unlikely that he had the time or motive to write this review during that tumultuous period. From November 1917 to November 1918, he was engaged in various unsuccessful economic endeavors around Bombay. He assumed a professorship of political economy at Sydenham College in Bombay in November 1918. The most likely hypotheses are that he penned this review shortly after acquiring the book in London during the spring of 1917 or during the interim period after Baroda, where he eventually set his sights on the economics position in Sydenham. As Keer notes, Ambedkar had the initiative to write Lord Sydenham to get the government's recommendation for the post at Sydenham College; it is possible that this review article was part of the general preparations for showing his qualifications and intellectual acumen for such a post. For more on this period, see Keer, *Dr. Ambedkar: Life and Mission*, 37–40.

12. Bhimrao R. Ambedkar, *The Problem of the Rupee*, in *Dr. Babasaheb Ambedkar Writings and Speeches* (Bombay: Government of Maharashtra, 1989), 6:330; and Ambedkar, "The Evolution of Provincial Finance in British India," in *Dr. Babasaheb Ambedkar Writings and Speeches*, 6:54.

13. Ambedkar, *The Problem of the Rupee*, in *Dr. Babasaheb Ambedkar Writings and Speeches*, 6:614.

14. "The Journal," *Journal of the Indian Economic Society* 1, no. 1 (1918): 1.

15. "The Journal," 3 (emphasis in original).

16. This anecdote could *not* be a reference to Harold Laski, since he joined the London School of Economics in 1920.

17. See Keer, *Dr. Ambedkar: Life and Mission*.

18. Bertrand Russell, *Principles of Social Reconstruction* (1916; repr., London: George Allen and Unwin, 1917). As noted by Ambedkar, the review focused on the 1917 British reprint edition (bearing the same title) of this book. The American edition of Russell's book, published in 1917, had the new title *Why Men Fight*.

19. Bhimrao R. Ambedkar, "Mr. Russell and the Reconstruction of Society," in *Dr. Babasaheb Ambedkar Writings and Speeches* (Bombay: Government of Maharashtra, 1979), 1:483.

20. Interestingly enough, I have never come across a copy of Russell's 1917 book in any of the caches of books previously owned by Ambedkar. Perhaps this could serve as some evidence that he wrote this review earlier—with the inference being that his

copy was lost on the torpedoed steamer in 1917—but the short time between the actual (re)publication of this book and Ambedkar's departure from London weighs against this hypothesis.

21. Robert B. Westbrook, *John Dewey and American Democracy* (Ithaca, NY: Cornell University Press, 1991), 136.
22. Bertrand Russell, "Pragmatism," in *Philosophical Essays* (New York: Simon and Schuster, 1966), 110–11.
23. Russell, "Pragmatism," 111.
24. Russell, "Pragmatism," 124.
25. For more on these thinkers, see Jane Duran, "Russell on Pragmatism," *Russell: The Journal of the Bertrand Russell Archives* 14 (1994): 31–37; and Tom Burke, *Dewey's New Logic: A Reply to Russell* (Chicago: University of Chicago Press, 1998).
26. John Dewey, "Three Contemporary Philosophers," in *The Middle Works of John Dewey*, ed. Jo Ann Boydston (Carbondale: Southern Illinois University Press, 1982), 12:244–50. For more on the intersecting visits of Russell and Dewey in China, see Jessica Ching-Sze Wang, *John Dewey in China: To Teach and to Learn* (Albany: State University of New York Press, 2007).
27. *1917 Syllabus*, 5.
28. Ambedkar, "Mr. Russell and the Reconstruction of Society," 1:483.
29. Russell, *Principles of Social Reconstruction*, 24–28.
30. Russell, *Principles of Social Reconstruction*, 26.
31. Russell, *Principles of Social Reconstruction*, 29–30.
32. There is evidence of similar reactions from Ambedkar as reader. I remember coming across such a material trace in his copy of *The Life of Jesus*, written by Ernest Renan, now held at Milind College in Aurangabad. After underlining a line by Renan about the "Semitic race" having "the glory of having made the religion of humanity," Ambedkar the reader placed a large exclamation point in the margin indicating his disagreement with this Western assessment. For him, traditions such as Buddhism would surely serve as a glorious religion of humanity as well as or better than Judaism or Christianity.
33. Russell, *Principles of Social Reconstruction*, 30.
34. Russell, *Principles of Social Reconstruction*, 30.
35. See the essays collected in Bertrand Russell, *Justice in Wartime* (Chicago: Open Court Publishing, 1916).
36. Russell, *Principles of Social Reconstruction*, 33.
37. Russell, *Principles of Social Reconstruction*, 33–34.
38. Russell, *Principles of Social Reconstruction*, 33–34.
39. Russell, *Principles of Social Reconstruction*, 224.
40. Russell, *Principles of Social Reconstruction*, 224.
41. Russell, *Principles of Social Reconstruction*, 155.
42. Russell, *Principles of Social Reconstruction*, 234.
43. Russell, *Principles of Social Reconstruction*, 228.
44. Tadd L. Ruetenik, "Social Meliorism in the Religious Pragmatism of William James," *Journal of Speculative Philosophy* 19 (2005): 238–49; Tadd L. Ruetenik, "Meliorism," in *Encyclopedia of American Philosophy*, ed. John Lachs and Robert Talisse (New York: Routledge Press, 2008), 498–501; and Scott R. Stroud, "What Does Pragmatic Meliorism Mean for Rhetoric?," *Western Journal of Communication* 74, no. 1 (2010): 43–60.
45. Ambedkar, "Mr. Russell and the Reconstruction of Society," 1:483.

46. Ambedkar, "Mr. Russell and the Reconstruction of Society," 1:484.
47. Ambedkar acquired his earliest copy of this work in January 1917 while studying in London.
48. John Dewey, *Democracy and Education*, vol. 9 of *The Middle Works of John Dewey*, ed. Jo Ann Boydston (Carbondale: Southern Illinois University Press, 1985), 20.
49. Dewey, *Democracy and Education*, 188.
50. For example, *Dubs*, 141.
51. Ambedkar referred to Russell's 1925 piece on nonviolence in the *Atlantic* in his own article in *Janata* on August 10, 1940; in an April 1, 1950, letter preserved in the Maharashtra State Archives, we also see that Ambedkar requested a copy of Russell's Reith Lectures from an administrator at All India Radio. Ambedkar's personal copy of Russell's *The Theory and Practice of Bolshevism*, 2nd ed. (London: George Allen and Unwin, 1949) survives in the archives of Milind College.
52. Ambedkar, "Mr. Russell and the Reconstruction of Society," 1:484.
53. Ambedkar, "Mr. Russell and the Reconstruction of Society," 1:485.
54. Ambedkar, "Mr. Russell and the Reconstruction of Society," 1:485.
55. Ambedkar, "Mr. Russell and the Reconstruction of Society," 1:485 (emphasis in original).
56. Ambedkar, "Mr. Russell and the Reconstruction of Society," 1:485.
57. Ambedkar, "Mr. Russell and the Reconstruction of Society," 1:485.
58. Ambedkar, "Mr. Russell and the Reconstruction of Society," 1:485.
59. See Max Jammer, *Concepts of Force* (Mineolo, NY: Dover, 1999), 7.
60. See the analysis of the mergers and disjunctions between Gandhi and Ambedkar on force in Aishwary Kumar, *Radical Equality: Ambedkar, Gandhi, and the Risk of Democracy* (Palo Alto, CA: Stanford University Press, 2015). See also Joan V. Bondurant, *Conquest of Violence: The Gandhian Philosophy of Conflict* (Berkeley: University of California Press, 1967); Mary Elizabeth King, *Gandhian Nonviolent Struggle and Untouchability in South India* (New Delhi: Oxford University Press, 2015); and Ramachandra Guha, *Gandhi: The Years That Changed the World 1914–1948* (New York: Alfred A. Knopf, 2018).
61. Ambedkar, "Mr. Russell and the Reconstruction of Society," 1:486.
62. Ambedkar, "Mr. Russell and the Reconstruction of Society," 1:486.
63. *Dubs*, 219 (emphasis in original).
64. *Dubs*, 219 (emphasis in original).
65. *Dubs*, 219.
66. *Dubs*, 220.
67. Dewey's views of Buddhism were likely skewed by his correspondence with Scudder Klyce (1879–1933) before and during Ambedkar's semesters with Dewey.
68. *Dubs*, 218 (emphasis in original). The distinctions enunciated in these lectures also inspired Hu Shih's account of constructive pacificism, which diverges in important ways from Ambedkar's appropriation of Dewey on force. For more on Hu and force, see Jerome B. Grieder, *Hu Shih and the Chinese Renaissance* (Cambridge, MA: Harvard University Press, 1970), 59.
69. *Dubs*, 218.
70. *Dubs*, 219.
71. *Dubs*, 219.
72. *Dubs*, 219.
73. *Dubs*, 219.
74. In 1940, Ambedkar returns to Russell's view of all force being violent (including his

1925 article in the *Atlantic*), but this time explicitly equates it to Gandhi's approach to nonviolence. See Bhimrao R. Ambedkar, "Mess of Indian Politics—2," *Janata*, August 10, 1940.

75. See the tensions over this term in Bertrand Russell, "The Ethics of War," *International Journal of Ethics* 25, no. 2 (January 1915): 127–42; Ralph Barton Perry, "Non-Resistance and the Present War—A Reply to Mr. Russell," *International Journal of Ethics* 25, no. 3 (April 1915): 307–16; Bertrand Russell, "War and Non-Resistance," *Atlantic Monthly* 116, no. 2 (August 1915): 266–74; and Bertrand Russell, "The War and Non-Resistance: A Rejoinder to Professor Perry," *International Journal of Ethics* 26, no. 1 (October 1915): 23–30.

76. John Dewey, "In Response," in *Later Works of John Dewey*, ed. Jo Ann Boydston (Carbondale: Southern Illinois University Press, 1984), 5:421 (emphasis added).

77. For various uses of "passive resistance" by Gandhi, as well as his efforts to summon the public's help in renaming his method, see Dennis Dalton, *Mahatma Gandhi*, 8–9, 26–27; see also Gandhi's and Tagore's early use of the term in Ramachandra Guha, *Gandhi*, 78, 182.

78. For the relation between Tolstoy and Gandhi, consult Martin Green, *Tolstoy and Gandhi, Men of Peace* (New York: Basic Books, 1983); and Martin Green, *The Origins of Nonviolence: Tolstoy and Gandhi in Their Historical Settings* (University Park: Pennsylvania State University Press, 1986). For useful accounts of Gandhi's method, see Ajay Skaria, *Unconditional Equality: Gandhi's Religion of Resistance* (Minneapolis: University of Minnesota Press, 2016); and Faisal Devji, *The Impossible Indian: Gandhi and the Temptation of Violence* (Cambridge, MA: Harvard University Press, 2012).

79. Ambedkar, "Castes in India," in *Dr. Babasaheb Ambedkar Writings and Speeches*, 1:14 (emphasis in original).

80. *Dubs*, 220.

81. *Dubs*, 220.

82. *Dubs*, 220–21.

83. Ambedkar, "Mr. Russell and the Reconstruction of Society," 1:486.

84. John Patrick Diggins, "John Dewey in Peace and War," *American Scholar* 50, no. 2 (1981): 214.

85. Satyabrata Rai Chowdhuri, *Leftism in India, 1917–1947* (New Delhi: Sage, 2017), 6–7.

86. *Dubs*, 221.

87. *Dubs*, 222.

88. *Dubs*, 222.

89. *Dubs*, 222.

90. *Dubs*, 222–23.

91. John Dewey, "Force and Coercion," in *The Middle Works of John Dewey*, ed. Jo Ann Boydston, vol. 10 (Carbondale: Southern Illinois University Press, 1982).

92. Dewey, "Force and Coercion," 246.

93. *Dubs*, 223.

94. *Dubs*, 223.

95. *Dubs*, 217.

96. Ambedkar, "Mr. Russell and the Reconstruction of Society," 1:486.

97. See also Alexander Livingston, "Between Means and Ends: Reconstructing Coercion in Dewey's Democratic Theory," *American Political Science Review* 111, no. 3 (2017): 522–34.

98. For accounts of the role of humiliation in caste oppression, see Gopal Guru, ed., *Humiliation: Claims and Contexts* (New Delhi: Oxford University Press, 2009).

99. Ambedkar had a lifelong concern with the harms of social boycott. It arises in the second issue of *Mook Nayak* in 1920, before the Simon Commission in 1929, in his *States and Minorities* memorandum from 1946, and in *The Buddha and His Dhamma* (1957).

100. Russell, *Principles of Social Reconstruction*, 155.

101. Russell, *Principles of Social Reconstruction*, 156.

102. Ambedkar, "Mr. Russell and the Reconstruction of Society," 1:487.

103. Ambedkar, "Mr. Russell and the Reconstruction of Society," 1:487.

104. Ambedkar, "Mr. Russell and the Reconstruction of Society," 1:488.

105. Ambedkar, "Mr. Russell and the Reconstruction of Society," 1:489 (emphasis in original).

106. Ambedkar, "Mr. Russell and the Reconstruction of Society," 1:491.

107. Ambedkar, "Mr. Russell and the Reconstruction of Society," 1:491. For another review of Russell's book, see C. Delisle Burns, "Principles of Social Reconstruction," *International Journal of Ethics* 27, no. 3 (1917): 384–87.

108. Ambedkar, "Mr. Russell and the Reconstruction of Society," 1:491.

109. Ambedkar, "Mr. Russell and the Reconstruction of Society," 1:492 (emphasis in original).

110. Ambedkar, "Mr. Russell and the Reconstruction of Society," 1:492.

111. Ambedkar, "Mr. Russell and the Reconstruction of Society," 1:492.

112. Ambedkar, "Mr. Russell and the Reconstruction of Society," 1:492.

113. Leo Tolstoy, *A Confession and What I Believe*, trans. Aylmer Maude (London: Oxford University Press, 1932). Ambedkar's annotated copies of this book and Tolstoy's *What Then Must We Do?* are preserved in the archives at Siddharth College in Mumbai. Both works are marked in Ambedkar's own hand with his signature and "20/7/1936" inside the cover. Ambedkar would later recommend Tolstoy's biography to his second wife, Savita, in their correspondence in March 1948.

114. This quotation, along with Ambedkar's markings and note, occurs in Tolstoy, *Confession and What I Believe*, 37.

CHAPTER THREE

1. Dhananjay Keer, *Dr. Ambedkar: Life and Mission* (Bombay: Popular Prakashan, 1990), 39.

2. Eleanor Zelliot, *Ambedkar's World: The Making of Babasaheb and the Dalit Movement* (New Delhi: Navayana, 2013), 65–66.

3. Zelliot, *Ambedkar's World*, 66.

4. Zelliot, *Ambedkar's World*, 66.

5. H. C. Sadangi, *Emancipation of Dalits and Freedom Struggle* (New Delhi: Isha Books, 2008), 160–61.

6. Eleanor Zelliot, *From Untouchable to Dalit: Essays on the Ambedkar Movement* (New Delhi: Manohar, 1996), 67.

7. Bhimrao R. Ambedkar, "Evidence before the Southborough Committee," in *Dr. Babasaheb Ambedkar Writings and Speeches* (Bombay: Government of Maharashtra, 1979), 1:276.

8. S. Anand, "Sanskrit, English and Dalits," *Economic and Political Weekly*, July 24, 1999, 2054.

9. Anand, "Sanskrit, English and Dalits," 2056.

10. B. R. Kamble, trans., *Mook Nayak* (Kolhapur: Dr. Babasaheb Ambedkar Research Institute in Social Growth, 2010), 10.

11. Many articles published in the first year (1920) of Ambedkar's newspaper, *Mook Nayak*, harshly criticize this approach.

12. Ambedkar, "Evidence before the Southborough Committee," 1:263–64.

13. Ambedkar, "Evidence before the Southborough Committee," 1:263.

14. For more on this strategy, see Christophe Jaffrelot's account in *Dr. Ambedkar and Untouchability: Fighting the Indian Caste System* (New York: Columbia University Press, 2005).

15. Arun P. Mukherjee, "B.R. Ambedkar, John Dewey, and the Meaning of Democracy," *New Literary History* 40 (2009): 347–48.

16. Scott R. Stroud, "Pragmatism and the Methodology of Comparative Rhetoric," *Rhetoric Society Quarterly* 39 (2009): 353–79; "Useful Irresponsibility? A Reply to Mao on the Purpose(s) of Comparative Rhetoric," *Rhetoric Society Quarterly* 41 (2011): 69–74; and Bruce Ziff and Pratima V. Rao, "Introduction to Cultural Appropriation: A Framework for Analysis," in *Borrowed Power: Essays on Cultural Appropriation*, ed. Ziff and Rao (New Brunswick, NJ: Rutgers University Press, 1997), 1–30. For more on the ethics of appropriation, see James O. Young and Conrad G. Brunk, eds., *The Ethics of Cultural Appropriation* (West Sussex, UK: Wiley-Blackwell, 2012).

17. Arun P. Mukherjee, "B.R. Ambedkar, John Dewey, and the Meaning of Democracy," *New Literary History* 40 (2009): 347–48.

18. Keya Maitra, "Ambedkar and the Constitution of India: A Deweyan Experiment," *Contemporary Pragmatism* 9 (2012): 301–20.

19. Ambedkar, "Evidence before the Southborough Committee," 1:248.

20. Ambedkar, "Evidence before the Southborough Committee," 1:248–49.

21. See the biographical essays in in Bhimrao R. Ambedkar, "Waiting for a Visa," in *Dr. Babasaheb Ambedkar Writings and Speeches*, vol. 12 (Bombay: Government of Maharashtra, 1993).

22. John Dewey, *Democracy and Education*, vol. 9 of *The Middle Works of John Dewey*, ed. Jo Ann Boydston (Carbondale: Southern Illinois University Press, 1985), 7 (emphasis added).

23. Dewey, *Democracy and Education*, 7 (emphasis added).

24. Dewey, *Democracy and Education*, 7 (emphasis added).

25. Ambedkar, "Evidence before the Southborough Committee," 1:248.

26. Dewey, *Democracy and Education*, 90 (emphasis added).

27. The social application of *endosmosis* stems originally from Henri Bergson; Dewey incorporates this usage into his *Democracy and Education* (1916). Ambedkar most likely picked up this term and its meaning from Dewey, not from Bergson's fuller philosophy; indeed, Ambedkar echoes the exact place that Dewey uses it, as well as Dewey's expanded phraseology of *social* endosmosis.

28. Ambedkar, "Evidence before the Southborough Committee," 1:251.

29. Dewey, *Democracy and Education*, 25 (emphasis added).

30. Dewey, *Democracy and Education*, 129 (emphasis added).

31. Dewey, *Democracy and Education*, 90 (emphasis added).

32. John Dewey, "The Ethics of Democracy," in *The Early Works of John Dewey*, ed. Jo Ann Boydston (Carbondale: Southern Illinois University Press, 1969), 1:244.

33. Ambedkar, "Evidence before the Southborough Committee," 1:251.

34. John Dewey, "Reconstruction in Philosophy," in *The Middle Works of John Dewey*, ed. Jo Ann Boydston (Carbondale: Southern Illinois University Press, 1982), 12:181.

35. Dewey, *Democracy and Education*, 318.

36. This situationally adapted aspect of Ambedkar's arguments is often missed by those looking at the *historical progression* that Ambedkar and his movement indicate, or by those who see his texts as fragments or expressions of a larger, and largely unified and consistent, *theory or doctrine* lying just below the surface in any imperfect utterance or specific persuasive message. This also is a path that many comparative accounts of Ambedkar and Dewey tread, though not without some usefulness.

37. Keith Miller, *Voice of Deliverance: The Language of Martin Luther King, Jr. and Its Sources* (New York: The Free Press, 1992); and Scott R. Stroud, "Echoes of Pragmatism in India: Bhimrao Ambedkar and Reconstructive Rhetoric," in *Recovering Overlooked Pragmatists in Communication: Extending the Living Conversation about Pragmatism and Rhetoric*, ed. Robert Danisch (Cham: Palgrave Macmillan, 2019), 79–103.

38. Gary Saul Morson, *The Words of Others: From Quotations to Culture* (New Haven, CT: Yale University Press, 2011), 42 (emphasis in original).

39. Morson, *Words of Others*, 130. See also Ruth Finnegan, *Why Do We Quote? The Culture and History of Quotation* (Cambridge: OpenBook Publishers, 2011), 191.

40. Finnegan, *Why Do We Quote?*, 257.

41. Keith Houston, *Shady Characters: The Secret Life of Punctuation, Symbols, and Other Typographical Marks* (New York: W. W. Norton, 2013), 197–204.

42. Morson, *Words of Others*, 78.

43. See W. V. O. Quine, *Mathematical Logic* (Cambridge, MA: Harvard University Press, 2009); and Donald Davidson, *Inquiries into Truth and Interpretation* (New York: Clarendon Press, 2001).

44. Morson, *Words of Others*, 37.

45. Morson, *Words of Others*, 38.

46. Morson, *Words of Others*, 38 (emphasis in original).

47. Finnegan, *Why Do We Quote?*, 171.

48. Wilhelm Halbfass, *Tradition and Reflection: Explorations in Indian Thought* (Albany: State University of New York Press, 1991).

49. Halbfass, *Tradition and Reflection*, 227.

50. Halbfass, *Tradition and Reflection*, 227.

51. Bhimrao R. Ambedkar, *Annihilation of Caste*, in *Dr. Babasaheb Ambedkar Writings and Speeches*, vol. 1 (Bombay: Government of Maharashtra, 1979).

52. Ambedkar, *Annihilation of Caste*, 1:79.

53. Dewey, *Democracy and Education*, 24 (emphasis added).

54. Bhimrao R. Ambedkar, "The Buddha and the Future of His Religion," in *Dr. Babasaheb Ambedkar Writings and Speeches* (Bombay: Government of Maharashtra, 2003), 17:pt.2:98.

55. For more context, see Leonard J. Waks and Andrea R. English, eds., *John Dewey's Democracy and Education: A Centennial Handbook* (New York: Cambridge University Press, 2017).

56. Ambedkar, *Annihilation of Caste*, 1:79.

57. Dewey, *Democracy and Education*, 81.

58. Dewey, *Democracy and Education*, 81–82 (emphasis added).

59. Mukherjee, "B.R. Ambedkar, John Dewey, and the Meaning of Democracy," 350.

60. Mukherjee, "B.R. Ambedkar, John Dewey, and the Meaning of Democracy," 350 (emphasis in original).
61. John Dewey, "Outlines of a Critical Theory of Ethics," in *The Early Works of John Dewey*, ed. Jo Ann Boydston (Carbondale: Southern Illinois University Press, 1969), 3:322 (emphasis removed).
62. Dewey, *Democracy and Education*, 84.
63. Bhimrao R. Ambedkar, "Mr. Russell and the Reconstruction of Society," in *Dr. Babasaheb Ambedkar Writings and Speeches*, 1:488–91.
64. See Suraj Yengde, *Caste Matters* (Delhi: Penguin, 2019) for a contemporary account of caste-conditioned experience in India.
65. For more on Gandhi and Ambedkar, see Jaffrelot, *Dr. Ambedkar and Untouchability*; Gail Omvedt, *Ambedkar: Towards an Enlightened India* (New York: Penguin Books, 2004); and Vijay Mankar, *Poona Pact: Historical Harms by Gandhi, Gandhism, and Congress* (Nagpur: Blue World Series, 2013).
66. Ambedkar, *Annihilation of Caste*, 1:95.
67. John Dewey, "Experience and Nature," in *The Later Works of John Dewey*, ed. Jo Ann Boydston (Carbondale: Southern Illinois University Press, 1981), 1:172 (emphasis added). Ambedkar's annotated 1929 edition of this book can be found in the Ambedkar Collection at Siddharth College in Mumbai.

CHAPTER FOUR

1. See Anand Teltumbde, *Mahad: The Making of the First Dalit Revolt* (Delhi: Aakar, 2016).
2. Bhimrao R. Ambedkar, "Unfortunately I Was born a Hindu Untouchable but I Will Not Die a Hindu," in *Dr. Babasaheb Ambedkar Writings and Speeches*, vol. 17, pt. 2 (Bombay: Government of Maharashtra, 2003).
3. Nanak Chand Rattu, *Little Known Facets of Dr. Ambedkar* (New Delhi: Focus Impressions, 2001); Devi Dayal, *Daily Routine of Dr. Ambedkar* (New Delhi: Samyak Prakashan, 2011); and Shankranand Shastri, *My Experiences and Memories of Dr. Babasaheb Ambedkar* (Delhi: Gautam Book Center, 2012).
4. Nanak Chand Rattu, *Reminiscences and Remembrances of Dr. B.R. Ambedkar* (New Delhi: Falcon Books, 1995), 122.
5. Many of his personal books also contain small check marks next to specific chapters of interest in the table of contents.
6. H. J. Jackson, *Marginalia: Readers Writing in Books* (New Haven, CT: Yale University Press, 2002), 100.
7. Jackson, *Marginalia*, 87.
8. Christopher S. Queen, "A Pedagogy of the Dhamma: B. R. Ambedkar and John Dewey on Education," *International Journal of Buddhist Thought and Culture* 24 (2015): 12.
9. V. Geetha does an admirable job giving her readers a sense for the many books that possibly influenced Ambedkar's thought in the 1940s in her examination of Siddharth College's archive. See "Unpacking a Library: Babasaheb Ambedkar and His World of Books," *Wire*, October 29, 2017, https://thewire.in/caste/unpacking -library-babasaheb-ambedkar-world-books. Her method usefully emphasizes the content of many of the books he owned, not the specific patterns of annotation or marking he made within them, differing from the method that I employ in this chapter. Both methods have their value and limitations. It is curious that J. D. Elam advances a theory of Ambedkar as a *reader* by only looking at what Ambedkar *writes*,

combined with an explicit resistance to using the data of Ambedkar's actual engagement with the material texts he read (but did not always cite or quote). See Elam's *World Literature for the Wretched of the Earth* (New York: Fordham University Press, 2021), 47.

10. Dayal, *Daily Routine of Dr. Ambedkar,* 78–79.
11. In my examination of annotations among all his books preserved at Siddharth College, Milind College, Rajgraha, the Symbiosis Institute, and other collections, I can discern no sustained pattern to these marking styles.
12. In my discussions with Vijay Surwade and Anandraj Ambedkar, another explanation emerged: Ambedkar had different pencils lying on the various tables he used for his frequent reading sessions throughout his personal library (such as at Rajgruha). This most likely explains the alternating red and blue markings that are present in many of his books; they indicate different sessions of reading the same book.
13. In my research at Siddharth College in Mumbai, I have located three copies of Dewey's *Democracy and Education* that Ambedkar owned, with two being extensively annotated. There is a paperback copy of *Democracy and Education* preserved at Milind College in Aurangabad. Two copies of Dewey and Tufts's 1908 *Ethics* (published in London in 1910) are preserved at Siddharth College, both extensively annotated. See Scott R. Stroud, "What Did Bhimrao Ambedkar Learn from John Dewey's *Democracy and Education?*," *Pluralist* 12, no. 2 (2017): 78–103.
14. The copy that I analyze here is the Macmillan 1916 edition. I refer to the passages he marked by using the page numbers in John Dewey, *Democracy and Education*, vol. 9 of *The Middle Works of John Dewey*, ed. Jo Ann Boydston (Carbondale: Southern Illinois University Press, 1985).
15. Dewey, *Democracy and Education*, 4.
16. Dewey, *Democracy and Education*, 5
17. Dewey, *Democracy and Education*, 6.
18. Dewey, *Democracy and Education*, 6.
19. Dewey, *Democracy and Education*, 7.
20. Dewey, *Democracy and Education*, 7.
21. Dewey, *Democracy and Education*, 9, 17.
22. Dewey, *Democracy and Education*, 23.
23. Eleanor Zelliot, *From Untouchable to Dalit: Essays on the Ambedkar Movement* (New Delhi: Manohar, 1996).
24. Dewey, *Democracy and Education*, 21.
25. Dewey, *Democracy and Education*, 80.
26. Dewey, *Democracy and Education*, 79.
27. Dewey, *Democracy and Education*, 82.
28. Dewey, *Democracy and Education*, 88–89.
29. Dewey, *Democracy and Education*, 90–91.
30. Dewey, *Democracy and Education*, 90. Here we see Bergson's term "endosmosis," accessed by Ambedkar through Dewey's reception and alteration of the French philosopher's concept.
31. Dewey, *Democracy and Education*, 92. We shall see ideas from this passage appear in *Annihilation of Caste* later in this chapter.
32. Dewey, *Democracy and Education*, 93. This line is also echoed later in Ambedkar's life in his "Prospects of Democracy in India" address for a Voice of America radio broadcast on May 20, 1956.

33. Ambedkar marks four passages in colored pencil in this section of Dewey, *Democracy and Education*, 94–95.

34. Dewey, *Democracy and Education*, 7–8.

35. Bhimrao R. Ambedkar, "Evidence before the Southborough Committee," in *Dr. Babasaheb Ambedkar Writings and Speeches* (Bombay: Government of Maharashtra, 1979), 1:248–49; and Ambedkar, *Annihilation of Caste*, 1:51.

36. An extended account of Ambedkar's engagement with *Democracy and Education* can be found in Stroud, "What Did Bhimrao Ambedkar Learn from John Dewey's *Democracy and Education?*"

37. I analyze here the extensively annotated copy that contains more than one hundred pages marked in all the styles and colors of emphasis Ambedkar used.

38. John Dewey and James H. Tufts, *Ethics*, in *The Middle Works of John Dewey*, ed. Jo Ann Boydston (Carbondale: Southern Illinois University Press, 1985), 5:6.

39. For the differences between the 1908 *Ethics* and the 1932 *Ethics*, see Abraham Edel, *Ethical Theory and Social Change: The Evolution of John Dewey's Ethics, 1908–1932* (New Brunswick, NJ: Transaction Publishers, 2001); and Roberto Frega and Steven Levine, eds., *John Dewey's Ethical Theory: The 1932 Ethics* (New York: Routledge, 2021).

40. The textual apparatus for the critical edition of the *Ethics* indicates that "George Bell and Sons" accompanies "Henry Holt and Company" on the rare British reissue. See John Dewey, *Ethics*, in *The Middle Works of John Dewey*, ed. Jo Ann Boydston (Carbondale: Southern Illinois University Press, 1985), 5:554.

41. Queen, "Pedagogy of the Dhamma," 8.

42. Scott R. Stroud, "The Influence of John Dewey and James Tufts' *Ethics* on Ambedkar's Quest for Social Justice," in *The Relevance of Dr. Ambedkar: Today and Tomorrow*, ed. Pradeep Aglave (Nagpur: Nagpur University Press, 2017), 33–54.

43. Edel, *Ethical Theory and Social Change*, 44.

44. Dewey and Tufts, *Ethics*, 5:7.

45. Dewey and Tufts, *Ethics*, 5:13.

46. Dewey and Tufts, *Ethics*, 5:8.

47. Dewey and Tufts, *Ethics*, 5:15.

48. Dewey and Tufts, *Ethics*, 5:42.

49. Dewey and Tufts, *Ethics*, 5:54.

50. Dewey and Tufts, *Ethics*, 5:74.

51. Dewey and Tufts, *Ethics*, 5:194.

52. Dewey and Tufts, *Ethics*, 5:194.

53. Dewey and Tufts, *Ethics*, 5:383.

54. Dewey and Tufts, *Ethics*, 5:383.

55. Dewey and Tufts, *Ethics*, 5:301 (emphasis in original).

56. Dewey and Tufts, *Ethics*, 5:167.

57. Dewey and Tufts, *Ethics*, 5:295.

58. Dewey and Tufts, *Ethics*, 5:399.

59. Dewey and Tufts, *Ethics*, 5:431.

60. Christophe Jaffrelot, *Dr. Ambedkar and Untouchability: Fighting the Indian Caste System* (New York: Columbia University Press, 2005).

61. *Times of India*, September 19, 1932, in *Source Material on Dr. Babasaheb Ambedkar and the Movement of Untouchables* (Bombay: Government of Maharashtra, 1982), 1:85.

62. *Source Material on Dr. Babasaheb Ambedkar*, 1:88.

63. *Source Material on Dr. Babasaheb Ambedkar*, 1:88.
64. *Times of India*, February 6, 1933, in *Source Material on Dr. Babasaheb Ambedkar*, 1:107.
65. Mohandas K. Gandhi, "The Caste System," *Young India*, December 8, 1920, in *The Collected Works of Mahatma Gandhi* (Ahmedabad: Navijivan Trust, 1966), 19:83–85.
66. Plato held a similar view based on classes tracking individual nature; this surely explains why Ambedkar was attentive to Dewey's critiques of Plato's politics and educational scheme.
67. *Times of India*, February 6, 1933, in *Source Material on Dr. Babasaheb Ambedkar*, 1:106.
68. These potential reasons for Ambedkar's "retirement" in 1935 are discussed in a report contained in *Times of India*, July 25, 1935, in *Source Material on Dr. Babasaheb Ambedkar*, 1:133.
69. Bhimrao R. Ambedkar, "Unfortunately I Was Born a Hindu Untouchable but I Will Not Die a Hindu," in *Dr. Babasaheb Ambedkar Writings and Speeches* (Bombay: Government of Maharashtra, 2003), 17:pt.2:95.
70. "The Bombay Depressed Classes' Conference," in *Indian Annual Register, July–December 1935*, ed. H. N. Mitra (New Delhi: Gian Publishing House, 1947), 316.
71. The performative aspect was key; Ambedkar discussed conversion earlier, but he did not personally and publicly proclaim his own plans until the 1930s.
72. *Bombay Chronicle*, October 15, 1935, in *Source Material on Dr. Babasaheb Ambedkar*, 1:134.
73. *Bombay Chronicle*, October 16, 1935, in *Source Material on Dr. Babasaheb Ambedkar*, 1:135.
74. *Times of India*, November 30, 1935, in *Source Material on Dr. Babasaheb Ambedkar*, 1:137.
75. *Source Material on Dr. Babasaheb Ambedkar*, 1:137.
76. *Source Material on Dr. Babasaheb Ambedkar*, 1:138.
77. *Source Material on Dr. Babasaheb Ambedkar*, 1:138.
78. *Annihilation of Caste* (London: Verso, 2016), 183n–184n.
79. Dhananjay Keer, *Dr. Babasaheb Ambedkar: Life and Mission* (Bombay: Popular Prakashan, 1990), 266.
80. Ambedkar, *Annihilation of Caste*, 1:27.
81. Keer, *Dr. Babasaheb Ambedkar: Life and Mission*, 267.
82. Eleanor Zelliot, *Ambedkar's World: The Making of Babasaheb and the Dalit Movement* (New Delhi: Navayana, 2013).
83. Ambedkar's own heavily annotated copies of each of these texts survive in Siddharth College's archives.
84. Ambedkar, *Annihilation of Caste*, 1:47.
85. Ambedkar, *Annihilation of Caste*, 1:47.
86. Dewey, *Democracy and Education*, 126 (emphasis added).
87. Ambedkar, *Annihilation of Caste*, 1:48.
88. Dewey, *Democracy and Education*, 326–27 (emphasis added).
89. Ambedkar, *Annihilation of Caste*, 1:51.
90. Dewey, *Democracy and Education*, 91 (emphasis added).
91. Ambedkar, *Annihilation of Caste*, 1:56.
92. Dewey and Tufts, *Ethics*, 5:75 (emphasis added).
93. Ambedkar, *Annihilation of Caste*, 1:57 (emphasis in original).
94. Ambedkar, *Annihilation of Caste*, 1:57.

95. Dewey, *Democracy and Education*, 89 (emphasis added).

96. Dewey, *Democracy and Education*, 93 (emphasis added).

97. Arun P. Mukherjee, "B.R. Ambedkar, John Dewey, and the Meaning of Democracy," *New Literary History* 40 (2009): 353.

98. Mukherjee, "B.R. Ambedkar, John Dewey, and the Meaning of Democracy," 353.

99. Ambedkar, *Annihilation of Caste*, 1:51.

100. Dewey, *Democracy and Education*, 7 (emphasis added).

101. Ambedkar, *Annihilation of Caste*, 1:51.

102. Ambedkar, *Annihilation of Caste*, 1:51.

103. Dewey, *Democracy and Education*, 7 (emphasis added).

104. Ambedkar, *Annihilation of Caste*, 1:51.

105. Dewey, *Democracy and Education*, 18 (emphasis added).

106. Dewey, *Democracy and Education*, 18.

107. Ambedkar, *Annihilation of Caste*, 1:64; and Dewey, *Democracy and Education*, 87. Versions of this "one word-many things" argument form appear in Ambedkar's *What Congress and Gandhi Have Done to the Untouchables* ("nation") and *The Buddha and His Dhamma* ("religion").

108. Ambedkar, *Annihilation of Caste*, 1:64.

109. Dewey and Tufts, *Ethics*, 5:386 (emphasis added).

110. Ambedkar, *Annihilation of Caste*, 1:64.

111. Dewey, *Democracy and Education*, 89 (emphasis added).

112. Ambedkar, *Annihilation of Caste*, 1:65.

113. Dewey, *Democracy and Education*, 89 (emphasis added).

114. Ambedkar, *Annihilation of Caste*, 1:57.

115. Dewey, *Democracy and Education*, 90–91 (emphasis added).

116. Ambedkar, *Annihilation of Caste*, 1:58.

117. Dewey and Tufts, *Ethics*, 5:490 (emphasis added).

118. Shankranand Shastri, *My Experience and Memories of Dr. Babasaheb Ambedkar* (Delhi: Gautam Book Centre, 2012).

119. Ambedkar, *Annihilation of Caste*, 1:75.

120. Ambedkar, *Annihilation of Caste*, 1:75.

121. Dewey and Tufts, *Ethics*, 5:5:301–2 (emphasis added). For the revisions in the 1932 revision of *Ethics*, see John Dewey and James Hayden Tufts, *Ethics*, vol. 7 of *The Later Works of John Dewey*, ed. Jo Ann Boydston (Carbondale: Southern Illinois University Press, 1985), 280.

122. Ambedkar, *Annihilation of Caste*, 1:75.

123. Ambedkar, *Annihilation of Caste*, 1:75.

124. Ambedkar, *Annihilation of Caste*, 1:75.

125. Ambedkar, *Annihilation of Caste* 1:76.

126. Concerning rhetorically problematic situations, see Lloyd F. Bitzer, "The Rhetorical Situation," *Philosophy and Rhetoric* 1 no. 1 (1968): 1–14; and Richard E. Vatz, "The Myth of the Rhetorical Situation," *Philosophy and Rhetoric* 6, no. 3 (1973): 154–61.

127. Ambedkar, *Annihilation of Caste*, 1:56.

128. Ambedkar, *Annihilation of Caste*, 1:73.

129. Ambedkar was unable to attend an All-India Depressed Classes Conference in Lucknow, so *Annihilation of Caste* was read by someone else in his stead. See Zelliot, *Ambedkar's World*, 156–57.

130. John Dewey, "The Reflex Arc Concept in Psychology," in *The Early Works of John*

*Dewey*, ed. Jo Ann Boydson (Carbondale: Southern Illinois University Press, 1972), 5:96–110.

131. Ambedkar, *Annihilation of Caste*, 1:68.
132. Ambedkar, *Annihilation of Caste*, 1:46.
133. Ambedkar, *Annihilation of Caste*, 1:47.
134. Ambedkar, *Annihilation of Caste*, 1:50.
135. For Ambedkar's work on legislative reform, see Martha Nussbaum, "Ambedkar's Constitution: Promoting Inclusion, Opposing Majority Tyranny," in *Assessing Constitutional Performance*, ed. Tom Ginsburg and Aziz Huq (Cambridge: Cambridge University Press, 2016), 295–336; Sukhadeo Thorat and Narender Kumar, eds., *B.R. Ambedkar: Perspectives on Social Exclusion and Inclusive Policies* (Delhi: Oxford University Press, 2008); and Aakash Singh Rathore, ed., *B.R. Ambedkar: The Quest for Justice*, vols. 1–5 (Delhi: Oxford University Press, 2020).
136. Robert T. Oliver, "Caste as Rhetoric in Being," in *Communication and Culture in Ancient India and China* (Syracuse: Syracuse University Press, 1971).
137. Ambedkar, *Annihilation of Caste*, 1:59.
138. Ambedkar, *Annihilation of Caste*, 1:59.
139. Bhimrao R. Ambedkar, "Away from the Hindus," in *Dr. Babasaheb Ambedkar Writings and Speeches*, vol. 5. (Bombay: Government of Maharashtra, 1989). The dating of this collection can be approximated by its reference to the 1951 Indian census.
140. Ambedkar, "Away from the Hindus," 5:419.
141. Ambedkar, *Annihilation of Caste*, 1:59.
142. Ambedkar, *Annihilation of Caste*, 1:65.
143. Ambedkar, *Annihilation of Caste*, 1:67.
144. Ambedkar, *Annihilation of Caste*, 1:67.
145. Ambedkar, *Annihilation of Caste*, 1:75.
146. Ambedkar, *Annihilation of Caste*, 1:74.
147. Ambedkar, *Annihilation of Caste*, 1:75.
148. Ambedkar, *Annihilation of Caste*, 1:76.

CHAPTER FIVE

1. Bhimrao R. Ambedkar, "Art of Public Speaking Could Be Developed," in *Dr. Babasaheb Ambedkar Writings and Speeches* (Bombay: Government of Maharashtra, 2003), 17:pt.3:384.
2. Bhimrao R. Ambedkar, "The Minority Must Always Be Won Over; It Must Never Be Dictated To," in *Dr. Babasaheb Ambedkar Writings and Speeches*, 17:pt.3:378.
3. Ambedkar, "Minority Must Always Be Won Over," 17:pt.3:381.
4. Dhananjay Keer, *Dr. Babasaheb Ambedkar: Life and Mission* (Bombay: Popular Prakashan, 1990), 251.
5. Bhimrao R. Ambedkar, "What Way Emancipation?," in *Dr. Babasaheb Ambedkar Writings and Speeches*, 17:pt.3:123.
6. Keer, *Dr. Babasaheb Ambedkar: Life and Mission*, 273.
7. Ambedkar, "What Way Emancipation?," 17:pt.3:117.
8. Ambedkar, "What Way Emancipation?," 17:pt.3:118.
9. Ambedkar, "What Way Emancipation?," 17:pt.3:119.
10. Dewey published "A Common Faith" in 1933, but it did not seem to reach or influence Ambedkar (he did not cite, mention, or echo it, nor did he own a copy). John Dewey, "A Common Faith," in *The Later Works of John Dewey*, ed. Jo Ann Boydston, vol. 9 (Carbondale: Southern Illinois University Press, 1986).

11. Ambedkar, "What Way Emancipation?," 17:pt.3:121.

12. Ambedkar, "What Way Emancipation?," 17:pt.3:122.

13. Ambedkar, "What Way Emancipation?," 17:pt.3:122.

14. Ambedkar, "What Way Emancipation?," 17:pt.3:122.

15. Ambedkar, "What Way Emancipation?," 17:pt.3:122.

16. Ambedkar, "What Way Emancipation?," 17:pt.3:122.

17. Ambedkar, "What Way Emancipation?," 17:pt.3:122.

18. Bhimrao R. Ambedkar, *Annihilation of Caste*, in *Dr. Babasaheb Ambedkar Writings and Speeches* (Bombay: Government of Maharashtra, 1979), 1:60. The elements in this passage can be identified in Dewey's discussion of Plato and education in *Democracy and Education*, vol. 9 of *The Middle Works of John Dewey*, ed. Jo Ann Boydston (Carbondale: Southern Illinois University Press, 1985), 96.

19. Ambedkar, "What Way Emancipation?," 17:pt.3:123.

20. John Dewey, "The Ethics of Democracy," in *The Early Works of John Dewey*, ed. Jo Ann Boydson (Carbondale: Southern Illinois University Press, 1969), 1:244.

21. These letters can be found in the *B. R. Ambedkar Papers*, Microfilm Roll No. 1, Nehru Memorial Museum and Library, New Delhi. For more details, see Scott R. Stroud, "Creative Democracy, Communication, and the Uncharted Sources of Bhimrao Ambedkar's Deweyan Pragmatism," *Education & Culture: The Journal of the John Dewey Society* 34, no. 1 (2018): 61–80. Ambedkar's typed copy of Dewey's 1939 speech, most likely sent by Kadam, is preserved in the Maharashtra State Archives.

22. Bhimrao R. Ambedkar, "People Cemented by Feeling of One Country, One Constitution and One Destiny, Take the Risk of Being Independent," in *Dr. Babasaheb Ambedkar Writings and Speeches*, 17:pt.3:25.

23. Ambedkar, "People Cemented by Feeling of One Country," 17:pt.3:30.

24. Dewey, "Ethics of Democracy," 233 (emphasis added).

25. Bhimrao R. Ambedkar, "Mr. Russell and the Reconstruction of Society," in *Dr. Babasaheb Ambedkar Writings and Speeches*, 1:488; and Bhimrao R. Ambedkar, "Evidence before the Southborough Committee," in *Dr. Babasaheb Ambedkar Writings and Speeches*, 1:251.

26. Ambedkar, "Evidence before the Southborough Committee," 1:256.

27. Bhimrao R. Ambedkar, "Educate, Agitate, Organize, have Faith and lose no Hope," in *Dr. Babasaheb Ambedkar Writings and Speeches*, 17:pt.3:276.

28. Consult Robert B. Westbrook, *John Dewey and American Democracy* (Ithaca, NY: Cornell University Press, 1991), 13–33; and Steven Rockefeller, *John Dewey: Religious Faith and Democratic Humanism* (New York: Columbia University Press, 1992), 76–98.

29. George S. Morris, "Philosophy and Its Specific Problems," *Princeton Review* 9 (1882): 227.

30. Jennifer Welchman, *Dewey's Ethical Thought* (Ithaca, NY: Cornell University Press, 1995), 21. See also Robert J. Roth, *John Dewey and Self-Realization* (Englewood Cliffs, NJ: Prentice-Hall, 1962); Scott R. Stroud, "Constructing a Deweyan Theory of Moral Cultivation," *Contemporary Pragmatism* 3, no. 2 (2006): 99–116; and Donald J. Morse, *Faith in Life: John Dewey's Early Philosophy* (New York: Fordham University Press, 2011).

31. For more on Hall and his animosity toward idealistic strains of philosophy, see Dorothy Ross, *G. Stanley Hall: The Psychologist as Prophet* (Chicago: University of Chicago Press, 1972).

32. For more on the Wundt-Hall connection, see John Shook, *Dewey's Empirical Theory of Knowledge and Reality* (Nashville, TN: Vanderbilt University Press, 2000), 73–79.
33. Shook, *Dewey's Empirical Theory of Knowledge and Reality*, 45–47.
34. John Dewey, *Psychology*, vol. 2 of *The Early Works of John Dewey*, ed. Jo Ann Boydston (Carbondale: Southern Illinois University Press, 1967), 310–314.
35. Rockefeller, *John Dewey*, 135–56.
36. Dewey, "Ethics of Democracy," 1:229.
37. Dewey, "Ethics of Democracy," 1:231.
38. Dewey, "Ethics of Democracy," 1:232.
39. Dewey, "Ethics of Democracy," 1:232.
40. Dewey, "Ethics of Democracy," 1:232.
41. See John Dewey, "From Absolutism to Experimentalism," in *The Later Works of John Dewey*, ed. Jo Ann Boydston (Carbondale: Southern Illinois University Press, 1984), 5:147–48.
42. Dewey, "Ethics of Democracy," 1:237 (emphasis in original).
43. Dewey, "Ethics of Democracy," 1:237.
44. Dewey, "Ethics of Democracy," 1:237.
45. Dewey, "Ethics of Democracy," 1:238.
46. Dewey, "Ethics of Democracy," 1:239.
47. Dewey, "Ethics of Democracy," 1:239.
48. Dewey, "Ethics of Democracy," 1:240.
49. Dewey, "Ethics of Democracy," 1:241.
50. Dewey, "Ethics of Democracy," 1:241.
51. Dewey, "Ethics of Democracy," 1:243.
52. Dewey, "Ethics of Democracy," 1:243.
53. Dewey, "Ethics of Democracy," 1:243–44.
54. For more on Dewey, personality, and the social gospel movement, see Rockefeller, *John Dewey*, 164–65.
55. Dewey, "Ethics of Democracy," 1:244.
56. Jennifer Welchman, *Dewey's Ethical Thought*, 29.
57. Dewey, *Psychology*, 315.
58. Dewey, *Psychology*, 351 (emphasis in original).
59. Dewey, *Psychology*, 351 (emphasis in original).
60. George S. Morris, *Philosophy and Christianity* (New York: Robert Carter and Brothers, 1883), 207.
61. Dewey, *Psychology*, 360.
62. Dewey, *Psychology*, 361.
63. Dewey, *Psychology*, 357.
64. Dewey, "Ethics of Democracy," 1:237.
65. See Morse, *Faith in Life*.
66. Ambedkar, "What Way Emancipation?," 17:pt.3:122.
67. Ambedkar, "What Way Emancipation?," 17:pt.3:123.
68. Shook, *Dewey's Empirical Theory of Knowledge and Reality*, 216.
69. James A. Good, *A Search for Unity in Diversity: The "Permanent Hegelian Deposit" in the Philosophy of John Dewey* (Lanham, MD: Lexington Books, 2006), 155–58.
70. Good, *A Search for Unity in Diversity*, 156.
71. Quoted in Good, *Search for Unity in Diversity*, 156.
72. Paul Stob, *Intellectual Populism: Democracy, Inquiry, and the People* (East Lansing: Michigan State University Press, 2020).

73. John Dewey, "Outlines of a Critical Theory of Ethics," in *The Early Works of John Dewey*, ed. Jo Ann Boydson (Carbondale: Southern Illinois University Press, 1969), 3:303.

74. Dewey, "Outlines of a Critical Theory of Ethics," 3:301.

75. Dewey, "Outlines of a Critical Theory of Ethics," 3:322 (emphasis removed).

76. Ambedkar, "What Way Emancipation?," 17.pt.3:122.

77. Bhimrao R. Ambedkar, "Away from the Hindus," in *Dr. Babasaheb Ambedkar Writings and Speeches* (Bombay: Government of Maharashtra, 1989), 5:409–12; and Charles A Ellwood, *The Reconstruction of Religion: A Sociological View* (New York: Macmillan, 1922), 39–43. Illustrating Ellwood's and Ambedkar's interest in the intersection of Deweyan psychology and the emerging field of sociology, Ambedkar also draws upon Ellwood's *Sociology in its Psychological Aspects* (New York: D. Appleton, 1912), 356–57.

78. Stephen Turner, "A Life in the First Half-Century of Sociology: Charles Ellwood and the Division of Sociology," in *Sociology in America: The American Sociological Associations Centennial History*, ed. Craig Calhoun (Chicago: University of Chicago Press, 2007), 115–54.

79. Ambedkar, "What Way Emancipation?," 17:pt.3:123.

80. Ambedkar, "What Way Emancipation?," 17:pt.3:123.

81. Dewey, "Ethics of Democracy," 1:244.

82. I'm indebted to Mangesh Dahiwale for his insights on the Marathi terms used in this speech.

83. Dewey, *Psychology*, 285 (emphasis in original).

84. Bhimrao R. Ambedkar, "Ranade, Gandhi and Jinnah," in *Dr. Babasaheb Ambedkar Writings and Speeches*, 1:218–19.

85. Bhimrao R. Ambedkar, "Philosophy of Hinduism," in *Dr. Babasaheb Ambedkar Writings and Speeches* (Bombay: Government of Maharashtra, 1987), 3:36.

86. Ambedkar, "Philosophy of Hinduism,"3:99.

87. Ambedkar, "Philosophy of Hinduism,"3:66.

88. Ambedkar, "Philosophy of Hinduism,"3:66. See also Scott R. Stroud, "Excessively Harsh Critique and Democratic Rhetoric: The Enigma of Bhimrao Ambedkar's *Riddles in Hinduism*," *Journal for the History of Rhetoric* 25, no. 1 (2022): 2–30.

89. Ambedkar, "What Way Emancipation?," 17:pt.3:124.

90. Ambedkar, "What Way Emancipation?," 17:pt.3:126.

91. Aakash Singh Rathore, *Ambedkar's Preamble: A Secret History of the Constitution of India* (Delhi: Vintage Books, 2020), 127.

92. K. M. Munshi, *Indian Constitutional Documents: Pilgrimage to Freedom, 1902–1950* (Bombay: Bharatiya Vidya Bhavan, 1967), 193–94.

93. Ambedkar, "What Way Emancipation?," 17:pt.3:129.

94. Ambedkar, "What Way Emancipation?," 17:pt.3:130.

95. Ambedkar, "What Way Emancipation?," 17:pt.3:130–31.

96. Ambedkar, "What Way Emancipation?," 17:pt.3:145.

97. Devi Dayal, *Daily Routine of Dr. Ambedkar* (New Delhi: Samyak Prakashan, 2011), 54.

98. T. Christmas Humphreys, *Karma and Rebirth*, 3rd ed. (London: John Murray, 1948). Ambedkar's annotated copy of this book is held in the Ambedkar Collection at Siddharth College in Mumbai.

99. Ambedkar, "What Way Emancipation?," 17:pt.3:127.

100. Ambedkar, "What Way Emancipation?," 17:pt.3:128.

101. Ambedkar, "What Way Emancipation?," 17:pt.3:128.

102. Ambedkar, "What Way Emancipation?," 17:pt.3:128.

103. Ambedkar, "What Way Emancipation?," 17:pt.3:131.

104. Soumyabrata Choudhury, *Ambedkar and Other Immortals: An Untouchable Research Programme* (Delhi: Navayana, 2018), 59 (emphasis in original).

105. Choudhury, *Ambedkar and Other Immortals*, 59 (emphasis in original).

106. Ambedkar, "What Way Emancipation?," 17:pt.3:132.

107. Ambedkar, "What Way Emancipation?," 17:pt.3:137.

108. Ambedkar, "What Way Emancipation?," 17:pt.3:128.

109. Ambedkar, "What Way Emancipation?," 17:pt.3:128.

110. Ambedkar, "What Way Emancipation?," 17:pt.3:128.

111. Ambedkar, "What Way Emancipation?," 17:pt.3:146.

112. "Dr. Ambedkar and Religion," *Free Press Journal*, May 18, 1950, in *Source Material on Dr. Babasaheb Ambedkar and the Movement of Untouchables*, ed. B.G. Kunte (Bombay: Government of Maharashtra, 1982), 1:369.

113. Keer, *Dr. Babasaheb Ambedkar: Life and Mission*, 476.

114. Bhimrao R. Ambedkar, "I Shall Devote Rest of My Life to the Revival and Spread of Buddhism," in *Dr. Babasaheb Ambedkar Writings and Speeches*, 17:pt:3:410.

115. Ambedkar, "I Shall Devote Rest of My Life to the Revival and Spread of Buddhism," 17:pt:3:410.

116. Bhimrao R. Ambedkar, "Buddhism Will Once Again Be the Religion of This Country," in *Ambedkar Speaks*, ed. Narendra Jadhav (New Delhi: Konark Publishers, 2013), 2:294.

117. Ambedkar, "Buddhism Will Once Again Be the Religion of This Country," 2:294.

118. Ambedkar, "Buddhism Will Once Again Be the Religion of This Country," 2:294.

119. Ambedkar, "Buddhism Will Once Again Be the Religion of This Country," 2:294.

120. Ambedkar, "Buddhism Will Once Again Be the Religion of This Country," 2:295.

121. Ambedkar, "Buddhism Will Once Again Be the Religion of This Country," 2:295.

122. Ambedkar, "Buddhism Will Once Again Be the Religion of This Country," 2:295.

123. Ambedkar, "Buddhism Will Once Again Be the Religion of This Country," 2:295.

124. Ambedkar, "Buddhism Will Once Again Be the Religion of This Country," 2:295.

125. Bhimrao R. Ambedkar, "The Tide of Buddhism Would Never Recede in India," in *Dr. Babasaheb Ambedkar Writings and Speeches*, vol. 17, pt. 3.

126. Ambedkar, "Tide of Buddhism Would Never Recede in India," 17:pt.3:517.

127. Ambedkar, "Tide of Buddhism Would Never Recede in India," 17:pt.3:518.

128. Recounted in Keer, *Dr. Babasaheb Ambedkar: Life and Mission*, 493.

129. Keer, *Dr. Babasaheb Ambedkar: Life and Mission*, 492–496.

130. Bhimrao R. Ambedkar, "The Buddha Dhamma Will Be the Savior of the World," in *Dr. Babasaheb Ambedkar Writings and Speeches*, 17:pt.3:527.

131. Keer, *Dr. Babasaheb Ambedkar: Life and Mission*, 495–99.

132. "Ambedkar Mystery," *National Standard*, May 12, 1950, in *Source Material on Dr. Babasaheb Ambedkar*, 1:369.

133. M. K. Pradhan, "Dr. Ambedkar and Buddhism," *Indian Express*, January 8, 1955, in *Source Material on Dr. Babasaheb Ambedkar*, 1:423 (emphasis in original).

134. "Ambedkar," *Times of India*, January 2, 1955, in *Source Material on Dr. Babasaheb Ambedkar*, 1:423 (emphasis in original).

135. For example, see "Conversion of Harijans: No Solution, Says Mr. Rajbhoj," *Times of India*, October 19, 1956, 11.

136. Caliban, "Stray Musings: An Opposition Leader Wanted," *Times of India*, October 21, 1956, 8.

137. Ambedkar, "Buddha Dhamma Will Be the Savior of the World," 17:pt.3:524.

138. Ambedkar, "Buddha Dhamma Will Be the Savior of the World," 17:pt.3:533.
139. Keer, *Dr. Babasaheb Ambedkar: Life and Mission*, 499.
140. Eleanor Zelliot, *Ambedkar's World: The Making of Babasaheb and the Dalit Movement* (New Delhi: Navayana, 2013), 169. See also Ambedkar, "Buddha Dhamma Will Be the Savior of the World," 17:pt.3:528.
141. Christophe Jaffrelot, *Dr. Ambedkar and Untouchability: Fighting the Indian Caste System* (New York: Columbia University Press, 2005), 134.
142. Ambedkar, "Buddha Dhamma Will Be the Savior of the World," 17:pt.3:530.
143. Keer, *Dr. Babasaheb Ambedkar: Life and Mission*, 500.
144. Keer, *Dr. Babasaheb Ambedkar: Life and Mission*, 500–501.
145. Ambedkar, "Buddha Dhamma Will Be the Savior of the World," 17:pt.3:531–32.
146. Ambedkar, "Buddha Dhamma Will Be the Savior of the World," 17:pt.3:534–35.
147. Ambedkar, "Buddha Dhamma Will Be the Savior of the World," 17:pt.3:535–36.
148. See also Shaunna Rodrigues, "Self-Respect as a Primary Political Ideal: Ambedkar's Challenge to Political Theory," in *B.R. Ambedkar: The Quest for Justice*, ed. Aakash Singh Rathore, vol. 1 (Delhi: Oxford University Press, 2020).
149. Ambedkar, "Buddha Dhamma Will Be the Savior of the World," 17:pt.3:536.
150. Ambedkar, "Buddha Dhamma Will Be the Savior of the World," 17:pt.3:536.
151. Jaffrelot, *Dr. Ambedkar and Untouchability*, 119–31; and Gauri Viswanathan, *Outside the Fold: Conversion, Modernity, and Belief* (Princeton, NJ: Princeton University Press, 1998).
152. Ambedkar, "Buddha Dhamma Will Be the Savior of the World," 17:pt.3:537.
153. Ambedkar, "Buddha Dhamma Will Be the Savior of the World," 17:pt.3:541–42.
154. Ambedkar, "Buddha Dhamma Will Be the Savior of the World," 17:pt.3:542.
155. Ambedkar, "Buddha Dhamma Will Be the Savior of the World," 17:pt.3:542.
156. Ambedkar, "Buddha Dhamma Will Be the Savior of the World," 17:pt.3:544.
157. Ambedkar, "Buddha Dhamma Will Be the Savior of the World," 17:pt.3:542.
158. Ambedkar, "Buddha Dhamma Will Be the Savior of the World," 17:pt.3:543.
159. Ambedkar, "Buddha Dhamma Will Be the Savior of the World," 17:pt.3:544.
160. Ambedkar, "Buddha Dhamma Will Be the Savior of the World," 17:pt.3:544.
161. Ambedkar, "Buddha Dhamma Will Be the Savior of the World," 17:pt.3:545.
162. Ambedkar, *Annihilation of Caste*, 1:73.
163. Eugene E. White, *Puritan Rhetoric: The Issue of Emotion in Religion* (Carbondale: Southern Illinois University Press, 2009).
164. Amartya Sen, *The Argumentative Indian* (New York: Farrar, Straus, and Giroux, 2005).
165. John Dewey, "Ethical Principles Underlying Education," in *The Early Works of John Dewey*, ed. Jo Ann Boydston (Carbondale: Southern Illinois University Press, 1972), 5:55.
166. Viswanathan, *Outside the Fold*, 225.
167. Viswanathan, *Outside the Fold*, 228.
168. Christopher Queen, "Dr. Ambedkar and the Hermeneutics of Buddhist Liberation," in *Engaged Buddhism: Buddhist Liberation Movements in Asia*, ed. Christopher S. Queen and Sallie B. King (Albany: State University of New York Press, 1996), 67.
169. Gregory H. Spencer, "The Rhetoric of Malcolm Muggeridge's Gradual Christian Conversion," *Journal of Communication and Religion* 18 (1995): 55–64; and Charles J. G. Griffin, "The Rhetoric of Form in Conversion Narratives," *Quarterly Journal of Speech* 76 (1990): 152–63.
170. Sonja K. Foss and Cindy L. Griffin, "Beyond Persuasion: A Proposal for an Invitational Rhetoric," *Communication Monographs* 62, no. 1 (1995): 4.

171. Foss and Griffin, "Beyond Persuasion," 5.
172. Bhimrao R. Ambedkar, "Ranade, Gandhi and Jinnah," in *Dr. Babasaheb Ambedkar Writings and Speeches*, 1:240.
173. Ambedkar, "Ranade, Gandhi and Jinnah," 1:240 (emphasis added).

CONCLUSION

1. Pradeep Gokhale, "Dr. Ambedkar as a Philosopher: Beyond Reductionism," in *The Philosophy of Dr. B. R. Ambedkar*, ed. Pradeep Gokhale (Pune: IPQ Publications, 2008).
2. For example, Isabel Wilkerson, *Caste* (New York: Random House, 2020).
3. John Dewey, *Democracy and Education*, vol. 9 of *The Middle Works of John Dewey*, ed. Jo Ann Boydston (Carbondale: Southern Illinois University Press, 1985), 89.
4. Dewey, *Democracy and Education*, 89.
5. Sukhadeo Thorat, "Foreword," in *Dr. Ambedkar and Democracy*, ed. Christophe Jaffrelot and Narender Kumar (New Delhi: Oxford University Press, 2018).
6. Bhimrao R. Ambedkar, speech presented on November 25, 1949, in *Dr. Babasaheb Ambedkar Writings and Speeches* (Bombay: Government of Maharashtra, 1994), 13:1216.
7. Ambedkar, speech presented on November 25, 1949, 13:1216.
8. Bhimrao R. Ambedkar, "My Philosophy of Life," in *Dr. Babasaheb Ambedkar Writings and Speeches* (Bombay: Government of Maharashtra, 2003), 17:pt.3:503.
9. Bhimrao R. Ambedkar, "Conditions Precedent for the Successful Working of Modern Democracy," in *Dr. Babasaheb Ambedkar Writings and Speeches*, 17:pt.3:472–86.
10. Bhimrao R. Ambedkar, "The Hindu Social Order: Its Essential Principles," in *Dr. Babasaheb Ambedkar Writings and Speeches* (Bombay: Government of Maharashtra, 1987), 3:96.
11. Bhimrao R. Ambedkar, "States and Minorities," in *Dr. Babasaheb Ambedkar Writings and Speeches* (Bombay: Government of Maharashtra, 1979), 1:409.
12. Bhimrao R. Ambedkar, "The Hindu Social Order: Its Essential Principles," in *Dr. Babasaheb Ambedkar Writings and Speeches*, 3:96.
13. Ambedkar, "Hindu Social Order," 3:96.
14. For instance, see Pradeep Gokhale, "Dr. Ambedkar on the Trio of Principles: Liberty, Equality and Fraternity," *Dialogue Quarterly, A Journal of Astha Bharati* 17, no. 3 (2016): 66–80; and Aakash Rathore Singh, *Ambedkar's Preamble: A Secret History of the Constitution of India* (Delhi: Vintage Books, 2020).
15. Bhimrao R. Ambedkar, "Riddles in Hinduism," in *Dr. Babasaheb Ambedkar Writings and Speeches* (Bombay: Government of Maharashtra, 1987), 4:283.
16. Ambedkar, "Riddles in Hinduism," 4:283.
17. Bhimrao R. Ambedkar, "Riddle 22: Brahma Is Not Dharma," Maharashtra State Archives, 8.
18. Ambedkar, "Riddles in Hinduism," 4:283.
19. Ambedkar, "Riddle 22," Maharashtra State Archives, 9.
20. Ambedkar, "Riddle 22," Maharashtra State Archives, 9–10.
21. Bhimrao R. Ambedkar, "Is Gandhi a Mahatma?," in *Dr. Babasaheb Ambedkar Writings and Speeches* (Bombay: Government of Maharashtra, 2003), 17:pt.2:67; and Bhimrao R. Ambedkar, "The Minority Must Always Be Won Over; It Must Never Be Dictated To," in *Dr. Babasaheb Ambedkar Writings and Speeches*, 17:pt.3:378.
22. Bhimrao R. Ambedkar, "Publications by Dr. B. R. Ambedkar," Maharashtra State Archives, 1.

23. Bhimrao R. Ambedkar, "Buddha or Karl Marx," in *Dr. Babasaheb Ambedkar Writings and Speeches*, 3:451.

24. For Ambedkar's engagement with Marx, see Scott R. Stroud, "Pragmatism, Persuasion, and Force in Bhimrao Ambedkar's Reconstruction of Buddhism," *Journal of Religion* 97, no. 2 (2017): 214–43; and Ajay Skaria, "Ambedkar, Marx, and the Buddhist Question," *South Asia* 38 (2015): 450–65.

25. Ambedkar, "Buddha or Karl Marx," 3:451.

26. Ambedkar, "Buddha or Karl Marx," 3:450.

27. Ambedkar, "Buddha or Karl Marx," 3:462.

28. I detail some of the changes between these editions, and their interplay with Dewey's pragmatism, in Scott R. Stroud, "Creative Democracy, Communication, and the Uncharted Sources of Bhimrao Ambedkar's Deweyan Pragmatism," *Education & Culture: The Journal of the John Dewey Society* 34, no. 1 (2018): 61–80.

29. Bhimrao R. Ambedkar, "Buddha and the Future of His Religion," in *Dr. Babasaheb Ambedkar Writings and Speeches*, 17:pt.2:98.

30. Bhimrao R. Ambedkar, *The Buddha and His Dhamma*, vol. 11 of *Dr. Babasaheb Ambedkar Writings and Speeches* (Bombay: Government of Maharashtra, 1992).

31. Ambedkar, *Buddha and His Dhamma*, 128.

32. Ambedkar, *Buddha and His Dhamma*, 359.

33. Ambedkar, *Buddha and His Dhamma*, 359.

34. Ambedkar, *Buddha and His Dhamma*, 359.

35. Ambedkar, *Buddha and His Dhamma*, 389.

36. Ambedkar, *Buddha and His Dhamma*, 389.

37. Ambedkar, *Buddha and His Dhamma*, 389.

38. Ambedkar, *Buddha and His Dhamma*, 346.

39. Ambedkar, *Buddha and His Dhamma*, 346.

40. Ambedkar, *Buddha and His Dhamma*, 346.

41. Ambedkar, *Buddha and His Dhamma*, 347.

42. For instance, see Gail Omvedt, *Dalits and the Democratic Revolution: Dr Ambedkar and the Dalit Movement in Colonial India* (Delhi: SAGE Publications, 1994); Dag-Erik Berg, *Dynamics of Caste and Law: Dalits, Oppression and Constitutional Democracy in India* (Cambridge: Cambridge University Press, 2020); Christophe Jaffrelot, *Dr. Ambedkar and Untouchability: Fighting the Indian Caste System* (New York: Columbia University Press, 2005); Luis Cabrera, *The Humble Cosmopolitan: Rights, Diversity, and Trans-state Democracy* (Oxford: Oxford University Press, 2019); Adele M. Fiske, "Religion and Buddhism among India's New Buddhists," *Social Research* 36, no. 1 (1969): 123–57; and Christopher S. Queen and Sallie B. King, eds., *Engaged Buddhism Buddhist Liberation Movements in Asia* (Albany: State University of New York Press, 1996).

43. Ambedkar, "Buddha or Karl Marx," 3:450.

44. Ambedkar, "Buddha or Karl Marx," 3:461.

45. Bhimrao R. Ambedkar, "Buddha or Karl Marx," in *Dr. Babasaheb Ambedkar Writings and Speeches*, 17:pt.3:554.

46. Ambedkar, "Buddha or Karl Marx," 17:pt.3:554.

47. Gail Omvedt, *Seeking Begumpura* (Delhi: Navayana, 2009).

48. J. D. Elam, in *World Literature for the Wretched of the Earth* (New York: Fordham University Press, 2021), 57, asserts that Dewey "likely" had read Ambedkar's *Annihilation of Caste* by 1939 (an identical version of this claim, albeit with the stronger assertion that there is "proof" that Dewey read Ambedkar, appears in his essay

"Of Castes and Crowds," in *B.R. Ambedkar: The Quest for Justice*, ed. Aakash Singh Rathore [Delhi: Oxford University Press, 2020]). The single piece of evidence given for this claim in both places is far from conclusive. Elam points to one line that Dewey writes in his 1939 "Creative Democracy—The Task Before Us" address as proof of Dewey's thought being influenced by Ambedkar's text: "For everything which bars freedom and fullness of communication sets up barriers that divide human beings into sets and cliques, into antagonistic sects and factions, and thereby undermines the democratic way of life." As far as evidence goes for a claim of exposure or influence, this is very weak. Dewey does not cite or quote Ambedkar's 1936 text here in 1939 (or elsewhere), and none of the distinctive phrases or terms in this line ("way of life," "sets," "factions," "cliques," "fullness") appear in Ambedkar's 1936 text. Judging from the meticulous cataloging in Jo Ann Boydston, *John Dewey's Personal and Professional Library* (Carbondale: Southern Illinois Press, 1982), Dewey did not own any version of *Annihilation of Caste*, a text that was published by a small Bombay printer in 1936 and 1937 in a run of a few thousand copies before Dewey's 1939 essay was penned. Our desire for symmetry in influence aside, it seems unlikely that Dewey had Ambedkar's speech in his hands before 1939 (if at all). A more likely hypothesis is that Dewey is continuing a point he has pushed for a long time. Most decisively, we see Dewey talking in this exact fashion about democracy—even with the addition of "castes"—well *before* he met Ambedkar or allegedly read his 1936 address. In August 1912, Dewey tells his audience in a public lecture on suffrage, "You can't have a real democracy where there is caste and cliques or sets" ("Professor for Suffrage," *New York Times*, August 9, 1912, 3). These themes of communication and community division into antagonistic groups appear in Dewey's *Democracy and Education* (1916), and also appear (in reconstructed form) in Ambedkar's 1936 work. There could be a story of Dewey's reception of Ambedkar's work waiting to be told, but better evidence will be required to tell it.

# INDEX

act, social environment and, 31
action: coercive government, 57; "general springs to," 30; habitualized, 31; intelligent, 92; "springs of," 83
activities: appropriative, 108; communicative, 176; meliorative, 260; mental-physical, 192; occupational, 161
act of reflection, 55
adaptation, 11, 29, 36, 93
Adlerblum, Nima, 7–12, 60, 218, 271n30
advocacy, persuasive, 243
agency, 63, 95, 149–50, 153, 170, 197, 199–200, 208–9; *ahimsa*, 87, 257–58, 261; effective, 243; individual, 44, 243; and power, 102; and self-realization, 233; willful, 45, 208, 211, 226
Ambedkar, Bhimrao: and Ramabai Ambedkar, 155; and Savita Ambedkar, 2, 5, 9, 218, 221; and Buddhism, 11, 223, 228, 232, 254–55, 267; and Columbia University, 4, 9–10, 15, 21, 35, 42, 185; and communism, 253; on conversion, 18, 120, 211, 213, 219, 221, 235, 260; on fraternity, 168, 255; and Hinduism, 133; and K. A. Keluskar, 147; on liberty and equality, 255; and meliorism, 17, 71; and Navayana Buddhism, 235–39, 241–63; Navayana Pragmatism and, 239, 241, 243–44, 247–51, 253–56, 258–59, 261–62; reconstructive rhetoric and, 125–26, 140–41, 153, 179; on Bertrand Russell,

72, 83, 90, 128; and social democracy, 248–49
*Annihilation of Caste* (Ambedkar), 122, 134, 157–58, 163, 172, 175–76
anticaste thought, 12, 105, 133, 237
appeals: persuasive, 134, 213; reconstructive, 226
Arya Samaj, 157–58, 175
association, 36, 41, 43, 45, 59, 111, 168, 194–95, 245; associated life, 35–36, 41, 43, 49–50, 54, 153, 248; and groups, 36; modes of, 163; and the socialized individual, 43
attitude: fraternity as, 250–51, 260; individual, 126; personal, 150, 178; respect as, 163, 226; socialized, 111
attraction-repulsion, 30, 50, 63, 179, 233
autonomy, 168, 174, 223, 231, 234, 243–44, 249

Brahminism, 98, 166, 215, 240, 256
Buddha, 3, 121, 218, 221, 236, 252, 258, 261; Karl Marx and, 252, 261; teachings, 223, 226, 254, 256, 261; young Ambedkar and, 11
*Buddha and His Dhamma* (Ambedkar), 1, 237, 247, 254–55
Buddhism, 208, 215–16, 218–21, 223–29, 231–33, 247, 253, 261–62; and conversion, 213; equality and, 216; and pragmatism, 156, 172